# Manual of PEDIATRIC NURSING

# CAREPLANS

### Second Edition

Department of Nursing
The Hospital for Sick Children
Toronto, Canada

Edited by Voirrey Broe

Little, Brown and Company   Boston   Toronto

Library of Congress Cataloging in Publication Data

Hospital for Sick Children. Dept. of Nursing.
  Manual of pediatric nursing careplans.

  Bibliography: p.
  Includes Index.
  1. Pediatric nursing—Handbooks, manuals, etc.
2. Children—Hospital care—Handbooks, manuals, etc.
I. Broe, Voirrey. II. Title. III. Title: Pediatric
nursing careplans. IV. Title: Manual of pediatric
nursing care plans. [DNLM: l. Patient Care Planning.
2. Pediatric Nursing. WY 159 H828m]
RJ245.H67  1985       610.73′62       85-205

ISBN 0-316-37389-3

Library of Congress Catalog Card No. 85-205


ISBN 0-316-37389-3

9  8  7  6  5  4  3  2  1

SEM

Published simultaneously in Canada
by Little, Brown & Company (Canada) Limited

Printed in the United States of America

To Matthew and Gregory
and our patients and their families

**INTO LIFE**

by **Pauline Redsell Fediow**

This statue stands in the surgical waiting room of
The Hospital for Sick Children, Toronto.
It is depicted in the Hospital's official coat of
arms, exemplifying the motto:

**"Care for what the child may become."**

# Foreword

We hope that all nursing professionals who serve and care for infants and children in children's hospitals or pediatric wards in general hospitals will find this book useful as a guide for the development of their nursing careplans.

The careplans in this text were developed by the nursing staff of The Hospital for Sick Children, Toronto. The idea of a pediatric hospital in Toronto was conceived by Elizabeth McMaster, who became the Hospital's first Director of Nursing. In April, 1875, she and a small group of dedicated women opened a six-bed hospital for children in a small rooming house. They named the house after the already famous children's hospital established 21 years earlier at Great Ormond Street in London, England. The stated purpose of this hospital was the care and cure of sick children.

In the beginning, the women decided that they could treat children from birth to age 12 as outpatients; however, because of the limitations of their nursing skills, they could accept as inpatients only children between the ages of 2 and 10 years. Further, no child with smallpox or any other "incurable" disease would be admitted.

Now, over a century later, the nursing staff care for almost three hundred thousand children a year in a complex 700-bed treatment center that is within walking distance of the original institution. The Hospital is internationally renowned for its pediatric treatment, teaching, and research. Patients and students come from around the world to receive care and teaching from the highly skilled and knowledgeable staff.

This compilation of pediatric nursing careplans is a fine and fitting tribute not only to the Hospital, but to its patients, their families and to the nursing staff who made it happen. Throughout the development of this project, the contributors have been sustained by the guidance and patience of Voirrey Broe, Nursing Manual Coordinator, and Carla Salvador, Assistant Editor, Medical Publications. Without their leadership and perseverance, the second edition of this book would not have been compiled.

J. Douglas Snedden
President and Chief Executive Officer

# Preface

The material in this *Manual of Pediatric Nursing Careplans* was developed out of our need for a system of planning patient care that would be accessible, current, and easily understood. Over the years we have used various formats and approaches to planning care. In the early days our careplans consisted mostly of doctors' diagnoses and orders, along with some standard routines. At the same time much information was passed on verbally from nurse to nurse. But we found these systems unsatisfactory: they did not ensure consistency and continuity of care; nurses were discouraged from writing detailed careplans because of the time involved; also, experienced pediatric nurses were not always available as resources.

For nurses at The Hospital for Sick Children, the turning point came when we read Marlene Mayers' *A Systematic Approach to the Nursing Care Plan* (New York: Appleton-Century-Crofts, 1972). This book, and a workshop conducted by Mayers, convinced us that we should implement a program to develop pediatric standard careplans for use within the Hospital. We are indebted to her for her work in developing this system of planning nursing care and her encouragement of us in writing the pediatric careplans.

In developing our standardized careplans we used a modification of the format described by Mayers. We define usual problems (actual and potential); objectives that indicate the problem has been prevented, is resolving, or has been resolved; the length of time during which one might expect the problem to occur or persist; and nursing orders designed to prevent or solve the problem.

Standard careplans, which emphasize the usual, common, and predictable, reflect the many similarities among patients without obviating the need to assess patients as individuals. Used in conjunction with other data, they enable nurses to provide a systematic and organized approach to nursing care that can be applied to any ward or clinic setting. A standardized pediatric careplan reminds experienced nurses of the usual problems encountered by the patient and parent with the disease or treatment and provides information for less-experienced personnel such as students and newly graduated nurses, and for relief nurses.

In our old system of care planning, the problem of a patient not drinking well would probably have been stated as "inadequate fluid intake" and the nursing orders might have read "push fluids" or "patient must drink 600 ml per shift." How much more purposeful our actions can be when the problem is defined as "patient reluctant to drink because he has a sore throat" or "patient refusing fluids because he is not used to drinking from a cup."

Almost 9 years have passed since we wrote our first standard careplan (for pertussis). Now we have more than 170 plans approved and in use. The slow but worthwhile process is ongoing. The standard careplan committee continues to review the careplans, paying particular attention to suitability for use by nurses relatively unfamiliar with the disease or condition. Existing plans are updated as necessary and reviewed at specified intervals and new careplans are being developed. Some plans have been withdrawn because treatment is changing and others updated to reflect the changes. In addition, during the past year all of the material has been put on a word processor, a time-consuming and often frustrating project but one that enables us to update and improve our careplans more easily. It also ensures that the careplans will be integrated into the Hospital's computerized patient care planning system.

We have been overwhelmed by the positive responses to the 1st edition of this book from across Canada and the United States, and from overseas. It is very gratifying to hear from so many of you that the book meets your needs. Students, new staff nurses, and nurses working in small hospitals or rural areas have found it particularly helpful. Experienced nurses have found it a handy reference and many hospitals are able to use the careplans with little or no modification.

The 2nd edition of the Manual contains 160 careplans. The format is the same as in the 1st edition but many plans have been extensively revised, to reflect changes in medical and nursing management of patient care, and new careplans have been added.

The nursing orders relating to management of home care and follow-up have been expanded. Written instructions referred to in planning for home care exist in this Hospital in the form of printed manuals, booklets, or instruction sheets. For example, for dialysis we have a manual for parents, another for older children, and a coloring book for younger children. Booklets containing information about diseases such as heart conditions or tumors are prepared and distributed on the wards. Instruction sheets for conditions such as head injury or scabies are given out in the appropriate clinics. In addition, written material is available as preparation for tests such as intravenous pyelography. Only a few samples of this type of information have been included in the Manual.

I wish to express my sincere appreciation to the members of the Standards Careplan Committee: Rebecca Frank, Janine Jurimae, Eva McLaughlin, and Muriel Richardson; and to Shirley Avery, Marilyn Booth, Lynn Dirks, Andrea Frewin, Carolyn McAllister, Elizabeth Nicholl, and Donalda Parks; and also to the many nurses at The Hospital for Sick Children who have contributed to the development and maintenance of our careplan system. I am also grateful for the assistance of the Hospital's Medical Publications Department in the preparation of the manuscript. It has been a particular pleasure for me to work with Carla Salvador (Assistant Editor). Without her support and encouragement the second edition would not have become a reality.

Voirrey Broe, R.N., R.S.C.N.
Nursing Manual Coordinator

# Contents

# Abbreviations and Symbols

The following standard abbreviations are used in the careplans:

| | | | | |
|---|---|---|---|---|
| a.c. | before meals | | H₂0 | water |

a.c. — before meals
ADH — antidiuretic hormone
ad. lib. — as desired
a.m. — morning
ASA — acetylsalicylic acid (Aspirin)
AV — arteriovenous
b.i.d. — twice a day
BP — blood pressure
BUN — blood urea nitrogen
C — celsius
Ca — calcium
CBC — complete blood count
cc — cubic centimeter (measuring gases)
Cl — chloride(s)
cm — centimeter
CNS — central nervous system
CO2 — carbon dioxide
CPP — cerebral perfusion pressure
CSF — cerebrospinal fluid
CV — central venous
CVP — central venous pressure
d.a.t. — diet as tolerated
dr — doctor (intern/house physician, consultant, etc.)
ECG — electrocardiogram
EEG — electroencephalogram
ENT — ear, nose, and throat (otorhinolaryngology)
ESR — erythrocyte sedimentation rate
ET tube — endotracheal tube
g — gram
g/dl — grams per deciliter
GI — gastrointestinal
Hb — hemoglobin
HCl — hydrochloric acid
Hct — hematocrit
Hg — mercury
HIR — head injury routine
hr — hour
h.s. — at bedtime

H₂0 — water
ICP — intracranial pressure
ICU — intensive care unit
i.m. — intramuscular(ly)
IMV — intermittent mandatory ventilation
ITP — idiopathic thrombocytopenic purpura
i.v. — intravenous(ly)
IVP — intravenous pyelogram
K — potassium
kg — kilogram
L — left
ml — milliliter (measuring fluids)
mm — millimeter
mmol — millimole
Na — sodium
NG tube — nasogastric tube
n.p.o. — nothing by mouth
N saline — normal saline solution
O2 — oxygen
OR — operating room
PAR — postanesthetic (recovery) room
p.c. — after meals
PEEP — positive end-expiratory pressure
pH — hydrogen ion concentration
p.m. — after noon
p.o. — by mouth
p.r.n. — as necessary
PT — prothrombin time
PTT — partial thromboplastin time
PUF — polyurethane foam
q2h, q3h, etc. — every 2 hours, every 3 hours, etc.
q.i.d. — 4 times a day
R — right
RBC — red blood count
RH — relative humidity
RT — respiratory technologist
SG — specific gravity
SGOT — serum glutamic oxaloacetic transaminase

| | | | |
|---|---|---|---|
| *stat* | immediately | **TV** | television |
| **TcPO2** | transcutaneous partial pressure of oxygen (arterial) | **VS** | vital signs |
| **t.i.d.** | 3 times a day | **WBC** | white blood count |
| **TLC** | "tender loving care" | < | less than |
| **TPR** | temperature, pulse, and respiration | > | greater than |

# Introduction to the Standard Careplans

Standard careplans are designed to provide nurses with written information for practical use. The present format is the one we have found most useful, but nurses elsewhere may wish to modify it. Furthermore, some of our careplans are based on or include treatments or equipment not used in some other hospitals: in such circumstances, the principles of care can be retained and the details adapted to the situation.

It must be borne in mind that (whatever their format or method of use) *standard careplans do not replace a patient's individual careplan*—they are a component of it. Standard careplans concern "usual" problems, and each patient has individual reactions, difficulties, and strengths. For example, the clinical course may differ from that anticipated: this "unusual" problem would necessitate additional planning to supplement or replace part of the standard careplan.

Each standard careplan lists the problems anticipated as a result of the stated condition or treatment and details the patient's long-term and short-term goals, the time by which such patients usually achieve them (except for Stresses of Hospitalization, which continue throughout the hospital stay), and the nursing actions we think will be required for their achievement. In short, we use the standard careplans as basic documents, obviating both the need for detailed recording "from scratch" for each patient and the possibility that even the most careful, experienced nurse may forget some usual aspect(s). Wherever possible we have outlined independent nursing actions, but the nursing implications of actions or instructions by other members of the health care team are included. Throughout, we have tried to give enough information to permit a nurse unfamiliar with a given condition to provide safe, intelligent nursing care.

Use of the standard careplans requires a clear understanding of their structure.

### "Goals for Discharge or Maintenance"
These goals constitute the signs, symptoms, or behavior that nurses expect to see or hear from the patient or members of his family by the time the patient leaves their care. "See Objectives" entered in this space indicates that the problems will be resolved when the short-term objectives have been met. Some problems may never be resolved; but we hope that, by the time the patient is discharged or transferred, members of his family will be demonstrating knowledge, attitudes, and skills that will allow optimal care in the future.

### "Usual Problems"
Throughout, we have defined problems as the difficulties or concerns of the patient and/or members of his family. The focus is on what the patient experiences, not on the problems that a nurse encounters as she cares for him. Under "Usual Problems" we have identified those that are present in most cases and potential problems that will develop if effective preventive action is not taken. Whenever possible the reason for the problem has been stated, to provide the nurse with more knowledge on which to base adaptations of care. When the cause is not stated, the problem stems directly from the title condition.

The standard careplans do not include *unusual* problems, which are difficulties or concerns of the *individual patient*. Such problems should be written on the patient's own careplan (see An Illustrative Case, which follows). We use the same method as for usual problems—identifying the patient's/parents' objectives, timing, and specific nursing orders—to deal with and solve each unusual problem.

### "Objectives"
The objectives are the signs, symptoms, or behavior expected when the problem is resolved or prevented. They state what the patient or members of his family will be doing and saying or physical changes in the patient that indicate progress or the prevention of deleterious developments.

### "Timing"
Timing indicates the usual time by which the corresponding objective is achieved. Some time intervals can be identified precisely in terms of hours or days, whereas others may depend on many variables; for the latter, the timing indicates either the end of a phase of therapy or the patient's discharge from hospital. As stresses connected with hospitalization *per se* are operative throughout a patient's stay, attempts to minimize them must be continued until he leaves. Therefore, no timings are stated in the Stresses of Hospitalization careplans.

Good nursing care requires attention at all times to all of the patient's current problems and awareness of other potential problems. Frequent checking of the careplans will ensure that no aspects are overlooked and will enable the nurse to evaluate the patient's actual progress in relation to that expected. For precise timings, a helpful practice is to note actual dates against the timings (e.g., under "By 3 days," write "July 8").

If the patient and/or members of his family have not achieved an objective by the time stated, the nurse should reevaluate the situation in regard to that problem. Why has the objective not been achieved? Are both the problem and objective still relevant, or should either be changed to accommodate factors that have developed or come to light in the interim? Are the nursing orders adequate, or should they be expanded or modified? Also, has failure to achieve this objective revealed another, previously unidentified, problem?

Thus, timing is a very important feature of these standard nursing careplans, corresponding to time limits for achievement of objectives (such as response to therapy) set by other members of the health care team.

### "Nursing Orders"
The nursing orders detail the actions to be taken by nurses caring for the patient to maintain continuity of the patient's care. For some nursing orders, further in-

formation about the reasons for particular orders has been included in parentheses.

The term "designated nurse" indicates the need for continuity of relationship between the patient and family and one member of the nursing staff.

### "Procedures" and "Instructions to Parents"

The standard careplans outline methods in some nursing orders but are not intended to replace a hospital's routine protocols. When nursing procedures are mentioned, refer to that section of your institution's procedures manual.

All parents are instructed orally in the home care of their child and are given this information in writing. Examples of instructions and information for parents of children with some specific conditions are included after the relevant plans.

### How to Use the Standard Careplans

The *patient careplan*, for overall nursing care, is initiated on admission to the hospital or on first attendance at the clinic. It includes:

1. A nursing history, recording information obtained during the nursing interview and from observation of the patient and members of his family
2. Doctor's orders
3. Hospital routines
4. Standard careplans:
   a. Stresses of Hospitalization careplan appropriate to the patient's stage of development
   b. Careplans relating to the reason for hospital admission or clinic attendance (e.g., diagnosis, treatment)
5. Identification of any unusual problems and of measures for dealing with them.

After reviewing this composite patient careplan, the nurse should be able to give appropriate, consistent care. Assessment continues throughout the patient's stay in hospital. Observations and evaluations of the suitability of planning and efficacy of care are recorded in the patient's progress notes, which include the nursing discharge-summaries.

### An Illustrative Case

The patient careplan evolved for "William (Billy) Hill" will serve to illustrate how the standard careplans are used. Billy, aged 8 years, was admitted to hospital with a fractured femur and abrasions of the left arm sustained in a car accident. He was treated in the emergency department and was admitted to the orthopedic ward on a Bradford frame with his left leg in a Thomas splint.

The morning of the accident, Billy had complained of a slightly sore throat, but his mother had decided it was not serious enough to keep him home from school. By afternoon, when he was admitted to the hospital, his temperature was 38.5°C and he had some clear nasal discharge.

The nurse who admitted Billy interviewed his mother. She recorded a nursing history (Figure 1) and attached to this the standard careplans for Stresses of Hospitalization (young schoolchild), Fractured Femur, and Pyrexia, and relevant plans referred to therein. Both Mrs. Hill and Billy were upset by the accident, but the nurse felt they were coping well and that there were no nursing problems beyond those outlined in the standard careplans. She referred to these plans on Billy's patient careplan and established the next day as the time for reassessment. On the front of the patient careplan she recorded pertinent information from the history and the doctor's orders; on the back she wrote "No unusual problems."

By the next morning Billy had copious nasal discharge. His temperature had risen to 39.7°C during the night. The nurses decided that, to prevent chest complications, nursing measures were required beyond those outlined in the standard careplan for the immobilized patient (referred to in the Fractured Femur careplan). They therefore crossed out the previous evening's assessment and recorded planning for this unusual problem.

Two days later a nurse pointed out that Billy was eating little from his meal trays except desserts. She learned that he had had many visitors, most of whom had brought candy, cookies, or chips; he was eating so many snacks that he was not hungry at mealtime. After discussion with Mrs. Hill, the nurses recorded a plan for a consistent approach to Billy's diet.

The patient careplan evolved for Billy by day 5 of his admission is shown in Figure 2.

```
100002        WARD 6F
HILL - WILLIAM (BILLY)
05-07-84       1630 HR
FRACTURED FEMUR. L.
DOB 20-06-76   M    SP
ORTHOPEDIC -- MONTCLAIR
```

**INFORMATION ABOUT INTERVIEW:** INFORMANT: *MOTHER*

**LANGUAGE OF PARENTS:** *ENGLISH*  OF CHILD: *ENGLISH*

**INTERPRETER?** (NAME & PHONE #)

**UNUSUAL CIRCUMSTANCES INFLUENCING INTERVIEW:** *MOTHER UPSET + CRYING, FEELS GUILTY ABOUT THE ACCIDENT. WORRIED ABOUT OTHER CHILDREN LEFT WITH A NEIGHBOR*

**CIRCUMSTANCES LEADING TO THIS HOSPITALIZATION:** WHY DID YOU BRING YOUR CHILD TO HOSPITAL?

**WHAT HAS THE DOCTOR TOLD YOU ABOUT YOUR CHILD'S ILLNESS?** TESTS, SURGERY, ETC.,

*BILLY WAS HIT BY A CAR ON THE WAY HOME FROM SCHOOL.*
*DOCTOR SAYS HE HAS BROKEN HIS LEFT LEG AND WILL HAVE TO BE IN TRACTION FOR*
*3 WEEKS, THEN HE WILL BE PUT IN A CAST. ALSO, HE HAS SOME SCRAPES*
*ON HIS ARM. HE SEEMS TO BE GETTING A COLD - HAS A SORE THROAT*

**MEDICATIONS:** (INCLUDE LATEST DOSE), TREATMENTS AT HOME;  **ALLERGIES:** FOOD, DRUG, OTHER

*EGGS + WOOL*
*CAUSES A RASH ON FACE + BODY*

**PREVIOUS HOSPITALIZATION:** NO ☐  YES ☑  HOSPITAL: *HSC.*

**WHAT WAS ADMISSION FOR?** CHILD'S AND PARENTS' REACTIONS TO HOSPITALIZATION?

*HAD TONSILS + ADENOIDS OUT WHEN HE WAS 6 YRS. OLD. WAS IN OVERNIGHT*
*NO UNUSUAL PROBLEMS*

**HOME BACKGROUND:** NICKNAME; SIBLINGS (NAMES AND AGES); PETS; OTHER IMPORTANT FAMILY MEMBERS;
RESPONSIBILITIES AT HOME AND IN COMMUNITY; FROM OUT - OF - TOWN?

*BROTHER - JIM, AGE 3 YR        SISTER - ANGELA, AGE 10 YR*
*FATHER HAS A NEW JOB AND WILL BE OUT OF TOWN UNTIL JULY 11.*
*FAMILY HAS A PUPPY NAMED SANDY*
*BILLY BELONGS TO THE CUB SCOUTS*

**VISITING PLANS:** *MOTHER WILL COME IN EACH EVENING. GRANDMOTHER + UNCLE ON WEEKENDS.*

**WAYS PARENTS WOULD LIKE TO PARTICIPATE IN CARE:** *MOTHER WOULD LIKE TO HELP BILLY WITH HIS*
*SUPPER, THEN BATHE + SETTLE HIM FOR THE NIGHT*

**HABITS OF DAILY LIVING:** FOOD AND FLUIDS: LIKES AND DISLIKES. SPECIAL SLEEP HABITS

**USUAL BATHROOM HABITS:** BED - WETTER, BLADDER EXPRESSION, ENEMA ROUTINES OR LAXATIVES.

*LIKES MOST FOODS - ESPECIALLY DESSERTS*
*FAVORITE DRINK - GINGER ALE         ALLERGIC TO EGGS*
*USUALLY SLEEPS ON STOMACH*

33384

POMR (26)

**Figure 1.** *Example of a nursing history.*

3

**RECREATION AND SOCIABILITY:**

FAVOURITE ACTIVITIES: (GAMES, HOBBIES, ETC.,)  LIKES BICYCING.  PLAYS BASEBALL + HOCKEY

ENJOYS CARD GAMES AND MAKING MODELS.    NOT VERY FOND OF READING.

LIKES TV AND RECORDS

RELATIONSHIPS WITH OTHER PEOPLE: PEERS, SIBLINGS, ADULTS

GETS ALONG WELL WITH MOST PEOPLE , IS NOT SHY WITH STRANGERS

PLAYS WITH A GROUP OF NEIGHBORHOOD BOYS

SCHOOL: NAME OF SCHOOL, GRADE, COURSE, PROGRESS

CENTENNIAL SCHOOL - GRADE 3      TEACHER - MRS. ROBERTS

BELONGINGS BROUGHT TO HOSPITAL   NONE

MOTHER WILL BRING IN SOME T-SHIRTS , ALSO SOME OF BILLY'S GAMES

CAPABILITIES OF PHYSICALLY &/OR MENTALLY HANDICAPPED CHILD: LIMITATIONS, RESTRICTIONS, MOBILITY,

FEEDING, SPEECH, SELF - CARE, ETC. SPECIAL BRACES, GLASSES

QUESTIONS ASKED BY PARENT &/OR PATIENT:   WILL BILLY BE IN MUCH PAIN ?

HOW WILL HE EAT WHEN HE IS LYING FLAT ON HIS BACK ?

HOW LONG WILL HE BE IN HOSPITAL ?

PERTINENT OBSERVATIONS MADE DURING INTERVIEW: (PARENTS' REACTIONS AND CONCERNS, PARENT - CHILD INTERACTION)

MOTHER VERY UPSET + CRYING , BLAMES HERSELF FOR THE ACCIDENT - SHOULD HAVE

KEPT BILLY AT HOME WHEN HE COMPLAINED OF A SORE THROAT.

IS MAKING REALISTIC PLANS FOR VISITING BILLY + CARING FOR HER OTHER CHILDREN

SHE WAS ABLE TO SETTLE BILLY BEFORE SHE LEFT.

NURSING OBSERVATIONS OF PATIENT ON ADMISSION: (PHYSICAL APPEARANCE, ADJUSTMENT TO HOSPITAL)

IS IN A THOMAS HIP SPLINT AND ON A BRADFORD FRAME. TRACTION IS INTACT

LEFT PEDAL PULSE IS STRONG , CAN MOVE TOES, L THIGH IS QUITE SWOLLEN

HAS SOME CLEAR NASAL DISCHARGE.    T 38°C (oral).

PROBLEMS IDENTIFIED FOR THE PATIENT CARE PLAN:

PROLONGED IMMOBILIZATION

MAINTENANCE OF TRACTION

ALLERGIES TO EGGS + WOOL

PYREXIA

SEPARATION FROM FAMILY

DATE JULY 5, 1984 SIGNATURE Janet Greene  R.N.

**Figure 1** (*Continued*).

4

# THE HOSPITAL FOR SICK CHILDREN                              PATIENT CARE PLAN

NAME: WILLIAM (BILLY) HILL       AGE: 8 YEARS      DIAGNOSIS: FRACTURED FEMUR (L)

ADMISSION DATE: JULY 5, 1984      DOCTOR: MONTCLAIR      NURSE: JANET GREENE

HISTORY AND SPECIAL INFORMATION  HIT BY CAR ON WAY HOME FROM SCHOOL
HAS A FRACTURE OF THE LEFT FEMUR + SOME ABRASIONS ON LEFT ELBOW
IS IN A THOMAS HIP SPLINT + ON A BRADFORD FRAME
T 38°C (oral), SEEMS TO HAVE A COLD, HAS SOME CLEAR NASAL
DISCHARGE

| SPECIAL POINTS TO OBSERVE | CHART | STANDARD CARE PLANS | FAMILY VISITING & PARTICIPATION |
|---|---|---|---|
| PEDAL PULSE (L FOOT) | q2h | FRACTURED FEMUR | MOTHER WILL VISIT IN EVE |
| ABRASIONS | daily + p.r.n | PYREXIA | TO HELP ½ SUPPER, BATHING & |
| NASAL DISCHARGE | q.8h | STRESSES OF HOSP. | SETTLING HIM. |
| COUGH | q.8h | - YOUNG SCHOOLCHILD | RELATIVES WILL VISIT ON |
|  |  |  | WEEKENDS - FATHER IS OUT |
|  |  |  | OF TOWN UNTIL JULY 11 |

| | INSTRUCTIONS | ACTIVITY | TIME | INSTRUCTIONS |
|---|---|---|---|---|
| TEMP | q.4h, q2h if temp ↑ | BATH | 1900 | BED - MOTHER WILL DO IN PM. |
| P&R | q.4h, CHECK AIR ENTRY | BEDREST | ✓ | ON FRAME, ON BACK |
| BP | | SCHOOL | 1030 | SCHOOLTEACHER WILL COME TO ROOM |
| PUPILS | | O.T. | | |
| INTAKE | | PHYSIO | | |
| OUTPUT | | RECREATION | 1400 | VOLUNTEER WILL COME TO ROOM |
| WEIGHT | | CLOTHING | NO POOL | SIDE-FASTENING SHORTS. OWN T-SHIRTS |

DIET: SELECTIVE MENU                                 DIET RESTRICTIONS & PREFERENCES
ENCOURAGE FOOD HIGH IN ROUGHAGE                 ALLERGIC TO EGGS
(FRUITS + VEGETABLES) + FINGER FOODS            LIKES GINGER ALE

| DATE | MEDICATIONS & TREATMENTS | TIME | DATE | SPECIAL TESTS AND PROCEDURES | TIME |
|---|---|---|---|---|---|
| July 5 | TYLENOL 325mg p.o q.4h, p.r.n. for temp ↑ 38.5°C | | | | |
| July 6 | NOVAHISTINE ELIXIR 5ml p.o q.i.d. | 0800 1200 1600 2000 | | | |
| | | | | | |
| | | | | | |
| | | | | | |
| | | | | | |
| | | | | | |
| | | | | | |
| | | | | | |

33358

**Figure 2.** *Example of a patient's careplan.*

5

| NURSING GOALS FOR DISCHARGE OR MAINTENANCE | DISCHARGE PLANNING REFERRALS |
|---|---|
| WILL BE GOING HOME IN A HIP SPICA MOTHER DEMONSTRATES CORRECT CAST CARE, TURNING, AND BEDPAN TECHNIQUES | PUBLIC HEALTH NURSE TO ARRANGE TRANSPORTATION HOME + RETURN TO CLINIC, AND HOME-SCHOOLING RED CROSS TO ARRANGE FOR HOSPITAL BED, BEDPAN + URINAL AT HOME |

| DATE | UNUSUAL PROBLEMS | OBJECTIVES | TIMING | NURSING ORDERS | SIGNATURE |
|---|---|---|---|---|---|
| July 5 | NO UNUSUAL PROBLEMS | REASSESS | JULY 6 | | J. Greene RN |
| July 6 | POTENTIAL CHEST PROBLEMS DUE TO UPPER RESPIRATORY TRACT INFECTION | NO CHEST PROBLEMS, ADEQUATE AIR ENTRY TO ALL LOBES | July 10 | a. ENCOURAGE DEEP-BREATHING + COUGHING, q2h DURING DAY, q4h AT NIGHT  b. INCREASE FLUID INTAKE TO AT LEAST 240 ml q2h WHILE HE IS AWAKE  c. OBSERVE FOR INCREASED NASAL DISCHARGE, COUGH, DECREASED AIR ENTRY + REPORT TO DR IF PRESENT. | J. Greene RN |
| July 8 | Potential delay in healing due to poor nutrition (eating candy + chips before meals, eating only dessert) | Is eating at least ½ of each meal. Is selecting a more balanced menu. | July 14 | a. Limit candy, etc., to after meals and only if he has eaten part of each course.  b. Encourage mother to take candy home. Suggest that small books or toys are brought instead.  c. Help patient with menu selection – do nutrition teaching.  d. Ensure that meals are attractively served.  e. Give positive reinforcement for eating meals | K. Barnes RN |

Figure 2 (Continued).

# Stresses of Hospitalization

Pediatric nursing care requires appreciation of the physical, emotional, spiritual, and social needs of both the child and his family. A child is a unique individual, part of a particular family—nuclear and extended—and of a specific community—neighborhood, friends, school, and social organizations. These are a child's support systems; they must be taken into account by all caregivers when a child enters the hospital environment. The child's parents, especially, are an integral part of their child's hospital experience. They, also, require care and they contribute to their child's care.

Most of the knowledge of the psychosocial effects of hospitalization on children has evolved over the last 30 years. Valuable work by Bowlby [1952, 1969, 1973], Spitz [1965], Robertson [1970], Robertson and Robertson [1971], and Anna Freud [1972] has alerted caregivers in the health sciences to the needs of children who are ill or in institutions. Erikson [1963, 1968] described the child as a developing individual with specific needs, skills, and tasks to be recognized at various stages of his growing years, and Piaget's theory of cognitive development [1972] indicated a further dimension. Increasing awareness of mental health has fostered preventive approaches to care. For example, Petrillo and Sanger [1972, 1980], McCollum [1975], and Hofmann, Becker, and Gabriel [1976] have written about the well-being of infants, children, and adolescents who are ill or in hospital. These concepts have challenged those working in pediatric health care to conduct further research into the special needs of children and to provide for them in child-care facilities and programs.

Child development is a continuous progression through stages, from complete dependence upon the mother to maturation as an independent adult. We have chosen to use the following classification of stages:

1. Infant stage: birth to 18 months
2. Toddler stage: 18 months to 3 years
3. Preschool stage: 3 to 5–6 years
4. Young schoolchild stage: 6 to 9–10 years
5. Preadolescence: girls, 9 to 11 years; boys, 10 to 12 years
6. Adolescence:
   a. Early adolescence: girls, 11 to 13 years; boys, 12 to 14 years
   b. Mid adolescence: girls, 13 to 16 years; boys 14 to 17 years
   c. Late adolescence: 16 to 18+ years

A complete careplan was formulated for each of these stages, considering adolescence as one stage that extends from the upheaval associated with endocrine changes through the child's struggle for independence to the achievement of a degree of independence and a sense of his identity.

Because the stages progress, each building on the preceding one, the ages assigned as well as the content of the plans overlap. Growth and development proceed at different rates in different individuals and are influenced by many factors, such as culture, climate, birth order, and nutrition, to name but a few. In addition, consideration must be given to children who are handicapped. Therefore, the ages assigned to these stages should be used only as guidelines. For example, menarche may occur in one girl at 11 years of age and in another at 14; the adolescent growth spurt usually begins earlier in a girl than in a boy; and a mentally retarded preschool child may have attained the level of physical development characteristic of his chronological age. Thus, judgment is needed in selecting the appropriate Stresses of Hospitalization careplan for each child.

Children experience stress when they are in hospital. A child is brought to hospital because he is ill or has been injured. Hospitalization, whether it is brief or prolonged, usually disrupts a child's development and his family's functioning.

The stresses of hospitalization for pediatric patients that are identified in the careplans are as follows.

1. **Separation.** Hospitalization separates a child from his usual environment and support systems—his family, home, friends, and sphere of activity.

2. **Illness.** Illness is any unhealthy condition of the body or emotional disturbance; for the purposes of the careplans this includes injury and sensations associated with his illness (e.g., pain, nausea, itching, and malaise). The state of being ill itself engenders problems; these are the subject of the Stresses of Hospitalization careplans. In addition there are the emotional problems specific to certain illnesses, such as the self-image of a child with heart disease; these are included under the relevant diagnosis in the main section of careplans.

3. **Altered activity and stimulation.** Both the hospital environment and the specific aspects of treatment alter a child's usual level of motor functioning, sensory input (visual, auditory, olfactory, gustatory, and tactile), and psychosocial interactions. Decreased activity and stimulation, such as bed rest, traction, and restriction of visitors, result in degrees of deprivation; increased activity and stimulation, such as several tests in one day, a noisy environment, and too many visitors, result in overstimulation. In some circumstances a new normal level of activity may be called for, temporarily (e.g., during traction) or permanently (increased, as after correction of a defect; or decreased, for a child with an acquired chronic disorder).

4. **Painful procedures.** These are the diagnostic and treatment procedures, including surgery, that a child perceives as painful. He may experience actual pain and/or fear of pain associated with bodily insults imposed by hospital personnel (diagnostic procedures

7

such as finger-prick, myelogram, or sigmoidoscopy; treatment procedures such as injection, change of dressing, or surgery).

Children's reactions to specific stresses depend upon many factors: their perception of them, their past experiences with them, their parents' reactions to them, their religious and cultural background, their present developmental stage, etc. Their feelings about and reactions to these stresses are expressed through their verbal and nonverbal behavior (e.g., regression, withdrawal, physical tension, irritability, outbursts of temper, and stoicism) in hospital and/or afterward at home. The nurse must assess each child and his particular circumstances to understand what feelings his behavior reflects, and must interpret the actual behavior in relation to the expected behavior. Also, the child's parents need to understand and appreciate this behavior.

The child's family is his link between his home life and the hospital. The nurse's role includes caring for the child *and* his parents, and fostering parental participation in the child's care, so that impairment of the child's development and of his family's functioning is minimized. *The pediatric nurse is an advocate of both the child and his family.*

The following Stresses of Hospitalization careplans reflect this philosophy by identifying the stresses that children experience in hospital, establishing the patient's goals and individual objectives, and outlining nursing actions to achieve the desired results. These careplans complement the medical and surgical ones, providing a basis for comprehensive nursing care.

## References

Bowlby, J.  *Maternal Care and Mental Health* (2nd ed.). Geneva: World Health Organization, 1952.

Bowlby, J.  *Attachment and Loss.* Vol. I. *Attachment.* New York: Basic Books, 1969.

Bowlby, J.  *Attachment and Loss.* Vol. II. *Separation: Anxiety and Anger.* New York: Basic Books, 1973.

Erikson, E. H.  *Childhood and Society* (2nd ed.). New York: Norton, 1963, pp. 247–274.

Erikson, E. H.  *Identity, Youth and Crisis.* New York: Norton, 1968.

Freud, A.  The role of bodily illness in the mental life of children. In S. I. Harrison and J. F. McDermott (Eds.), *Childhood Psychopathology. An Anthology of Basic Readings.* New York: International Universities Press, 1972, pp. 572–584.

Hofmann, A. D., Becker, R. D., and Gabriel, H. P.  *The Hospitalized Adolescent. A Guide to Managing the Ill and Injured Youth.* New York: Free Press, 1976.

McCollum, A. T.  *Coping with Prolonged Health Impairment in Your Child.* Boston: Little, Brown, 1975.

Petrillo, M., and Sanger, S.  *Emotional Care of Hospitalized Children. An Environmental Approach.* Philadelphia: Lippincott, 1972, (2nd ed.) 1980.

Piaget, J.  The stages of the intellectual development of the child. In S. I. Harrison and J. F. McDermott (Eds.), *Childhood Psychopathology. An Anthology of Basic Readings.* New York: International Universities Press, 1972, pp. 157–166.

Robertson, J.  *Young Children in Hospital* (2nd ed.). London: Tavistock, 1970.

Robertson, J., and Robertson, J.  Young children in brief separation. A fresh look. *Psychoanalytic Study of the Child* 26:264–315, 1971.

Spitz, R. A.  *The First Year of Life.* New York: International Universities Press, 1965, pp. 3–16.

# Stresses of Hospitalization:
# Infant Stage (Birth to 18 Months)

The birth of an infant occurs after months of anticipation and preparation by his family. The circumstances that precede the birth inevitably influence the milieu into which the child is born. Each family member begins to compare the actual child with the wished-for child. The members gradually adjust their expectations, and then they can form an attachment with the new baby.

Within the family, a special relationship forms between the mother (usually the primary caregiver) and her baby. The infant is primarily a receiver (of care, food, sensations, etc.), taking in through his mouth (e.g., he sucks a nipple, a pacifier, and his hands) and his senses (visual, auditory, and tactile). During the first year, he is increasingly able to communicate his needs more specifically and respond when they are met. As his mother consistently meets his needs, a trusting relationship is established. From the second month of life, he perceives himself and his mother as one unit. A few

months later he begins to realize his separateness from his mother; gradually, a smile specifically for his mother develops, indicating that a special bond has formed between them. It is during this time that he may experience "stranger-anxiety." Around the end of the first year, as his motor skills progress from crawling to tentative walking, he practices moving away from his mother but will experience anxiety when separated from her.

Hospitalization of an infant disrupts this developing relationship and can create feelings of insecurity for both the mother and her infant. When an infant is hospitalized, it is important that he continue his development. Also, the special relationship between a mother and her baby (bonding) must be promoted. The nurse, therefore, must consider care for the mother as much a part of her role as care for the infant.

### Goals for Discharge or Maintenance
**I.** The infant experiences minimal stresses of hospitalization.
**II.** The parents understand these stresses and are prepared to help their infant recover from them.

| Usual Problems/Objectives | Nursing Orders |
|---|---|
| **1a.** Separation of an infant from his mother at birth.<br><br>**Objectives.** The infant and mother experience minimal effects of separation:<br><br>(1) They develop a satisfying, appropriate relationship.<br><br>(2) The mother gains confidence in her ability to care for her infant. | On admission of infant, identify the mother's primary supportive person (e.g., husband, mother, or friend) and his or her role as defined by the mother. Spend time with this person, gathering information about the pregnancy, labor, delivery, and postpartum events. Encourage the father to be a link between the mother and infant (e.g., by visiting his wife after seeing their infant). Also, have him hold the infant whenever possible. If possible, see or talk with the mother—whether she is in this or another hospital or at home—and ensure that she has opportunities to discuss her baby's condition and treatment with the medical staff. Describe his appearance (e.g., color of hair, shape of face). If her baby was born prematurely, explain the characteristics of a premature infant to her and correct any misconceptions she may have.<br><br>Ensure that the designated nurses have assessed their own feelings about the infant and are communicating a positive attitude; this will foster a positive attitude in the mother. Plan with the mother ways of maintaining her communication with medical and nursing personnel, by daily telephone calls or other means, while she is separated from her baby.<br><br>If the mother can come to the hospital, encourage the father to be present the first time she visits their baby: his acceptance of the situation may help to allay her anxiety. Beforehand, describe to her the infant's present condition and prepare her for equipment she may see. Since her infant was born either prematurely or with a health problem, remember that she will probably feel disappointment, guilt, anger, and/or blame. Recognize that she will need to work through these feelings. Assess her need for additional assistance to cope with |

continued

| Usual Problems/Objectives | Nursing Orders |
|---|---|
| **1a. (Continued).** | her feelings and plan coordinated intervention (e.g., by a social worker, community nurse, or psychiatrist). |
| | *Respect the mother's special status* and provide an environment conducive to mothering (e.g., privacy and a comfortable chair). Encourage and provide opportunities for the mother to have contact with her infant: getting to know her baby comprises many experiences—visual (eye-to-eye and face-to-face), auditory (recognizing her baby's cry and sounds), and tactile (touching, holding, and cuddling). Give her tasks to perform for her baby, such as changing the diaper under him, especially if he is too ill for her to feed him. Be with the mother when she is with her child. Help her to interpret cues to her baby's needs and to meet them; praise her attempts to develop her ability to meet them; support her efforts at nurturing. Assess the present status of her mothering activities, and help her to progress (e.g., from seeing, to gently talking to, exploring, holding, cuddling, rocking, bathing, and feeding her infant). Determine her wishes about feeding her baby (breast or bottle). If she wants to breast-feed him, and this is appropriate for both of them, plan a realistic program (e.g., she can pump her milk and bring it in). Identify situations in which she may need some guidance and offer assistance without usurping her position as mother. If this is her first child, remember that the mother's anxiety and uncertainty will be even greater and that she may be fearful. |
| | *If the mother cannot come to the hospital,* ensure as consistent an assignment of nurses as possible to provide at all times a caregiver who knows the infant's needs. Identify the reasons that prevent the mother from coming to see her baby; explore ways of overcoming these barriers so that, if possible, the mother may come to the hospital in sufficient time before discharge to become acquainted with her baby, to begin to form a relationship with him, and to learn to care for him. |
| | In planning for discharge, identify community resources to help the mother adjust to mothering her infant at home. |
| **1b.** Separation of an infant from his mother after he has been at home. | Spend time with the mother to gather information about the pregnancy, labor, delivery, and postpartum events; her baby's daily activities (e.g., patterns of feeding, sleeping, and play) and comfort measures and objects; and to get to know the infant in his mother's presence. Plan nursing care to include patterns already established, and encourage the mother to participate in her baby's care. Ensure a consistent assignment of nurse(s) to promote a trusting relationship with the parents and to provide the infant with continuity of caregivers. Ensure that the designated nurses have assessed their own feelings about the infant and are communicating a positive attitude. This will foster a positive attitude in the mother. |
| **Objectives.** The infant and his mother experience minimal effects of separation: | |
| (1) They continue/develop a satisfying, appropriate relationship. | |
| (2) The mother maintains/gains confidence in her ability to care for her infant. | |
| | *Respect the mother's special status* and provide an environment conducive to mothering (e.g., privacy and a comfortable chair). Encourage consistent visiting to en- |

| Usual Problems/Objectives | Nursing Orders |
|---|---|
| **1b. (Continued).** | hance continuity of the developing mother–infant relationship. This schedule should provide optimal opportunities for the mother and the nurse to plan and share the infant's care (e.g., can the mother room-in with her baby?).<br><br>*If the mother can come to the hospital,* find out how she feels about the schedule and the sharing of care. Accept her decisions about the degree of her involvement and recognize her feelings (e.g., fearfulness, insecurity, and possibly resentment of the nurses' competence and close relationship with her infant). Recognize that she will find separation difficult and encourage her to express her feelings. Maximize her involvement: recognize her need to participate in planning her infant's care (e.g., if she has been breast-feeding her baby, assess the possibility of continuing this). The baby will probably cry when his mother has to leave, so be available to help her adjust to this temporary separation; if appropriate, suggest that she wait beyond her baby's view to hear him stop crying. Help her to keep in touch when she and the baby are separated (e.g., encourage her to telephone from home to be assured that her baby has settled). When his mother leaves, stay with the infant and comfort him until he settles. During her absence, talk to him about his mother; ask the parents to bring a favorite toy or a security object or, for older infants, pictures of family members. Hold, cuddle, and rock the baby often.<br><br>*If the mother cannot come to the hospital,* ensure as consistent an assignment of nurses as possible, to provide at all times a caregiver who knows the infant's needs. Identify the reasons that prevent the mother from coming to see her baby and explore ways of overcoming these barriers. Establish regular contact with the mother, by telephoning or by writing letters and sending photographs of her baby. Be sensitive to her feelings about separation from her infant: encourage her to express her feelings and listen to her; help her to identify and solve problems. Ensure that she is kept informed of her baby's progress by both nursing and medical staff. Recognize her need to participate in planning her infant's care (e.g., does she have specific requests or suggestions? Are there clothes or other items that she would like to send?). In planning for discharge, identify community resources to help the mother adjust to mothering her infant at home. |
| **2. Illness.**<br><br>**Objectives**<br><br>**a.** The infant experiences minimal stress from his illness and achieves optimal recovery from the stress.<br>**b.** The parents adjust to their infant's illness. | Respond immediately to any discomfort expressed by the infant (e.g., touch him, rock or cuddle him, offer a pacifier).<br><br>Spend time with the parents to ascertain what they know about their infant's illness. Ensure that they are kept informed about his illness and his progress; reinforce this information and rectify any misconceptions. Identify and help them to get in touch with other health care team members who can help them understand.<br><br>Help the parents to express their feelings and concerns. |

continued

| Usual Problems/Objectives | Nursing Orders |
|---|---|
| **2. (Continued).** | Offer your support. If you think they need it, help them get in touch with other supportive persons (e.g., clergy, social worker). |
| | Encourage the mother to be as actively involved in her baby's care as is comfortable for her. Help the parents provide care within the limitations imposed by the illness; e.g., if their baby is too ill to be held, encourage them to stroke, touch, and talk softly to him. Acknowledge their participation in their baby's care. |
| | Help the parents to prepare for caring for their baby at home (e.g., teach them any treatments to be done at home, so they can be comfortable with them). If necessary, identify persons and agencies in the community who can help them, and ensure that they can make the desired contacts. |
| **3.** Altered activity and stimulation.<br><br>**Objective.** The infant engages in normal activity and experiences normal stimulation to the limit of his capabilities. | Spend time with the mother to learn about her baby's usual level of activity. Assess his level of development (sensory, motor, language, and psychosocial); identify his developmental gains, and plan care to include stimulation to maintain them (e.g., a mobile, rattle, or stuffed animal; a stroller). While giving care, repeat the infant's sounds and talk to him; provide as much eye-to-eye, face-to-face contact as possible. An occupational therapist or recreationist can help in devising a systematic plan to maintain or advance the infant's development. Involve the parents in this planning and implementation. Their baby's "infant-stimulation plan" should be at his bedside for use by everyone caring for him. |
| | Assess the infant's hospital environment to determine whether he is receiving too little stimulation (deprivation), too much (overstimulation), or what is normal for him. |
| | *If there is insufficient stimulation,* identify areas in which activity and stimulation can be increased and plan for this (e.g., provide brief periods in different body positions or out of restraints; hang brightly colored mobiles within his view; use a music box, busy-box, rattle, infant's exerciser, walker; bounce him playfully on your knee). Encourage the parents to participate and acknowledge their involvement. |
| | *If there is too much stimulation,* identify areas in which activity and stimulation can be decreased at least temporarily (e.g., turn lights off, decrease noise, limit the number of people in the vicinity, play soft music, and stroke him). Organize the nursing care to include definite rest periods and ensure that the infant does rest. Encourage his parents to participate and acknowledge their involvement. |
| **4.** Painful procedures (clinical, investigational, surgical) and fear of them.<br><br>**Objectives**<br><br>  **a.** The infant experiences minimal pain from the procedures. | Explain and interpret all procedures to the parents; encourage their involvement and implement their decisions. Ascertain whether an analgesic might be necessary for the infant, and if so, when to give it.<br><br>During the procedure use the infant's security objects |

| Usual Problems/Objectives | Nursing Orders |
|---|---|
| **4. (Continued).**<br><br>  **b.** The infant and his parents are not unduly fearful of or anxious about the procedures. | (e.g., a pacifier or blanket). If appropriate, hold him securely, so the procedure can be done efficiently and as quickly as possible (reducing the duration of discomfort) and to let him know that he has not been deserted. Talk soothingly to him throughout the procedure.<br><br>Afterward, allow the infant to discharge his tension through mobility and crying. If appropriate, encourage the parent to hold, stroke, touch, and talk softly to him until he settles; offer guidance to them. If the parents are not available or their participation is inappropriate, the designated nurse will provide these comfort measures. |

# Stresses of Hospitalization: Toddler Stage (18 Months to 3 Years)

Toddlers are beginning to discover their environment. Gross and fine motor skills, language, and bowel and bladder control are important milestones in the development of their independence. The toddlers' developing motor ability and limited impulse-control necessitate provision of a safe environment with appropriate supervision, so that they can enjoy new experiences and practice their newly acquired skills. Play is a necessary part of the toddlers' day: it enables them to express their feelings and to learn (e.g., finding out what things are, how they work, and what to do with them). Their mother continues to be their main source of security, and their relationship with her fosters their growth and development. *When a toddler is in hospital, the staff must supplement the mother's role in these areas without usurping it.* Rooming-in is the most effective model of care for this age group.

Young toddlers (18 to 24 months) have mastered the art of walking. They see themselves as separate from their mother but need to assure themselves frequently of their mother's presence. In the hospital, therefore, they display separation anxiety and are constantly concerned about their mother's whereabouts. In separating toddlers from their family and the security of their mother's presence, illness and hospitalization threaten their attempts at independence and growing self-control, usually resulting in regressive behavior. At this stage, children are egocentric in their thinking, actions, and feelings. Illness and treatment arouse fears and fantasies. They are likely to interpret separation from family, home, and secure surroundings as abandonment or as punishment for something they have done wrong, or both. The nurse must demonstrate through her care her appreciation of these stresses experienced by a toddler, his mother, and other family members; she must provide an environment that reduces the anxiety of separation and promotes continuing development of the child's autonomy.

### Goals for Discharge or Maintenance
I. The child experiences minimal stresses of hospitalization.
II. The parents understand these stresses and are prepared to help their child recover from them.

| Usual Problems/Objectives | Nursing Orders |
|---|---|
| **1.** Separation from parents and siblings.<br><br>**Objectives.** The child and his family experience minimal effects of separation:<br><br>**a.** They continue their satisfying relationship.<br><br>**b.** The mother maintains confidence in her ability to care for her child. | On admission, introduce the child and his parents to the ward area (playroom, washroom, the child's room, and his roommates) and usual routines (e.g., hospital pamphlets and daily routines).<br><br>If appropriate, suggest that the child wear his own clothes while he is in hospital.<br><br>Spend time with the parents to learn:<br><br>–How their child responds to new situations.<br><br>–What experiences he has had with separation from the family and how he reacted.<br><br>–Whether he has previous hospital experiences (when, for what, for how long; clinic visits; what he recalls; how he reacted).<br><br>–What preparation the child has had for the present hospitalization (e.g., what he has been told about hospital, parents' availability, expected procedures).<br><br>–What comfort measures they use when their child is upset or uncomfortable; what his comfort objects are (e.g., blanket, bottle, stuffed toy). Ask for these objects to be brought in.<br><br>–Their plans to be with their child (who will be coming to see him, how often).<br><br>Ensure consistent assignment of nurses, to establish a trusting relationship with the child and his parents: the toddler needs to be able to identify consistent caring person(s). Promote continuity of parent–child–sibling relationships. Encourage consistent visiting, preferably daily; this gives the child confidence that his parents |

| Usual Problems/Objectives | Nursing Orders |
|---|---|
| 1. (Continued). | will return. Provide opportunities (out of hearing distance of the child) to discuss with his mother her feelings and her wishes for involvement in his care. Encourage her participation (e.g., if the mother wishes to bathe her child, arrange this), and each time she comes, make it possible for her to discuss her involvement. If appropriate, plan with parents for the siblings to visit.<br><br>Provide an environment conducive to mothering (e.g., privacy and a comfortable chair) and respect the mother's special status. Identify areas in which she may need guidance and supervision; offer assistance but do not usurp her role as mother. Be sensitive to mother–child interactions, so as not to interrupt what may be a significant time for them. The toddler is more apt to express his feelings about separation in his mother's presence (e.g., crying when she arrives and protesting when she leaves). Explore with the mother her feelings about and her interpretation of her child's reactions to separation. Offer suggestions to the mother to help decrease the effects of separation on her child (e.g., leaving reassuring objects—pictures of family, familiar clothing such as pajamas and slippers, toys from home—and telephoning). Help her handle situations: e.g., when she leaves, her child will probably cry and protest—when the mother is preparing to leave, be available to help them both to deal with the temporary separation. Encourage the mother to be honest with her child about her leaving and to let him and the nurse know when she plans to return. Help the child by staying with him, comforting him, and engaging him in an activity until he settles; help the mother by encouraging her to telephone from home for assurance that he has settled. Ensure that the mother is aware that toddlers usually regress when they are in hospital, and reassure her that although this regression may continue for some time after discharge, it is temporary. Commend the mother's participation in her child's care.<br><br>Help the child to deal with periods of separation from his mother. Talk about home experiences (e.g., have photographs of the family for the child to see, handle, and talk about), his mother's care for him, etc. When you can honestly interpret the situation, express the child's feelings for him: "I know you miss Mummy; she misses you, too. Mummy knows where you are and is coming to see you after lunch." Help the child to interpret and understand hospitalization. Assure him, often, that his parents will take him home when he is well. Ensure that the child receives comfort from caregivers and his comfort objects. Spend time with him, other than for treatment, to foster a relationship. Incorporate play and happy exchanges during care (e.g., when bathing and feeding). Use verbal and nonverbal expressions to convey to the child that you care.<br><br>Bedtime is an especially vulnerable time for the toddler. If his mother is unable to be there, stay with him and help him settle (e.g., read a story, talk about the day's events); help him perform his usual bedtime rituals, and provide special comforts (e.g., hold him on your lap, and |

continued

| Usual Problems/Objectives | Nursing Orders |
|---|---|
| **1. (Continued).** | tuck him into his bed with his favorite toys and blankets). Nighttime presents special problems (e.g., sleep disturbances): ensure that the child receives the attention and comfort he needs to feel secure during the night in what is to him a strange environment.<br><br>If the parents cannot come to see their child, recognize the anxiety they are feeling as a result of being separated from him. Encourage continuing communication by telephone or letters; ask the parents to send photographs of family and pets. Try to establish a schedule of incoming telephone calls, so that you have up-to-date information (from medical staff also) when they call; if at all possible, have the child speak with his parents. (Recognize that the toddler is missing his parents, especially his mother.)<br><br>Offer the parents suggestions for their child's management after his return home. Prepare them for potential emotional reactions (e.g., nightmares, tantrums, clinging, or regressive behavior). These reactions may start in hospital and continue or cease at home; they may start only after his return home; or they may be the same or different in the two settings. |
| **2. Illness.**<br><br>**Objectives**<br><br>**a.** The child and his parents adjust to his illness.<br><br>**b.** The child experiences minimal stress from his illness and achieves optimal recovery from the stress. | Spend time with the parents to learn about their child's experiences with illness and his response, and assess what they know about his present illness. Identify other health care team members who can give them information and help them understand their child's condition. Ensure that any desired contacts are made (e.g., with the dietitian, doctor).<br><br>Assess how the parents feel about their child's illness and its effects on the family. Plan approaches to help them deal with their feelings so they can help their child. (Toddlers are very receptive to their parents' reactions; therefore, the nurse should be aware that parental attitudes and responses affect how toddlers perceive their illness.)<br><br>If the parents are comfortable with their feelings and can be honest and supportive with their child, help them continue this approach. Some parents want to talk with their child about his illness but are uncomfortable with their feelings and need guidance. Recognize their need to express their concerns (e.g., fears, anxieties, even guilt) about their child's illness and ensure that they receive assistance to do so. Assess the parents' need for additional assistance; advise them of appropriate sources of help (e.g., social worker, clergy) and ensure that any contacts they desire are made. Other parents are neither comfortable with their feelings nor want to talk with their child about his illness: recognize that they, also, need to express their feelings. Assess their need for assistance, and put them in touch with appropriate sources of help. In collaboration with other health care team members, share your concerns openly but tactfully with the parents about their child's need for information concerning his illness and treatment and for continuing comfort from them. |

| Usual Problems/Objectives | Nursing Orders |
|---|---|
| **2. (Continued).** | Provide opportunities for parents to talk freely, beyond their child's hearing, about his illness. Ascertain what they have told their child and how they perceive his response(s) to his illness. The toddler cannot distinguish between distress from within and that which is imposed: anything that causes him discomfort (e.g., whether it is abdominal pain or a finger-prick) requires recognition of his feelings and immediate comforting. Discuss and plan with the parents how to talk with the toddler about his illness (e.g., whether to communicate information to him through play or words) and what comfort measures they use or think are suitable in the present circumstances.

Observe the toddler's behavior to learn how he feels and what he thinks about his illness. If he can talk, transferring the hurt to a toy is less anxiety-producing than talking about himself (e.g., "What made Teddy sick?" "Why does Teddy's leg hurt?"). Help him clarify his thinking: offer information that is simple, direct, and related to his experiences (e.g., "Teddies don't get sick because they are bad—children don't, either." "Teddy's leg hurts to let him know that his leg isn't working right and needs to be fixed [mended]"). Help the toddler appreciate what he *can* do, so he does not generalize his illness to his whole body ("It's only Teddy's leg that is sore; he can still sit up in bed and play with his toys").

Praise the parents for participation in their child's care, and evaluate the approach with them frequently.

If appropriate, help the parents prepare to care for their child at home (e.g., teach them any treatments that need to be continued, so they can do them properly and confidently). Tell the parents about sources of help and community agencies, and help them make any necessary contacts. |
| **3.** Altered activity and stimulation.<br><br>**Objective.** The child engages in normal activity and experiences normal stimulation to the limit of his capabilities. | Learn as much as possible from parents about their child's activities and psychosocial development (e.g., daily routines, motor skills, and language development). Assess the child's level of development, and plan with his parents how to maintain it. Schedule his day to include familiar routines and habits, refraining from extra expectations that would impose additional stress while he is in the hospital (e.g., weaning from the bottle, removing his pacifier, or beginning toilet-training). As the toddler has no sense of time, link explanations to daily activities to help him with time-orientation (e.g., "Mummy comes after your breakfast," or "We'll read a book and then get washed for lunch"). Recognize his pride in accomplishing tasks and praise him for his attempts.

Identify areas in which the toddler needs direction or supervision and provide it. Assess the environment for potential hazards and remove them. Include playful interactions during his routine care (e.g., during his bath, allow him to splash water, sail boats, and fill and empty containers). Ensure that he has appropriate play materials at all times; utilize hospital play programs designed for his age group. |

continued

| Usual Problems/Objectives | Nursing Orders |
|---|---|
| **3. (Continued).** | Recognize the toddler's limited tolerance for delayed gratification and offer immediate alternatives (e.g., if he may not eat or drink for a while, remove him from a room where other children are eating and engage him in some activity he enjoys). |
| | Assess the child's hospital environment and determine whether he is receiving too little stimulation (deprivation), too much (overstimulation), or what is normal for him. |
| | *If there is insufficient stimulation*, try to identify areas where it can be increased. Discuss the limitations of activity and plan alternatives with his parents; e.g., if bed rest is ordered, provide a change of scenery (place his bed near a window), music, bed toys, and toys with moving parts. Join in his activities (e.g., read him a story, play with him with a toy), promoting activity to the limit of the restrictions. If possible, have other children play with him. (Even if they cannot participate, toddlers benefit from watching and listening to others.) |
| | *If there is too much stimulation*, discuss and plan with his parents how to decrease it. Provide quiet times as well as definite rest periods in an appropriate environment. Help the parents to understand their child's needs for quiet activities (e.g., soft music, stories) and include their suggestions. Be sensitive to the possibility that the schedule of tests, treatments, and procedures may not allow the child sufficient time to recover, and be aware of his reactions to them; discuss your concerns with the medical staff. |
| **4.** Painful procedures (clinical, investigational, surgical) and fear of them.<br><br>**Objectives**<br>**a.** The child experiences minimal pain from procedures.<br>**b.** The child and his parents are not unduly fearful of or anxious about procedures. | If at all possible, refrain from having the toddler experience painful procedures in his own bed; he should be able to think of his bed as a secure place in what is to him a strange environment. Tell parents about all the procedures their toddler is about to experience. If they understand the reason for a procedure and know what will happen before, during, and after it, they can support and comfort their child. (Parents know their children better than anyone else does and know what helps them. Acknowledge the parents' decisions, suggestions, and any assistance they offer in the procedure.) |
| | Ensure that preparation occurs at a suitable time (usually just beforehand), and keep in mind the child's previous experience with procedures. Ensure that what you tell him is within his comprehension. Use visual aids (e.g., a doll or stuffed animal and safe hospital equipment); encourage the toddler to handle and familiarize himself with these before and after a procedure. Limit explanations to the external body part involved and what the child will see and hear. Refrain from using words such as "bad" or "nasty" for disease and "shots" for injections; many toddlers interpret these words in relation to punishment or violence or both, increasing their feelings of being punished with hospitalization. Take your cues from how the toddler is reacting to the visual aids. Talk honestly about the pain he will feel: let the child know how his parents and you will help him |

| Usual Problems/Objectives | Nursing Orders |
|---|---|
| **4. (Continued).** | (e.g., tell the child you will stay with him [*and do so*] throughout and after the procedure).<br><br>Allow the toddler to express his hurt, and help his parents understand his need for expression and protest. Use comfort measures (e.g., talk soothingly to him during the procedure and hold, hug, and rock him immediately afterward). Make sure that he takes his comfort objects with him into situations that are painful or might frighten him. Ensure that any pain is controlled (by positioning, quiet, and/or analgesics) and that the environment is conducive to recovery. Tell the toddler when the procedure is over and stay with him until he settles. Encourage his parents to comfort him. If the parents cannot be present, the nurse must assume the primary supporting role.<br><br>Be aware of the toddler's exposure to other children who are undergoing or have undergone painful procedures: what he sees and hears increases his own fear and stimulates fantasies. Be sure he knows that the other children are all right and that he is comforted. |

Preschoolers can tolerate brief separations and move more easily than toddlers from the security of their home environment into the wider world of their neighborhood. Their attachment to their family though, is still their most important association. They have achieved some mastery of gross and fine motor skills. Also, their language skills have developed sufficiently for them to express some of their feelings, ask questions, and understand answers, but their facility in using language may exceed their understanding of the answers or of words used by adults.

Preschoolers' language, creativity, inquisitiveness, and urge for locomotion contribute to an intrusive, aggressive style. They have a vivid imagination and fantasy life which is reflected in their play. For example, they imitate significant roles: they pretend to be someone they admire (e.g., father, mother) and thus enjoy the power associated with the role; they pretend to be someone or something they fear (e.g., doctor, tiger) and thus try to master the fear by assuming an active rather than a passive role. As they become more aware of the differences between themselves and others, including sexual differences, they are increasingly aware of their sexual identity. This may be expressed in two ways: through heightened curiosity of which they should not be ashamed, and through periods of modesty for which they need privacy.

Illness and hospitalization, and especially painful and intrusive procedures, stimulate fantasies of bodily harm which prompt toddlers to view these experiences as punishment for real or imagined misdeeds. Their parents (especially the mother) are their chief support when they encounter the stresses of hospitalization. These children are very receptive to their parents' reactions, but they are also beginning to form attachments to other significant persons. They are sensitive to the attitudes (facial expressions, tone of voice, and gestures) and feelings of those around them (parents, hospital staff, and other patients).

Preschoolers need thoughtful preparation and explanations of procedures, and opportunities to voice their feelings and concerns about all aspects of their illness and hospitalization. Play facilitates this process: children in this age group use play to master experiences. Therefore, a preschooler's nurse should incorporate opportunities for play throughout the child's stay in hospital. In addition, preadmission programs are very helpful for this age group.

## Goals for Discharge or Maintenance
I. The child experiences minimal stresses of hospitalization.
II. The parents understand these stresses and are prepared to help their child recover from them.

| Usual Problems/Objectives | Nursing Orders |
|---|---|
| 1. Separation from mother, father, siblings, and peers.<br><br>**Objectives.** The child and his family experience minimal effects of separation:<br><br>a. They continue their satisfying relationship.<br><br>b. The parents maintain confidence in their ability to care for their child. | On admission, introduce the child and his parents to the ward area (playroom, washroom, the child's room, and roommates) and usual routines (e.g., hospital pamphlets and daily routines).<br><br>If appropriate, suggest that the child wear his own clothes while he is in the hospital.<br><br>Spend time with the parents to learn:<br><br>–How their child responds to new situations.<br><br>–What experiences he has had with separation from the family and how he reacted.<br><br>–Whether he has previous hospital experiences (admitted when, for what, for how long; clinic visits; what he recalls; how he reacted).<br><br>–What preparation the child has had for the present hospitalization (e.g., what he has been told about the hospital, parents' availability, expected procedures).<br><br>–What comfort measures they use when their child is upset or uncomfortable; what his comfort objects are (e.g., blanket, stuffed toy). Ask for these objects to be brought in.<br><br>–Their plans to be with their child (who will be coming to see him, how often). |

| Usual Problems/Objectives | Nursing Orders |
|---|---|
| **1. (Continued).** | Ensure a consistent assignment of nurses to establish a trusting relationship with the child and his parents: the preschooler needs to be able to identify consistent caring person(s). Promote continuity of parent–child–sibling relationships. Encourage consistent visiting, preferably daily; this gives the child confidence that his parents will return. Provide opportunities to discuss with the parents their child's care, out of hearing distance of the child. Encourage parents' participation in their child's care (e.g., if the mother wishes to bathe her child, arrange this) and each time they come give them an opportunity to discuss their involvement. Identify areas in which the parents may need some guidance and supervision, and offer it without usurping their position. Be sensitive to parent–child interactions, so as not to interrupt what may be a significant time for them. The preschooler is more apt to express his feelings about separation in his parents' presence (e.g., crying when they visit and protesting when they leave). Explore with the parents their feelings about and interpretations of their child's reactions to separation. Help the parents to handle these situations. For example, when the mother leaves, her child will probably cry and protest; be available to help them deal with this temporary separation. Encourage parents to be honest with their child about leaving and to let him and the nurse know when they plan to return. Help the child by staying with him, comforting him, and engaging him in an activity until he settles; help the parents by encouraging them to telephone from home for assurance that he has settled.

Offer suggestions to the parents to help decrease the effects of the separation on their child (e.g., by leaving reassuring objects—picture of family, familiar clothing such as pajamas and slippers, toys from home—and telephoning). Commend the parents' participation in their child's care. If appropriate, plan with the parents when siblings may visit. Encourage them to bring in information about the child's friends (neighborhood, nursery school, or kindergarten). Help them appreciate how their child is dealing with the separation.

Bedtime is an especially vulnerable time for the preschooler. If his mother is unable to stay until bedtime, help him to settle to sleep by reading a story to him, for instance, or talking about the day's events. Help the child perform his usual bedtime rituals, and provide special comforts (e.g., by holding him on your lap and tucking him into bed with his favorite toys and blanket). Nighttime presents special problems (e.g., sleep disturbances): ensure that the child receives the attention and comfort he needs to feel secure during the night in what is to him a strange environment.

If the parents cannot come to see their child, recognize the anxiety they are feeling as a result of being separated from him.

Encourage continuing communication between the parents and the nursing and medical staff (e.g., by telephone) and between the parents and their child (e.g., by telephone, letters, and photographs). Recognize that |

continued

| Usual Problems/Objectives | Nursing Orders |
|---|---|
| **1. (Continued).** | this young child is missing his parents and siblings immensely.<br><br>The preschooler has already begun the socialization process (playing, sharing, learning from and supporting each other). Plan group activities with other preschoolers (e.g., sitting together for meals, playing games, listening to stories or music), to continue the development of this process.<br><br>Ensure that the parents are aware that preschoolers usually regress when they are in hospital. Reassure them that, although this regression may continue for some time after discharge, it is temporary. |
| **2. Illness.**<br><br>**Objectives**<br><br>**a.** The child and his parents adjust to his illness.<br><br>**b.** The child experiences minimal stress from his illness and achieves optimal recovery from the stress. | Spend time with the parents and their child to learn about his experiences with illness and his response to them. Assess what the parents know about his present illness. Identify other health team members who can give them more information and help them understand, and ensure that desired contacts are made (e.g., with the dietitian, doctor).<br><br>Assess how the parents feel about their child's illness and its effects on the family. Plan approaches to help them deal with their feelings so they can help their child. (Preschoolers are very receptive to their parents' reactions; therefore, nurses should be aware that parental attitudes and responses affect how a child perceives his illness.)<br><br>If the parents are comfortable with their feelings and can be honest and supportive with their child, help them continue this approach. Some parents want to talk with their child about his illness but are uncomfortable with their feelings and need guidance. Recognize their need to express their concerns (e.g., fears, anxieties, even guilt) about their child's illness and ensure that they receive assistance to do so. Assess their need for additional assistance; advise them of appropriate sources of help (e.g., social worker, clergy) and ensure that any contacts they desire are made. Other parents are neither comfortable with their feelings nor want to talk with their child about his illness: recognize that they, also, need to express their feelings. Assess their need for assistance, and put them in touch with appropriate sources of help. In collaboration with other health team members, share your concerns openly but tactfully with the parents about their child's need for information concerning his illness and treatment and for continuing comfort from them.<br><br>Provide opportunities for the parents to talk freely, beyond their child's hearing, about his illness. Ascertain what they have told their child and how they perceive his response(s) to his illness. The preschooler cannot distinguish between distress from within and that which is imposed: anything that causes him discomfort (e.g., whether it is abdominal pain or a finger-prick) requires recognition of his feelings and immediate comforting. Discuss and plan with parents how to talk with their child about his illness (e.g., who will teach; words and |

| Usual Problems/Objectives | Nursing Orders |
|---|---|
| **2. (Continued).** | explanations the child needs to know; how to reinforce information). They may become more comfortable about their own approach by watching and learning from the nurse. |
| | Learn about what the child knows, how he feels, and what he thinks about his illness. Use toys and play activities to obtain this information. For a child of this age, talking about a toy (stuffed animal, doll) is less anxiety-producing than talking about himself (e.g., "What made Teddy sick?" "Why does Teddy's leg hurt?"). Help him clarify his thinking. Offer information that is simple, direct, and related to his experiences (e.g., "Teddies don't get sick because they are bad—children don't either." "Teddy's leg hurts to let him know that his leg isn't working right and needs to be fixed [mended]"). When talking with him, discuss the healthy parts of his body and what he *can* do, so that he doesn't generalize his illness to his whole body (e.g., "It's only Teddy's leg that is sore; he can still sit up in bed and play with his puzzles"). Encourage the child to ask questions and express his feelings. Encourage him to tell you when he is not feeling well (e.g., tiredness, headache, or nausea), and respond by comforting him. His knowledge of the body is limited to what he sees, feels, and uses, and explanations must reflect this. Therefore, direct your teaching to the body part involved and talk about what is happening now and what will happen when the condition is controlled or improved. Be sensitive to verbal and nonverbal expressions; anticipate and rectify any misconceptions. Praise the parents' participation in their child's treatment, and evaluate approaches with them often. |
| | Preschoolers are becoming aware of sexual differences and need privacy. Pull the curtains and allow privacy for their toilet, allow them to wear underwear, etc. Recognize and accept their capacity for curiosity and fantasy (e.g., they should not be scolded or made to feel guilty for their inquisitiveness). |
| | If appropriate, help parents to prepare to care for their child at home (e.g., teach them any treatments that need to be continued, so they can do them properly and comfortably). Tell the parents about sources of help and community agencies, and assist them in making contacts. |
| **3.** Altered activity and stimulation.<br><br>**Objective.** The child engages in normal activity and experiences normal stimulation to the limit of his capabilities. | Learn as much as possible from the parents about their child's activities and psychosocial development (e.g., daily routines, language development, motor skills, and relationships with children and adults). Assess the child's level of development and discuss with his parents how to maintain it. Plan the child's day to include his familiar routines and habits. Recognize that his concept of time is more defined than the toddler's; he is aware of the day's events and routines, and he has some understanding of the concepts of past and future. |
| | Ensure that preschoolers continue as much as possible the self-care they have learned and praise their efforts. |

continued

| Usual Problems/Objectives | Nursing Orders |
|---|---|
| **3. (Continued).** | They are proud of these skills and relinquishing them threatens their self-esteem. Recognize the need to channel energy constructively; provide activities within the limits imposed by the child's illness. Recognize the child's need for gratification and offer alternatives to sources denied him (e.g., if he may not eat or drink, remove him from the room where other children are eating and substitute an activity that interests him). |
| | Assess the preschooler's hospital environment and determine whether he is receiving too little stimulation (deprivation), too much (overstimulation), or what is normal for him. |
| | *If there is insufficient stimulation,* try to identify how stimulation can be increased. Discuss the limitations of activity and plan alternatives with the parents and child; e.g., when the child's mobility is limited, provide toys with moving parts (windmills) or toys that move (cars) or opportunities to ride in a wheelchair or on a stretcher. Promote as much independence as restrictions will allow (e.g., participation in daily routines, choice of play). Involve parents in promoting activity and stimulation for their child. Include other preschoolers in his activities whenever possible. |
| | *If there is too much stimulation,* discuss with the parents and child how to decrease it (e.g., remove the child from other children; position for rest). Schedule quiet periods (e.g., time for stories) and see that he is not disturbed when his parents are there. Be sensitive to the possibility that the schedule of tests, treatments, and procedures may not allow the child sufficient time to recover, and be aware of his reactions to them: discuss your concerns with the medical staff. |
| **4.** Painful procedures (clinical, investigational, surgical) and fear of them.<br><br>**Objectives**<br><br>**a.** The child experiences minimal pain during procedures.<br><br>**b.** Before the procedures, the child and his parents are not unduly fearful of or anxious about them.<br><br>**c.** After the procedures, the child verbalizes feelings about them, the pain, and his efforts to control the pain during the procedure. | If at all possible, refrain from having the preschooler exposed to painful procedures in his own bed. He should be able to feel that his bed is a secure place in what is to him a strange environment. Tell parents about all procedures their child is about to experience. If they understand the reason for the procedure and know what will happen before, during, and after it, they can support and comfort him. (Parents know their children better than anyone else does and they know what helps them. Acknowledge their decisions, suggestions, and any assistance they offer in the procedure.)<br><br>Ensure that preparation occurs in sufficient time for the preschooler to ready himself, and make certain that what you tell him is within his comprehension. Use visual aids (e.g., dolls, stuffed animals, or puppets; safe hospital equipment); encourage him to handle and familiarize himself with these before and after the procedure. (Repetition provides an opportunity to master a situation.) Limit explanations to the external body part involved and what he will see and hear. Refrain from using words such as "bad" or "nasty" for disease and "shots" for injections. Many preschoolers interpret these words in relation to punishment or violence, |

| Usual Problems/Objectives | Nursing Orders |
|---|---|
| 4. (Continued). | increasing their feelings of being punished with hospitalization.<br><br>Recognize the child's feelings and encourage his (verbal and nonverbal) expression of them. Take your cues from how he reacts to the visual aids. Whenever appropriate, reinforce often that he should not blame himself for the hospitalization or illness and that the procedure is limited. Talk honestly about the pain he will feel. Let him know how his parents and you will help him.<br><br>Increasing awareness of sexual identity brings concern for the intactness and safety of the genitals. Therefore, preschoolers view the removal of their underwear and the insertion of catheters, suppositories, or rectal thermometers as threats to their bodies. Explain why these measures are done, and reassure the child that they are temporary and will not alter his body permanently. Try to ascertain his fears and fantasies about painful procedures, and rectify any misconceptions revealed during play and conversation (e.g., reassure the child that the incision will not fall apart when the stitches are removed).<br><br>Recognize that preschool children feel very vulnerable when their bodies are exposed. Convey the message that you respect them and that you recognize their need to be told when the intrusion is to begin and for an assurance of privacy and comfort. Offer the child some control in situations (e.g., "Which arm can we use for your blood test?"), *but do not give a choice if there is none.* Stay with the child throughout and after the procedure. Allow him to express his hurt (e.g., "It will feel like an 'ouch'; yell if you feel like it"). Comfort him during the procedure (e.g., talking softly) and afterward (e.g., stroking, holding him). See that the child has his security objects with him in painful and stressful situations. Ensure that any pain is controlled (e.g., analgesics, positioning, and/or quiet) and that the environment is conducive to his recovery.<br><br>Tell the child when the procedure is over. Be available as much as possible, and be aware of his reactions to the procedure and any alteration in his body. Acknowledge his assistance with the procedure. *Do not say,* "You are a good boy"; a child interprets such words as "good" and "bad" as a reflection of worth rather than of ability to cope. Rather, make statements like "you held very still for your blood tests" or "you helped the doctor do your test." Encourage parents to comfort their child. Acknowledge the parents' involvement in the procedure; help them to deal with their child's need for protest and expression of hurt. If they cannot be present, the nurse must assume the primary supporting role.<br><br>Be aware of the child's exposure to other children undergoing painful procedures; what he sees stimulates his own fear and fantasies. Be sure he knows that the other children are all right and that he is comforted. |

6683

Young school children are ready to engage in formal, systematic activities. They enjoy challenges: planning, exploring, collecting, creating, questioning, learning, producing, and building. Visible achievements give them a sense of competence. Their inquisitiveness and continuing development of physical skills allow them to be adventurous. They are competitive and have a sense of fair play. Their widening range of interests takes them beyond their family into the community, where they participate with peers and adults in both spontaneous and organized activities (e.g., games with rules). Forming clubs and gangs with peers of the same sex provides them with the opportunity to organize part of their lives according to rules they establish. Adherence to these rules is strictly enforced by the group. They will, however, test the limits of rules which they view as imposed by adults. In short, this is a time of learning the skills necessary to live sociably and cooperatively in the world beyond their homes.

Illness and hospitalization interrupt their daily routines and social contacts. They worry about falling behind in school and being unable to compete. Fears and fantasies of abandonment, pain, and mutilation are matters of concern. Many young schoolchildren regress while they are in hospital. The more mature ones are beginning to understand the concept of permanence; they may fear permanent impairment and even death. Young schoolchildren see a nurse as a caring adult who provides them with information, helps them understand the hospital environment, and enables them to deal realistically with what is happening to them. Preadmission programs are very helpful for this age group.

## Goals for Discharge or Maintenance
I. The child experiences minimal stresses of hospitalization.
II. The parents understand these stresses and are prepared to help their child recover from them.

| Usual Problems/Objectives | Nursing Orders |
|---|---|
| 1. Separation from family, peers, and daily activities.<br><br>**Objective.** The child experiences minimal effects of separation. | On admission, introduce the child and his parents to the ward area (playroom, washroom, the child's room, and roommates) and usual routines (e.g., hospital pamphlets and daily routines).<br><br>If appropriate, suggest that the child wear his own clothes while he is in the hospital.<br><br>Spend time with the parents to learn:<br><br>–How their child responds to new situations.<br><br>–What experiences he has had with separation from the family and how he reacted.<br><br>–Whether he has previous hospital experiences (admitted when, for what, for how long; clinic visits; what he recalls; how he reacted).<br><br>–What preparation the child has had for the present hospitalization (e.g., what he has been told about the hospital, parents' availability, expected procedures).<br><br>–How they comfort their child when he is upset or disturbed—ask the parents to bring his favorite toy.<br><br>–Their plans to be with their child (who will be coming to see him, how often, or if they will be staying with him).<br><br>Ensure a consistent assignment of nurses to establish a trusting relationship with the child and his parents: the young schoolchild needs to be able to identify consistent caring person(s). Promote continuity of patient–child–sibling relationships. Encourage consistent visiting, as often as possible, to maintain contact within the family.<br><br>Encourage the parents to participate in their child's care and discuss their feelings about this each time they |

| Usual Problems/Objectives | Nursing Orders |
|---|---|
| **1. (Continued).** | come. Identify areas in which they may need some guidance and supervision and offer assistance without usurping their position. Be sensitive to parent–child interactions, so as not to interrupt what may be a significant time for them. Help the parents deal honestly with their child when they have to leave him, and encourage them to tell him when they will return. Acknowledge their help in their child's care.

If the parents cannot come to the hospital, recognize the anxiety they are feeling as a result of being separated from their child. Try to establish a schedule of incoming telephone calls so that current information is available from both nursing and medical staff. Recognize that the child is missing his family, particularly his parents. Encourage continuing communication by telephone and/or letters and photographs; if at all possible, have the child speak with his parents when they call. Ask the parents if they will allow their child to telephone them, and how often, and help him do this. Encourage him to write letters, or send cards he has made, to parents, siblings, and peers.

Encourage continuing contact with the child's friends (e.g., messages brought by his parents, telephone calls, and/or visits by his teacher), and foster his activities with peers inside the hospital (e.g., eating together, playing games, and joint projects). Provide opportunities for the child to discuss his feelings about the separation, and give him the chance to make decisions, so he can maintain some control over his situation (e.g., contact with peers, keeping up with school work). |
| **2. Illness.**<br><br>**Objectives**<br>**a.** The child and his parents adjust to his illness.<br><br>**b.** The child experiences minimal stress from his illness and achieves optimal recovery from the stress. | Spend time with the parents and their child, separately and together, to learn about the child's experiences with illness and his response. Assess what the parents know about their child's present illness. Identify health team members who can give them information and help them understand, and ensure that desired contacts are made (e.g., with the doctor, dietitian). Assess what the parents feel about their child's illness and its effects on the family. Plan approaches to help them deal with their feelings, so they can help their child. (Young schoolchildren are very receptive to their parents' reactions; therefore, nurses should be aware that parental attitudes and responses affect how a child perceives his illness.)

If the parents are comfortable with their feelings and can be honest and supportive with their child, help them continue this approach. Some parents want to talk with their child about his illness but are uncomfortable with their feelings and need guidance. Recognize their need to express their concerns (e.g., fears, anxieties, even guilt) about their child's illness and ensure that they receive assistance to do so. Assess their need for additional assistance; advise them of appropriate sources of help (e.g., social worker, clergy) and ensure that any contacts they desire are made. Other parents are neither comfortable with their feelings nor want to talk with their child about his illness; recognize that they, |

continued

| Usual Problems/Objectives | Nursing Orders |
|---|---|
| **2. (Continued).** | also, need to express their feelings. Assess their need for assistance, and put them in touch with appropriate sources of help. In collaboration with other health team members, share your concerns openly but tactfully with the parents about their child's need for information concerning his illness and treatment and for continuing comfort from them. |
| | Provide opportunities for the parents to talk freely, beyond his hearing, about their child's illness. Ascertain what they have told their child and how they perceive his response(s). Discuss and plan with them how to talk with their child about his illness (e.g., how and when information will be communicated). Recognize that the parents may feel comfortable watching and learning from the nurse. |
| | Young schoolchildren learn quickly and eagerly. Therefore, their learning about their illness is a necessary component of the teaching plan. In teaching, use simple medical terms for parts of the body. Direct your teaching to the body part involved; talk about what is happening now and what will happen when the condition is controlled or improved. Use visual aids (e.g., dolls, body-outline drawings, and safe hospital equipment) to make descriptions more understandable. Encourage the child to ask questions and express his feelings. Assess how much information he wants and can handle; reinforce information already given until he indicates readiness for more. Praise the parents for any involvement in their child's care, and evaluate the approach together frequently. |
| | If appropriate, help the child's parents prepare to care for him at home (e.g., teach them any treatments that need to be continued, so they can do them properly and comfortably). Tell them about sources of help and community agencies, and assist them in making contacts. |
| **3.** Altered activity and stimulation.<br><br>**Objective.** The child engages in normal activity and experiences normal stimulation to the limit of his capabilities. | Learn as much as possible from the child and his parents about the child's activities and psychosocial development (e.g., daily routines, language and communication skills). Assess the child's level of development and, with his parents, plan ways to maintain it. Plan the child's day to include familiar routines, habits, and activities. Provide opportunities for tasks and age-appropriate activities within his capabilities, but be available to offer assistance. Recognize the child's limitations in tolerating delay in gratification and offer alternative sources of gratification; help him to express constructively his feelings about the limits imposed by his illness. Ensure both active and quiet times throughout the day. |
| | Assess the child's hospital environment, and determine whether the stimulation he is receiving is too little (deprivation), too much (overstimulation), or what is normal for him. |
| | *If there is insufficient stimulation,* try to identify areas where stimulation can be increased. Discuss limitations of the child's activity and plan alternatives with him |

| Usual Problems/Objectives | Nursing Orders |
|---|---|
| **3. (Continued).** | and his parents (e.g., for a child restricted to bed, arrange for peers or staff or both to join in his activities). Maintain as much of the child's independence as the restrictions imposed by his illness will allow. Encourage the parents to help provide their child with contact, communication, and activities.

*If there is too much stimulation*, discuss and plan with the parents and child how to decrease it. Provide quiet times as well as definite rest periods in an appropriate environment. Try to schedule time for you to be alone with the child to help him deal with his feelings. Be sensitive to the possibility that the schedule of tests, treatments, and procedures may not allow the child sufficient time to recover, and be aware of his reactions to them; discuss your concerns with the medical staff. |
| **4.** Painful procedures (clinical, investigational, surgical) and fear of them.<br><br>**Objectives**<br><br>**a.** The child experiences minimal pain during procedures.<br><br>**b.** Before the procedures, the child and his parents are not unduly fearful of or anxious about them.<br><br>**c.** After the procedures, the child verbalizes feelings about them, the pain, and his efforts to control the pain during the procedure. | Discuss with the parents their wishes for involvement in preparations and comply with their decisions. For each procedure, use an appropriate method to prepare the child (e.g., with stories, pictures, discussions, and play with equipment). Tell the child what he will see, hear, and feel; who will be with him; how he can help with the procedure; how long it will take; and who will be with him afterward. Ensure that he receives accurate information about the effects of the procedure. Recognize his concern about his appearance and body functions afterward (e.g., scars, loss of hair, prosthesis) and his need for assistance to deal with any alterations. If appropriate, discuss with him how he can cope with these and offer suggestions (e.g., clothing, wig, makeup).

Encourage questions, reinforce explanations, and rectify misconceptions; proceed with further explanations when the child is ready. Emphasize that the procedure is limited to a specific time and specific part of the body. Talk honestly about the pain he will feel and how you will help him. Encourage him to express his feelings.

Recognize that young schoolchildren feel very vulnerable when their bodies are exposed. Let them know that you respect them and that you recognize their need to be told when the intrusion is to be started and for assurance of privacy and comfort. Acknowledge their need to be in control. When possible, allow them to make some decisions about the procedure (e.g., "Which arm can we use for your blood test?" "Do you want to go to the x-ray department in a wheelchair or walk?"), *but do not offer a choice if there is none.*

Recognize that a child may ask for a few minutes to compose himself before a procedure. Acknowledge his assistance with the procedure; encourage expression of his hurt, and tell him that it is all right to cry. Ensure that any pain due to the procedure is controlled (e.g., by analgesics, positioning, and/or quiet) and that the environment is conducive to recovery. Be available as much as possible, and be aware of the child's responses to the procedure and to any alteration in his body.

Afterward, use visual aids to help the child talk about what has happened to him, to help him increase his |

continued

| Usual Problems/Objectives | Nursing Orders |
|---|---|
| 4. (Continued). | understanding. When the stress is behind him, a child is more able to ask questions; be sure to rectify any misconceptions he may have. Help parents appreciate that questions and concerns may continue after their child returns home. Ensure that they have accurate knowledge and encourage them to discuss his concerns openly and honestly with the child. |

During the preadolescent stage, hormonal changes lead to the appearance of secondary sex characteristics and the beginning of the rapid physical growth that marks the onset of prepuberty. These alterations are accompanied by an upsurge of sexual feelings. Sexual curiosity is expressed verbally (e.g., jokes, whisperings, secrets) and nonverbally (e.g., looking at pictures in magazines). There is, however, a striking difference in the way preadolescent boys and girls relate to those of the opposite sex: boys tend to turn away from girls, but girls more readily express heterosexual interest. At the same time, both boys and girls often choose from among their friends a special friend or chum of the same sex. This relationship signifies the first movement toward intimacy with a person beyond the family circle.

Although their thinking is still factual, preadolescents are progressing toward abstract thought. They have some understanding of body parts and functions, but still have difficulty dealing with body processes they cannot observe or do not experience.

Preadolescents have well-established daily routines and activities (e.g., school, sports, clubs). Their increased motor skills and coordination, together with their competitiveness and the need to conform to group expectations, prompt them to take risks. Although life is broadening for them, home is still very much the center of their life. They begin to compare their family life (e.g., rules, customs, status) with the family life of their friends. They come to the realization that their parents are not omnipotent or omniscient.

Illness and hospitalization interrupt their daily routines, activities, and social contacts. They may worry about pain, mutilation, and death. The natural changes taking place in their bodies at this time heighten their awareness of their bodies, causing them to focus on their illness, intrusive procedures, and any potential or actual alterations to their body that may result. Preadolescents can use their hospital experience to learn more about their body, their illness and its management, and occupational roles. The nurse has the opportunity to channel this energy and interest constructively.

### Goals for Discharge or Maintenance
I. The child experiences minimal stresses of hospitalization.
II. The parents understand these stresses and are prepared to help their child recover from them.

| Usual Problems/Objectives | Nursing Orders |
|---|---|
| **1.** Separation from family, peers, and daily activities.<br><br>**Objective.** The child experiences minimal effects of separation. | On admission, introduce the child and his parents to the ward area (playroom, washroom, the child's room, and roommates) and usual routines (e.g., hospital pamphlets and daily routines).<br><br>If appropriate, suggest that the child wear his own clothes while he is in the hospital.<br><br>Spend time with the parents to learn:<br><br>–How their child responds to new situations.<br><br>–What experiences he has had with separation from the family and how he reacted.<br><br>–Whether he has previous hospital experiences (admitted when, for what, for how long; clinic visits; what he recalls; how he reacted).<br><br>–What preparation the child has had for the present hospitalization (e.g., what he has been told about hospital, parents' availability, expected procedures).<br><br>–How they comfort their child when he is upset or disturbed; what are his objects of solace.<br><br>–Their plans to be with their child (who will be coming to see him, how often).<br><br>Ensure a consistent assignment of nurses to establish a trusting relationship with the child and his parents. Promote continuity of family–child relationships, and |

continued

| Usual Problems/Objectives | Nursing Orders |
|---|---|
| **1. (Continued).** | encourage consistent visiting as often as possible. Each time the parents come to the ward, discuss their feelings and their wishes concerning involvement in their child's care; encourage their participation and organize nursing care to include this. Identify areas in which the parents may need some guidance and supervision and offer assistance without usurping their position. Be sensitive to parent–child interactions, so as not to interrupt what may be a significant time for them. When the parents are leaving, encourage them to tell their child when they will return. Commend the parents for their participation in their child's care. |
| | If the parents cannot come to the hospital, recognize the anxiety they may be feeling as a result of being separated from their child. Encourage communication by telephone or letters or both, and suggest that the child have photographs (family members, pets, etc.). Try to establish a schedule of incoming telephone calls from the parents so that current nursing and medical information is available. If possible, have the child speak with his parents. Ascertain whether the parents will allow their child to telephone them, and how often, and help him do this. Encourage the child to write letters and make cards to send to his parents, siblings, and friends. |
| | Ensure that the child can maintain contact with outside friends (e.g., messages brought in by his parents, telephone calls, visits by his teacher). Help the child to socialize with his hospital peers (e.g., eating together, playing games, joint projects) to help him form relationships. |
| | Provide opportunities for the child to discuss his feelings about separation. Plan with him ways to minimize his concerns, anxiety, and loneliness. If at all possible, arrange for him to continue his schooling and usual routines and wear his own clothing. |
| **2. Illness.** **Objectives** **a.** The child and his parents adjust to his illness. **b.** The child experiences minimal stress from his illness and achieves optimal recovery from the stress. | Assess what the parents know about their child's illness. Identify other health care team members who can provide more information and help the parents with their understanding, and ensure that they can get in touch with appropriate persons (e.g., doctor, dietitian). Assess what the parents feel about their child's illness and its effects on the family. Plan approaches to help them deal with their feelings, so they can assist their child. |
| | If the parents are comfortable with their feelings and can be honest and supportive with their child, help them continue this approach. Some parents want to talk with their child about his illness but are uncomfortable with their feelings and need guidance. Recognize their need to express their concerns (e.g., fears, anxieties, even guilt) about their child's illness and ensure that they receive assistance to do so. Assess their need for additional help; advise them of appropriate sources (e.g., social worker, clergy) and ensure that any contacts they desire are made. Other parents are neither comfortable with their feelings nor want to talk with their child |

| Usual Problems/Objectives | Nursing Orders |
|---|---|
| **2. (Continued).** | about his illness: recognize that they, also, need to express their feelings. Assess their need for assistance, and put them in touch with appropriate sources of help. In collaboration with other health team members, share your concerns openly but tactfully with the parents about their child's need for information concerning his illness and treatment and for continuing comfort from them. |
| | Provide opportunities for the parents to talk freely, beyond their child's hearing, about his illness. Ascertain what they have told their child, how he responded to this information, and their interpretation of his feelings about it. Discuss and plan with the parents how to talk with their child about his illness (e.g., how and when information will be communicated). |
| | Preadolescents are very receptive to ideas and new information. Therefore, their learning about their illness is a necessary component of the teaching plan. Use simple medical terms for external and internal parts of the body. Direct teaching to the body part involved and rectify any misconceptions they may have. Talk about what is happening now and what will happen when the illness is controlled or improved. Use visual aids (e.g., body-outline drawings, diagrams, booklets, and safe hospital equipment) to make descriptions more understandable. |
| | Encourage the child to ask questions and to express his feelings. Assess how much information he wants and can handle, and reinforce the information given until the child indicates a readiness for more. Try to ensure: (1) that the child has a basic understanding of his body, how it works, and how his illness is affecting it; (2) that he understands what he can and cannot do now and will be able to do when the illness is resolved; (3) that he can distinguish between discomfort caused by illness and by external means; and (4) that he expresses his discomfort and receives and responds to comforting. |
| | Anticipate the child's need for comfort and offer it, including comfort measures identified by his parents. |
| | Praise the parents for their participation in their child's care and evaluate the approaches with them frequently. Recognize the preadolescent's need for gratification and provide alternatives to sources denied him (e.g., if he cannot visit play areas, arrange suitable group or individual play sessions in his room). |
| | If appropriate, help the parents prepare to care for the child at home (e.g., teach them any treatments that need to be continued, so they can do them properly and comfortably). Tell them about outside sources of help and community agencies, and enable them to make any necessary contacts. |
| **3.** Altered activity and stimulation.<br>**Objective.** The child engages in normal activity and experiences normal stimulation to the limit of his capabilities. | Learn as much as possible from the child and his parents about the child's activities and psychosocial development (e.g., daily routines, language and communication skills). Assess the child's level of development, |

continued

| Usual Problems/Objectives | Nursing Orders |
|---|---|
| **3. (Continued).** | and outline the routines and activities he is likely to encounter in the hospital. Plan with the child and his parents ways to maintain his level of independence and control over his environment, within the limits imposed by his illness. |
| | Recognize the child's abilities and interests and provide opportunities for him to use them. Plan with the child both active and quiet times throughout the day. Encourage him to participate in age-appropriate activities (e.g., with peers, hospital programs). Recognize his need to channel energy constructively, and provide activities (particularly projects that require skill; e.g., building models) to meet this need within the limitations of the illness and treatments. |
| | Assess the child's hospital environment and determine whether he is receiving too little stimulation (deprivation), too much (overstimulation), or what is normal for him. |
| | *If there is insufficient stimulation,* try to identify areas where stimulation can be increased. Discuss the limitation of activity and plan alternatives with the child and his parents (e.g., if he is restricted to bed, arrange for his peers to visit him for group activities and/or for staff to provide diversions). Encourage the parents' participation in providing their child with contact, communication, and activities. |
| | *If there is too much stimulation,* plan with the parents and child how to decrease it. Ensure definite quiet periods and rest every day in a quiet environment. Explain to the child's parents his need for quiet activities and encourage their participation. Be sensitive to the possibility that the schedule of tests, treatments, and procedures may not allow the child sufficient time to recover: help the child express his feelings about them, and discuss your concerns with the medical staff. |
| **4.** Painful procedures (clinical, investigational, surgical) and fear of them.<br><br>**Objectives**<br><br>**a.** The child experiences minimal pain during procedures.<br><br>**b.** Before the procedures, the child and his parents are not unduly fearful of or anxious about them.<br><br>**c.** After the procedures, the child verbalizes feelings about them, the pain, and his efforts to control the pain during the procedure. | Discuss with the parents their wishes for participation in preparation for the procedure (and, if appropriate, during it), and abide by their decision. At a suitable time, prepare the child for each procedure, using visual aids, stories, pictures, and discussions, handling equipment, etc., to convey information. Let the child know who will be with him, how he can help with the procedure, how long it will take, and who will be with him afterward.<br><br>Ensure that preadolescents receive accurate information about the effects of a procedure, and recognize their concern about their appearance and body functions afterward (e.g., scars, loss of hair, or prosthesis). Recognize their need for assistance to deal with these alterations: help them, offer suggestions (e.g., clothing, wigs, makeup), and, if desirable, enlist the help of other health team members. Encourage questions and reinforce explanations. If appropriate, emphasize that the procedure is limited to a specific time and part of the body. Rectify any misconceptions the child may have, and proceed with further explanations when he is ready. |

| Usual Problems/Objectives | Nursing Orders |
|---|---|
| 4. (Continued). | Encourage the child to express his feelings. If appropriate, arrange for him to discuss/learn with peers who have had or will be having the same procedure. (For preadolescents, peer support is an important aid to adjustment.)<br><br>Recognize that preadolescents feel very vulnerable when their bodies are exposed. Let them know that you respect them and that you recognize their need for notification of the intrusion before it begins and an assurance of privacy and comfort. Be aware that they may ask for a few minutes to compose themselves before a procedure. Talk honestly about the pain they will feel and how you will help them.<br><br>Acknowledge the child's need to be in control. Give him the opportunity to make some decisions concerning the procedure (e.g., "Which arm can we use for your blood test?" "Do you want to go to the x-ray department in a wheelchair or walk?"), *but do not offer a choice if there is none.*<br><br>Acknowledge the child's assistance with the procedure. Encourage expression of his hurt, and tell him that it is all right to cry. Ensure that any pain due to the procedure is controlled (e.g., by analgesics, positioning, and/or quiet) and that the environment is conducive to recovery. Be available as much as possible, and be aware of the child's responses to the procedure and to any alteration in his body.<br><br>Afterward, provide opportunities to discuss with the child what has happened to him; use visual aids to help increase his understanding. (With the stress behind him, a child is more able to ask questions.) Rectify any misconceptions he may have. Help the parents appreciate that questions and concerns may continue after their child returns home: ensure that they have accurate knowledge and encourage them to discuss the child's concerns openly and honestly with him. |

**Early adolescence (girls, 11 to 13 years; boys, 12 to 14 years)**

**Mid adolescence (girls, 13 to 16 years; boys, 14 to 17 years)**

**Late adolescence (16 to 18+ years)**

The nursing care of adolescents must demonstrate appreciation of their need to contribute to reaching their health goals. If this need is satisfied, they can emerge from the experience of hospitalization with a sense of being a worthwhile person and with their self-esteem intact. The nurse has the opportunity to provide a therapeutic relationship, through which she can help adolescents view situations realistically, to rectify any misinterpretations they may have, and to help them participate in their treatment.

### Early Adolescence

Early adolescence begins with puberty and is characterized by significant biological, psychological, and social changes. Young adolescents focus attention on their changing bodies, comparing them with their peers'. The changes influence their perceptions of their body image; therefore, *normalcy and acceptance by their peers are to be sought at all costs*. They form close attachments to friends of the same sex; only later will they form heterosexual relationships. With early adolescence comes the beginning of coherent abstract thinking and the questioning of rules, values, and expectations as the developing child begins to strive for independence.

Illness and hospitalization heighten the young adolescent's awareness of his or her body and concern for its well-being. Fears and fantasies (which may or may not be based on accurate interpretation of information) often accompany this concern. Many at this stage of development are fearful of loss of body control; of being unloved, unattractive, or disabled; and even of death. But the enforced dependence of illness and hospitalization may appear less threatening if they can maintain their dependent relationships with parents and assume new ones with staff.

### Mid Adolescence

Mid adolescence begins when young persons have developed a sufficient sense of their biological changes and sufficient identity with their peers to allow them to explore relationships with the opposite sex. Their struggle for emancipation from the family is intensified by their need to achieve self-worth, self-control, and independence. Their association with peers offers them the opportunity to belong to a significant group outside the family, to test their emerging individuality, and to try out various modes of behavior. Conflicts arise between adolescents and their parents over such issues as peer-group mores versus family mores, their idealism versus their parent's realism, their strivings for independence versus their dependence, and the parents' struggle to accept their child's emerging autonomy. Their responses to situations vary within a continuum from submission to rebellion.

In this phase of adolescence the young person is extremely vulnerable to the stresses of illness and hospitalization, interfering as they do with the complex developmental processes. Enforced dependence confronts these adolescents with the dilemma of their conflicting needs to be independent and to be cared for and their determination not to allow themselves to regress. Potential or actual loss of physical attractiveness and functioning threatens their acceptability to their peers and their own emerging identity. Their ever-increasing awareness of their body and its functions exaggerates their fears of painful procedures because of fears and fantasies engendered by real or imagined intrusions into their body. What they perceive as the greatest threat of all—their inability to control what is happening to themselves—can be overwhelming.

### Late Adolescence

Late adolescence is a period of resolution of the tasks of mid adolescence. Older adolescents are thinking of such issues as education and career choices, marriage, children, and life-style—their whole future. They have almost achieved autonomy, as illustrated by their ability to make decisions. The establishment of a stable sexual identity allows them to form close relationships with members of the opposite sex. Simultaneously, relationships with their family become more mature, progressing toward open communication and respect.

Because they have a more stable sense of their independence, older adolescents are more capable of dealing with the imposed dependence of illness and hospitalization. But the stresses threaten their barely established identity and life-style as well as their aspirations for the future.

### Goals for Discharge or Maintenance
I. The adolescent experiences minimal stresses of hospitalization.
II. The parents understand these stresses and are prepared to help their child recover from them.

| Usual Problems/Objectives | Nursing Orders |
|---|---|
| **1.** Separation from family, peers, daily activities, and life-style.<br><br>**Objective.** The adolescent experiences minimal effects of separation. | On admission, orient the adolescent and his parents to the hospital environment and routines (e.g., ward, recreation rooms; introduce him to peers or roommates).<br><br>If appropriate, suggest that the adolescent wear his own clothes while he is in the hospital. |

| Usual Problems/Objectives | Nursing Orders |
|---|---|
| **1. (Continued).** | Spend time with the adolescent and his parents (individually and together) to learn: |
| | –How he responds to new situations. |
| | –What experience he has had with separation from the family and how he reacted. |
| | –Whether he has previous hospital experiences (admitted when, for what, for how long; clinic visits; what he recalls; how he reacted). |
| | –What preparation he has had for the present hospitalization, including expected procedures. |
| | –How his parents comfort him when he is upset. |
| | –When members of the family will come to see him. |
| | –His favorite activities and hobbies. [As appropriate, encourage him to continue with these activities and interests (e.g., bring in his guitar, flute, needlework).] |
| | –Friends' plans for visiting him, arrangements to continue schooling, etc. |
| | –Encourage the adolescent to decorate his room or bedside unit to reflect his life-style/family/interests (e.g., posters, photographs of family members, magazines). |
| | Encourage consistent visiting and as often as possible. Promote continuity of the adolescent's supports by encouraging his relationships with family members and friends, and urge him to make decisions about the visiting arrangements. |
| | Ensure a consistent assignment of nurses to establish a trusting relationship with the adolescent and his family. Ascertain from the adolescent and his parents the degree to which they would like or he would like them to participate in his care. (There may be a conflict between the striving for emancipation, which reaches a peak in mid adolescence, and the dependence forced upon adolescents by illness. Therefore, they may be ambivalent about parental involvement in their care.) Help the adolescent and his parents resolve issues to their mutual satisfaction. Be sensitive to parent–child interactions, so as not to interrupt what may be a significant time for them. |
| | If no family members can come to the hospital, recognize the anxiety they may feel. Ensure continuing communication between the adolescent/staff and family/friends by telephone calls, letters, photographs, etc. |
| | Recognize that the adolescent needs contact with as many as possible of the staff members involved in his care, and ensure that he gets this attention. Allot time each day, other than treatment time, to spend with him: the relationship that develops between the adolescent and the nurse establishes trust and security and conveys interest in his worth as an individual. Encourage conversation, expression of feelings, and special diversions. |

continued

| Usual Problems/Objectives | Nursing Orders |
|---|---|
| **1. (Continued).** | Offer opportunities *in private* for the adolescent to ask questions, volunteer information, and relate his concerns. (Bear in mind that many adolescents find it difficult to express their concerns; make sure they know of your availability and interest.) Be receptive to his sharing of information with you. Recognize the adolescent's need, as a maturing individual, for privacy and for confidentiality of information about himself, but convey the message that, as a member of the health care team committed to working together for his well-being, you may need to relate to other members what he tells you, to help him reach his health goal. *Make certain he knows that information about patients is never shared with other patients or other patients' families.* |
| | Adolescents may ask that information be kept from their parents. The nurse must observe certain principles: |
| | –Do not promise to keep information confidential if you do not intend to or cannot do so. |
| | –Respect the fact that adolescents are in the process of developing a private inner life. |
| | –Remember that adolescents are not independent adults and still require support and guidance from caring adults (usually their parents). |
| | –Try to preserve/promote mutual respect and sharing between adolescents and their parents. |
| | Encourage peer relationships on the ward and within hospital programs. (These friendships provide an opportunity for adolescents to feel accepted, and sharing experiences can help them to overcome restrictions on their outside interests.) |
| **2.** Illness.<br><br>**Objectives**<br><br>**a.** The adolescent and his parents adjust to his illness.<br><br>**b.** The adolescent experiences minimal stress from his illness and achieves optimal recovery from the stress. | Discuss with the adolescent (and, in the case of a young adolescent, listen for information about) his understanding of and feelings about the illness, and its effects on his daily activities, family, and relationships with friends. Identify his confidants (e.g., parents, friends, sister, brother, girlfriend, or boyfriend). |
| | Discuss with the parents their concerns and how their child's illness affects the rest of the family. Determine their interpretation and understanding of the illness and how they perceive their child's feelings about it. Rectify any misconceptions they may have and provide opportunities for them to learn more about the illness and treatments (e.g., from the surgeon, dietitian). |
| | If the parents are comfortable with their feelings and can be honest and supportive with their adolescent child, help them continue this approach. Some parents want to talk with their child about his illness but are uncomfortable with their feelings and need guidance. Recognize their need to express their concerns (e.g., fears, anxieties, even guilt) about the illness and ensure that they are enabled to do so. Assess their need for additional help; advise them of appropriate sources (e.g., social worker, clergy) and ensure that any contacts they |

| Usual Problems/Objectives | Nursing Orders |
|---|---|
| 2. (Continued). | desire are made. Other parents are neither comfortable with their feelings nor want to talk with their adolescent child about his illness; recognize that they, also, need to express their feelings. Assess their need for assistance, and put them in touch with appropriate sources. In collaboration with other health care team members, share your concerns openly but tactfully with the parents about an adolescent's need for information about his illness and treatment and for continuing comfort and support from them. |
| | Provide opportunities for the parents to talk freely, beyond their child's hearing, about his illness. Find out what they have told him, how he responded to this information, and their interpretations of his feelings about it. |
| | Based on the combined assessment of the adolescent and parents, plan how and what to teach them about his illness, to rectify misconceptions, and to be in keeping with what he wants to know. Tactful, sensitive communication is the key: often, the adolescent's anxiety precludes his asking for information or understanding fully what is told him. Teach him useful medical terms, and encourage and help him to seek answers to his questions from appropriate health care team members (e.g., the surgeon, dietitian). Involve him in the planning of his treatment program, and acknowledge his compliance with the requirements. Evaluate and update teaching plans regularly to take into account any changes in his needs. |
| | Adolescents are capable of mature coping mechanisms to deal with the stress of illness: denial, intellectualization, compensation and projection, regression, withdrawal, and acting-out. Recognize which mechanisms are effective for your patient and respect the manner of coping. Bear in mind, however, that the adolescent's abstract thinking results in a rich but often distorted fantasy life that frequently leads to misinterpretation of information. |
| | Anticipate the adolescent's need for comfort and offer it. Encourage him to express discomforts associated with the illness (e.g., nausea) and any suggestions he has to alleviate them. |
| | Help the adolescent identify his feelings; indicate your acceptance of them and, if necessary, discuss alternative means of expressing them. Set limits on unacceptable behavior and react appropriately (e.g., praise, withdrawal of privileges). Praise *any* attempts at constructive expression of his feelings. If you think that the adolescent needs further help in dealing with his feelings, ensure that he talks with the appropriate person (e.g., social worker, psychiatrist). |
| | Assist the adolescent and his parents to anticipate care required after discharge, so that preparations can be made (e.g., any treatments that need to be done at home must be taught before discharge, so both the patient and his parents can be comfortable with them). Identify |

continued

| Usual Problems/Objectives | Nursing Orders |
|---|---|
| **2. (Continued).** | sources of help and support and community agencies and help them make any desired contacts. |
| **3.** Altered activity and stimulation.<br><br>**Objective.** The adolescent engages in normal activity and experiences normal stimulation to the limit of his capabilities. | Gather information from the adolescent about his daily activities, interests, friends, etc. Assess his level of development and plan with him ways to maintain his present level of independence and control over his environment.<br><br>Outline the activities and hospital routines he is likely to encounter, so he can anticipate and adjust to them. *Recognize that accepting delay in gratification is as difficult for many adolescents as for younger children.*<br><br>Allow the adolescent to make decisions whenever possible; e.g., "You can have a bath or a shower. Which would you prefer?" "You may select your menu. If you have any questions, I'll discuss them with you." "Wear your own clothes if you would like to." Recognize his abilities and interests and provide opportunities for him to use or further them. Praise all efforts to maintain or enhance his life-style.<br><br>Assess the adolescent's hospital environment and determine whether he is receiving too little stimulation (deprivation), too much (overstimulation), or what is normal for him.<br><br>*If there is insufficient stimulation,* try to identify areas where it can be increased. Discuss any necessary limitations of activity and plan alternatives with the patient (e.g., telephone calls, letter-writing, challenging projects, and/or socializing with peers). Encourage the involvement of family, special friends, and school in arranging contacts, communication, and activities, within the limitations imposed by the illness.<br><br>*If there is too much stimulation,* plan with the adolescent how to decrease it. Provide opportunities for resting during the day (turn off the TV, limit the number of people entering the room, etc.) and ensure that he has uninterrupted sleep at night. Discuss with the parents and visitors the cause and effects of overstimulation, and involve them in efforts to decrease it. Be sensitive to the possibility that the schedule of tests, treatments, and procedures may not allow the adolescent sufficient time for recovery: help him express his feelings about them, and discuss your concerns with the medical staff. |
| **4.** Painful procedures (clinical, investigational, surgical) and fear of them.<br><br>**Objectives**<br><br>**a.** The adolescent experiences minimal pain during procedures.<br><br>**b.** Before the procedures, the adolescent and his parents are not unduly fearful of or anxious about them.<br><br>**c.** After the procedures, the adolescent verbalizes | Ensure that the adolescent knows about each procedure, the reason for it, and that he has opportunities to express concerns, ask questions, and prepare himself for it. Assure him that he will learn the results (*and see that he does*). Be specific about the details of the procedure; the body parts involved; what he will see, hear, and feel; and how long it will take. Talk honestly about the pain he will feel; tell him how you will help him and whether an analgesic will be prescribed.<br><br>Ensure that adolescents receive accurate information about the effects of a procedure, and recognize their |

| Usual Problems/Objectives | Nursing Orders |
|---|---|
| **4. (Continued).**<br><br>feelings about them, the pain, and his efforts to control the pain during the procedure. | concern about their appearance and body functions afterward (e.g., scars, loss of hair, or prosthesis). Recognize that they need help to deal with these alterations; if appropriate, discuss with them how to deal with these, and offer suggestions (e.g., clothing, wigs, makeup).<br><br>Acknowledge the adolescent's need to have some control over the situation, and allow him time to compose himself. If he requests that family or certain staff members be involved in the procedure, try to arrange this or explain why it is not possible. Encourage him to help with the procedure. Include him in some decision-making (e.g., "Which arm would you rather have the i.v. in?") and acknowledge his assistance.<br><br>Recognize that adolescents feel extremely vulnerable when their body is exposed: provide privacy and comfort throughout procedures and afterward. At all times, convey your respect for them and your recognition of their need to be notified before intrusion begins and of an assurance of privacy and comfort. Let them know that it is all right to cry, but remember that maintaining self-control may be very important to them.<br><br>Ensure that any pain due to the procedure is controlled (e.g., with analgesics, positioning, and/or quiet) and that the environment is conducive to recovery. Ensure that you are available as much as possible; be aware of the adolescent's responses to the procedure and to any alteration of his body.<br><br>Afterward, provide opportunities for the adolescent to talk about what has happened to him: with the stress behind him, he is more able to ask questions. Rectify any misconceptions he may have and help him increase his understanding. Help the parents appreciate that questions and concerns may continue after their child returns home: ensure that they have accurate knowledge and encourage them to discuss his concerns openly and honestly with him. |

**Goals for Discharge or Maintenance**
See Objectives.

| Usual Problems/Objectives/Timing | Nursing Orders |
|---|---|
| **1.** Patient/parents anxious and concerned about the abdominal pain.<br><br>**Objectives.** Patient/parents express their concerns and are able to cope with explanations given.<br><br>**Timing.** As soon as possible. | **a.** Explain to patient/parents the importance of reporting signs and symptoms for diagnosis of pain.<br><br>**b.** Assess and record:<br>– Location of pain.<br>– Type and degree of pain (e.g., continuous or intermittent; ache or stabbing pain).<br>– Precipitating factors.<br>– Factors that reduce or relieve the pain.<br><br>**c.** Test urine for blood and protein as ordered; record results.<br><br>**d.** Notify dr of any significant signs and symptoms.<br><br>**e.** Maintain patient on bed rest when he has pain.<br><br>**f.** Administer analgesic as ordered. |
| **2.** Potential nausea and vomiting.<br><br>**Objective.** Nausea and vomiting reduced.<br><br>**Timing.** 24 hr. | **a.** Consult dr about progression to diet as tolerated. Start with small amounts of clear fluids, increase to full fluids, then provide soft diet unless contraindicated.<br><br>**b.** Record amount, type, and time of oral intake.<br><br>**c.** Record any episodes of nausea.<br><br>**d.** Administer antiemetic as ordered.<br><br>**e.** If patient vomits, record time, amount, and description of emesis (e.g., presence of bile, blood, or undigested food).<br><br>**f.** Provide an environment free of unpleasant sights and odors. |
| **3.** Potential abdominal distention due to bleeding, flatus, ascites, constipation, or abdominal mass.<br><br>**Objective.** Early detection of abdominal distention.<br><br>**Timing.** Until cause of abdominal pain is resolved or treated. | **a.** Observe for abdominal distention.<br><br>**b.** If abdomen becomes distended:<br>– Notify dr.<br>– Measure abdominal girth at umbilicus *stat*, then q6–8h.<br><br>**c.** Record stool data:<br>– Number.<br>– Color.<br>– Consistency.<br>– Mucus.<br>– Blood.<br><br>**d.** Test stools for occult blood and record results (use Hematest tablet, not stick). |

continued

| Usual Problems/Objectives/Timing | Nursing Orders |
|---|---|
| **4.** Patient/parents anxious about tests.<br><br>**Objective.** Patient/parents understand need for tests to determine cause of pain.<br><br>**Timing.** As soon as possible. | **For each test:**<br><br>**a.** Explain to patient/parents the reason for the test, what will be done, and when.<br><br>**b.** Prepare patient according to his ability to understand (following hospital procedure).<br><br>**c.** If appropriate, arrange for parents to be present or to accompany their child to the place where testing will be done (e.g., radiology).<br><br>**d.** Ensure that dr tells the patient/parents the test result as soon as it is known. |

## Goal for Discharge or Maintenance

Parents understand and are willing to comply with home care and follow-up.

| Usual Problems/Objectives/Timing | Nursing Orders |
|---|---|
| **1.** Potential injury due to uncontrolled muscular activity and/or loss of consciousness.<br><br>**Objective.** No injuries.<br><br>**Timing.** Until seizure is over and/or until discharge. | **a.** *If patient is on the floor.* Remove surrounding furniture and toys.<br><br>**b.** *If patient is in bed.* Remove hard, sharp, or hot objects; place pillows or pads along sides of bed.<br><br>**c.** Loosen patient's clothing, especially around the neck.<br><br>**d.** Turn patient on his side and support/protect his head, if not contraindicated.<br><br>**e.** Do not restrain patient, attempt to open his mouth, or use tongue depressors and mouth gags.<br><br>**f.** Stay with the patient; have someone else notify the dr *stat.*<br><br>**g.** Do not take patient's temperature orally.<br><br>**h.** Ensure that patients with known seizure disorders wear helmets or other protective devices when out of bed. |
| **2.** Potential aspiration of secretions and/or vomitus, due to malfunction of throat muscles and temporary loss of gag reflex.<br><br>**Objectives.** No aspiration; patent airway.<br><br>**Timing.** Until seizure is over. | **a.** Have $O_2$ and suction equipment next to bed. Administer p.r.n.<br><br>**b.** Place patient semiprone to allow secretions to drain from the mouth.<br><br>**c.** Ensure that mouth and nose are clear. If necessary, suction secretions to maintain a patent airway. |
| **3.** Potential delay in diagnosis and treatment because seizures have not been observed or described accurately.<br><br>**Objective.** Seizures are observed and recorded in detail.<br><br>**Timing.** Until discharge. | **a.** Describe and record events that led up to seizure. For example:<br>– Bright/flashing lights.<br>– Noise or excitement.<br>– Emotional outbursts.<br><br>**b.** Describe patient's appearance during onset. For example:<br>– Cry or other sound.<br>– Change in facial expression.<br>– Random activity.<br>– Position of head (turned to side, straight).<br>– Unilateral or bilateral posturing.<br><br>**c.** Record time of onset and duration.<br><br>**d.** Describe and record:<br>– Site of commencement.<br>– Tonic phase, if present (length, parts of body involved).<br>– Clonic phase (twitching or jerking movements, |

continued

| Usual Problems/Objectives/Timing | Nursing Orders |
|---|---|
| **3. (Continued).** | parts of body involved and sequence, lack of movement in any extremity).<br><br>–Color changes (pallor, flushing, cyanosis).<br><br>–Sweating.<br><br>–Position of mouth (e.g., deviating to one side), tongue bitten, frothing at mouth.<br><br>–Position of eyes and pupil reaction.<br><br>–Character of respirations.<br><br>–Involuntary urination or defecation.<br><br>**e.** Describe postictal state (e.g., drowsiness, confusion, change in ability to move, changes in speech or sensation). Record length of postictal sleep.<br><br>**f.** Notify dr if seizure is followed by other seizures in rapid succession or if duration of seizure seems excessive. |
| **4.** Family fearful and anxious, lacking knowledge of disorder.<br><br>**Objective.** Patient and family members express their feelings.<br><br>**Timing.** Before discharge. | **a.** Reinforce dr's explanation about probable cause of seizure(s).<br><br>**b.** Teach safety precautions, medication, and care during and after seizure.<br><br>**c.** Ensure that parents have appointment for follow-up, and know what to do and whom to contact if child has another seizure. |

# Careplan 12    Isolation: Psychological Aspects

**Goals for Discharge or Maintenance**
See Objectives.

| Usual Problems/Objectives/Timing | Nursing Orders |
|---|---|
| **1.** Patient's fear and anxiety due to lack of understanding of reasons for isolation and of isolation techniques.<br><br>**Objective.** Patient/parents express understanding of the need for isolation and of isolation techniques.<br><br>**Timing.** 24 hr. | **a.** Explore patient's/parents' understanding of isolation; correct misconceptions.<br><br>**b.** Explain technique used and reason for isolation:<br>–Give explanations appropriate to patient's age level (*avoid using words such as "dirty," "bad," or "bugs"*).<br>–*Emphasize that this is not a punishment.*<br><br>**c.** Dress child in up-patient clothing when appropriate.<br><br>**d.** If mask precautions are necessary, allow the child to see uncovered faces at his cubicle window (especially important for young infants). |
| **2.** Loneliness, as shown by frequent use of call-bell, apathy, or excessive sleeping.<br><br>**Objective.** Patient participates in all activities allowed.<br><br>**Timing.** Until discharge. | **a.** Allow time for patient to express his feelings.<br><br>**b.** Plan the day's activities *with the patient*; include schooling and visits by recreationist if at all possible.<br><br>**c.** Supply patient with crafts, toys, TV, etc., appropriate to his age and interests.<br><br>**d.** When leaving the room, state reason for leaving and approximate time of return.<br><br>**e.** Make certain child knows how to use the call-bell.<br><br>**f.** Encourage parents to visit. Allow a peer or sibling to visit if at all possible, particularly if patient is an adolescent.<br><br>**g.** Encourage parents to bring a favorite toy or game from home. |
| **3.** Potential lack of privacy, due to physical structure of unit.<br><br>**Objective.** Privacy maintained as much as possible.<br><br>**Timing.** Until discharge. | **a.** For child's personal hygiene, draw window blinds and place a sign on door to knock and wait before entering.<br><br>**b.** Provide commode/potty-chair if appropriate.<br><br>**c.** Provide pajamas rather than open-back gowns. |
| **4.** Parents/patient anxious because of fear of communicable disease or lack of understanding of restrictions.<br><br>**Objective.** Parents/patient express understanding of the disease and reasons for isolation.<br><br>**Timing.** As soon as possible. | **a.** Teach parents isolation techniques and explain reasons for restrictions.<br><br>**b.** Stress the need for visiting.<br><br>**c.** Encourage parents' participation in child's care and activities.<br><br>**d.** Spend time with parents: discuss child's condition and encourage expression of their feelings about his isolation.<br><br>**e.** Arrange for dr to talk with parents as needed. |
| **5.** Potential regression in behavior, due to prolonged isolation. | *See* nursing orders for problems 1 (separation) and 3 (altered activity and stimulation) in the patient's Stresses of Hospitalization careplan. |

**Goals for Discharge or Maintenance**
See Objectives.

| Usual Problems/Objectives/Timing | Nursing Orders |
|---|---|
| **1.** Potential skin breakdown due to unrelieved pressure on skin, loss of sensation, and incontinence of urine and stool.<br><br>**Objective.** Skin clear and intact.<br><br>**Timing.** Until patient is mobile. | **a.** Turn patient at least q2h, from side to side, prone, and on back, unless contraindicated.<br><br>**b.** If patient is incontinent, wash and dry him thoroughly after each voiding and stool. Use good perineal technique.<br><br>**c.** Use alternating-pressure mattress, plastic-bubble sheeting, or sheepskin, together with flannelette sheets. Frequently check that sheets are dry and wrinkle-free.<br><br>**d.** Ensure that patient's nutrition is maintained.<br><br>**e.** Assess patient's skin thoroughly b.i.d. |
| **2.** Potential joint fixation, contractures, wristdrop and footdrop, and loss of muscle mass.<br><br>**Objectives.** No joint fixation, contractures, or wristdrop or footdrop. Minimal loss of muscle mass.<br><br>**Timing.** Until patient is mobile. | **a.** Help patient with active and/or passive movements of all joints through their range of motion, unless contraindicated.<br><br>**b.** Use foot-board or foot-rest and bed-cradle.<br><br>**c.** Position limbs with sandbags, orthopedic pillows, or rolled towels, p.r.n. |
| **3.** Potential loss of muscle tone.<br><br>**Objectives.** Patient is able to flex and extend limbs. Muscle strength and tone preserved.<br><br>**Timing.** Until patient is mobile. | **a.** In consultation with physical therapist, establish suitable routine exercises for all movable parts of patient's body, to be done at least t.i.d.; assist p.r.n. |
| **4.** Potential constipation due to change in activity and diet.<br><br>**Objective.** Normal defecation at least every 3 days.<br><br>**Timing.** Until discharge. | **a.** Record accurately the frequency and consistency of stools.<br><br>**b.** Obtain order for laxative, enema, or stool-softener if no stools are passed for 3 days.<br><br>**c.** Increase roughage in diet. |
| **5.** Potential urinary problems (e.g. infection, renal calculi)<br><br>**Objectives.** Urine clear, with normal odor. Stable fluid intake and urine output. No dysuria.<br><br>**Timing.** Until discharge. | **a.** Establish and maintain reasonable fluid intake.<br><br>**b.** Observe for pain on voiding, frequency or retention, and odor.<br><br>**c.** Increase intake if urine is concentrated.<br><br>**d.** Report unusual difficulties to dr.<br><br>**e.** Offer cranberry juice, diluted with water or ginger ale, t.i.d. (Cranberry juice increases urine acidity, helps prevent bacteriuria, and retards calculus formation.) |
| **6.** Potential risk of thrombophlebitis or thrombus/embolus, particularly in older children.<br><br>**Objectives.** Normal respiration. No pain. Good pedal pulse; no vascular inflammation or tenderness; early detection of embolus. | **a.** Turn patient and establish exercises as noted in nursing orders 1(a), 2(a), and 3(a).<br><br>**b.** Whenever you are in the room, observe patient for:<br>–Temperature change in a leg.<br>–Leg sensitive to pressure. |

| Usual Problems/Objectives/Timing | Nursing Orders |
|---|---|
| **6. (Continued).**<br>**Timing.** Until discharge or until patient is mobile. | –Aching or cramping in a leg, especially in the calf or when the patient dorsiflexes the foot.<br>–Dyspnea.<br>–Confusion.<br>–Sudden elevation of temperature.<br>–Petechiae, especially on chest.<br>–Sudden increase in restlessness.<br>**c.** Report any of above to dr *stat*. |
| **7.** Potential hypostatic pneumonia.<br>**Objective.** No chest congestion.<br>**Timing.** Until discharge. | **a.** Ensure that child coughs and deep-breathes, t.i.d., and more often if he is prone to respiratory infection.<br>**b.** Encourage and assist movement and exercises as outlined in nursing orders 1(a) and 3(a).<br>**c.** Suction p.r.n. |
| **8.** Potential boredom and/or frustration over dependence on others.<br>**Objective.** Patient expresses ability to cope with restricted activity and some acceptance of dependence.<br>**Timing.** By discharge or when patient becomes mobile. | **a.** Help patient to plan day's activities, including school, occupational therapy, and recreation.<br>**b.** Encourage patient to express concerns and feelings.<br>**c.** Encourage independent activity within limits of disorder (e.g., bathing, feeding himself).<br>**d.** Praise patient's efforts. |

## Goals for Discharge or Maintenance
**I.** Quiet, dignified death.
**II.** The child's family are helped to cope with the death and to make realistic plans.

**Note:** Comprehensive care by a health team is especially important for a dying child and his family. The situation is stressful for everyone involved, and the nurses should be able to discuss problems with other staff members (e.g., psychiatrist, social worker) as they arise.

| Usual Problems/Objectives/Timing | Nursing Orders |
|---|---|
| **1.** Pain (most likely in a child with leukemia or other neoplasia).<br><br>**Objective.** Patient expresses reasonable comfort and/or appears comfortable. Parents assess that child appears comfortable.<br><br>**Timing.** Until death. | **a.** Assess level of pain at least q2h for efficacy of analgesic. Discuss with dr if change in analgesic appears indicated. (Remember that pain from bone involvement can disappear and reappear within minutes. Do not withhold analgesic.)<br><br>**b.** Plan care so that procedures are done after analgesic has been given.<br><br>**c.** Position patient comfortably; support painful limbs with pillows.<br><br>**d.** Apply warmed towels or hot-water bottle to painful area(s).<br><br>**e.** If abdomen distended, place patient in semi-Fowler's position.<br><br>**f.** Minimize disturbing stimuli, but provide gentle diversions (e.g., music; read to patient) when appropriate. |
| **2.** Dyspnea (most likely in a child with heart disease or pulmonary disorder).<br><br>**Objective.** Dyspnea is minimized.<br><br>**Timing.** Until death. | **a.** Whenever breathing is a problem, remain with child constantly to reassure him with your presence.<br><br>**b.** Position patient comfortably, with head of bed elevated.<br><br>**c.** Administer $O_2$ as ordered, by hood or mask or in croup tent.<br><br>**d.** If patient's distress increases, notify dr. |
| **3.** Weakness and fatigue.<br><br>**Objective.** Patient appears less fatigued.<br><br>**Timing.** Until death. | **a.** Plan undisturbed rest periods.<br><br>**b.** Assist in daily activities p.r.n.<br><br>**c.** If patient is fatigued, restrict visitors to short periods or quiet sitting.<br><br>**d.** Modify or omit procedures (e.g., bed-making) if not essential to patient's comfort. |
| **4.** Potential skin breakdown.<br><br>**Objective.** Skin clean and intact.<br><br>**Timing.** Until death. | **a.** Help patient to change position at least q2h.<br><br>**b.** Use alternating pressure mattress or sheepskin together with flannelette sheets.<br><br>**c.** Ensure that sheets are dry and wrinkle-free. |
| **5.** Family's anxiety and grief as they become aware of imminence of child's death.<br><br>**Objective.** Family members display their feelings and talk about their concerns and fears.<br><br>**Timing.** Until death. | **a.** Encourage parents to discuss their fears and concerns and help them to start planning realistically for the future.<br><br>**b.** Designated nurse to be present when dr talks to parents.<br><br>**c.** Designated nurse to establish supportive rapport |

| Usual Problems/Objectives/Timing | Nursing Orders |
|---|---|
| **5. (Continued).** | with family; spend 15–20 min daily with parents, away from patient's room, listening to their concerns and wishes; assist parents with their explanations to siblings/relatives, as needed. |
| | **d.** Explain all procedures and tests carefully, and try to anticipate needs (e.g., for information on condition), to avoid frustrations and misunderstanding. |
| | **e.** Recognize that family may channel anger toward staff. Avoid retaliation. |
| | **f.** Restrict staff entering the room to only those responsible for care. |
| | **g.** If parents are staying with their child: |
| | –Make them as comfortable as possible, providing bed or bed-chair. |
| | –Assess parents' level of fatigue. |
| | –Request sedation order for parents if necessary. |
| | –Encourage parents to leave the child to take meals. Make sure that someone is with the child; accompany parents to cafeteria; etc. |
| | **h.** When parents visit, notify dr in charge of their child (to answer questions, explain any change in condition, etc.). |
| | **i.** Ask family members if they wish to talk to a member/minister of their religious denomination. |
| | **j.** Ensure that someone (e.g., dr or social worker) has advised the parents whom to contact about funeral arrangements. |
| **6.** Patient is emotional, anxious, or angry, because of separation from family members, pets, etc., and/or fears of mutilation and death. **Objectives.** Contact is maintained between child, family members, and friends. Patient appears comforted and satisfied with information. **Timing.** Until death. | **a.** Encourage child to discuss fears and concerns and help him cope with them. |
| | **b.** Avoid medical discussion in vicinity of patient. |
| | **c.** Clarify with dr and parents what the child has been told. If parents do not want their child to know the prognosis, tell them that their wishes will be respected but that if he asks questions he will be answered truthfully and they will be informed. |
| | **d.** Encourage and help family to participate in the child's care. Include siblings in visiting plans (make special arrangements for young ones). |
| | **e.** Provide child with suitable age-appropriate toys or activities to give an outlet for emotions, fears, and concerns. |
| | **f.** Designated nurse(s) to spend time each shift sitting with and listening to patient, other than when doing treatments. |
| | **g.** Assess and record the best method of preparing child for procedures and tests. |
| | **h.** If child becomes very irritable and demanding, remain calm and try to anticipate his needs, but be firm about carrying out necessary procedures. |
| | **i.** If another child dies on the ward and the patient asks |

continued

| Usual Problems/Objectives/Timing | Nursing Orders |
|---|---|
| **6. (Continued).** | about it, tell him the truth; take time to answer his questions to his satisfaction, and ensure that he has settled reasonably well before you leave him. |
| **7.** Patient's/family's potential feeling of abandonment because staff have difficulty coping psychologically with impending death.<br><br>**Objective.** Staff provide appropriate, consistent support for the child and family.<br><br>**Timing.** Until death. | **a.** Provide emotional support for the child and his family.<br><br>**b.** Plan conferences to allow nurses to discuss their feelings about death, their involvement with the child and his family, and reactions to a "no resuscitation" decision. Include other health care workers as appropriate.<br><br>**c.** Provide opportunities for the nurse designated to care for the child to air her feelings to other staff members.<br><br>**d.** Ensure that the designated nurse has opportunities for frequent periods, however brief, out of the room. Help her with the patient's physical care. Provide opportunities for reassignment if necessary.<br><br>**e.** With other health care workers, discuss approaches, resolve problems, and coordinate information given to family.<br><br>**f.** Arrange for dr and parents to meet daily. Be present at meeting and clarify information given.<br><br>**g.** Answer family's questions honestly. Share feelings with them as appropriate.<br><br>**h.** When indicated, provide continuous nursing care so child and family will not feel left alone.<br><br>**i.** If no resuscitation is ordered, allow child to die quietly, surrounded by those who love him. |
| **8.** Family distress at the time of the child's death.<br><br>**Objective.** Family members express their feelings, and staff support and comfort them.<br><br>**Timing.** Before the family leave the hospital. | **a.** Help the family to cope with their child's death.<br><br>**b.** Designated nurse (preferably one who has known the child and his family) should stay in the room.<br><br>    –Allow parents to touch, hold, and embrace their child.<br><br>    –Be alert for indications that the family might wish to be alone with their child for a while (if they do, leave the room but stay nearby).<br><br>**c.** Offer assistance in placing telephone calls for parents and be ready to support other family members if needed.<br><br>**d.** Suggest that family members go to a quiet room while their child is bathed; a nurse should accompany them if they so desire. Assure them that they can return to the child's room and that the nurse will stay with them if they wish her to.<br><br>**e.** If a dr other than their own certified the child's death, reassure the parents that their own dr has been notified.<br><br>**f.** While attending to the child's physical care, gather his personal belongings so that his parents will not |

| Usual Problems/Objectives/Timing | Nursing Orders |
|---|---|
| **8. (Continued).** | have to do this. Do not put personal belongings in the shroud; return all of them to the family.<br><br>**g.** Ensure that a nurse escorts the family from the floor when they are ready to go home.<br><br>**h.** Encourage the family to telephone or return to visit at a later date, if they wish; emphasize interest in helping them. |
| **9.** Potential family concerns: (a) language barrier; (b) unauthorized autopsy if permission has been refused; (c) who will take their child from the hospital; and (d) inability to leave hospital.<br><br>**Objectives.** Identification of and compassionate attention to the problem(s).<br><br>**Timing.** As appropriate. | **a.** Obtain assistance from an interpreter.<br><br>**b.** Reassure family that their child's body will not be disturbed and that autopsy is done only when authorized by parents.<br><br>**c.** Explain that a nurse will take their child to the Quiet Room and that the undertaker will arrange for removal from the hospital.<br><br>**d.** Kindly but firmly, help parents to leave; if necessary, arrange for their transportation home. Reassure them that their child will be handled carefully and respectfully. Emphasize interest in having them telephone or visit when they feel able to. |

# Careplan 15  Unconscious Patient

**Goals for Discharge or Maintenance**
See Objectives

| Usual Problems/Objectives/Timing | Nursing Orders |
|---|---|
| **1.** Potential aspiration due to lack of pharyngeal reflex.<br><br>**Objective.** No aspiration.<br><br>**Timing.** Until patient is fully conscious. | **a.** Position the patient to prevent aspiration.<br>**b.** Have $O_2$ and suction set up at bedside and other emergency equipment available.<br>**c.** Aspirate airway as needed.<br>**d.** If an airway is in use, ensure that it is in correct position.<br>**e.** If patient is on nasogastric (NG) tube feedings, ensure that he is positioned on R side during feeding and for at least 30 min afterward.<br>**f.** If patient has endotracheal (ET) or tracheotomy tube, see appropriate careplans. |
| **2.** Potential increased intracranial pressure.<br><br>**Objective.** Early detection of increased intracranial pressure.<br><br>**Timing.** Ongoing, until cause of unconsciousness has been resolved. | **a.** Elevate head of bed 10–15 degrees.<br>**b.** Position patient to avoid pressure on neck veins.<br>**c.** *See* Careplan 71: Increased Intracranial Pressure. |
| **3.** Potential cerebral hypoxia due to underlying condition or obstructed airway.<br><br>**Objective.** No hypoxia. Early detection of problems.<br><br>**Timing.** Ongoing, until resolution of underlying condition. | **a.** Maintain patent airway. Give $O_2$ as indicated.<br>**b.** Administer medications as ordered to prevent cerebral edema.<br>**c.** Monitor vital signs q1h until stable, then q2–4h.<br>**d.** Check pupil reaction and level of consciousness q1h or as ordered.<br>**e.** Observe for and record any tremors, twitching, seizure activity, and signs of meningeal irritation (e.g., high pitched cry, nuchal rigidity, opisthotonos).<br>**f. Infants.** Measure occipital-frontal circumference daily. Assess status of fontanelle (full or sunken, tense or soft).<br>**g.** Monitor fluid intake and output. |
| **4.** Potential delay in diagnosis or treatment due to inaccurate observations.<br><br>**Objective.** Observations are recorded in detail. Changes are reported promptly.<br><br>**Timing.** Ongoing. | **a.** Assess patient's level of consciousness. (Be aware that there are different levels of unconsciousness. Patient may be able to hear you and understand what is going on.)<br>**b.** Observe for and record:<br>– Changes in spontaneous behavior.<br>– Resistance to care.<br>– Response to verbal commands.<br>– Response to noxious stimuli.<br>– Type of verbalization or crying. |

| Usual Problems/Objectives/Timing | Nursing Orders |
|---|---|
| **5.** Potential corneal ulceration or eye infection due to loss of corneal reflex, depressed lacrimation, and nonclosure of eye.<br><br>**Objective.** No corneal ulceration or eye infection.<br><br>**Timing.** Until fully conscious. | **a.** Cleanse eye area with N saline q2h.<br>**b.** Instill eye drops per dr's orders.<br>**c.** If unconsciousness is likely to be prolonged and patient's eyes are open constantly:<br>  –Ensure that ophthalmology consultation is arranged.<br>  –If eyelid closure is ordered, *see* Careplan 85: Vision Defects.<br>**d.** Protect patient's eyes when suctioning, etc. (if the catheter or fluid from it touches the eyelids infection may occur). |
| **6.** Potential halitosis, furred tongue, and mouth infection, due to mouth-breathing and nonstimulation of salivary glands.<br><br>**Objectives.** Teeth, tongue, and gums clean; lips moist; no stomatitis.<br><br>**Timing.** Until discharge. | **a.** Perform oral hygiene q2h. Follow hospital procedure for mouth care.<br>**b.** Swab tongue and lips with mineral oil (liquid paraffin) q4h. |
| **7.** Potential prolonged immobilization. | *See* Careplan 13: Prolonged Immobilization. |
| **8.** Parents' anxiety about their child's condition and progress.<br><br>**Objective.** Parents express concerns and appear able to cope with explanations given.<br><br>**Timing.** As soon as possible. | **a.** Designated nurse to establish supportive rapport with family.<br>**b.** Explain procedures and care.<br>**c.** Encourage and assist parents in helping with their child's care (e.g., touching and talking to him). |
| **9.** Potential anxiety of patient, due to altered communication.<br><br>**Objective.** Patient appears to relax when he is talked to or held.<br><br>**Timing.** Until patient is fully conscious. | **a.** *Assume that patient can hear you talking.*<br>**b.** Talk normally to patient, calling him by name, especially during care and procedures.<br>**c.** Provide soft music.<br>**d.** Avoid medical discussion in vicinity of patient.<br>**e.** Handle equipment quietly.<br>**f.** Provide tactile stimulation (if this does not provoke undesirable muscle response). For example: Hold patient's hand, stroke limbs and forehead; infant, hold and cuddle. |
| | **Note.** When cause of unconsciousness has been diagnosed, see appropriate careplans for specific care and follow-up. |

# Careplan 16  Outpatient Surgery

**Goals for Discharge or Maintenance**
See Objectives.

| Usual Problems/Objectives/Timing | Nursing Orders |
|---|---|
| **1.** Anxiety about impending surgery, anesthesia, unfamiliar environment, and fear of separation.<br><br>**Objectives.** Parent and child voice questions and concerns and state an understanding of information given. They appear reasonably calm.<br><br>**Timing.** Before surgery. | **a.** Reinforce information given previously to child/parent by surgeon, etc.<br><br>**b.** Explain to child and parent, as simply as possible, specific relevant routines (e.g., blood test, vital signs, "special sleep," and a rest afterward) and whether a dressing will be applied.<br><br>**c.** Reassure child that he will be going home today (e.g., his clothes are being kept in the pre-op room) and that his parent will stay at the hospital until he is ready to leave.<br><br>**d.** Answer questions simply and truthfully.<br><br>**e.** If there is a language barrier, call an interpreter; ask her to ensure that child and parent understand the procedures. |
| **2.** Potential delay or postponement of surgery because of upper respiratory infection, fever, rash, communicable disease, or recent oral intake.<br><br>**Objectives:** Minimal delay in surgery; parents understand reason for delay.<br><br>**Timing:** Before surgery. | **a.** Report to anesthetist and surgeon immediately any unusual signs or symptoms.<br><br>**b.** Reinforce dr's explanation to parents, to ensure that they understand why surgery has been delayed or postponed.<br><br>**c.** If surgery is postponed, repeat instructions about not eating or drinking before surgery when he comes next time. |
| **3.** Potential delay or postponement of surgery because of arrival at wrong time or without proper information or correct consent.<br><br>**Objective.** Minimal delay in surgery.<br><br>**Timing.** Before surgery. | **a.** If child arrives at the wrong time, try to sort out the problem and fit the operation into the day's schedule.<br><br>**b.** Refer problems about consent to charge nurse.<br><br>**c.** Keep parents informed of progress and try to relieve their anxiety. |
| **4.** *Postoperatively.* | *See* Careplan 19: Anesthetized Patient: Immediate Postoperative Care (in PAR/Recovery Room). |
| **5.** *If patient has a cast applied to limb:* Potential impairment of circulation, and/or nerve damage, due to pressure.<br><br>**Objective.** Adequate circulation to extremity.<br><br>**Timing.** At discharge from postanesthetic room (PAR). | **a.** Elevate limb.<br><br>**b.** Explain to child the need to keep the limb still until cast is dry.<br><br>**c.** Observe color, blanching, sensation, warmth, and movement of limb and whether child appears to be in pain.<br><br>**d.** Report significant signs to dr.<br><br>**e.** Give analgesic if ordered. |
| **6.** Potential injury while patient is disoriented or weak or has fainted.<br><br>**Objective.** No injury. | **a.** When patient is ready to go home, help him to sit up slowly, then have him wait until dizziness has subsided. |

continued

| Usual Problems/Objectives/Timing | Nursing Orders |
|---|---|
| **6. (Continued).**<br>**Timing.** Until discharge from PAR. | **b.** Sit patient in a chair for a few minutes before he tries to walk.<br>**c.** If patient faints, return him to bed; raise foot of bed. Take BP, pulse, and respiration, and apply cold cloth to his forehead.<br>**d.** Children too big to be carried should be transported in a wheelchair to leave the hospital.<br>**e.** Instruct parent to take child home in a private car *with two adults*, or in a taxi—not by public transportation.<br>**f.** Inform parents that the child may be sleepy and disoriented for a while. He should be kept indoors and quiet for 24 hr. |
| **7.** Apprehension due to fear, pain, and separation from parents.<br>**Objective.** Patient appears calm.<br>**Timing.** Before discharge. | **a.** Hold and comfort young children.<br>**b.** Give analgesic, if ordered, when patient is responding and breathing normally.<br>**c.** *Dental patients.* Apply ice-pack to face.<br>**d.** Give child a drink if this is ordered.<br>**e.** Distract child with age-appropriate toy.<br>**f.** Assure the child that his parent is waiting for him and that he will be going home *soon*.<br>**g.** Return the child to his parent as quickly as possible. |
| **8.** Parental concern about home care.<br>**Objective.** Parents describe accurately the care required at home and demonstrate their ability to cope with it.<br>**Timing.** By discharge. | **a.** Reinforce dr's instruction for care at home.<br>**b.** Explain how to increase diet from clear fluids to normal foods.<br>**c.** Reinforce dr's teaching about giving analgesic or other medication at home.<br>**d.** Ensure that parents know signs of developing problems (e.g., increased temperature, bleeding from incision, or blood seeping through dressing, cast problems). Give them written instructions; ensure that they understand them.<br>**e.** Ensure that arrangements have been made for follow-up and that parents know what they are. |

# THE HOSPITAL FOR SICK CHILDREN
## PERIOPERATIVE NURSING RECORD
### PRE-OP

NAME COMMONLY USED _____

LANGUAGE SPOKEN AT HOME _____

WHO WILL VISIT POST-OP _____

WHERE THEY WILL BE     ROTUNDA ☐     HOME ☐     WORK ☐

PHONE NUMBER _____

DATE:

PRE-OP TEACHING GIVEN TO PATIENT     YES ☐     NO ☐

DETAILS

---

PRE-OP TEACHING GIVEN TO PARENTS     YES ☐     NO ☐

DETAILS

---

SPECIAL FAMILY SITUATIONS/SPECIFIC PROBLEMS OF CHILD

---

NURSING FOLLOW UP NEEDED ON

---

| PRE-OP CHECK LIST | YES | NO | N/A | O.R. | SPECIAL NOTE |
|---|---|---|---|---|---|
| ARMBAND CORRECT & LEGIBLE | | | | | PLEASE BE SENSITIVE TO: |
| ALLERGIES NOTED | | | | | |
| RED ARMBAND IN PLACE | | | | | BLINDNESS |
| ANAESTHETIC SHEET COMPLETE | | | | | DEAFNESS |
| SICKLE CELL TEST DONE | | | | | ANXIETY |
| SPECIFIC CONSENT COMPLETE | | | | | MEDICATION |
| OLD HISTORY ON CHART | | | | | FAMILY PROBLEM |
| TOY, SECURITY OBJECT (DESCRIBE) | | | | | LANGUAGE |
| | | | | | OTHER |
| NAIL POLISH REMOVED | | | | | |
| VALUABLES, JEWELLERY REMOVED | | | | | |
| DENTURES | | | | | |
| CONTACT LENS | | | | | |
| HEARING AID | | | | | |
| OTHER | | | | | |
| WHERE ARE THEY? | | | | | SIGNATURE OF O.R. NURSE |
| BLOOD ORDERED | | | | | |
| BLOOD AVAILABLE | | | | | SPECIAL INFORMATION |
| PHOTOS TAKEN | | | | | |
| ENEMA ORDERED | | | | | |
| ENEMA GIVEN | | | | | |
| PRE-OP SCRUB | | | | | |
| HAIR BRAIDED | | | | | |
| HAIR SHAMPOOED | | | | | |
| VOIDED PRE-OP | | | | | |
| TIME VOIDED | | | | | |
| | | | | | |

SIGNATURE OF WARD/UNIT NURSE _____

**Goals for Discharge or Maintenance**
I. The patient undergoes anesthetic and surgical intervention without incident.
II. The patient is transferred to Postanesthetic Room (PAR) or Intensive Care Unit (ICU) in a stable condition.

| Usual Problems/Objectives/Timing | Nursing Orders |
|---|---|
| **1.** Potential anxiety due to:<br>–Fear of the unknown.<br>–Strange environment.<br>–Fear of needles.<br>–Separation from parents.<br>–Previous experience in hospital.<br><br>**Objective.** Patient talks to staff and is relaxed and cooperative.<br><br>**Timing.** Until anesthetized. | **a.** Remove your mask to talk to the child.<br>**b.** Introduce yourself.<br>**c.** Check patient's name band for proper identification.<br>**d.** Find out how much patient knows about surgery.<br>**e.** Assess patient's level of anxiety.<br>**f.** Give age-appropriate explanations.<br>**g.** Reinforce where parents will be.<br>**h.** Discuss with patient any special requests (e.g., no needles). Inform anesthesiologist if appropriate.<br>**i.** Call for an interpreter as necessary.<br>**j.** Provide diversionary toys or games.<br>**k.** Cuddle patient when appropriate.<br>**l.** Ensure that the patient is not left alone in the OR playroom or corridor. |
| **2.** Potential delay in surgery related to the combination of anesthetic drugs and the patient's medical status.<br><br>**Objectives.** No delay in surgery; early detection of problems.<br><br>**Timing.** Until anesthetized. | **a.** Check data in patient's chart (temperature, weight, hemoglobin, urinalysis, etc.).<br>**b.** Weigh patient again or take temperature if results are questionable. Notify anesthesiologist if laboratory results are not within expected parameters. |
| **3.** Potential cancellation of surgery or postoperative complications because patient has an infection.<br><br>**Objective.** No infection or its early detection.<br><br>**Timing.** Before anesthetic. | **a.** Check for infection (pustules, upper respiratory infection, coughing, communicable disease).<br>**b.** Take patient's temperature if he feels warm.<br>**c.** Notify anesthesiologist or surgeon if an infection is suspected.<br>**d.** Pay attention to the child's remarks. |
| **4.** Potential aspiration due to a full stomach, vomiting, loose tooth, dentures, or foreign body in mouth.<br><br>**Objective.** No aspiration.<br><br>**Timing.** Until recovered from anesthetic. | **a.** Ask child if he has eaten and refer to chart (no solids within 6 hr—no fluids within 4 hr).<br>**b.** Check the mouth pre-operatively for loose teeth, chewing gum, or other objects.<br>**c.** Return dentures and dental prosthesis to the ward unless otherwise instructed.<br>**d.** Have suction ready and working during induction and extubation.<br>**e.** Stay with patient during induction and extubation.<br>**f.** Turn patient on his side and put him in Trendelenburg's position and suction mouth if he vomits.<br>**g.** Accompany patient to PAR or ICU with anesthesiologist.<br>**h.** Take suction tip with you to PAR or ICU. |

| Usual Problems/Objectives/Timing | Nursing Orders |
|---|---|
| 5. Potential injury (e.g., cuts, cautery burns), due to jewelry. Also, potential loss of jewelry.<br>**Objectives.** No injury; no loss of jewelry.<br>**Timing.** Ongoing. | **a.** Check pre-operatively for presence of jewelry.<br>**b.** Return jewelry to the ward or tape it in place on the patient. |
| 6. Potential injury due to fall from stretcher or table if side-rails are not in position or if mattress slips from OR table.<br>**Objective.** No falls.<br>**Timing.** Until patient is in PAR or ICU. | **a.** Keep side-rails up on beds at all times.<br>**b.** Never leave patient alone.<br>**c.** Restrain patient with jacket as indicated.<br>**d.** Clamp mattress to OR table.<br>**e.** Use Velcro restraint straps on OR table.<br>**f.** Use the canvas restraint strap and buckle it before moving the table laterally.<br>**g.** Have enough people to transport patient safely. |
| 7. Potential hypothermia due to a cold room, lack of nourishment, lack of clothing, lack of activity.<br>**Objective.** Normal temperature maintained.<br>**Timing.** Until patient is in PAR or ICU. | **a.** Have thermometer to monitor patient's temperature (axillary, nasopharyngeal, or rectal).<br>**b.** Warm the room using the thermostat if necessary.<br>**c.** Cover patient with warm blankets.<br>**d.** Use warming blanket for children 2 years or under.<br>**e.** Use hot water bottles as necessary.<br>**f.** Have blood warmer available as necessary. |
| 8. Potential hypoxia due to difficult intubation.<br>**Objective.** Intubation facilitated.<br>**Timing.** Until endotracheal (ET) tube is in place. | **a.** Stay with the patient until he is intubated and stable.<br>**b.** Assist the anesthesiologist as necessary.<br>**c.** Have O₂ and suction readily available whenever the patient is in the room. |
| 9. Potential loss of dignity due to exposure of the patient.<br>**Objective.** No loss of dignity.<br>**Timing.** Until patient is in PAR or ICU. | **a.** Cover the patient as necessary.<br>**b.** Tell patient postoperatively that he is back in his own bed. This tends to prevent restlessness and undue exposure. |
| 10. Potential injuries, pressure areas, or respiratory embarrassment due to incorrect positioning, lack of padding and protective covering, or lengthy surgery.<br>**Objective.** No pressure areas, injuries, or respiratory embarrassment.<br>**Timing.** Until patient is in PAR or ICU. | **a.** Position patient carefully (refer to positioning and draping procedure in OR Manual).<br>–Protect pressure areas.<br>–Restrain arms.<br>–Avoid hyperextension of limbs.<br>–Extend bed and use foot extension for tall patients.<br>–Use ripple mattress for long-term patients.<br>–Check that equipment is in good repair (e.g., safety locks, brakes). |
| 11. Potential hyperthermia due to sensitivity to anesthetic agents, room being hot, or warming blanket being too hot. | **a.** Put temperature probe in place and turn on the monitor.<br>**b.** Check the accuracy of the thermometer. |

continued

| Usual Problems/Objectives/Timing | Nursing Orders |
|---|---|
| **11. (Continued).**<br>**Objective.** Patient maintains normal temperature.<br>**Timing.** Until patient is in PAR or ICU. | **c.** Control room temperature.<br>**d.** Check the temperature of the warming blanket.<br>**e.** If patient's temperature is ↑, turn off warming blanket and initiate cooling measures as ordered by dr.<br>**f.** Refer to hospital protocol for malignant hyperthermia if indicated. |
| **12.** Potential respiratory arrest due to adverse reaction to anesthetic drugs, aspiration of foreign body, improper positioning, or interrupted airway.<br>**Objective.** Breathing normal.<br>**Timing.** Until patient has recovered from anesthetic. | **a.** Stay with the patient.<br>**b.** Have $O_2$ and suction available.<br>**c.** Help anesthesiologist as directed.<br>**d.** Position patient to assist respiratory function.<br>**e.** Observe the patient during postoperative transfer for symptoms of laryngospasm. |
| **13.** Potential cardiac arrest due to adverse effects of surgery or anesthesia.<br>**Objective.** Normal heart rate.<br>**Timing.** Until patient has recovered from anesthetic. | **a.** Monitor the heart action with ECG.<br>**b.** Stay with the patient during induction and extubation.<br>**c.** Recognize symptoms of impending cardiac arrest (e.g., weak or no pulse, blanched skin, no breathing).<br>**d.** In the event of an arrest stay in room with the anesthesiologist and assist with the cardiac arrest routine. |
| **14.** Potential burns due to improper use of hot water bottles, electric warming blanket, skin prep solutions, grounding, or cautery equipment.<br>**Objective.** No burns.<br>**Timing.** Until surgery is completed. | **a.** Be sure temperature of hot water bottles and warming blanket are no more than 40°C.<br>**b.** Be sure the patient is properly grounded to electrosurgical unit.<br>**c.** Use prep sheets carefully.<br>**d.** Use double thickness flannelette sheet over warming blanket.<br>**e.** Check patient's skin postoperatively (for reddened areas, etc.). |
| **15.** Potential acidosis or alkalosis due to changes in physiology under anesthesia.<br>**Objective.** Early diagnosis and treatment of acidosis or alkalosis.<br>**Timing.** Until patient has recovered from anesthetic. | **a.** Provide arterial line equipment.<br>**b.** Provide blood gas syringe and heparin.<br>**c.** Do blood gas analysis.<br>**d.** Ensure that specific drugs likely to be used are at hand. |
| **16.** Potential shock due to positioning, decreased blood volume, or adverse reaction to drug therapy.<br>**Objective.** Prevention or early diagnosis of shock.<br>**Timing.** Until patient has recovered from anesthetic. | **a.** Provide sphygmomanometer.<br>**b.** Move the patient slowly and gently.<br>**c.** Lower legs from elevated position (stirrups) slowly.<br>**d.** Watch for respiratory difficulty or skin reaction.<br>**e.** Provide equipment for i.v. infusion. |
| **17.** Potential adverse reaction to surgery due to foreign bodies left in situ.<br>**Objective.** No foreign bodies left in patient. | **a.** Make sure all surgical counts are correct.<br>**b.** Note on tally board mounted on wall when throat pack is in place. |

| Usual Problems/Objectives/Timing | Nursing Orders |
|---|---|
| **17. (Continued).**<br><br>**Timing.** Before patient leaves OR. | **c.** Make sure that any needle in use in the surgical field is returned to the scrub nurse. |
| **18.** Potential hypovolemia due to blood loss.<br>**Objective.** No excessive fluid loss.<br>**Timing.** Until surgery is completed. | **a.** Weigh sponges before and after surgery to estimate blood loss. Record the loss.<br>**b.** Provide equipment for i.v. infusion.<br>**c.** Provide equipment for central venous pressure (CVP) line.<br>**d.** Provide syringe and tubes for typing and cross-matching.<br>**e.** Fill out requisition for typing and cross-matching, label blood tubes, and send them to blood bank.<br>**f.** Send for blood as needed.<br>**g.** Check blood with anesthesiologist before it is hung.<br>**h.** Measure urine output.<br>**i.** Measure irrigation and infiltration.<br>**j.** Use graduated bottle for suctioned blood and fluids. |
| **19.** Potential injury to patient due to restlessness during transport.<br>**Objectives.** Maintain body temperature within normal range; prevent shock; prevent injury.<br>**Timing.** Until patient is in PAR or ICU. | **a.** Cover patient with warm blankets.<br>**b.** Move patient from table to bed gently.<br>**c.** Have enough people to make the move gently and safely.<br>**d.** Put the side-rails up.<br>**e.** Talk to patient. |

**Goals for Discharge or Maintenance**
 I. The patient tolerates room air.
 II. The patient is restored to optimal level of consciousness.

| Usual Problems/Objectives/Timing | Nursing Orders |
|---|---|
| **1.** Potential asphyxia or hypoxia due to airway obstruction.<br><br>**Objectives.** Patent airway; normal respiration.<br><br>**Timing.** Until transfer from PAR. | **a.** Place patient on side, with neck extended (if not contraindicated).<br><br>**b.** On entry to PAR give patient humidified $O_2$ by mask at 8 liters/min, for 30 min at least, or until patient is fully awake.<br><br>**c.** Remain with patient until gag reflex has returned to normal.<br><br>**d.** Allow metal, rubber, or plastic airway to remain in place until patient begins to waken and is trying to reject it. If airway appears to be obstructed, lift mandible forward. |
| **2.** Potential aspiration of vomitus and/or excessive secretions.<br><br>**Objective.** No aspiration.<br><br>**Timing.** Until transfer from PAR. | **a.** Ensure that patient is positioned on side (or in semiprone position after awake).<br><br>**b.** Maintain patient on n.p.o. for 4 hr or as ordered.<br><br>**c.** Suction as necessary (e.g., when secretions are heard in naso- and oropharynx. |
| **3.** Potential hypovolemia due to blood loss.<br><br>**Objectives.** Early detection of blood loss.<br><br>**Timing.** Until transfer from PAR. | **a.** Monitor vital signs:<br>  –Temperature, q1h.<br>  –Pulse, respirations, and BP, q15 min.<br>  –Notify dr *stat* if there are any significant changes.<br><br>**b.** Maintain i.v. fluids as ordered.<br><br>**c.** Report excessive/unusual blood loss.<br><br>**d.** Report biochemistry and hematology results to dr. |
| **4.** Potential hypothermia or hyperpyrexia due to cold OR or reaction to anesthetic agent.<br><br>**Objective.** Temperature stable at 37°C ±1°.<br><br>**Timing.** Before transfer from PAR. | **a.** Record patient's temperature on admission to PAR and q15 min if indicated (use thermistor).<br><br>**b.** If patient's temperature is below 36°C, apply warmed blankets.<br><br>**c.** If patient is hyperpyrexic:<br>  –Use only light covering.<br>  –Remove excess bedding or clothing.<br>  –Use tepid water sponging, cooling blanket, as ordered.<br><br>**d.** If temperature cannot be returned to normal within 1 hr, report to anesthesiologist. |
| **5.** Potential injury while patient is unconscious or during emergence excitement.<br><br>**Objective.** No injuries.<br><br>**Timing.** Until transfer from PAR. | **a.** Keep side-rails up.<br><br>**b.** Restrain patient as ordered or as appropriate for type of surgery.<br><br>**c.** Sedate patient as ordered.<br><br>**d.** Guide patient's movements as necessary to prevent |

| Usual Problems/Objectives/Timing | Nursing Orders |
|---|---|
| **5. (Continued).** | injury. (Be aware that the patient cannot complain of pain such as pricking of open safety pin or pressure from clamp.) |
| **6.** Potential fear and apprehension due to disorientation.<br><br>**Objective.** Patient is awake, alert, and oriented.<br><br>**Timing.** Before transfer from PAR. | **a.** Assume that the patient can hear. Avoid medical discussion when in his vicinity. (The patient's ability to hear returns more quickly than other senses as he emerges from the anesthetic.)<br><br>**b.** Continually orient and reassure patient that surgery is over and that he is in the recovery room.<br><br>**c.** Explain procedures (e.g., administration of sedation, equipment being used). |

# Careplan **20** Anesthesia with Ketamine: Immediate Postoperative Care (in PAR/Recovery Room and After Return to Ward)

**Goals for Discharge or Maintenance**
See Objectives.

| Usual Problems/Objectives/Timing | Nursing Orders |
|---|---|
| **1.** *Anesthetized patient.* | *See* Careplan 19: Anesthetized Patient: Immediate Postoperative Care in (PAR/Recovery Room) |
| **2.** Potential emergence phenomena (e.g., vivid dreams, illusions, hallucinations, aimless crying).<br>**Objective.** No or minimal emergence phenomena.<br>**Timing.** Until end of stay in PAR. | **a.** Minimize environmental stimuli:<br>–Avoid loud noises.<br>–Talk softly.<br>–Dim lights.<br>–Place patient at end of PAR or in single room.<br>–Ensure minimal disturbance when taking pulse and BP.<br>**b.** Label bed to indicate that patient has had ketamine (Ketalar). |
| *In PAR and after return to ward*<br>**3.** Other potential significant effects (e.g., nystagmus, incoordination, dry mouth or excessive salivation, diaphoresis, hypertension, and/or tachycardia).<br>**Objective.** Patient appears relaxed.<br>**Timing.** 24 hr postop. | **a.** *Safety precautions*<br>–Keep side-rails up.<br>–Allow patient out of bed only with supervision and/or assistance.<br>**b.** Give mouth care, sponge patient, and change linen, p.r.n.<br>**c.** Report hypertension or tachycardia to dr. |

# Careplan 22 Newborn Infant Undergoing Anesthesia

## Goals for Discharge or Maintenance
I. Patient undergoes anesthetic and surgical intervention without incident.
II. Patient is returned to ward in a stable condition.

| Usual Problems/Objectives/Timing | Nursing Orders |
|---|---|
| **1.** Potential loss of body heat due to cool temperature of the operating room (OR), lack of food and slowed metabolism, or exposure to temperature changes during transportation to and from OR.<br><br>**Objective.** Infant's normal temperature maintained.<br><br>**Timing.** Until transferred to ward. | **a.** Warm the room to 30°C (85°F).<br><br>**b.** Place warming blanket on the table under a double thickness of flannelette sheet.<br><br>**c.** Keep incubator plugged in at all times.<br><br>**d.** Use heating lamp during induction and extubation.<br><br>**e.** Keep rectal and esophageal thermometers available.<br><br>**f.** Use warm prep solutions.<br><br>**g.** Notify ward 20 min before end of surgery that the infant will be returning.<br><br>**h.** Keep a warm blanket available for use after extubation.<br><br>**i.** Ensure that elevator is available to transport patient before unplugging the incubator. |
| **2.** Potential hypoxia due to difficult intubation.<br><br>**Objective.** Intubation facilitated.<br><br>**Timing.** Until endotracheal (ET) tube is taped in place and infant is stable. | **a.** Have newborn anesthetic tray with specialized anesthetic equipment available.<br><br>**b.** Ensure that $O_2$, metal suction tip, and suction catheter are available at all times when the infant is in the OR.<br><br>**c.** Hold the infant's head and shoulders securely to facilitate an "awake" intubation. (The legs and arms should be left free.)<br><br>**d.** Steady the infant's head until the ET tube is securely taped in place and the anesthesiologist no longer needs nursing assistance. |
| **3.** Potential dehydration due to lack of fluid intake and blood loss.<br><br>**Objective.** Infant is adequately hydrated.<br><br>**Timing.** Until return to ward. | **a.** Ensure that a cut-down tray is available.<br><br>**b.** Have size 3 and size 5 feeding tubes and angiocatheters available to attach to i.v. tubing.<br><br>**c.** Provide i.v. infusion set.<br><br>**d.** Tape i.v. securely in place.<br><br>**e.** Restrain limb with a padded tongue depressor.<br><br>**f.** Have blood filter available.<br><br>**g.** Weigh all sponges and record blood loss on tally board mounted on wall/count worksheet.<br><br>**h.** Record all irrigations. |
| **4.** Potential overhydration due to overinfusion of i.v. fluids.<br><br>**Objective.** No overhydration.<br><br>**Timing.** Until return to ward. | **a.** Set up i.v. with a 250-ml unit of fluid, a Pedatrol, and a mini-drip (60 gtts/ml).<br><br>**b.** Clamp Pedatrol at source and at 10 ml level. |

| Usual Problems/Objectives/Timing | Nursing Orders |
|---|---|
| **5.** Potential drying of respiratory tract due to anesthetic agents.<br>**Objective.** Moist mucous membranes.<br>**Timing.** Until return to ward. | **a.** Maintain maximum humidity.<br>**b.** Have special anesthetic humidifier with thermometer box available. |
| **6.** Potential shock due to surgical intervention or adverse reaction to anesthetic.<br>**Objective.** Early diagnosis of the symptoms of shock.<br>**Timing.** Until infant returns to ward. | **a.** Apply newborn-size stethoscope to chest.<br>**b.** Apply adult-size ECG electrodes to limbs.<br>**c.** Apply newborn-size BP cuff and attach it to oscillometer.<br>**d.** Have Doppler BP equipment available.<br>**e.** Ensure that infant's face can be seen clearly (to ensure early detection of changes in color). |
| **7.** Potential aspiration due to vomiting.<br>**Objective.** No aspiration.<br>**Timing.** Until infant returns to ward. | **a.** Provide NG tube for emptying the stomach.<br>**b.** Keep suction ready and turned on. |
| **8.** Potential respiratory arrest during transport.<br>**Objective.** Infant breathing well.<br>**Timing.** Until transfer to ward is completed. | **a.** Ensure that arrangements have been made to transport patient quickly (e.g., elevator booked).<br>**b.** Ensure that an OR nurse attends the baby with the anesthesiologist during transfer from the OR to ward. |

# Careplan 23    Newborn Infant: Apnea

**Goals for Discharge or Maintenance**
See Objectives.

| Usual Problems/Objectives/Timing | Nursing Orders |
|---|---|
| **1.** Potential brain damage due to hypoxia.<br><br>**Objective.** Baby initiates and maintains adequate respiration.<br><br>**Timing.** Until discharge. | **a.** Observe and/or monitor constantly. Check that flowmeters and $O_2$ concentration remain constant.<br><br>**b.** Observe for bradycardia, cyanosis, mottling, and pallor.<br><br>**c.** Note precipitating events:<br><br>–Constipation (check time, consistency, and amount of last stool).<br><br>–Feeding.<br><br>–Low hemoglobin.<br><br>–Position.<br><br>–Frequent suctioning to remove mucus.<br><br>**d.** When apnea occurs:<br><br>–Check for regurgitation; suction p.r.n.<br><br>–Stimulate baby (e.g., rub soles of feet; pinch earlobes to stimulate crying; hold in sitting position and stroke body).<br><br>–*Do not bang the incubator.* |
| **2.** Potential continuing apnea despite stimulation. Potential resumption of apnea after resuscitation, due to hyperventilation resulting from lengthy resuscitation.<br><br>**Objective.** Adequate, stable respiration.<br><br>**Timing.** As soon as possible. | **a.** If stimulation is insufficient to overcome apnea, call for assistance; suction well and begin resuscitation *stat*. Ventilate at 60 breaths/min via face mask and hand ventilator, with $O_2$ at ordered concentration. Use just enough pressure to see chest move in response. Continue only until baby becomes pink.<br><br>**b.** *After color response.* Insert orogastric tube (size 8 polyethylene tubing will do) to decompress stomach. Leave tube in place until infant's condition improves.<br><br>**c.** If color fades and spontaneous respirations do not resume, stimulate or ventilate intermittently p.r.n.<br><br>**d.** When pink color returns, *stop* insufflation.<br><br>**e.** Record periods of apnea (time, duration, color, apical rate) and type of stimulation required. |

# Careplan 24   Newborn Infant: Oxygen Therapy

**Goal for Discharge or Maintenance**
Baby tolerates room air.

| Usual Problem/Objective/Timing | Nursing Orders |
|---|---|
| 1. Potential complications due to incorrect $O_2$ concentration: (a) brain damage from *hypoxia*; (b) lung and/or eye damage from *hyperoxia*.<br><br>**Objective.** $O_2$ concentration maintained constantly as ordered.<br><br>**Timing.** Until $O_2$ is discontinued. | **a.** Observe: color, respiratory rate and depth, heart rate, and baby's activity.<br><br>**b.** Check $O_2$ concentration at baby's face q1h. (Ordered and actual concentration must not differ by more than 1%.)<br><br>**c.** At beginning of each shift, if $O_2$ concentration is incorrect, or when change in $O_2$ concentration is ordered, check that:<br>  –Equipment is working properly (nebulizer, flowmeter, resuscitation bag); replace faulty equipment *stat*.<br>  –$O_2$ tubing does not contain condensed water.<br>  –$O_2$ concentration from resuscitation bag is as ordered.<br><br>**d.** If infant is on $TcPO_2$ monitor, *see* Careplan 27: Newborn Infant Undergoing Transcutaneous Oxygen Monitoring.<br><br>**e.** Check each blood-gas value and compare with normal; if anomalous, **notify charge nurse** *stat*. |

**Goal for Discharge or Maintenance**
Microbilirubin within normal limits.

| Usual Problems/Objectives/Timing | Nursing Orders |
|---|---|
| | **Note:** Record each period of phototherapy, in the chart *and* on the incubator. |
| **1.** Potential eye damage due to continuous exposure to light.<br><br>**Objective.** Eyes not exposed to phototherapy light.<br><br>**Timing.** Until end of phototherapy. | **a.** Cover infant's eyes with eye-pads and black cotton fabric while he is under phototherapy light.<br><br>**b.** Check with neonatologist/ophthalmologist whether the phototherapy is to be continuous or intermittent. |
| **2.** Potential eye infection and lack of visual stimulation, due to continuous wearing of eye-pads.<br><br>**Objective.** No redness or discharge.<br><br>**Timing.** Until end of phototherapy. | **a.** Change eye-pads t.i.d. Turn off the lamp before removing eye-pads.<br><br>**b.** Check eyes for redness and discharge.<br><br>**c.** When changing pads, cleanse eyes with normal saline and absorbent cotton.<br><br>**d.** When infant is not under lamp (e.g., when feeding), leave eye-pads off and provide visual stimuli. |
| **3.** Potential dehydration due to increased bilirubin excretion, causing diarrhea and increased output of (amber-colored) urine.<br><br>**Objective.** Adequate hydration.<br><br>**Timing.** 2 days after end of phototherapy. | **a.** Ensure at least minimal required intake (p.o. and i.v.) q3h.<br><br>**b.** Check level of hydration q3h; if infant is dehydrated, notify dr.<br><br>**c.** Record number and consistency of stools. |
| **4.** Potential excoriation of buttocks, due to diarrhea and urinary excretion of bilirubin.<br><br>**Objective.** Clear skin.<br><br>**Timing.** 2 days after end of phototherapy. | **a.** Clean and dry infant thoroughly after each stool and voiding. Apply thin coating of protective cream or paste over buttocks, to protect skin.<br><br>**b.** Check incubator for cleanliness and odor; clean q8h. |
| **5.** Potential hyperbilirubinemia due to inadequate exposure to light.<br><br>**Objective.** Entire body surface exposed to constant, even light.<br><br>**Timing.** Until end of phototherapy. | **a.** Change baby's position at least q3h.<br><br>**b.** Remove all infant's clothing except mitts and eye-pads before putting him under the lamp.<br><br>**c.** Take mitts off during feeding and to exercise hands.<br><br>**d.** Report flickering or burned-out light *stat*. |
| **6.** Potential kernicterus.<br><br>**Objective.** Early detection of signs and symptoms.<br><br>**Timing.** Until discharge. | **a.** Check each microbilirubin result and compare with normal levels.<br><br>**b.** Observe for irritability, jitteriness, lethargy, poor sucking, or hypotonia. |
| **7.** Potential elevation of temperature by phototherapy lights.<br><br>**Objective.** Temperature within normal limits.<br><br>**Timing.** Until end of phototherapy. | **a.** Record rectal temperature q3h and adjust incubator temperature if necessary. If appropriate, *see* Careplan 26: Newborn Infant in Servocontrol (Controlled-temperature) Incubator. |

# Careplan 26 — Newborn Infant in Servocontrol (Controlled-Temperature) Incubator

**Goals for Discharge or Maintenance**
See Objectives.

| Usual Problems/Objectives/Timing | Nursing Orders |
|---|---|
| **1.** Potential hyperthermia or hypothermia due to incorrect setting or positioning of ISC probe.<br><br>**Objective.** Infant's temperature maintained at normal level while probe is being used.<br><br>**Timing.** Until use of probe is discontinued. | **a.** Prepare equipment:<br>–Set Control Point Adjust at 36.8°C–36.9°C (skin-temperature setting).<br>–Set Red Line Adjust at 38°C (high-temperature alarm system).<br>–Clean end of probe with an alcohol swab.<br><br>**b.** Tape probe securely to infant's skin, over vascular soft tissue such as liver. (If the probe is not *securely* taped, it will register a falsely low reading and the incubator temperature will rise.)<br><br>**c.** If infant is lying on abdomen, tape ISC probe securely to soft tissue of back. (If infant lies on probe, it will register a falsely high reading and the incubator temperature will drop.)<br><br>**d.** If phototherapy is to be applied:<br>–Cut a small piece of aluminum foil and place it *over* the end of the probe (not around it).<br>–Place probe in desired position, with foil uppermost.<br>–Cover probe and foil with transparent tape. (This reflects phototherapy light away from the probe, preventing overheating and a consequent drop in incubator temperature.)<br><br>**e.** If patient continues to lose heat, check possible cause (e.g., evaporation) and institute appropriate measures (*see* Careplan 30: Premature Infant: General Care). |
| **2.** If infant has sepsis: Potential increase in metabolic stress, due to use of ISC probe.<br><br>**Objective.** No additional metabolic stress.<br><br>**Timing.** Until sepsis clears.<br><br>**Note:** When high fever develops, the ISC probe records it, the incubator temperature drops, and the infant's metabolism increases to maintain his higher temperature. The end result is increased physiological stress in addition to the sepsis. | **a.** Remove probe; use manual temperature setting for incubator.<br><br>**b.** Regulate incubator temperature according to infant's age and weight (*see* Careplan 30: Premature Infant: General Care).<br><br>**c.** Record axillary temperature q2–3h; simultaneously, record incubator temperature. |

# 27

## Newborn Infant Undergoing Transcutaneous Oxygen Monitoring

**Goals for Discharge or Maintenance**
See Objectives.

| Usual Problems/Objectives/Timing | Nursing Orders |
|---|---|
| | **Note:** Transcutaneous oxygen monitoring (TcPO$_2$) probes are applied and changed by the respiratory technologist. |
| **1.** Potential burns due to prolonged contact with TcPO$_2$ probe.<br><br>**Objective.** No burns.<br><br>**Timing.** Until monitoring is discontinued. | **a. Infants weighing less than 1500 g.**<br>—Heat probe to 43°C.<br>—Change probe site q2h.<br>**b. Infants weighing more than 1500 g.**<br>—Heat probe to 44°C.<br>—Change probe site q3–4h.<br>**c.** Check probe site area carefully for redness and blistering. If present, change probe site *stat*. (Sometimes the area under the probe becomes red—this usually fades within a few hours.) |
| **2.** Potential excoriation of skin due to irritation from adhesive ring.<br><br>**Objective.** Early detection of skin problems.<br><br>**Timing.** Until monitoring is discontinued. | **a.** Remove adhesive ring *gently*. Use oil or water to soften adhesive, p.r.n.<br>**b.** Ensure that infant's skin is kept clean and dry.<br>**c.** If skin is excoriated, ensure that probe is reapplied well away from the affected site. |
| **3.** Potential delay of or inappropriate treatment, due to inaccurate values.<br><br>**Objective.** Early detection of equipment problems or faulty procedure.<br><br>**Timing.** Until monitoring is discontinued. | **a.** Ensure that there is a tight seal between the adhesive ring and skin (a leak in the seal will cause a false high reading on the monitor).<br>**b.** Handle equipment gently to prevent damage to the membrane and wiring.<br>**c.** Ensure that infant is not lying on probe (this will cause a false low reading).<br>**d.** Check that alarms are set and turned *on*.<br>**e.** If a significant drop in the TcPO$_2$ reading occurs:<br>—Check infant's color and general status.<br>—Notify dr *stat* if infant's color is poor.<br>—Notify respiratory technologist if infant's color is good (equipment may need changing).<br>**f. Extremely cold infant.** Inaccurate values may be recorded if probe is placed in a poor blood flow area. |
| **4.** Potentially inappropriate levels of blood O$_2$ (too high or too low), due to failure to maintain appropriate oxygenation.<br><br>**Objective.** Appropriate oxygenation maintained.<br><br>**Timing.** Continuing. | **a.** Observe monitor read out frequently (maintain set range, usually 60 to 80 mm Hg for term infants; 50 to 70 mm Hg for preterm infants).<br>**b.** If readings are high, the FIO$_2$ must be decreased slowly (by 5% until the readings are in the range ordered by dr.<br>**c.** Observe infant for change in color (cyanosis, pallor) and in chest sounds.<br>**d.** If infant's condition deteriorates or TcPO$_2$ drops suddenly, notify dr *stat*. Be prepared to start resuscitation. |

# Careplan 28  Newborn Infant: Umbilical Vessel Catheter

**Goals for Discharge or Maintenance**
See Objectives.

| Usual Problems/Objectives/Timing | Nursing Orders |
|---|---|
| 1. Potential hemorrhage and possible exsanguination due to disconnection of system, bleeding around catheter site, or removal or dislodgement of catheter. **Objective.** Prevention or early detection of hemorrhage. **Timing.** Until 12 hr after catheter is removed. | **a.** Ensure unobstructed view of insertion site. *Do not cover site with dressings.* After catheter insertion, cleanse old blood from site (use sterile swabs and sterile water). **b.** Observe constantly for oozing/bleeding around the catheter site and connections. **c.** Restrain infant p.r.n. **d.** Check frequently that all connections are tight and that i.v. tubing is positioned correctly (to prevent traction on catheter). **e.** Maintain method used by dr to stabilize catheter and stopcock. **f.** After catheter is removed by dr: –If oozing present, apply firm pressure to cord stump (using sterile gauze pads) for several minutes. –If oozing persists, notify dr. **g.** If catheter becomes dislodged: –Apply firm pressure to cord stump *stat*. –Notify dr *stat*. |
| 2. Potential anemia due to blood sampling. **Objective.** No excessive/unnecessary blood sampling. **Timing.** Until after catheter is removed. | **a.** Record in detail the amount of blood removed; include this amount in fluid balance record. **b.** Record tests for which blood has been drawn (to prevent duplication of sampling). **c.** Know infant's most recent Hb and Hct. |
| 3. Potential impairment of circulation to lower extremities by vasospasm. **Objective.** Adequate peripheral circulation. **Timing.** Until catheter is removed. | **a.** Before catheter is inserted, assess color and bruising of lower limbs. (Sometimes it is difficult to discern cause of cyanosis after catheterization.) **b.** Observe constantly for color and warmth of buttocks and feet (especially toes) and for blanching of legs. If significant changes occur in color of lower extremities, notify dr *stat*. |
| 4. Potential infection of umbilical cord and/or sepsis from catheter. **Objective.** No infection. **Timing.** Until catheter is removed. | **a.** Encourage all staff members to use correct aseptic technique during catheter placement and blood samplings. **b.** Observe for inflammation and discharge from cord stump and for signs of sepsis (*see* Careplan 30: Premature Infant: General Care). **c.** Use Micropore membrane-filter on i.v. line (to prevent entry of contaminants into bloodstream). **d.** Change i.v. bag, tubing, and filter, q24h. (Contaminants will grow through filter after 24 hr.) **e.** For sampling. Clean flushing syringe and stopcock with alcohol, then disconnect flushing syringe and attach sampling syringe. |

83

continued

| Usual Problems/Objectives/Timing | Nursing Orders |
|---|---|
| **4. (Continued).** | **f.** Change flushing syringe whenever fluid becomes contaminated with blood and p.r.n.<br><br>**g.** When catheter is removed, send tip for culture and sensitivities. |
| **5.** Potential invasive measures for blood sampling if catheter becomes obstructed and must be removed.<br><br>**Objective.** Catheter patent (for infusions and/or blood samplings).<br><br>**Timing.** Until catheter is removed. | **a.** Provide flushing system as ordered by dr to clear line after blood sampling.<br><br>**b.** Always use an infusion pump to maintain correct i.v. rate.<br><br>**c.** If a three-way stopcock is being used, check that i.v. flow is not turned off accidentally.<br><br>**d.** If blood refluxes into catheter, check connections. If problem is not resolved, notify dr *stat*. |
| **6.** Potential emboli of air or blood clots introduced into the system.<br><br>**Objective.** Prevention or early detection of air or clots in the system.<br><br>**Timing.** Until catheter is removed. | **a.** If blood is collecting in catheter, check all connections.<br><br>**b.** If there is air in the i.v. tubing, aspirate it.<br><br>**c.** If patient's status changes suddenly (e.g., respiratory rate, pulse, and/or color) notify dr *stat*.<br><br>**d.** *See* nursing orders for problem 5. |
| **7.** Potential fluid and electrolyte imbalance due to inadequate monitoring of intake and output or to inappropriate flushing solution.<br><br>**Objective.** Fluid and electrolyte balance maintained.<br><br>**Timing.** Until catheter is removed. | **a.** Use an infusion pump to administer i.v. solutions.<br><br>**b.** Ensure that the flushing solution is the same as the i.v. solution (it should *not* be N saline, which gives rise to hypernatremia: this is especially deleterious for premature infants).<br><br>**c.** Record fluid intake in detail, including the amount of flushing solution used (after blood sampling).<br><br>**d.** Record number of times infant urinates, or (if requested by dr) details of output. Include amounts of blood taken as part of output.<br><br>**e.** Observe constantly for signs of fluid overload:<br><br>–Edema.<br>–Tachypnea.<br>–Tachycardia.<br>–Diuresis.<br>–Rales. |
| **8.** Potential organ damage caused by placement of catheter and/or irritation from rapid infusion of hyperosmolar fluids: (a) necrotizing enterocolitis; (b) cerebral hemorrhage.<br><br>**Objective.** Prevention or early detection of problems.<br><br>**Timing.** Until catheter is removed. | **a.** Ensure that roentgenogram is taken after placement, to ensure that umbilical catheter is in correct position. (Umbilical venous line in the inferior vena cava; umbilical arterial line in the abdominal aorta.)<br><br>**b.** Infuse medication or hyperosmolar solution *slowly* through an umbilical catheter. (Rapid infusion of a bolus of $Ca^{++}$ or sodium bicarbonate into an umbilical line changes vascular flow through the brain and can cause cerebral hemorrhage. Peripheral i.v. lines should be used for any rapid infusions.)<br><br>**c.** Notify dr *stat* if any signs/symptoms of necrotizing enterocolitis occur:<br><br>–Abdominal distention. |

| Usual Problems/Objectives/Timing | Nursing Orders |
|---|---|
| 8. (Continued). | –Bile-stained vomitus. |
| | –Frank blood in stools or tarry stools. |
| | If the first two signs are evident, test all stools for occult blood. |
| **Note:** Umbilical *arterial* lines are inserted only if the infant is so ill that frequent blood sampling is required. They should be removed by a dr, by the fifth day at the latest. Umbilical *venous* lines are inserted for exchange transfusions only; they are left in place if another exchange may be needed. | |

# Careplan 29 — Newborn Infant (Premature or Term): Care During Ventilator Support

**Goals for Discharge or Maintenance**
See Objectives.

| Usual Problems/Objectives/Timing | Nursing Orders |
|---|---|
| | **General Nursing Orders**<br>**a.** The infant must be observed continuously.<br>**b.** Equipment for administering mechanical ventilation (bag and mask), and emergency treatment of pneumothorax (23 gauge needle, syringe, container of sterile water, or chest drain tray) must be at patient's bedside.<br>**c.** In the event of mechanical failure, start manual ventilation *stat* and notify the unit's technician or respiratory technologist, as appropriate. |
| **1.** Potential airway obstruction due to:<br>–Aspirated meconium (before and/or after intubation).<br>–Secretions in ET tube.<br>–Kinking or displacement of ET tube into bronchus or esophagus.<br>–Condensation of water vapor in ventilator tubing.<br>–Airway damage due to initial intubation (swelling), or repeated intubations (scarring, strictures).<br>**Objective.** Patent airway.<br>**Timing.** Until extubated. | **a.** Position respirator close to infant's side to prevent pull on lines and kinking.<br>**b.** Use pads to support infant's head and the ET tube.<br>**c.** Support ET tube manually when handling and turning infant.<br>**d.** Assess bilateral air entry, color, and respiratory effort at least q1h.<br>**e.** Observe for and report signs of airway obstruction *stat:*<br>–Chest retraction.<br>–Minimal air entry.<br>–Agitation.<br>–Sudden, inexplicable deterioration in infant's condition.<br>**f.** Suction ET tube p.r.n. (usually q2–3h). Follow hospital procedure. Instill N saline before suctioning as per dr's orders.<br>**g.** Observe and record characteristics of secretions (amount, consistency, color).<br>**h.** Ensure optimum humidification of gas in ventilator tubing. (Pediatric size ET tubes are small in diameter and can easily become obstructed by thickened secretions.)<br>**i.** If infant is in an incubator, the amount of ventilator tubing outside the incubator should be kept to a minimum. (The warm temperature in the incubator helps decrease the amount of condensation in the tubing.)<br>**j.** Empty the water that condenses in the delivery tubing p.r.n., usually about every 15 min. (Water condensation in the delivery tubing may cause obstruction and sudden flooding of the trachea.) |
| **2.** Potential atelectasis due to:<br>–Instability of lung function. | **a.** Ensure that ordered positive pressure is maintained. Notify respiratory technologist if there are any problems with this. |

| Usual Problems/Objectives/Timing | Nursing Orders |
|---|---|
| **2. (Continued).**<br>–Accumulated secretions or mucous plug in airway.<br>–ET tube suctioning (blocking airway and removing air from lungs).<br>**Objective.** Adequate lung expansion.<br>**Timing.** Until extubated. | **b.** Reposition infant, q2h, from side to side.<br>**c.** Do chest physiotherapy as ordered.<br>**d.** "Sigh" infant after ET suctioning. Use bag or machine to give 2 or 3 deep breaths to infant before adjusting to regular cycle. |
| **3.** Potential pneumothorax/pneumomediastinum due to:<br>–Decreased lung compliance.<br>–Positive-pressure ventilation.<br>**Objective.** Early detection of pneumothorax or pneumomediastinum.<br>**Timing.** Until extubated. | **a.** Monitor and record cycling pressures at least q1h.<br>**b.** Observe and report *stat* any signs or symptoms of pneumothorax or pneumomediastinum.<br>  **i.** *Pneumothorax*<br>    –Tachypnea, tachycardia.<br>    –Cyanosis.<br>    –Diminished air entry.<br>    –Abnormal chest appearance.<br>    –Mediastinum/apical shift.<br>    –Sudden deterioration in condition.<br>  **ii.** *Pneumomediastinum*<br>    –Muffled heart/apical beat.<br>    –Bilateral air entry unchanged.<br>    –Decreased cardiac output.<br>    –Crepitus around neck and upper chest.<br>**c.** If pneumothorax is suspected, prepare for immediate emergency treatment (insertion of chest needle and drain). |
| **4.** Potential displacement of ET tube (usually into the esophagus), due to movement of or traction on tubing and machine.<br>**Objective.** ET tube remains in correct position.<br>**Timing.** Until extubation. | **a.** Position infant so that head is in line with body (no hyperextension or flexion).<br>**b.** Ensure that infant is positioned comfortably (on either side), and place pads to support head and ET tubing (infant is less likely to move around and pull on tubing).<br>**c.** Check stabilizing tapes on ET tube frequently.<br>**d.** Prevent traction on patient-ventilator lines.<br>**e.** Restrain infant p.r.n.<br>**f.** Ensure that emergency cart is close at hand in case reintubation is necessary. |

**Goals for Discharge or Maintenance**
I. Weight 2500 g: steady weight gain.
II. Infant feeding appropriately.
III. Parents handle infant comfortably and can cope with required home care and follow-up.

| Usual Problems/Objectives/Timing | Nursing Orders |
|---|---|
| **1.** Potential cold stress due to excessive heat loss.<br><br>**Objective.** Axillary/rectal temperature maintained at 36.5°–37°C. (Be aware that in small premature infants there may be no difference between skin and rectal temperature.)<br><br>**Timing.** Until discharge. | **a.** Maintain incubator at temperature appropriate for body weight:<br><br>Under 1000 g, 35°–36°C<br><br>1000–1500 g, 34°–35°C<br><br>1500–2000 g, 33°–34°C<br><br>2000–3000 g, 32°–34°C<br><br>Over 3000 g, 31°–33°C<br><br>**b.** Ensure that:<br><br>–Incubator is placed away from drafty areas.<br><br>–Incubator portholes are closed.<br><br>–Infant is placed in center of incubator (away from walls).<br><br>–Infant is dressed in hat and booties p.r.n.<br><br>**c.** Maintain relative humidity at 60–70% to decrease heat loss by evaporation (use nebulizer with compressed air).<br><br>**d.** Record infant's temperature q2–3h, or more frequently if hypo- or hyperthermic (record incubator temperature simultaneously).<br><br>**e.** Perform all care in the incubator until infant's condition is stable and his weight is at least 1400 g.<br><br>**f. Infants under 1500 g.** Maintain on servocontrol temperatures for first 10–14 days or until stabilized. *See* Careplan 26: Newborn Infant in Servocontrol (Controlled-temperature) Incubator.<br><br>**g. Infants under 1000 g.** Use heat shield or double-walled incubator to prevent heat loss by radiation.<br><br>**h.** Monitor daily weight gain or loss. (If metabolic energy is utilized to maintain temperature, weight gain may be retarded.)<br><br>**i.** When infant is transferred to crib, bundle and dress him warmly (including booties and hat). Check his temperature q3h and dress him accordingly.<br><br>**j.** If infant is cold (less than 36.5°C), rewarm slowly (1° per hr). Rapid rewarming may cause shock and apnea:<br><br>–Increase incubator temperature gradually within appropriate range.<br><br>–Maintain heated humidity. Pull as much of the nebulizer tubing as possible into the incubator. (Fluid in tubing outside incubator cools, causing pooling of water instead of fine misting.) |

| Usual Problems/Objectives/Timing | Nursing Orders |
|---|---|
| **1. (Continued).** | −If additional heat is required, external radiant heat may be applied with an overhead warmer. The heat shield and/or servocontrol probe must be removed before using the overhead warmer; place the warmer's probe on the infant. *Be careful not to heat the incubator's thermometer.*<br><br>−Wrap baby's body closely in clear, soft plastic (saran); leave face and head uncovered.<br><br>*These nursing orders may be used sequentially; the more vigorous methods may not be necessary.* |
| **2.** Potential failure to maintain a weight gain, due to intolerance of feeds or insufficient caloric intake.<br><br>**Objectives.** Steady, appropriate weight gain (average, 20–30 g per day); infant tolerates feeds and is contented afterwards.<br><br>**Timing.** Until discharge. | **a.** Weigh daily; if variation exceeds 80 g, recheck weight with another nurse and/or reweigh infant on another scale. Notify dr p.r.n.<br><br>**b.** Review diet every 2 days: check that caloric intake is adequate for weight (140–200 cal/kg/day); notify dr if insufficient.<br><br>**c.** Check dr's orders before initiating feedings (first feeding should be sterile water).<br><br>**d.** Check that total i.v. and p.o. intake equals the total ordered by dr.<br><br>**e.** Burp baby after both tube- and bottle-feeding.<br><br>**f.** Position baby on R side or abdomen, with head of cot slightly elevated, for 1/2 hr p.c. (to aid digestion and avoid aspiration).<br><br>**g.** If feedings are withheld, review periodically with dr when to restart them. Assess and discuss the necessity for i.v. fluids in the interim.<br><br>**h.** If feeds given via NG tube:<br>−Check NG tube placement before each feeding.<br>−Aspirate stomach before each feeding to check absorption.<br>−If aspirate is partially digested and less than 2 ml, refeed aspirate and continue with feeds.<br>−Increase by 1–2 ml per feeding, as tolerated, to total amount.<br>−If aspirate is greater than 2 ml, notify dr or charge nurse; follow their instructions.<br><br>**i.** When baby is 34–36 weeks' gestation or 1500 g:<br>−Try gradual change to bottle feedings (as ordered by dr). Offer one bottle feeding q8h for 1–2 days; then alternate bottle and tube feedings for 1–2 days; then offer the bottle at each feeding, as tolerated.<br><br>**j. Bottle-fed infants.**<br>−Increase feed by no more than 5 ml at a time.<br>−If baby tires or becomes distressed, ask for order to gavage p.r.n. (Signs and symptoms of inability to tolerate bottle feeding: slow feeder [>20 min], poor sucking or swallowing, and respiratory difficulty [60 breaths or more a minute].) |

continued

| Usual Problems/Objectives/Timing | Nursing Orders |
|---|---|
| **2. (Continued).** | **k.** When infant tolerates about 25 ml q2h, consult dr about changing to q3h feedings. (Infant's weight and the volume of the feed appropriate to the weight must be assessed.)<br><br>**Note:** *Feeding of breast milk is encouraged: the mother's expressed breast milk may be stored on the unit if it is going to be used within 48 hr. Otherwise, breast milk must be sent to Food Services to be frozen until needed. Tell the mother that she will be able to breast-feed her baby as his condition permits this.* |
| **3.** Potential sepsis due to immature immunologic response and decreasing maternal antibodies (particularly if baby is not being fed breast milk).<br><br>**Objective.** No sepsis.<br><br>**Timing.** Until discharge. | **a.** Check for signs/symptoms of potential sepsis:<br>–Decreased tolerance of feedings.<br>–Lethargy.<br>–Apnea and bradycardia.<br>–Jaundice.<br>–Fluctuation in temperature (hypothermia is more common).<br>–Mottling, pallor.<br><br>**b.** Instruct and supervise all staff and visitors in proper hand-washing and aseptic technique. Screen all staff and visitors for infectious diseases and exposure to infectious diseases.<br><br>**c.** Check infant's mouth for evidence of thrush when doing mouth care.<br><br>**d.** Maintain infant's skin integrity:<br>–Keep skin clean and dry.<br>–Limit use of soap.<br>–Cleanse after urination and stooling.<br>–Do not use medicated, commercial adhesive tapes (e.g., Band-Aids®).<br>–Remove adhesive tape carefully p.r.n. (use oil to loosen).<br>–Turn infant at least q2h to avoid pressure areas.<br>–Protect bony prominences of small premature infants by placing baby on sheepskin or plastic-bubble sheeting (ensure proper positioning to avoid pressure).<br><br>**e.** Perform mouth care q2h using sterile water and sterile cotton-tipped swabs.<br><br>**f.** Cleanse cord with alcohol daily after bath.<br><br>**g.** Record and report any discharge from eyes, umbilicus, etc.; cleanse appropriately.<br><br>**h.** Wipe incubator inside and out with sterile water q8h. Wash incubator completely with sterile water and chlorhexidine gluconate solution daily.<br><br>**i.** Transfer infant to fresh incubator q5 days *(put date on patient's careplan)*. Send used one for special cleaning in department of respiratory technology. |

| Usual Problems/Objectives/Timing | Nursing Orders |
|---|---|
| **4.** Potential constipation due to poor intestinal motility and infant's limited mobility.<br><br>**Objective.** Regular stooling pattern established.<br><br>**Timing.** Before discharge. | **a.** Check for:<br>–Intolerance of feeds.<br>–Abdominal distention.<br>–Apnea.<br>–Straining at stools.<br>–Stool size, frequency, and consistency (know difference between stool of infants fed breast milk vs formula).<br><br>**b.** Record and report any abnormalities or changes in infant's stooling.<br><br>**c.** Take temperature rectally to gently stimulate peristalsis unless contraindicated. Consult dr about administration of glycerin tip to aid stooling. |
| **5.** Potential respiratory distress due to pulmonary disease, upper airway obstruction, and immature respiratory center.<br><br>**Objectives.** No respiratory distress; respiratory rate within normal limits (40–60 breaths per min).<br><br>**Timing.** Until discharge. | **a.** Position infant on side or abdomen (never on back):<br>–Change infant's position q2h.<br>–When infant is on side: Place a small support under neck and behind back, to maintain position and ensure correct positioning for maintaining airway.<br>–When patient is on abdomen: Place a small roll under shoulders and another under groins, or place baby in knee-chest position.<br><br>**b.** Auscultate the chest for bilateral air entry and adventitious sounds (e.g., rales, rhonchi).<br><br>**c.** Suction nasopharynx p.r.n.:<br>–Suction the back of the oropharynx first to prevent aspiration of accumulated secretions; suction nasally.<br>–Use intermittent suction for 5–10 sec p.r.n. (*Continual suctioning can cause apnea through vagal stimulation.*)<br>–*Suction gently (never exceed 80–90 mm Hg)* with French catheter size 6 or 8, lubricated with sterile water to prevent tissue trauma.<br><br>**d.** Check for signs/symptoms of respiratory distress:<br>–Chest retractions.<br>–Nasal flaring.<br>–Tachypnea >60.<br>–Apnea.<br>–Expiratory grunt.<br>–Cyanosis.<br>Notify dr *stat* if any of these are present. |
| **6.** Potential exhaustion and general debilitation due to immaturity and lack of energy reserves.<br><br>**Objectives.** Adequate rest; weight gain.<br><br>**Timing.** Until discharge. | **a.** Plan care to provide maximal rest time between procedures.<br><br>**b.** Avoid excessive handling and overstimulation of infant. |

continued

| Usual Problems/Objectives/Timing | Nursing Orders |
|---|---|
| **7.** Potential damage to vital organs caused by biochemical imbalance (e.g., abnormal $PO_2$, blood glucose, calcium, bilirubin).<br><br>**Objective.** Early detection of symptoms.<br><br>**Timing.** Until discharge. | **a.** Check infant for:<br><br>–Jitteriness, twitching and/or tremors.<br><br>–Jaundice.<br><br>–Apnea and bradycardia.<br><br>–Color changes.<br><br>**b.** Monitor blood tests. Report abnormal results to dr or charge nurse. |
| **8.** Potential lack of maternal bonding:Infant Stage. | *Note especially* introduction and nursing orders for problem 1 in Careplan 1: Stresses of Hospitalization: Infant Stage. |
| **9.** Parental anxiety because of unexpected prematurity, unfamiliar surroundings and equipment, prolonged illness, uncertain outcome, or concern about ability to cope.<br><br>**Objectives.** Parents relaxed and comfortable when handling their baby, participating competently in his care, and making reasonable plans for home care (and if appropriate, discussing and accepting baby's limitations).<br><br>**Timing.** By discharge. | **a.** Talk to parents and create supportive atmosphere before their first visit to their baby:<br><br>–Describe and explain his general appearance.<br><br>–Explain how baby is being fed.<br><br>–Explain the purpose of equipment.<br><br>–Instruct them in scrub routine.<br><br>–Explain ward routines and rules for visitors.<br><br>–Encourage questions and expression of feelings about baby.<br><br>**b.** Accompany each parent into the room the first time he or she visits.<br><br>**c.** Assess parents' readiness for participation. If baby's condition allows, demonstrate handling. Encourage parents to touch and handle the baby, talk to him, and participate in his care (feeding, bathing, cuddling, etc.), with supervision.<br><br>**d.** Record parent-infant interactions and note progress.<br><br>**e.** If parents' anxiety is prolonged or severe, refer them to the neonatal clinical nurse specialist or social worker.<br><br>**f.** Ensure that parents are kept informed of plans to transfer their baby to another unit or hospital, if appropriate.<br><br>**g.** If infant is being discharged home, ensure that:<br><br>–Parents are comfortable in giving newborn care and know how to give treatments and/or medication, if ordered.<br><br>–Parents have written instructions for home care and follow-up.<br><br>–Parents have names and telephone numbers of persons to contact if they are concerned.<br><br>–Public health nurse has been notified. |

# Procedure for Tube-Feeding (Indwelling Nasogastric Tube)

## Purpose
To feed neonates whose sucking and/or swallowing reflexes are undeveloped.

## Equipment needed
Narrow micropore adhesive tape (¼-½ inch wide, depending on infant's size)
Red cloth (Mystic) tape, ¾ inch wide
Polyethylene feeding tube, size 5 (French)
Scissors
Diaper/blanket
Measuring tape
Stethoscope
Plastic syringe, 12 ml
pH testing paper
Plastic medicine cup, sterile (to hold formula/breast milk)
Formula/breast milk (warmed, if it has been refrigerated)

## Procedure for Inserting Tube (Figure 3A)

**1.** Cut 2 pieces of micropore adhesive tape, approximately 1½ inches in length.

**2.** Cut a piece of red tape, approximately 2 inches in length.

**3.** Place one piece of the white adhesive tape across the infant's upper lip (to act as a base).

**4.** Measure length of tube to be inserted (from tip of nose to ear lobe to tip of sternum, following curve of esophagus; add ½ inch to this length.)

**5.** Center piece of red tape over measured point and wrap around tube. (This will serve as a guide to indicate if tube has slipped out of position.)

**6.** Measure length of tube from red tape marker to distal end and record on flow sheet.

**7.** Position second piece of white tape over the red tape (covering half the width of the red tape) and criss-cross, leaving two wings to secure to base tape.

**8.** Bundle baby with a diaper or blanket.

**9.** Insert tube through the nostril, and advance it gently into the esophagus until the red marker is reached (just below nostril). Secure wings of the white tape to the base tape.

**10.** Remove restraint and settle infant.

## Procedure for Feeding (Figure 3B)

**1.** *The following checks must be made before every feeding to ensure that the tube is positioned properly:*

   –Check measurement of tube from red marker to distal end.

   –If there is a change in measurement (indicating that tape has loosened and tube has slipped further in or out), adjust tube or remove it and insert new one.

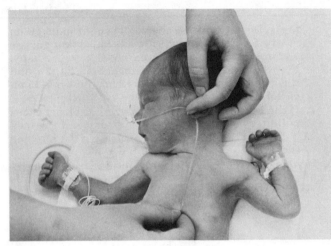

A

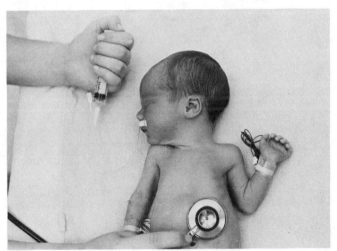

B

**Figure 3.** *Tube-feeding the neonate. A. Inserting tube. B. Procedure for feeding.*

   –Place stethoscope over upper L quadrant of abdomen. Introduce 1–2 cc of air rapidly through a syringe. Simultaneously, listen through the stethoscope. A distinct popping sound should be heard, indicating proper placement of the tube.

   –Gently aspirate tube. If there is aspirate, place a drop on pH testing paper (pH of gastric juices is 4–5). Record amount of aspirate and test result on flow sheet.

**2.** Aspirate tube to determine whether the previous feed has been absorbed:

   **a.** Aspirate of 1 ml is negligible.

   **b.** Aspirate of 2 ml is the upper limit of normal gastric residue; the baby must be watched for tolerance of

continued

## Procedure

feeds. Do not increase the volume of formula given at this feeding. The aspirate has important gastric electrolytes in it; therefore, refeed it to the baby. For example, if the feed is 15 ml of SMA 20 q2h, and the aspirate is 2 ml, refeed the 2 ml, then give 15 ml of SMA 20 (do not increase the amount).

c. If the aspirate is greater than 2 ml, subtract extra milliliters from the total. For example, if the feed is 15 ml of SMA 20, and the aspirate is 3 ml, refeed the 3 ml, then give 14 ml of SMA 20.

3. If you persistently or suddenly obtain large amounts of aspirate, notify the charge nurse or doctor; this may be a sign of sepsis and must be reported.

4. Position baby on his R side and elevate his head slightly.

5. Proceed with feeding by drawing up formula in a syringe and injecting it *slowly* (1 ml/min) into the tube.

6. At the end of the feeding, clear the tube by injecting ½-1 ml of air.

7. After every feeding, burp the baby and do mouth care.

8. Reposition baby, leaving him on his R side for ½ hr p.c.

9. Change the tube every 3 days or sooner, p.r.n. Note the date of change on the infant's careplan.

### Goals for Discharge or Maintenance
**I.** Patient/family show reasonable acceptance of any disability or scarring.
**II.** They can cope with home care and with the (possibly prolonged) follow-up.

This plan is divided into eight sections:

**A.** Acute phase: on admission
**B.** Acute phase: shock
**C.** Positioning
**D.** Burn site
**E.** Nutrition
**F.** Skin grafts
**G.** Emotional reactions
**H.** Home care and follow-up

| Usual Problems/Objectives/Timing | Nursing Orders |
|---|---|
| **A. Acute Phase: On Admission** | |
| **1.** Potential infection of burn. <br><br> **Objective.** No infection. <br><br> **Timing.** Continuing. | **a.** Perform admission procedure for burns (*see* example, page 107). <br><br> **b.** Follow hospital procedure for protective technique. |
| **2.** Potential dehydration due to increased capillary permeability and excessive loss of fluid through burned tissue. <br><br> **Objective.** Adequate hydration. <br><br> **Timing.** 24 hr. | **a.** Maintain i.v. infusion(s) as ordered. <br><br> **b.** Record intake and urinary output in detail q1h. <br>  –Determine SG of each urine specimen. <br>  –Under output, include estimated loss of fluid from burn. <br><br> **c.** If ordered, insert urinary catheter to facilitate measurement of output. <br><br> **d.** Notify dr if output is diminished (dr will establish parameter). |
| **3.** Potential anemia and/or electrolyte imbalance. <br><br> **Objective.** Early detection of anemia or electrolyte imbalance. <br><br> **Timing.** 24 hr. | **a.** Prepare for the tests that will be done to establish baseline data for subsequent monitoring of patient's condition. (Usual tests: WBC and differential, ESR, Hb, Hct; serum electrolytes; blood gases; blood typing and cross-match.) <br><br> **b.** Report all laboratory results to dr *stat*. |
| **B. Acute Phase: Shock** <br><br> **1.** Potential respiratory distress due to inhalation injury, obstructive edema, tight eschar formation, and/or oversedation. <br><br> **Objective.** Early detection of respiratory distress. <br><br> **Timing.** Day 3. | **a.** Examine nose and throat for soot and burned mucosa. Look for singed hair, eyelashes, and eyebrows and soot-flecked secretions. Report findings to dr *stat*. <br><br> **b.** Observe respiration closely; report signs of distress *stat*. <br><br> **c.** If patient is having sedation, observe very closely as respirations may be depressed, masking symptoms of distress. <br><br> **d.** Change patient's position q2h. If he is on an electric turning frame, tip the frame up and down slightly. If he is on an ordinary bed, turn him side to side. <br><br> **e.** Hyperextend neck to assist respiration. |

| Usual Problems/Objectives/Timing | Nursing Orders |
|---|---|
| **B.1. (Continued).** | **f.** Provide humidified $O_2$ via hood or croup tent as ordered.<br><br>**g.** Encourage patient to deep-breathe and cough q1h.<br><br>**h.** Follow physical therapist's instructions for postural drainage. |
| **2.** Potential hemorrhage: from injuries at time of accident; and/or due to erosion of blood vessels by debridement; and/or from deep fasciotomies.<br><br>**Objective.** Early detection of bleeding.<br><br>**Timing.** Day 3. | **a.** Elevate burned extremities.<br><br>**b.** Record TPR and BP q1h. If BP drops or pulse is rapid and thready, notify dr *stat*.<br><br>**c.** Do not reinforce any dressings (this could mask fresh bleeding).<br><br>**d.** If fresh bleeding occurs:<br><br>–Apply pressure *directly* to the area that is bleeding.<br><br>–Call for help; notify dr *stat*.<br><br>–If necessary, place patient in shock position (elevate foot of bed). |
| **3.** Potential fluid and electrolyte imbalance due to excessive loss of fluid through damaged tissues.<br><br>**Objective.** Fluid balance maintained.<br><br>**Timing.** Day 3. | **a.** Regulate rate of i.v. infusions very carefully.<br><br>**b.** Record intake and output in detail, q1h.<br><br>**c.** Encourage fluids p.o. as tolerated.<br><br>**d.** Observe burns for exudate: record amount (much or little), color, and consistency. |
| **4.** Potential oliguria due to renal shutdown caused by hypovolemia.<br><br>**Objective.** Normal hourly output for age:<br><br>    2 mo, 10–18 ml    3–5 yr, 25–30 ml<br>    1 yr, 15–20 ml    5–8 yr, 25–40 ml<br>    2–3 yr, 20–25 ml    8–14 yr, 25–50 ml<br><br>**Timing.** Day 3. | **a.** Record urine output and SG q1h.<br><br>**b.** Notify dr *stat* if, for 2 consecutive hours:<br><br>–Urine output is below normal.<br>–Urine output is excessive.<br>–SG exceeds 1.030. |
| **5.** Potential hypothermia due to excessive evaporation or exposure (if open-air treatment is being used).<br><br>**Objective.** Temperature within normal limits.<br><br>**Timing.** Day 3. | **a.** If patient is over 2 years of age, place him in hot, dry room. Maintain room temperature at 26°–33°C (80°–92°F).<br><br>**b.** Nurse children under 2 years of age in rooms with usual temperature and RH. (Their temperature control is not fully developed and they lose fluids quickly.)<br><br>**c.** Provide bed-cradle with cover(s) to prevent chilling.<br><br>**d.** Avoid drafts and limit exposure time during bathing and dressing procedures. |
| **6.** Potential pyrexia due to infection and/or trauma.<br><br>**Objective.** Temperature within normal limits.<br><br>**Timing.** Day 3. | **a.** If child is febrile:<br><br>–Reduce covers over bed; do not tuck them in.<br><br>–Force fluids, if tolerated.<br><br>–Give antipyretics, as ordered<br><br>–Take swabs for culture and sensitivities, as ordered.<br><br>**b.** If fever persists, lower room temperature to 24°C. |

continued

| Usual Problems/Objectives/Timing | Nursing Orders |
|---|---|
| **C. Positioning**<br>**1.** Potential breakdown of unburned skin, due to friction of body surfaces, splints, etc., and prolonged immobilization.<br><br>**Objective.** No further skin breakdown.<br><br>**Timing.** Until patient is fully mobile. | **a.** *See* Careplan 13: Prolonged Immobilization.<br><br>**b.** Change patient's position q1h (turn side to side, prone/supine, if extent of burn permits).<br><br>**c.** Gently massage unburned body prominences with soap and water p.r.n. Place polyurethane foam (PUF) pads under heels, elbows, and sacrum, p.r.n.<br><br>**d.** Maintain good body alignment, using towels or pads to support patient's position and prevent friction. Two examples are summarized as follows:<br><br>**(1) Burns of head and neck**<br><br>–*When patient is on back.* Hyperextend neck by placing small roll under nape of neck.<br><br>–*When patient is on abdomen.* Place small pad under forehead. If nearby skin is burned, make rolls of PUF instead of towels.<br><br>**(2) Burns of upper chest and arms**<br><br>–*When patient is on side.* Place rolled towels behind back and between legs.<br><br>–*When patient is on back.* Abduct legs and place rolled towels between them. Position feet in flexion, using footboard or sandbag. Position arms at 90-degree angle from body.<br><br>–*When patient is on abdomen.* Place rolled towels between ankles. Keep feet at 90-degree angle. Place a small roll of cloth or PUF under ankles (to raise feet off bed) or position feet over edge of mattress.<br><br>**e.** If splints are in use, remove *at least* q4h to inspect skin. If skin is being rubbed, pad edges of splints with gauze. *Correct position of limb must be maintained.* If splint is still causing problems, notify dr or physical therapist (adjustments can be made). |
| **2.** Contractures.<br><br>**Objective.** No or minimal contractures.<br><br>**Timing.** By discharge. | **a.** In collaboration with physical therapist, determine method of positioning patient to prevent contractures.<br><br>–**In bed.** *See* nursing orders C.1(d) and (e).<br><br>–**In chair (not wheelchair).** Elevate legs; support back to maintain upright position. If legs can be dangled, apply elasticized (tensor) bandages. Do not leave patient in chair for long periods. Start with ½ hr, then 1 hr if this is tolerated, t.i.d. or q.i.d. |
| **3.** Uncomfortable positioning.<br><br>**Objective.** Parents/patient understand reasons for positioning.<br><br>**Timing.** As long as positioning is necessary. | **a.** Explain to parents, as well as patient, the need for positioning (and splints) to prevent contractures (disfigurement).<br><br>**b.** Ensure that splints are checked by physical therapist at regular intervals.<br><br>**c.** Ensure that patient does not remove splints.<br><br>**d.** Health care team members to spend as much time as possible with patient (and, if appropriate, encourage |

| Usual Problems/Objectives/Timing | Nursing Orders |
|---|---|
| **C.3. (Continued).** | parents to do so), to divert his attention (by talking, reading, playing games, watching TV, listening to the radio, etc.). |
| **4.** Poor posture when walking, due to discomfort, pain, and/or increasing contractures resulting from prolonged immobilization.<br>**Objectives.** Improved posture and increased ambulation.<br>**Timing.** By discharge. | **a.** Encourage child to stand up straight, look ahead, and walk with heels on the ground.<br>**b.** Instruct patient to walk in shoes with rubber soles or barefoot (to prevent slipping).<br>**c.** Follow instructions given by physical therapist.<br>**d.** Apply tensor bandages to legs, if appropriate, over any bandages already in position.<br>**e.** Record distance walked; increase as tolerated.<br>**f.** Praise patient's attempts or progress. |
| **D. Burn Site**<br>**1.** Blistering.<br>**Objective.** Blistered area clean and healing.<br>**Timing.** Until blisters are healed. | **a.** Leave all blisters intact.<br>**b.** Protect blisters by dressings, positioning, careful handling, etc.<br>**c.** Debride blisters only when ordered by dr (usually, when the blisters break): remove blistered skin, using scissors and forceps.<br>**d.** **Blisters on lips.** *Do not break or remove.* Encourage patient not to lick his lips. Apply prescribed ointments sparingly. |
| **2.** Facial burns: Vision restricted by edema.<br>**Objective.** Parents/patient coping with explanations.<br>**Timing.** 48 hr. | **a.** Explain to patient/parent that swelling is only temporary.<br>**b.** Announce yourself when approaching child.<br>**c.** Explain all procedures fully to patient, before and during them.<br>**d.** Anticipate child's needs.<br>**e.** Cleanse patient's eyes p.r.n. with N saline.<br>**f.** Prevent child from rubbing eyes. |
| **3.** Potential discomfort due to serous oozing.<br>**Objective.** Patient dry and comfortable.<br>**Timing.** As long as oozing persists. | **a.** Place patient on PUF pad; change pad p.r.n. *Do not cover pad with bed linen.* Do not put any waterproof material *under* the pad (allow fluid to seep through to the bed linen underneath).<br>**b.** Use bed-cradle.<br>**c.** Keep burned area clean and as dry as possible. Try to prevent sticking.<br>**d.** Apply ointment as ordered by dr. |
| **4.** Potential restriction of circulation and/or respiration by eschar formation on circumferential burns.<br>**Objectives.** Adequate circulation to limbs; adequate air entry to lungs. | **a.** Elevate burned extremities on pillows.<br>**b.** Observe patient q15 min for increasingly difficult respiration (due to restricted movement of chest wall), and color, temperature, and swelling of limb(s). |

continued

| Usual Problems/Objectives/Timing | Nursing Orders |
|---|---|
| **D 4. (Continued).**<br>    **Timing.** 48 hr. | Notify dr *stat* if respiration is becoming difficult or if limb(s) are swelling, becoming paler or cool to touch, or pulses decreased or absent.<br>**c.** Have equipment (scalpel, dressings, and/or towels) ready in case dr must do an escharotomy.<br>**d.** *If escharotomies are done*, observe areas constantly for bleeding. At first sign of bleeding:<br>  –Apply pressure *directly* to the bleeding area.<br>  –Call for help; notify dr *stat*.<br>  –If necessary, place patient in shock position (head down), unless contraindicated (e.g., patient has upper body or facial edema). |
| **5.** Potential maceration due to rubbing of burn surfaces (neck, axillae, elbows, groins, and/or hands).<br>  **Objective.** No maceration.<br>  **Timing.** Until burn/graft healed. | **a. Neck area.** Place roll of PUF behind neck to maintain hyperextension. *No pillows.* Apply neck splint if ordered.<br>**b. Axillae and elbows.** Place PUF roll in each axilla to keep arms extended at 90 degrees; restrain at wrists. Use sandbags to maintain patient's position.<br>**c. Hands.** Apply N saline dressings lightly around each finger. Apply hand splints if ordered.<br>**d. Groins, legs, and feet**<br>  –Keep patient's legs extended and spread apart.<br>  –Place rolled PUF, or sandbags covered with PUF, between legs.<br>  –If patient is lying on his side, angle legs and feet and place PUF between them.<br>**e.** Keep burned areas clean. |
| **E. Nutrition**<br>  **1.** Potential loss of weight due to anorexia and/or frequent fasting for surgery.<br>  **Objective.** Patient's weight maintained or increasing.<br>  **Timing.** Continuing. | **a.** Record intake and output in detail.<br>**b.** Record caloric intake daily.<br>**c.** Discuss child's food preferences with family. Note any racial or religious differences or limitations.<br>**d.** Enlist help of dietitian to plan child's intake (calories and protein must be doubled).<br>**e.** Impress on parents/patient the importance of diet.<br>**f.** Provide small meals and frequent snacks, attractively served. If child's condition permits:<br>  –Help him to sit up to eat.<br>  –Encourage him to feed himself, but set time limit and then assist him.<br>  –Vary diet to regulate stool frequency. |
| **2.** Potential malnutrition resulting from ingestion of nonnutritious treats brought in by visitors, and resultant inability to eat the planned diet. | **a.** Explain to parents the importance of a nutritious diet to speed the healing of burns. Arrange for them to discuss their child's diet with a dietitian.<br>**b.** Recognize the mother's need to help her child. |

| Usual Problems/Objectives/Timing | Nursing Orders |
|---|---|
| **E.2. (Continued).**<br><br>**Objective.** Parents understand and accept the extra importance of a balanced, highly nutritious diet while burns are healing.<br><br>**Timing.** Until burns are healed. | –Allow food to be brought in, but advise the mother about selection and, when she brings it, ensure that it is appropriate.<br>–Include this intake in the record.<br>**c.** Encourage parents to be present at mealtimes. Show them how they can help (by positioning, feeding, etc.). |
| **F. Skin Grafts**<br>1. Potential sloughing of graft.<br><br>**Objective.** Graft healed.<br><br>**Timing.** 5 days postop. | **a.** *Handle patient very carefully.*<br>**b.** Position patient to prevent rubbing or sliding of graft.<br>**c.** If grafts are covered with Sofra-tulle (dressing impregnated with framycetin sulphate BP) only:<br>–Prevent wrinkling or folding of the tulle.<br>–If blebs form under the graft, clip the tulle with scissors; smoothe gently, using cotton-tipped applicators.<br>**d.** Restrain patient p.r.n. Ensure that restraints and splints do not interfere with grafts.<br>**e.** Remove crusting and dead grafts when ordered by dr.<br>**f. Leg grafts.** If patient is allowed to get up, apply elastic (tensor) bandage over existing leg bandages. |
| 2. Potential discomfort and bleeding from donor site.<br><br>**Objective.** Discomfort minimal and donor site healed.<br><br>**Timing.** 8–10 days. | **a.** Pressure dressings are left intact for 8–10 days. Remove them only if ordered by dr or if oozing is severe (see **c**).<br>**b.** If patient is uncomfortable, position him *off* the donor site.<br>**c.** Observe for oozing through dressings.<br>–If small amount, outline with pen on dressing; record.<br>–If large amount of oozing, *do not apply more dressings.* Remove outer layers, down to covering dressing (e.g., gauze impregnated with scarlet-red dye), and apply a fresh pressure dressing. Then place patient so that pressure is on donor site. Notify dr *stat*.<br>**d.** When the pressure dressing is removed:<br>–Trim the scarlet-red dressing as it begins to separate.<br>–If appropriate, place the child in a tub bath to speed removal of the scarlet-red dressing.<br>**e.** When the area has healed:<br>–Apply petrolatum liberally.<br>–Depending on the location of burn, give tub bath or sitz bath p.r.n. *Do not use soap.* |
| 3. Dry skin and potential itching due to diminution of oil secretion and sweating (graft and donor sites).<br><br>**Objective.** No skin breakdown by scratching. | **a.** Explain why the skin is dry (secretory and sweat glands burned away).<br>**b.** Explain importance of not scratching. |

continued

| Usual Problems/Objectives/Timing | Nursing Orders |
|---|---|
| **F. 3. (Continued).**<br>**Timing.** Continuing. | **c.** Keep patient's fingernails and toenails cut short. Restrain arms or hands p.r.n.<br><br>**d.** Apply petrolatum to all healed areas (graft and donor).<br><br>**e.** Apply cool, wet compresses to itchy areas.<br><br>**f.** Give antipruritics if ordered.<br><br>**g.** Provide oilated baths as ordered by dr.<br><br>**h.** Do not use soap on child's skin. |
| **4.** *After grafts and burns have healed:* Increased sensitivity to heat and cold.<br><br>**Objectives.** Ambient temperature feels comfortable to patient. Parents/patient know how to cope at home.<br><br>**Timing.** Continuing. | **a. Indoors.** Adjust temperature of room(s), according to child's sensation of warmth or coolness.<br><br>**b. Outdoors.** Protect healed areas from direct sunlight.<br><br>**c. Summer.** Cover sensitive areas with light clothing.<br><br>**d. Winter.** Dress child warmly in cold weather (to prevent frostbite). |
| **G. Emotional Reactions**<br><br>**1.** Disorientation, apathy, or agitation, due to suddenness of accident and unfamiliar environment.<br><br>**Objective.** Patient is alert, relatively calm, asking questions.<br><br>**Timing.** 24 hr. | **a.** If patient is disoriented, talk to him quietly; explain where he is and why.<br><br>**b.** If patient is apathetic, try to stimulate him; ask questions and encourage him to talk.<br><br>**c.** If patient is agitated, reduce stimuli; speak in a calm, reassuring manner.<br><br>**d.** Be alert to the possibility that the patient might have an undetected head injury.<br>–Do HIR q4h p.r.n. |
| **2.** Fright and anxiety about the accident, possible guilt feelings, fear of disfigurement or death and the strange environment.<br><br>**Objectives.** Fear and anxiety reduced; patient is talking about the accident.<br><br>**Timing.** By discharge. | **a.** Explain procedures and equipment to patient:<br>–Burn-bath/dressings.<br>–Blood tests.<br>–Gowns, masks, gloves, i.v. lines, etc.<br><br>**b.** Describe surroundings.<br><br>**c.** Explain to the patient who will be looking after him. If he does not need constant surveillance, instruct him how to call for a nurse.<br><br>**d.** If patient is isolated, *see* Careplan 12: Isolation: Psychological Aspects.<br><br>**e.** Ensure a consistent assignment of nurses, to establish trust and confidence.<br><br>**f.** Spend time with patient other than for treatments. Encourage expression of fears and concerns.<br><br>**g. Procedures and treatments**<br>–Assess need for analgesia before treatment.<br>–Offer a choice only when it is possible.<br>–State what must be done and why.<br>–Suggest ways in which the patient can participate. |

| Usual Problems/Objectives/Timing | Nursing Orders |
|---|---|
| **G.3.** Parents are distressed and bewildered and may have feelings of guilt about the accident and sudden hospitalization.<br><br>**Objective.** Parents express their concerns and talk to members of the health team, and later, their child, about the accident.<br><br>**Timing.** Continuing. | **Designated nurse:**<br>**a.** Stay with parents to reassure and comfort them.<br>**b.** As soon as they can cope with their feelings, explain:<br>  –Physical set-up of ward.<br>  –Gown, mask, and hand-washing routines.<br>  –Who will be looking after their child.<br>  –The initial routines (burn-bath, i.v. lines, blood tests, etc.).<br>  –Their child's appearance.<br>  –If exposure method is being used, explain the method, reason for its use, the room's high temperature, etc.<br>**c.** At parents' first visit, and at later visits if necessary, accompany them into their child's room; stay with them as long as necessary.<br><br>**General Nursing Orders**<br>**a.** Allow time for parents to express their concerns, away from the child's room. Reassure them that their reactions and fears are normal.<br>**b.** Consult social worker and/or psychiatrist about handling parents' stress and guilt feelings.<br>**c.** As the child's condition stabilizes, encourage patient and parents to talk to each other about the accident.<br>**d.** As long as you think necessary, restrict visitors to parents and close relatives (never more than two at a time). Encourage them to deal with their stress *away from* the child's room. |
| **4.** Disturbed sleep and nightmares; patient is reliving the accident.<br><br>**Objective.** Restful nighttime sleep.<br><br>**Timing.** 1 week. | **a.** Wake the patient when he appears to be having a nightmare.<br>**b.** Encourage him to talk to you about his nightmares the next day.<br>**c.** Report to dr/psychiatrist if nightmares persist. |
| **5.** Anxiety, frustration, and anger about treatments (baths, dressings) that are lengthy, uncomfortable, and seemingly endless.<br><br>**Objective.** Less anxiety and a reasonable degree of acceptance of the need for treatments.<br><br>**Timing.** Until skin is grafted. | **a.** Explain each procedure before you start.<br>**b.** Allow patient to just sit in the bath for a while (for young child, provide toys) before you start treatment.<br>**c.** Encourage patient to remove his dressings himself, but give him a time limit in which to do this.<br>**d.** Reassure child that it is all right to cry if it hurts, but he must understand the importance of keeping still while you are debriding, etc. Give the child something to squeeze or bite on, if appropriate.<br>**e.** *Only one nurse* should debride the burn. (It is frightening for a child to see several people picking at his skin with forceps; it also increases the pain.)<br>  –Limit debriding time to 30 min. |

continued

| Usual Problems/Objectives/Timing | Nursing Orders |
|---|---|
| **G.5. (Continued).** | —Wipe off as much eschar as possible with the old cream (this is less painful than debriding with forceps).<br><br>—Then use forceps and scissors.<br><br>—If patient shows interest, allow him to do some debriding.<br><br>**f.** Encourage parents to be with their child during his bath, even if for only a few minutes. |
| **6.** Patient's potential continuing dependence on others to perform for him activities normal for his age, after recovery from the acute phase.<br><br>**Objective.** Patient increasingly independent within the limits of his physical disability.<br><br>**Timing.** Until discharge. | **a.** Encourage patient to maintain or regain independence.<br><br>**b.** Explain to parents the importance of allowing their child to do things for himself, even if it is awkward and takes time.<br><br>**c. Mealtimes.** Hand splints can be removed at mealtime. Do not feed the child until he has tried to cope by himself.<br><br>—Place food within patient's reach.<br><br>—Prepare food so that it will be easy to eat.<br><br>—Provide padded cutlery and utensils that patient can manipulate.<br><br>—Place a nonslip rubber mat under plate, or use a plate guard.<br><br>—Provide a flexed straw or a nonspill cup.<br><br>**d.** Encourage patient to perform routine daily activities (brush teeth, comb hair, bathe, hold urinal, etc.), as appropriate.<br><br>**e.** Praise patient for all efforts made, however small. |
| **7.** Concern about altered body image.<br><br>**Objective.** Patient retains or regains feelings of self-worth and self-esteem.<br><br>**Timing.** Continuing. | **a.** Be careful of *your* facial expressions and comments while in patient's presence.<br><br>**b.** Help family members to accept child's appearance.<br><br>**c.** Encourage patient to talk about his appearance. If his face is burned and he wants to see it, give him a mirror. Answer all his questions, comfort him, and stay with him until you feel he is reasonably settled.<br><br>**d.** Encourage parents to treat their child as normal—as they did before the accident.<br><br>**e.** Explain to parents about scarring and contractures and how they will be managed.<br><br>**f.** Explain to the patient:<br><br>—Scars get redder, then fade gradually *(but do not reassure the patient that there will be no scars).*<br><br>—Contractures can be stretched; he will be returning to hospital later to have this done.<br><br>—He will return to hospital frequently, to see doctors and other therapists who will decide what will be done to improve his appearance.<br><br>—The importance of good hygiene and diet to keep intact skin clear for grafting. |

| Usual Problems/Objectives/Timing | Nursing Orders |
|---|---|
| **G.7. (Continued).** | **g.** Help patient with personal grooming, selection of clothes, etc. Enlist the help of all appropriate members of the health care team. |
| **8.** Patient's fear of rejection, particularly if burns are on exposed areas (especially the face).<br><br>**Objective.** Patient learns to cope with others' reactions to his appearance.<br><br>**Timing.** Before discharge. | **a.** If siblings and other significant family members have not seen the child since the accident, it is important they do so long before he returns home. Parents need help in arranging and coping with these visits. Provide guidance, support, and reassurance.<br><br>**b.** The patient should be introduced *gradually* to other people to experience their reactions to his appearance, by:<br>–Spending time with roommates.<br>–Walking around the ward.<br>–Going to playroom on the ward.<br>–Riding on the elevator.<br>–Going to main playroom.<br>–Going to snack bar or cafeteria within the hospital.<br>–Walking in public areas adjacent to the hospital.<br>Always accompany the child to his destination until he feels secure in meeting new people. Make sure he is dressed well in ordinary clothes (not pajamas), that his hair is combed, etc.<br><br>**c.** If possible, introduce him to a patient who has already been at home after being burned. Try to provide opportunities for the two sets of parents to meet.<br><br>**d.** If difficult situations arise, comfort the child and explain the other person's reaction. Stay with him until he has expressed his feelings and is calmer.<br><br>**e.** Help the child to realize that change in a person's appearance does not change his inner self or limit his potential achievements. |
| **H. Home Care and Follow-up**<br>**1.** Patient's/parents' concern about coping with care at home; potential failure to comply with instructions.<br><br>**Objectives.** Patient/parents:<br>–Know the exercise program thoroughly and understand its great importance.<br>–Cope with all aspects of care comfortably.<br>–State their intention to comply with all instructions, in the knowledge that the lengthy treatments will help the child to return to a normal life-style.<br><br>**Timing.** By discharge. | **Designated nurse:**<br>**a.** Explain dr's discharge orders. If an antipruritic has been prescribed, ensure that the parents have a prescription.<br><br>**b.** Ensure that patient/parents understand the importance of complying with instructions for home care and follow-up.<br><br>**c.** Teach them:<br>–Management of itchy, dry skin—cool baths and application of bath oil.<br>–Protection from heat and cold.<br>–Protection (but not overprotection) from injury.<br>–Exercise program (in conjunction with physical therapist). |

continued

| Usual Problems/Objectives/Timing | Nursing Orders |
|---|---|
| **H.1. (Continued).** | –Application of splints, elasticized pressure suit (e.g., Jobst), dressings, and bandages.<br><br>**d.** Check that all follow-up programs (physical therapy, schooling, etc.) have been arranged.<br><br>**e.** Ensure that the parents have instructions in writing and know whom to contact if they need help or advice. |

# Admission Procedure for Burn Patient

1. Remove the patient's clothing and/or bandages.
2. Shave off hair (except eyebrows) in the vicinity of burns.
3. Take swabs for culture and sensitivities, from the surface of burns, clear skin, and perineum.
4. Bathe the patient in a warm N saline tub bath; *or* perform warm N saline soaks of the burned area, using large gauze squares ("burn gauze") placed *evenly* over burn. Bathe or soak patient for 20 min.
5. Shampoo his hair.
6. Cover the stretcher with a sterile sheet.
7. Remove the patient from the tub (or discontinue soaks) and place him on the prepared stretcher.
8. Take repeat swabs for culture and sensitivities (from the surface of burns, clear skin, and perineum); take swabs from his nose and throat.
9. Debride the burn as ordered by the doctor. Using sterilized scissors, forceps, and gauze swabs, remove loose skin and eschar. (Blisters on the face, hands, feet, and perineum are usually left intact.) Do not debride for longer than 30 min.
10. Rinse the burned area with N saline.
11. If photographs are to be taken, arrange for them to be done at this time.
12. Apply topical ointment as ordered (usually silver sulfadiazine, SSD).
13. Place a pad of PUF on the patient's bed (this helps to prevent adherence of the burned area to bed linen).
14. Place the patient directly on the pad and position him appropriately with rolled towels or PUF, etc.

Careplan **32** Child Abuse, Suspected

**Goals for Discharge or Maintenance**
See Objectives.

| Usual Problems/Objectives/Timing | Nursing Orders |
|---|---|
| **1.** Patient's potential fear of and lack of trust in adults, due to abuse and/or neglect.<br><br>**Objectives.** Child is relaxed; allows adults to approach; interacts spontaneously with adults; is not abused while in hospital.<br><br>**Timing.** Until discharge. | **a.** Ensure that the child-abuse team has been contacted.<br><br>**b.** Ensure a consistent assignment of nurses.<br><br>**c.** Use a gentle, reassuring approach.<br><br>**d.** Plan a consistent routine for physical care and activity.<br><br>**e.** Do not initiate discussion about the source of injury.<br><br>**f.** If the child initiates discussion, allow him to express his feelings.<br><br>**g.** Do not discuss the abuser's behavior in the child's hearing.<br><br>**h.** Observe discreetly during family visits.<br><br>**i.** Document observations on Nursing Observations flow sheet on admission and as requested (Figure 4, page 109). |
| **2.** Potential negative attention-seeking behavior and disturbed peer relationships.<br><br>**Objectives.** Child socializes with peers. Decreased negative behavior.<br><br>**Timing.** As soon as possible. | **a.** Document observations of:<br>–Tantrums.<br>–Excessive crying.<br>–Fecal smearing.<br>–Vomiting.<br>–Bed-wetting.<br>–Aggressiveness.<br>–Refusing foods.<br><br>**b.** Anticipate situations likely to cause negative behavior (e.g., mealtime, bedtime), and give extra attention at that time.<br><br>**c.** Reward appropriate behavior with attention.<br><br>**d.** Use a firm, consistent approach.<br><br>**e.** Use constructive discipline (e.g., reason with the child; take him to his room until he settles).<br><br>**f.** Provide constructive, supervised play, and document the patient's behavior with other children. |
| **3.** Parents' potential embarrassment and/or hostility due to guilt or to fear of authority (e.g., hospital, Children's Aid Society).<br><br>**Objectives.** Parents appear less anxious and more relaxed and show interest in their child's care. They evidence changed behavior by using more appropriate methods in caring for their child. Parents express understanding and acceptance of plans made for their child.<br><br>**Timing.** By discharge. | **a.** Designated nurse to spend time with parents at every visit.<br><br>**b.** Be supportive and nonjudgmental.<br><br>**c.** Discuss with parents methods of discipline the staff have attempted, and results (successes *and* failures).<br><br>**d.** Encourage parents' participation in their child's care with nurse's assistance and supervision. Document amount and quality of involvement.<br><br>**e.** Place patient in a room with other children, so that the parents can observe other parents' attitudes and methods of dealing with their children. |

CHILD-ABUSE PROGRAM
NURSING OBSERVATIONS

The nurses' observations of the abused child and his family play an important part in the assessment of the family. A thorough evaluation is, in turn, very important in treatment planning.

In order to record the nurses' observations of the patient, the parent(s) and other visitors, the following form should be used at the admission and discharge assessment, at weekly intervals, and as requested. In both sections A & B, please tick one or more responses and/or comment in the spaces provided.

| Date of Admission_____ | Who accompanied child on admission_____ | |
| Date of Follow-up 1_____ | Date of Follow-up 2_____ | Date of Follow-up 3_____ |
| Signature _____ | Signature_____ | Signature_____ |

**A  OBSERVATIONS OF THE PATIENT**

**PATIENT'S REACTION TO MOTHER**

| | Admission | Follow-up 1 2 3 |
|---|---|---|
| anger | ☐ | ☐ ☐ ☐ |
| fear | ☐ | ☐ ☐ ☐ |
| lack of interest | ☐ | ☐ ☐ ☐ |
| pleasure | ☐ | ☐ ☐ ☐ |
| sadness | ☐ | ☐ ☐ ☐ |
| withdrawal | ☐ | ☐ ☐ ☐ |
| other | ☐ | ☐ ☐ ☐ |
| specify _____ | | |

**PATIENT'S REACTION TO FATHER**

| | Admission | Follow-up 1 2 3 |
|---|---|---|
| anger | ☐ | ☐ ☐ ☐ |
| fear | ☐ | ☐ ☐ ☐ |
| lack of interest | ☐ | ☐ ☐ ☐ |
| pleasure | ☐ | ☐ ☐ ☐ |
| sadness | ☐ | ☐ ☐ ☐ |
| withdrawal | ☐ | ☐ ☐ ☐ |
| other | ☐ | ☐ ☐ ☐ |
| specify_____ | | |

**PATIENT'S REACTION TO WARD-STAFF**

| | Admission | Follow-up 1 2 3 |
|---|---|---|
| appropriate | ☐ | ☐ ☐ ☐ |
| approval seeking | ☐ | ☐ ☐ ☐ |
| attention seeking | ☐ | ☐ ☐ ☐ |
| disinterested | ☐ | ☐ ☐ ☐ |
| fearful | ☐ | ☐ ☐ ☐ |
| provocative | ☐ | ☐ ☐ ☐ |
| withdrawn | ☐ | ☐ ☐ ☐ |
| other | ☐ | ☐ ☐ ☐ |
| specify_____ | | |

**PATIENT'S REACTION TO PEERS**

| | Admission | Follow-up 1 2 3 |
|---|---|---|
| aggressive | ☐ | ☐ ☐ ☐ |
| fearful | ☐ | ☐ ☐ ☐ |
| ingratiating | ☐ | ☐ ☐ ☐ |
| withdrawn | ☐ | ☐ ☐ ☐ |
| appropriate | ☐ | ☐ ☐ ☐ |
| other | ☐ | ☐ ☐ ☐ |
| specify_____ | | |

**PATIENT'S GENERAL BEHAVIOR**

| | Admission | Follow-up 1 2 3 |
|---|---|---|
| appropriate | ☐ | ☐ ☐ ☐ |
| destructive | ☐ | ☐ ☐ ☐ |
| hyperactive | ☐ | ☐ ☐ ☐ |
| nightmares | ☐ | ☐ ☐ ☐ |
| poor sleeper | ☐ | ☐ ☐ ☐ |
| poor eater | ☐ | ☐ ☐ ☐ |
| other | ☐ | ☐ ☐ ☐ |
| specify _____ | | |

Reaction to other visitors:  sibling(s); aunt; uncle; grandparent(s); other (please specify if possible)

Comments:_____

Does history of patient's behavior prior to admission seem the same or different from what you observed on the ward?

Comments:_____

Has child given any story of how injury occurred:  Yes ☐   No ☐   Was this elicited ☐   or volunteered ☐

Comments:_____

**Figure 4.** *Form for recording observations on possible child abuse.*

<u>B</u> OBSERVATION OF THE PARENT ─────────────────────────────

a) DOES THE PARENT SEEM INVOLVED WITH THE CHILD:        DOES PARENT SEEM:

|  | Admission | Follow-up 1 2 3 |  |  | Admission | Follow-up 1 2 3 |
|---|---|---|---|---|---|---|
| holding | ☐ | ☐ ☐ ☐ | | uninvolved with the child | ☐ | ☐ ☐ ☐ |
| bathing | ☐ | ☐ ☐ ☐ | | frustrated by child | ☐ | ☐ ☐ ☐ |
| changing diapers | ☐ | ☐ ☐ ☐ | | hostile (physical, verbal) | ☐ | ☐ ☐ ☐ |
| feeding | ☐ | ☐ ☐ ☐ | | other | ☐ | ☐ ☐ ☐ |
| playing | ☐ | ☐ ☐ ☐ | | specify | | |
| other | ☐ | ☐ ☐ ☐ | | | | |
| specify _____ | | | | | | |

_____        _____
_____        _____

b) REACTION OF PARENT TO WARD-STAFF:        c) REACTION OF PARENT TO OTHER PARENTS:

DOES PARENT SEEM:

|  | Admission | Follow-up 1 2 3 |  |  | Admission | Follow-up 1 2 3 |
|---|---|---|---|---|---|---|
| demanding | ☐ | ☐ ☐ ☐ | | little involvement | ☐ | ☐ ☐ ☐ |
| embarrassed | ☐ | ☐ ☐ ☐ | | talkative | ☐ | ☐ ☐ ☐ |
| guilty | ☐ | ☐ ☐ ☐ | | appropriate | ☐ | ☐ ☐ ☐ |
| hostile | ☐ | ☐ ☐ ☐ | | inappropriate | ☐ | ☐ ☐ ☐ |
| withdrawn | ☐ | ☐ ☐ ☐ | | specify _____ | | |
| appropriate | ☐ | ☐ ☐ ☐ | | | | |
| other | ☐ | ☐ ☐ ☐ | | | | |
| specify ____ | | | | | | |

_____        _____
_____        _____
                                        _____

d) VISITING PATTERN

FREQUENCY OF VISITS PER WEEK:        INDICATE AVERAGE LENGTH OF VISIT:

|  | 1 | 2 | 3 | 4 | 5 | 5+ |  |  | 10-30 min | 30-60 min | 1-1½ hr | 2+ hr |
|---|---|---|---|---|---|---|---|---|---|---|---|---|
| Mother | ☐ | ☐ | ☐ | ☐ | ☐ | ☐ | | | ☐ | ☐ | ☐ | ☐ |
| Father | ☐ | ☐ | ☐ | ☐ | ☐ | ☐ | | | ☐ | ☐ | ☐ | ☐ |
| Grandparents | ☐ | ☐ | ☐ | ☐ | ☐ | ☐ | | | ☐ | ☐ | ☐ | ☐ |
| Other | ☐ | ☐ | ☐ | ☐ | ☐ | ☐ | | | ☐ | ☐ | ☐ | ☐ |
| specify _____ | | | | | | | | | | | | |

e) Have the parents provided any history of the patient's injury:

If so, what did mother say: _____

_____

If so, what did father say: _____

_____

f) History provided by other relative: _____

_____

_____

Signature (admission) _____

**Figure 4** (*Continued*)

| Usual Problems/Objectives/Timing | Nursing Orders |
|---|---|
| 3. (Continued). | **f.** Do not diagnose or interpret behavior to parents. |
| | **g.** Designated nurse to maintain contact with child-abuse team for exchange of information and attend all meetings concerning the child. |
| | **h.** Explain to parents that they will be informed of discharge plans *by the child-abuse team*. |
| | **i.** Allow parents to discuss their feelings about the discharge plans. |

# Careplan 33

Drug Ingestion, Accidental *or* Intentional:
Post–Emergency Ward Care

## Goals for Discharge or Maintenance
I. Patient or parents display insight into reasons for ingestion.
II. Parents state correct knowledge concerning storage of toxic substances.

| Usual Problems/Objectives/Timing | Nursing Orders |
|---|---|
| **1.** Potential respiratory depression due to drug.<br><br>**Objective.** Normal respiration.<br><br>**Timing.** 24 hr. | **a.** Record vital signs, pupil reaction, and level of consciousness every ½ hr until stable, then q4h.<br><br>**b.** Check airway for obstruction; suction p.r.n.<br><br>**c.** If patient is unconscious, position him on side or abdomen with chin forward (to prevent aspiration). |
| **2.** Potential dehydration due to difficulty taking fluids orally.<br><br>**Objective.** Normal hydration.<br><br>**Timing.** 24 hr. | **a.** Maintain i.v. fluids as ordered.<br><br>**b.** If patient is conscious, offer fluids orally q½h (30–60 ml).<br><br>**c.** Record intake and output.<br><br>**d.** Observe for signs and symptoms of dehydration q4h. |
| **3.** Potential injury due to restlessness or during reduced consciousness.<br><br>**Objective.** No injury.<br><br>**Timing.** Until discharge. | **a.** Put side-rails up and pad them if necessary.<br><br>**b.** Remove hard or sharp objects.<br><br>**c.** Use restraints if necessary.<br><br>**d.** Observe patient frequently (at least q15 min) until conscious. |
| **4.** Potential loss of consciousness. | *See* Careplan 15: Unconscious Patient. |
| **5.** *Intentional ingestion.* | *See* Careplan 39: Suicidal Patient, Adolescent. |
| **6.** *Accidental ingestion:* Parents have potential guilt feelings about child's access to drug.<br><br>**Objectives.** Parents express guilt feelings and describe safety measures they have introduced or will introduce at home.<br><br>**Timing.** By discharge. | **a.** Spend time with parents (at least 15–20 min daily), encouraging conversation.<br><br>**b.** Do not be judgmental.<br><br>**c.** Teach safe storage of toxic substances.<br><br>**d.** Notify the public health nurse as necessary. |
| **7.** Potential impairment of mental function and disturbance of orientation, due to cerebral toxicity of ingested substance.<br><br>**Objective.** Patient oriented in time and space.<br><br>**Timing.** As soon as possible. | **a.** On every contact, orient patient to time and place, if appropriate.<br><br>**b.** Confirm reality. |

# Mental and Behavioral Disorders

*The standard careplans in this section are intended for
use by nurses caring for patients on general medical or
surgical wards.*

A patient with anorexia nervosa requires both medical and psychiatric intervention, as the manifestations of this syndrome are both physiological and psychological. Many of these patients are admitted to a medical unit for a total assessment because of their presenting problem of severe weight loss. There, they receive a complete physical and psychological assessment before the diagnosis of anorexia nervosa is established. A treatment program is then devised to meet the specific needs of the individual patient, parents, and family members. This program must establish a safe, caring, and controlled environment for the patient.

This careplan encourages a multidisciplinary team approach, the team consisting of all caregivers participating in the patient's treatment program (e.g., nurses, dietitian, pediatrician, ward residents, psychiatrist, social worker, occupational therapist). Each team member assesses the patient and contributes to the management program.

The nurse is a key member in both the assessment phase and treatment program. The nurse's relationship with the patient and family members, observations, assessments, interventions, and records are important components of the total management program. The nurse's assessment is derived from interpersonal relationship with, and observation of, the patient. Information about the patient's behavior, particularly in relation to food, must be recorded. For example:

–Daily assessment of food intake (detailed record of amount and type of food eaten, caloric count calibrated, food likes and dislikes).

–Habits and behaviors associated with food, meals, and eating (e.g., expression of lack of appetite, aversion to certain food, disgust at thought of food, hiding of food, preoccupation with food, stealing and hoarding of food, feelings of guilt after eating, self-induced vomiting, periods of starvation alternating with unsatisfying gorging, feeling full after eating).

–Patient's feelings and attitudes regarding gaining, losing, and/or maintaining weight (e.g., feelings related to a pursuit of thinness).

–Patient's activities, relationships, and mood (e.g., interest in and ability to be involved in age-appropriate activities of daily living, affect, feelings related to self-image, relationships with parents/ peers/staff).

Together the health care team devises the individual treatment program for the patient, which reflects the patient's stage of development and physical and psychological condition. The team determines:

1. Goals of the patient's hospital stay (e.g., weight goal, caloric intake expected).

2. Specific approaches to reach goals (e.g., behavioral modification program, individual and group psychotherapy, family lunch therapy sessions).

3. The role of each team member with the patient and family.

4. Specific and consistent conference times to evaluate patient's progress.

This careplan identifies the usual problems experienced by these patients and provides nursing orders that should be considered and adapted to the individual program.

### Goals for Discharge or Maintenance
Patient and parents have some understanding of anorexia nervosa and state their intention to adhere to follow-up plans.

| Usual Problems/Objectives/Timing | Nursing Orders |
|---|---|
| 1. Excessive weight loss and malnutrition because of patient's vigorous attempts to maintain a thin body (e.g., patient voluntarily refuses food even if hungry; patient involved in an intense, self-imposed, dieting/starvation regimen—states "doesn't feel hungry").<br><br>**Objective.** Patient eats required nutritional diet and/or achieves weight goal.<br><br>**Timing.** As soon as possible. | a. Ensure a consistent assignment of nurses, to establish supportive relationships and continuity of approach.<br><br>b. When the multidisciplinary team has decided on the treatment program: with the dr, explain approaches and goals to both the patient and parents. Clearly identify the roles of the caregivers involved in the program to decrease any misinterpretation of responsibilities (e.g., dr is responsible for overall program, discussing weight goals with patient and parents). Try to identify the patient's and parents' concerns and rectify misconceptions.<br><br>*Interpretation of the treatment program must be accurate and consistent; all information must be clearly recorded on the patient's chart.*<br><br>c. Discuss and approach food-related issues according to the individual program initiated. This should be |

| Usual Problems/Objectives/Timing | Nursing Orders |
|---|---|
| **1. (Continued).** | clearly defined (e.g., how to deal with the patient's feelings and behaviors/habits associated with food and eating). Remember that the patient is preoccupied with food-related issues; attention and interest in the patient must focus on other areas of development. A matter-of-fact delineation of goals is presented as part of the program (e.g., expected weight goal for discharge). Usually any discussion of food is discouraged and/or referred to the designated team member responsible for food-related issues (e.g., generally the dietitian, who establishes a relearning program about food, as well as providing an age-appropriate nutritional diet). |
| | **d.** Encourage and promote conversations and activities that concern subjects other than food. *See also,* nursing orders 3 (c, d, & e). |
| **2.** Parent-child relationship characterized by power struggles over the child's independence, especially in regard to food-related issues (e.g., parents deny their child's need for independence, child expresses ambivalence about becoming independent). <br><br> **Objective.** Improved parent-child relationship and communication. <br><br> **Timing.** As soon as possible. | **a.** Designated nurse(s) to spend time with parents to establish a relationship (e.g., explain nurse's role in program, listen and watch for expressions of feelings/concerns, direct them to appropriate team members for clarification of misconceptions/concerns, answer questions). <br><br> **b.** Record patient-family visits and interactions (e.g., who visits, how long, how often, what they do, their reactions/responses to each other, patient's reactions after visit). <br><br> **c.** Encourage patient to recognize and discuss feelings concerning issues related to independence from and dependence on parents. <br><br> **d.** Acknowledge and positively reinforce patient's efforts to make age-appropriate, independent decisions. <br><br> **e.** Commend parents' efforts to encourage and support their child's age-appropriate independence (e.g., decision-making behavior). <br><br> **f.** Acknowledge and encourage patient and parents to discuss issues related to their relationship. Refer them to appropriate team members for assistance/concerns (e.g., social worker, psychiatrist). Promote discussion about discharge and follow-up care. (The precise arrangements and their timing will depend on the individual program and the patient's progress.) |
| **3.** Patient has difficulty expressing feelings, making decisions, and relating to others [e.g., seeks attention in negative ways, negative manipulation (control) of environment, withdrawal]. <br><br> **Objectives.** Establishes relationships with designated nurse(s) and with other patients, particularly peers; seeks attention in age-appropriate ways; is positive and nonmanipulative. <br><br> **Timing.** As soon as possible. | **a.** Ensure that patient discusses issues with designated nurse(s). [If the patient directs issues, concerns, and questions to uninvolved staff members, the chance of resolving them is lessened, the development of a relationship with the designated nurse(s) impeded, and the probability of an inconsistent approach increased.] <br><br> **b.** Identify the patient's usual behavioral responses to staff, parents, and peers (e.g., disinterest, defiance, anger). Plan approaches with the team that will help the patient express feelings constructively and form worthwhile, meaningful relationships. |

continued

| Usual Problems/Objectives/Timing | Nursing Orders |
|---|---|
| **3. (Continued).** | **c.** Encourage and direct conversations to topics related to the patient's interests, school, friends, etc. Provide age-appropriate diversions that will promote conversation and social contacts (e.g., games, puzzles, projects), ask questions, and encourage answers. |
| | **d.** Help patient initiate contact with peers (e.g., choose an appropriate roommate, suggest joint peer projects). Acknowledge and encourage patient's attempts to participate and socialize. |
| | **e.** Foster the patient's strengths, talents, and skills. Encourage decision-making involving daily activities of living (e.g., personal grooming, recreational activities). (Such recognition helps the patient develop self-confidence and pride in own abilities.) |
| | **f.** Encourage patient to express feelings about the treatment program. Recognize that setting limits and expectations on the patient's behavior will promote emotional and behavioral reactions. Identify these reactions. Encourage the patient to express any feelings. Provide opportunities for the patient to learn constructive ways to handle these feelings (e.g., help the patient direct concerns and problems to appropriate health team members for problem-solving and resolution of issues, help patient engage in therapeutic activities). Record the patient's behavioral and emotional reactions and adjustment to the treatment program (e.g., expression of feelings, mood, activities). |
| **4.** Physical signs and symptoms associated with syndrome (e.g., emaciation, constipation, amenorrhea, hypothermia, lanugo, bradycardia, hypotension, dry skin, brittle hair, dependent edema). | **a.** On admission, record physical signs and symptoms. |
| | **b.** Record vital signs daily unless otherwise ordered. |
| **Objective.** Physical signs and symptoms are resolving. | **c.** Record patient's expression of symptoms. Recognize patient's concern about symptoms; encourage expression of feelings about them, and ensure that the medical staff answer questions related to these concerns. Reinforce dr's explanations. |
| **Timing.** As soon as possible. | **d.** Consult dr about management/treatment of individual signs/symptoms. |
| | **e.** Record and report to the medical staff *any* changes in the patient's condition. |
| | **f. Emaciation.** Ensure that weight records are accurate. (The exact weighing schedule and weight goal will depend on the individual treatment program.) Some factors to consider would be: |
| | –Weigh patient on same scales, in same clothing, at same time of day. |
| | –Remind patient to void before being weighed. |
| | –Be alert to attempts to distort weight (e.g., hiding articles in clothing to increase weight). Record any of this behavior and plan with team how best to deal with it. |

| Usual Problems/Objectives/Timing | Nursing Orders |
|---|---|
| **5.** Potential exhaustion due to high level of physical activity coupled with unawareness of or inability to recognize fatigue, [e.g., involved in rigorous self-devised exercise program, engages in little physical rest—always stands, rises early, preoccupied with work (schoolwork, housework, cooking)]. <br><br> **Objective.** Gradual resumption of age-appropriate physical activity associated with recognition of internal cues of fatigue. <br><br> **Timing.** As soon as possible. | **a.** Ascertain from patient and parents, and record, patient's usual interests and daily activities (e.g., typical day's activities/schedule, sports involvement, exercises). <br><br> **b.** With dr, explain to patient and parents: <br><br> **i.** The activity limitations and expectations of the treatment program (e.g., limitations are usually geared to low energy activities; expectations generally include cooperation and compliance with the treatment regimen). <br><br> **ii.** Why activity limitations are necessary for the patient's health and well-being. (These limitations have several purposes: <br><br> –They tend to break through the patient's and parents' denial by emphasizing that the patient is ill and needs rest. <br><br> –They restrict activity and therefore decrease caloric expenditure. <br><br> –They establish a step to initiate control when the patient is feeling out of control. <br><br> **iii.** What is required before the patient's activity level will be increased (e.g., often, an operant conditioning regimen combined with supportive psychotherapy is used; this personalized reward system must reflect a safe, caring, and controlled environment for the patient). <br><br> (Types and amounts of physical activity appropriate for the patient will depend on both the patient's physical and psychological needs and the specific role of activity in the treatment program. The health care team decides on this.) <br><br> **c.** Recognize and record events that precipitate the patient's increased restlessness and/or physical activity. Discuss with the team ways of helping the patient during these times. Often, limitations on the patient's activities increase the patient's anxiety. Therefore, methods of dealing with this increased anxiety must be established (e.g., expression of feelings in either words or constructive activities such as writing, crafts, or clay building; use of minimal doses of antianxiety medication). <br><br> **d.** Record on a regular basis the patient's ability to adhere to the activity limitations. |

# 35

## Depression in Adolescence: Primary Diagnosis or Secondary to Another Illness

**Goals for Discharge or Maintenance**
See Objectives.

| Usual Problems/Objectives/Timing | Nursing Orders |
|---|---|
| **1.** Patient has difficulty expressing feelings and relating to others.<br><br>**Objective.** Patient discusses feelings and concerns with assigned members of the health care team.<br><br>**Timing.** As soon as possible. | **a.** Ensure a consistent assignment of nurses to help the adolescent identify caregiver(s) to trust.<br><br>**b.** Encourage establishment of a multidisciplinary team of all caregivers involved (e.g., nurses, dr, psychiatrist, social worker, recreational therapist, teacher, physical therapist). Ensure that the team meets regularly (e.g., once a week) to exchange information and plan intervention.<br><br>**c.** Be receptive to and encourage the patient's attempts to interact and express his feelings, concerns, ideas, and/or questions. Plan to spend specific periods of time throughout the day with the patient and inform him that you will be doing this. Do not avoid the patient when he is silent and/or appears to reject you. Your consistent presence and efforts to establish a relationship convey your concern, interest, and care. Provide privacy for your conversations with the patient. Provide and use age-appropriate diversional activities to encourage conversations (e.g., cards, games, puzzles). Remember that feelings are often expressed nonverbally (e.g., crying, turning away). Recognize these behaviors as expressions of internal concerns. If you can interpret the patient's feelings accurately, identify them for him (e.g., "I know you are feeling sad . . . I'll sit with you for a while"). Acknowledge all the patient's attempts to express feelings.<br><br>**d.** Learn about the patient's usual activities and friendships. Encourage and promote opportunities to maintain these activities and continue communication with friends.<br><br>**e.** Record, daily, patient's behavior and relationships (e.g., activities, mood, concentration, interactions). |
| **2.** Potential withdrawal from people and loss of interest in activities of daily living.<br><br>**Objective.** Patient initiates and participates in age-appropriate activities and interactions with parents and staff.<br><br>**Timing.** As soon as possible. | **a.** Assess the patient's behavior related to meeting his own needs. Identify daily activities that need direction and those that the patient is doing for himself.<br><br>**b.** Devise a program with gradually increasing expectations to encourage and support age-appropriate independent behavior. Begin with promoting the adolescent's ability to meet his own needs, then incorporate psychosocial activities and expectations.<br><br>**c.** Acknowledge all his efforts toward establishing age-appropriate independence.<br><br>**d.** *See* nursing order 1 (c).<br><br>**e.** Encourage the patient to make decisions; promote his confidence in his ability to do so.<br><br>**f.** Recognize that adolescents want to be alone sometimes, but do not allow these periods to increase the patient's withdrawal. Behaviors such as closing the |

| Usual Problems/Objectives/Timing | Nursing Orders |
|---|---|
| **2. (Continued).** | door, pulling down blinds, and turning off lights, increase the adolescent's isolation; therefore, they should be discouraged.<br><br>**g.** Identify situations that trigger increased withdrawal (e.g., visitors, procedure, dr's interview, new roommate). Plan with the team approaches to deal effectively with these situations.<br><br>**h.** Recognize patient's expression of feelings of inadequacy and fear of failure. Offer support and direction. |
| **3.** Potential uncooperative, aggressive behavior, stemming from anger.<br><br>**Objective.** Patient recognizes his feelings of anger and learns constructive ways to deal with them.<br><br>**Timing.** As soon as possible. | **a.** Recognize that depressed adolescents often have difficulty expressing their anger constructively. Outward expressions of anger can be a first step in dealing with their internal feelings of distress. Their anger is often expressed through antisocial behaviors (e.g., swearing, rebellious back-talking, threats of physical abuse, testing the rules and regulations). Do not get caught up in an angry interaction. Report all such incidents to the health care team so consistent therapeutic intervention can be initiated and coordinated. If you are concerned for the safety of the adolescent or others due to the patient's angry outbursts/behavior, contact the dr immediately so the patient receives appropriate intervention (e.g., environmental safety and/or medication).<br><br>**b.** *With the health care team:* plan and evaluate the effect of approaches aimed at helping the patient deal constructively with his feelings of anger through appropriate physical activities. If possible, include an occupational therapist and/or physical therapist to plan activities through which he can discharge his aggressive energy (e.g., working with clay, playing basketball, running). Provide opportunities for the patient to talk about and deal with his anger, especially if this is related to issues of hospitalization and your expectations of him on the ward. Help him identify feelings; talk about causes and effects and constructive ways to handle situations. Acknowledge all attempts to deal constructively with his anger.<br><br>**c.** Refer the patient's questions and concerns related to his privileges, limitations, and/or expectations of his treatment program to the appropriate delegated health care team member (e.g., nurse, dr). This decreases the patient's opportunity to test and manipulate the expectations and approaches of his treatment program. |
| **4.** Patient has low self-image and low self-esteem, due to actual or anticipated loss of a person, status, or achievements (e.g., separation from or death of a person; school or job failure or dismissal; implications of surgery or chronic illness).<br><br>**Objective.** Patient talks about, understands, and adjusts to his loss(es).<br><br>**Timing.** As soon as possible. | **a.** *With the rest of the health care team:* Identify the loss that the patient is experiencing (the loss may be real or imaginary).<br><br>**b.** Identify how the patient views his loss (the important issue with a "loss" is the patient's perception of it in relation to himself and his future).<br><br>**c.** Devise a plan to help the patient begin to cope with his loss constructively. Identify the nurse's role in this plan. |

continued

| Usual Problems/Objectives/Timing | Nursing Orders |
|---|---|
| **4. (Continued).** | **d.** Identify and reinforce the patient's attributes to rebuild his self-esteem and self-image. *This image and approach must be conveyed with sincerity.* |
| **5.** Potential suicidal feelings due to inability to resolve depression. | *See* Careplan 39: Suicidal Patient, Adolescent. |
| **6.** Parents' potential emotional distress about their child's depression.<br><br>**Objective.** Parents recognize and discuss their concerns and appear less distressed.<br><br>**Timing.** As soon as possible. | **Designated nurse:**<br>**a.** Introduce yourself to the parents and explain your role. Spend time alone with them taking a nursing history, explaining, and answering their questions. Listen and watch for their expressions of feelings and concerns. Identify areas in which they need assistance; put them in touch with other team members who can help them, but assure them of your continuing support.<br><br>**b.** Explain all nursing management approaches and procedures. Explore the possibility of involving the parents in their child's management program. Acknowledge their involvement.<br><br>**c.** Encourage and include parents and their child in discussions about hospitalization, home plans, etc.<br><br>**d.** Record patient/family interactions:<br>–Who visits.<br>–How often, how long.<br>–What they do (activities).<br>–Patient's behavioral and emotional response.<br>–Parents/family members' reactions.<br>–Patient's reactions after family members (significant others) leave. |
| **7.** Patient's potential problems of separating from hospital and staff due to:<br>–Dependence established in hospital.<br>–Anxiety that his needs will not be met in the community.<br><br>**Objective.** Patient integrates into his community.<br><br>**Timing.** At discharge. | **a.** Discuss with the patient his concerns about leaving the hospital. Explain that, for everyone, separation brings mixed feelings of happiness, sadness, anxiety, and anger, and that adjustment to change takes time.<br><br>**b.** Discuss with the patient and his parents the plans they are making for his return home.<br><br>**c.** Ensure that the family know about appropriate community organizations, and help them get in touch.<br><br>**d.** Recognize the patient's desire to visit the ward after his return home, but ensure that he is (re-) establishing himself in the community. Recognize that frequent visits and phone calls to the ward may mean this is not happening. |

# 36

## Mealtime Problems in Physically Healthy Children Aged 2 Years and Older

**Goals for Discharge or Maintenance**
See Objectives.

| Usual Problems/Objectives/Timing | Nursing Orders |
|---|---|
| 1. Child is unwilling to stay at table for meals, due to short attention-span.<br><br>**Objective.** Child sits at table throughout meals.<br><br>**Timing.** Day 7. | **a.** Set expectations for child's stay at table:<br>**Day 1.** 10 min.<br>**Day 4.** 20 min.<br>**Day 7.** Through the meal.<br>**b.** Record length of time child is at the table.<br>**c.** Control diversions (e.g., turn TV off).<br>**d.** Position child comfortably but properly at table.<br>**e.** Bring him back to the table if he leaves before expected time has passed.<br>**f.** Praise him when he reaches expectation. |
| 2. Failure to use cutlery/utensils appropriately, due to lag in development or lack of training.<br><br>**Objective.** Child feeds himself and is acting appropriately.<br><br>**Timing.** Day 7. | **a.** Inform child of expectations for his behavior.<br>**b.** Establish appropriate consequences for not using cutlery (e.g., remove food if patient does not try to use cutlery). Allow for messiness, especially at first.<br>**c.** Praise child for correct use of cutlery and utensils. |
| 3. Poor nutrition, reflecting pattern at home.<br><br>**Objective.** Child eats a portion (½ to 1 tsp) of each food offered.<br><br>**Timing.** Day 7. | **a.** Give small portions, one course at a time.<br>**b.** Expect child to taste each food on plate (not necessarily finish it).<br>**c.** Give child pudding or dessert only after main course has been tasted.<br>**d.** Give praise when due. |
| 4. Potential recurrence of mealtime problem(s) at home, due to parents' inability or unwillingness to change habits.<br><br>**Objective.** Parents supervise meals in hospital.<br><br>**Timing.** As soon as possible. | **a.** Have parents visit at mealtime.<br>**b.** Explain methods used; inform parents of expectations.<br>**c.** Demonstrate methods for two meals, then get parents to supervise meals as often as possible.<br>**d.** Observe parents' supervision and be ready to support their authority. |

# Careplan 37

## Sleep Problems and Bedtime (Settling) Problems in Physically Healthy Children

**Goals for Discharge or Maintenance**
Child accepts bedtime without protest and sleeps restfully.

| Usual Problems/Objectives/Timing | Nursing Orders |
|---|---|
| 1. Difficulty settling at bedtime, or leaving bed frequently, due to separation from family, fear of the dark or abandonment, and/or attention-seeking.<br><br>**Objectives.** Child goes to bed or is put to bed without protest and stays there. Decreased expressions of fear.<br><br>**Timing.** 2 weeks. | a. Assess whether difficulty relates to fears concerning sleep or is an attention-seeking device.<br><br>b. Document sleeping pattern at home.<br><br>c. If possible, discuss with child his fears of the dark or of abandonment (e.g., what does the dark mean to him?).<br><br>d. Leave night-light on if needed and provide special toys, blanket, etc.<br><br>e. Give lots of TLC (cuddling, tell stories, etc.), and make night a pleasant time.<br><br>f. Give lots of reassurance at bedtime.<br><br>g. If appropriate, try to have parent settle the child at night. |
| 2. Restless sleep and/or frequent awakening due to anxiety.<br><br>**Objective.** Restful, unbroken sleep.<br><br>**Timing.** 2 weeks. | a. Assess sleep pattern.<br><br>b. When child awakens during night, assess whether he is having dreams, nightmares, or night terrors; talk about them and provide comfort.<br><br>c. If toddler is awake during night:<br>–Check for wetness and soothe him.<br>–Sit with him and soothe him.<br>–Cuddle him for 2 min or so.<br>–Do *not* take him out of room. |

# Careplan 38
## Speech Delay in Otherwise Normal, Healthy Young Children

**Goal for Discharge or Maintenance**
Speech developing.

| Usual Problems/Objectives/Timing | Nursing Orders |
|---|---|
| **1.** No speech.<br>**Objective.** Child babbles.<br>**Timing.** 2 weeks. | **a.** Talk and babble with child whenever care is given and especially during play.<br>**b.** Emphasize strong consonants, such as M, N, P, B, and K. Use combinations of sounds (e.g., ma-ma, ba-ba, goo-goo).<br>**c.** Praise child whenever he makes *any* sound. |
| **2.** Sounds or babbling only.<br>**Objective.** Child says single words.<br>**Timing.** 4 weeks. | **a.** Make up words appropriate for child's sounds (e.g., ba—ball, baby).<br>**b.** Praise child when he makes sounds, especially imitative ones. |
| **3.** Single words, but not to indicate or on recognition of objects.<br>**Objective.** Child says words to indicate objects.<br>**Timing.** 7 days. | **a.** Introduce an object to patient and say word; expect to hear the word back before giving object.<br>**b.** Give object only when correct word is said; praise child.<br>**c.** When child has learned a word/object association, introduce another word. |

# 39

## Suicidal Patient, Adolescent

1. Patient has decided and attempted to commit suicide.
2. Patient is potentially suicidal.

### Goals for Discharge or Maintenance
See Objectives.

| Usual Problems/Objectives/Timing | Nursing Orders |
|---|---|
| **1.** Patient is potentially dangerous to self due to helplessness/hopelessness about a specific situation, chronic loneliness, or specific yearning for a lost love relationship.<br><br>**Objectives:**<br><br>**a.** Patient expresses no further suicidal gestures or hints (verbal or nonverbal).<br><br>**b.** Patient expresses some increased appreciation of self-worth and hope, and appears to mean what he says.<br><br>**Timing.**<br><br>**a.** As soon as possible.<br><br>**b.** Before discharge.<br><br>(Long-term goal is to increase patient's self-esteem. This usually requires ongoing therapy and will not be achieved without follow-up after discharge.) | **a.** On admission, ensure a consistent assignment of nurses to establish an environment that promotes security, stability, and trust. Designated nurses to introduce themselves to the patient and explain their role. Spend time with the patient taking a nursing history and answering patient's questions. Listen and watch for expressions of feelings and areas of concern. Chart these observations (e.g., both verbal and nonverbal behaviors expressed).<br><br>**b.** If patient has not been assessed by dr/psychiatrist regarding his suicidal intent, observe the patient on a close-to-constant regimen (e.g., from at least every 15 min to constant observation) depending on your nursing assessment of his situation. Interim precautions and interventions to consider before a complete psychiatric assessment are:<br><br>–Patient to be in pajamas. Remove his clothes from room until the risk of leaving hospital has been assessed and a decision made about him wearing his clothes.<br><br>–Check room and personal belongings to identify and remove potentially harmful objects (e.g., sharp objects, nail polish, all medication). Tell the patient that these belongings will be locked up for safe keeping and returned when it is appropriate.<br><br>**c.** Ensure that a psychiatrist is called to assess the patient's suicidal intent and make recommendations on ward management issues, such as degree of observation required, visitors, and telephone privileges.<br><br>**Degrees of Nursing Observation**<br>**i.** *Constant Observation*<br>A nurse must be with the patient at all times in a 1:1 relationship. The patient must be in pajamas and his clothes removed from the room and sent home with parents. If possible, the patient should be in a single room. Check room and personal belongings for potentially harmful objects and remove these (e.g., matches, scissors, belts). Personal hygiene needs (bathing and toileting) are cared for in the patient's room. Be alert to the possibility that the patient may not comply with the treatment regimen (e.g., may remove i.v., may not swallow medication). Report any of this type of behavior to the dr/psychiatrist. Diversional activities must involve only safe materials (e.g., cards, puzzles, magazines),<br><br>**ii.** *Close Observation*<br>The frequency of observation must be specifically ordered (e.g., every 15 min *or* every 30 min). The patient must be assessed at these intervals for his physical and psychological state and the assessment recorded in the progress notes at the speci- |

| Usual Problems/Objectives/Timing | Nursing Orders |
|---|---|
| **1. (Continued).** | fied times. A specific verbal interaction with the patient and psychosocial and physical assessment must be made at least once an hour to establish the patient's physical and emotional status. As safe an environment as possible must be provided: the patient's room must be assessed for potentially harmful objects, which are then removed. Patient to remain in pajamas with clothes removed from room and sent home with parents. Patient has bathroom privileges. Diversional activities must involve only safe materials. |
| | **iii.** *Ward Privileges* <br> Patient is informed of the actual ward boundaries and expectations involved with ward privileges (e.g., bathroom privileges, walking in halls of ward, visiting other patients' rooms on the ward). Dr's orders must be written about whether the patient is to wear pajamas or may wear his own clothes. Appropriate explanations must be provided if patient is to stay in pajamas and clothes are removed from room. All off-ward privileges (e.g., cafeteria, recreational activities) require specific dr's orders. |
| | **Visitors** <br> In general, the visiting privileges of a suicidal patient are restricted. Therefore, decisions must be made and orders written on who may visit the patient, whether supervision is required of these visits/visitors, and how often and how long visits are to be. Visiting privileges are determined on an individual basis depending on the psychological assessment of the patient and his unique needs. Also, *see* problem 1 nursing order (k). |
| | **Telephone** <br> Decisions must be made and orders written related to telephone privileges (e.g., how often, what telephone, to whom). |
| | **d.** Be present when the assigned dr and/or psychiatrist explain the treatment plan to the patient and parents. Reinforce explanations that have been made about this program with the patient and his family. |
| | **e.** Encourage the establishment of a team of all caregivers working with the patient and family (e.g., nurses, pediatrician, psychiatrist, social worker, ward resident). Ensure that the team meets regularly and frequently to share information, assess patient's progress, evaluate management approaches, and establish new plans when necessary. With the appropriate team members explain any changes or new plans to patient and family and encourage them to express their feelings about these plans. |
| | **f.** Explain clearly and reinforce to the patient when necessary all nursing management approaches and procedures. For example: "We care about you and are here to help you. Therefore, we will be staying with you to help you understand (deal with) your feelings (thoughts, questions)." |

continued

| Usual Problems/Objectives/Timing | Nursing Orders |
|---|---|
| **1. (Continued).** | **g.** Allow patient to express feelings and thoughts (e.g., anger, sadness, disappointments, suicidal thoughts) but do not force the issue if he does not want to talk. (Sometimes a silent presence is very supportive.) Be a nonjudgmental listener. (A concerned listener can reinforce the patient's self-worth.) Some of the patient's feelings and thoughts may arouse frustration, anger, sadness, etc. within you. Share your feelings and concerns with colleagues in nursing and at multidisciplinary conferences, to deal with them and plan appropriate interventions that will assist both you and the patient. |
| | **h.** Show your interest and support in your relationship with the patient. Help identify and reinforce the patient's strengths (e.g., personality, physical appearance, intellect, skill at chess) and supports —both personal (family and friends) and professional (health care team members). |
| | **i.** If the patient shows any signs of increased stress (such as aggression or an increase in agitation, withdrawal, or verbalization of desire to harm self) *stay* with him. Assure him by actions and words that when he cannot control his behavior the staff will help him (e.g., "We will not let you harm yourself or others"). Report these signs immediately to the assigned dr/psychiatrist so the patient receives appropriate intervention (e.g., environmental safety and/or medication). |
| | **j.** Record, each shift, the patient's behavior, activities, feelings expressed, mood, and relationships he is forming with staff members and other patients. |
| | **k.** Acknowledge, observe, and record the patient's visitors (e.g., who visits, how often, for how long, activities and interactions, and patient's reactions to visitors and visits). Encourage the patient to talk about these visits and relationships. This assessment helps the health care team understand the significant people in the patient's life. |
| **2.** Family (and significant others) are emotionally distressed by their sense of failure/concern about their child (the patient).<br><br>**Objectives.** Family members and/or significant others recognize and express their concerns/feelings and experience less distress.<br><br>**Timing.** As soon as possible. | **a.** Designated nurses to introduce themselves to family members and explain role. Spend time with them alone taking a nursing history, explaining, and answering their questions. Listen and watch for their expressions of feelings and concerns. Identify areas in which they need assistance and put them in touch with other team members who can help with their needs. Assure them of your continuing support. |
| | **b.** Explain all nursing management approaches and procedures. Explore the possibility of involving parents in their child's treatment program on the ward. Acknowledge their involvement and participation. |
| | **c.** Acknowledge and make contact with parents/family members each time they come to see their child. Encourage expression of their concerns and questions. Identify appropriate resource staff to assist them with issues (e.g., psychiatrist, ward resident, social worker). |

| Usual Problems/Objectives/Timing | Nursing Orders |
|---|---|
| **2. (Continued).** | **d.** Record interactions between patients, parents, and other members of the family (e.g., who visits, how often, for how long, what they do, patient's/parents' behavior and emotional response, and patient's reactions when family leaves). |
| **3.** Depression. | *See* Careplan 35: Depression in Adolescence. |
| **4.** Potential difficulties related to discharge plans due to the patient's feelings about the plans.<br><br>**Objective.** Patient expresses his feelings and concerns related to discharge plans and experiences less distress.<br><br>**Timing.** Before discharge. | **a.** Ensure that the health care team discusses the plan for discharge (or the transfer of the patient to another facility), to coordinate the efforts of the team members.<br><br>**b.** Accompany the assigned dr and/or psychiatrist when discharge plans are discussed and explained to the patient and his family.<br><br>**c.** Encourage the patient's expression of feelings and concerns related to discharge plans. Record these feelings and concerns.<br><br>**d.** *See* nursing orders for problem 7 in Careplan 35: Depression in Adolescence. |

# Careplan 40 — Chickenpox (Varicella)

**Goals for Discharge or Maintenance**
See Objectives.

| Usual Problems/Objectives/Timing | Nursing Orders |
|---|---|
| **1.** *Isolation.* | **a.** *See* Careplan 12: Isolation: Psychological Aspects. <br> **b.** Follow hospital procedure for asepsis. |
| **2.** Potential infected lesions, which will result in scarring if scratched. <br> **Objective.** No infected lesions. <br> **Timing.** 7 days. | **a.** Ensure that patient's fingernails and toenails are short and clean. (Infants to wear mittens p.r.n.) <br> **b.** Handle child gently. <br> **c.** If itching is severe: <br>   –Add sodium bicarbonate to bathwater. <br>   –Request order for antihistamine to be given p.r.n. <br>   –For infant or toddler, use mitts on hands. <br> **d.** Supply with age-appropriate play materials for diversion. |
| **3.** Potential pyrexia. | *See* Careplan 10: Pyrexia. (Do not use fan: virus is airborne.) |
| **4.** Potential vesicles on oral mucous membranes. | *See* Careplan 128: Stomatitis. |
| **5.** Potential spread of infection in hospital and at home. <br> **Objective.** Spread of infection minimized. <br> **Timing.** As soon as possible. | **a.** Instruct parents to keep siblings (and patient, if discharged from hospital) at home and away from newborns for the duration of the incubation period (from day 10 to day 21 after contact). <br> **b.** **Patients undergoing immunosuppressive therapy.** If patient is exposed to disease, report to dr *stat*. (A life-threatening form of chickenpox can develop in these patients. It is recommended that immunoglobin or zoster plasma be given within 48 hr of contact.) |

## Goals for Discharge or Maintenance
Parents describe plan for appropriate home care.

| Usual Problems/Objectives/Timing | Nursing Orders |
|---|---|
| **1.** Reddened and/or excoriated skin in diaper area.<br><br>**Objective.** Child has clear, intact skin.<br><br>**Timing.** By day 3 if area is only reddened; by day 7 if skin is excoriated. | **a. Reddened skin only.** Wash child's perineum, buttocks, and groins with mild soap and water after each voiding and defecation. Rinse well and pat dry. For small infant, soak affected area in warm water; avoid using soap.<br><br>**b. Excoriated skin.** Use cotton fluffs and mineral oil (instead of soap and water) to clean affected area.<br><br>**c.** When child is up or is going to be held, smear protective cream or paste, as ordered, on buttocks and apply diaper. Do not use powder or oil, tightly pinned or double diapers, disposable diapers, or plastic pants.<br><br>**d.** When child is resting or sleeping, remove diapers and paste, and leave skin exposed to air.<br><br>**e.** Check child frequently. Change diaper/bedding as soon as possible after wetting or soiling.<br><br>**f.** Designated nurse to inform parents of plan of care. |
| **2.** Potential recurrence at home, due to lack of knowledge about management.<br><br>**Objective.** Parents express correct understanding of perineal care.<br><br>**Timing.** By discharge. | **a.** Designated nurse to assess previous home care methods.<br><br>**b.** Suggest other approaches that might be more successful.<br><br>**c.** Stress importance of changing child promptly.<br><br>**d.** Explain:<br>–Powder and oil tend to clog pores and cake on skin, retaining bacteria.<br>–Tight diapers and plastic pants increase production and retention of body heat and moisture.<br>–Disposable diapers may make rash worse.<br><br>**e.** Instruct parents:<br>–To soak soiled diapers in cold water, then wash diapers in hot water using mild soap; rinse well and dry.<br>–If rash persists, to rinse clean diaper in vinegar solution before drying (to neutralize ammonia produced when child urinates).<br>–If soiled diapers have a strong ammonia odor, to give child more water to drink between feedings (if not contraindicated). |

# 42

## Goals for Discharge or Maintenance
I. Parents know how to care for their child and can cope with this at home.
II. Family members are making realistic plans for the future.

| Usual Problems/Objectives/Timing | Nursing Orders |
|---|---|
| **1.** Bullae, resulting in denudation of skin. | **a.** *See* Careplan 49: Toxic Epidermal Necrolysis (Ritter's Disease).<br><br>**b.** For specific dressing procedures, see dr's orders.<br><br>**c.** Ensure that patient's nutritional intake is adequate. |
| **2.** Potential contractures by scar tissue.<br><br>**Objective.** Minimal or no contractures.<br><br>**Timing.** Throughout hospital stay. | **a.** Consult physical therapist about an exercise program.<br><br>**b.** Exercise patient's arms and legs during bath.<br><br>**c.** Place rolls (e.g., rolled bandages, PUF) in patient's hands before applying mittens.<br><br>**d.** Remove mittens at least q4h for finger exercises.<br><br>**e.** Handle gently to avoid skin trauma (blisters form at the site of any trauma). |
| **3.** Parent/child concerned about altered appearance and distressed over diagnosis and prognosis.<br><br>**Objectives.** Parents and child express their fears and concerns and state some understanding of the disease.<br><br>**Timing.** Before discharge. | **a.** Observe mother's reaction to child and her involvement in child's care.<br><br>**b.** If appropriate, encourage child to participate in his care.<br><br>**c.** Encourage and help family members to participate in child's care.<br><br>**d.** Spend time with family members, allowing them to express their fears and concerns.<br><br>**e.** Refer family to appropriate departments/authorities p.r.n. (dr, genetics department, social services, education, etc.) |
| **4.** Potential mismanagement at home, due to lack of knowledge.<br><br>**Objectives.** Family members demonstrate ability to care for child at home and express realistic plans for the future.<br><br>**Timing.** By discharge. | **a.** Reinforce dr's explanation about course of disease.<br><br>**b.** Teach parents how to carry out treatments that will be used at home. Assess parents' ability to care for child at home.<br><br>**c.** Refer for home care program and to public health nurse, if appropriate. |

# Careplan 43 Infectious Hepatitis

### Goals for Discharge or Maintenance
Patient/parents understand the mode of transmission and the course of hepatitis and will comply with follow-up care.

| Usual Problems/Objectives/Timing | Nursing Orders |
|---|---|
| **1.** *Isolation.* | **a.** Follow hospital procedure for asepsis.<br>**b.** *See* Careplan 12: Isolation: Psychological Aspects. |
| **2.** Nausea and/or vomiting and anorexia.<br>**Objective.** Adequate nutrition.<br>**Timing.** 7 days. | **a.** Offer small amounts of high-carbohydrate fluids q1–2h (e.g., fruit juices, carbonated beverages).<br>**b.** When nausea subsides, offer low-fat, high-carbohydrate diet in small servings.<br>**c.** If necessary, have the dietitian plan menus around the patient's likes and dislikes and ensure that child's meals are presented attractively. |
| **3.** Lassitude, headache, irritability, and jaundice.<br>**Objective.** Patient participates in own care without undue fatigue.<br>**Timing.** 3 weeks. | **a.** Daily, record degree of jaundice and color of stools and urine. Report any changes.<br>**b.** Plan care to provide undisturbed rest periods.<br>**c.** Assist patient with routine activities as necessary.<br>**d.** Maintain child on bed rest until jaundice clears. |
| **4.** Discomfort due to hepatic enlargement.<br>**Objective.** Patient is reasonably comfortable.<br>**Timing.** 7 days. | **a.** Position patient comfortably to reduce pressure on his abdomen.<br>**b.** Place his belongings within easy reach, to prevent him from stretching his right side.<br>**c.** Request sedation if necessary. |
| **5.** Potential itching due to increased bilirubin.<br>**Objective.** Scratching decreased or absent.<br>**Timing.** 7 days. | **a.** If patient is scratching:<br>–Add sodium bicarbonate to his bath water.<br>–Bathe him b.i.d. |
| **6.** Potential complications: hepatic coma or bleeding disorder.<br>**Objectives.** No undue confusion or tremors; no decline in level of consciousness.<br>**Timing.** Until discharge. | **a.** Report to dr any signs of mental confusion, emotional instability, or restlessness.<br>**b.** Report to dr if purpura develops or bleeding occurs. |
| **7.** Potential mismanagement at home due to lack of knowledge of disease process.<br>**Objective.** Patient/parents have adequate knowledge of the disease and its transmission.<br>**Timing.** Before discharge. | **a.** Teach family members about the illness, diet, and mode of transmission. Ensure that they observe strict hygiene. (If necessary, notify public health nurse.)<br>**b.** If appropriate, instruct patient to avoid alcohol for at least 6 months.<br>**c.** Ensure that patient has an appointment for follow-up at the clinic or dr's office. |

# Careplan  Mumps (Parotitis)

**Goals for Discharge or Maintenance**
See Objectives.

| Usual Problems/Objectives/Timing | Nursing Orders |
|---|---|
| 1. *Isolation.* | **a.** Follow hospital procedure for airborne infections.<br>**b.** *See* Careplan 12: Isolation: Psychological Aspects. |
| 2. Potential difficulty chewing and swallowing, due to parotid swelling and pain.<br>**Objective.** Patient has minimal discomfort when eating and/or drinking.<br>**Timing.** 5–7 days. | **a.** Offer a bland diet: initially semiliquid, then solid foods as tolerated.<br>**b.** Offer only nonacidic fluids.<br>**c.** Mouth care q2h and p.r.n.<br>**d.** Assess need for analgesic. |
| 3. Potential headache, fever, and malaise.<br>**Objectives.** No headache; minimal fever; patient is comfortable.<br>**Timing.** 4 days. | **a.** *See* Careplan 10: Pyrexia. (Do not use fan: virus is airborne.)<br>**b.** Dim lights and speak softly.<br>**c.** Provide age-appropriate materials for quiet play. |
| 4. Potential pain and swelling of testes (orchitis).<br>**Objective.** Discomfort reduced.<br>**Timing.** 8 days. | **a.** Ensure that patient has adequate bed rest.<br>**b.** Assure patient that this is a temporary condition caused by the mumps.<br>**c.** Apply ice-packs to reduce swelling.<br>**d.** Support scrotum (scrotal support or rolled towels).<br>**e.** Help patient to stand to void if he is having difficulty.<br>**f.** Assess need for analgesic. |
| 5. Potential complications: meningoencephalitis or aseptic meningitis.<br>**Objective.** Early detection of complications.<br>**Timing.** 10 days. | **a.** Observe carefully for, and report to dr if present:<br>  –Prolonged fever.<br>  –Prolonged or severe headache.<br>**b.** Report *stat*:<br>  –Stiff neck.<br>  –Vomiting.<br>  –Tremors or seizures.<br>  –Reduced level of consciousness.<br>  –Any deviation in pupil reaction. |
| 6. Anxiety about facial swelling (and orchitis).<br>**Objective.** Patient reassured that swelling will soon disappear.<br>**Timing.** 48 hr. | **a.** Ensure a consistent assignment of nurses.<br>**b.** Explain the disease process and reassure the patient that the swelling and pain are only temporary.<br>**c.** Allow opportunities for the patient to express feelings, verbally or through play.<br>**d.** **Preadolescent or adolescent boy.** Ask a male dr or male nurse to talk to patient if you think he might be worried about the possibility of sterility due to orchitis. |
| | **Note:** If siblings have not received mumps vaccine or had the disease, they are to be kept at home for the duration of the incubation period (from day 12 to day 21 after contact). |

# Careplan 45 Pertussis

## Goals for Discharge or Maintenance
I. Parent and/or child can cope with coughing paroxysms.
II. Child can tolerate normal diet.

| Usual Problems/Objectives/Timing | Nursing Orders |
|---|---|
| **1.** *Isolation.* | **a.** *See* Careplan 12: Isolation: Psychological Aspects.<br>**b.** Follow hospital procedure for asepsis. |
| **2.** Potential obstruction of airway by thick mucus or aspirated vomitus.<br><br>**Objective.** No obstruction or aspiration.<br>**Timing.** 2 weeks. | **a.** Place patient away from rooms of children with airborne infections.<br>**b.** Prop door open (e.g., with taped tongue depressors) and listen continuously for cough.<br>**c.** Observe for coughing spells: q1h with infant, q4h with child. *If infant is a silent cougher,* observe constantly or listen for cough and use apnea monitor.<br>**d.** Remain at bedside during paroxysm, and assess patient's ability to cope with cough.<br>**e.** Assist during paroxysms if necessary:<br><br>**Infant**<br>–Tip baby over your lap.<br>–Pat gently on back.<br>–Remove mucus with facial tissue.<br>–Hold him until he is calm.<br>–When he is in bed, always position him on abdomen or side.<br><br>**Child**<br>–Splint chest with arms, hands, or binder.<br>–Instruct him to support his own chest by holding elbows in and crossing arms over chest.<br><br>**f.** Use suction only if mucus is obstructing airway.<br>**g.** If child is cyanotic, administer O₂ and notify dr. |
| **3.** Potential dehydration, malnutrition, and weight loss, due to vomiting with cough.<br><br>**Objectives.** No weight loss; adequate hydration.<br>**Timing.** 2 weeks. | **a.** Withhold milk from diet until child can cough without vomiting or cyanosis.<br>**b.** Start on solid foods as soon as possible.<br>**c.** If food is vomited, feed again ½ hr later.<br>**d.** Feed infants on demand, in upright position; use small-holed nipple.<br>**e.** Weigh patient daily before breakfast.<br>**f.** Report frequent vomiting to dr.<br>**g.** Observe for signs of dehydration. |
| **4.** Potential exhaustion due to frequent and/or prolonged paroxysms.<br><br>**Objective.** No exhaustion.<br>**Timing.** 1 week. | **a.** Avoid waking or startling patient for procedures.<br>**b.** Omit procedures (e.g., bath, bed-making) if not essential to patient's comfort.<br>**c.** Provide undisturbed rest periods. |

| Usual Problems/Objectives/Timing | Nursing Orders |
|---|---|
| 5. Potential mismanagement at home, due to lack of understanding of disease.<br><br>**Objective.** Parents can cope with child during coughing paroxysms and feedings.<br><br>**Timing.** Before discharge. | a. Encourage and teach parents how to handle child when coughing.<br><br>b. Encourage and help parents to feed infant.<br><br>c. Instruct parents about milk restriction.<br><br>d. On discharge, inform parents that cough usually persists for several weeks.<br><br>e. Inform parents when quarantine period will be over (incubation period is from day 5 to day 21 after contact).<br><br>f. Check the child's immunization record. If appropriate, instruct parents about immunization for other diseases, and care of sibling contacts.<br><br>g. Ensure that parents have follow-up appointment. |

# Careplan 46 — Rubeola (Measles)

**Goals for Discharge or Maintenance**
See Objectives.

| Usual Problems/Objectives/Timing | Nursing Orders |
|---|---|
| **1.** *Isolation.* | **a.** Follow hospital procedure for airborne infections.<br>**b.** *See* Careplan 12: Isolation: Psychological Aspects. |
| **2.** Pyrexia. | *See* Careplan 10: Pyrexia. (Do not use fan: virus is airborne.)<br><br>—The fever may last up to 6 days. |
| **3.** Potential photophobia due to conjunctivitis.<br>**Objective.** Reduced discomfort.<br>**Timing.** 7 days. | **a.** Place patient in room away from sunlight and do not use bright lights near him.<br>**b.** Limit TV viewing.<br>**c.** **Older child.** Place cool pads (sterile water) on eyelids periodically. |
| **4.** Pharyngitis, coryza, and hacking cough, due to inflammation of laryngeal and tracheobronchial mucous membranes.<br>**Objective.** Symptoms gradually relieved.<br>**Timing.** 7 days. | **a.** Give frequent drinks of cool, nonacidic fluids.<br>**b.** Increase humidity in patient's room.<br>**c.** Give cough suppressants as ordered. |
| **5.** Potential malaise and/or anorexia.<br>**Objective.** Patient appears comfortable and is eating reasonably well.<br>**Timing.** 8 days. | **a.** Speak quietly when in patient's room.<br>**b.** Provide patient with age-appropriate materials for nonstimulating play, and join in activities to divert him.<br>**c.** Ensure adequate rest and uninterrupted sleep.<br>**d.** Offer frequent small meals attractively served. If no visitors are present, stay with patient while he is eating. |
| **6.** Potential otitis media, pneumonia, and/or encephalitis.<br>**Objective.** Early detection of complications.<br>**Timing.** **a.** Otitis media. 7 days.<br><br><br><br><br>**b.** Pneumonia. 7 days.<br><br><br><br><br>**c.** Encephalitis. Up to 2 weeks. | **a.** Report to dr:<br>—Complaints of earache.<br>—Discharge from ear.<br>—Pulling on ears.<br>—Irritability (particularly in infants).<br><br>**b.** Report to dr:<br>—Cough becoming more severe.<br>—Chest pain.<br>—Generalized aches and pains.<br>—Increasing pulse or respiration rate.<br><br>**c.** Report to dr:<br>—Prolonged fever.<br>—Headache.<br>—Vomiting.<br>—Drowsiness. |

# Careplan 47 Scabies

## Goals for Discharge or Maintenance
Parents/patient understand the condition and will comply with home care and follow-up.

| Usual Problems/Objectives/Timing | Nursing Orders |
|---|---|
| **1.** Potential cross-infection.<br>**Objective.** No cross-infection.<br>**Timing.** Until discharge. | **a.** Follow hospital procedure for asepsis.<br>**b.** *See* Careplan 12: Isolation: Psychological Aspects. |
| **2.** Severe itching.<br>**Objective.** Relief from itching.<br>**Timing.** As soon as possible. | Itching is intense. *Initiate treatment at once;* it is effective within 48 hr.<br>**a.** Reassure patient that the treatment, if done properly, will relieve the itching and clear the condition.<br>**b.** If you think patient is suffering unduly, consult dr about giving an antipruritic.<br>**c.** Bathe patient and shampoo his hair, then apply ointment, as ordered by dr, to whole body, paying special attention to wrists, between fingers, underarms, waist, and groins.<br>    **Older child.** Supervise bath and application of ointment.<br>**d.** Change all bed linen and clothing at each treatment.<br>**e.** *See* nursing orders for problem 3. |
| **3.** Potential secondary infection of lesions broken by scratching.<br>**Objective.** No secondary infection.<br>**Timing.** Until discharge. | **a.** Trim patient's fingernails and toenails and keep them short and clean. (Infants to wear mittens p.r.n.)<br>**b.** Impress on patient/parents the importance of not scratching.<br>**c.** Ensure that bed linen and clothing are clean. |
| **4.** Potential reinfection at home if the source of infection has not been identified and cleared.<br>**Objectives.** Parents can cope with information given and are willing to comply with instructions for home care.<br>**Timing.** Before discharge. | **a.** Before discharge, explain to parents the importance of treating all family members and household contacts simultaneously.<br>**b.** Assess parents'/patient's knowledge of basic hygiene; teach when indicated. If necessary, notify public health nurse and/or social services.<br>**c.** Ensure that parents know how to give treatments. If appropriate, have them perform treatment under supervision. (They or a public health nurse will treat the other members of the household and contacts at home.)<br>**d.** Instruct parents to change and wash all bed linen, personal clothing, and towels, *at each treatment.* (Use ordinary laundry methods and soap or detergent.)<br>**e.** Ensure that parents have written instructions for treatment and prescriptions for ointment and antipruritic. |

# Careplan 48   Stevens-Johnson Syndrome (Erythema Multiforme, Severe)

## Goal for Discharge or Maintenance
Skin lesions are healed.

| Usual Problems/Objectives/Timing | Nursing Orders |
|---|---|
| **1.** Potential secondary infection of skin and mucous membranes.<br>**Objectives.** No secondary infection, or its early detection.<br>**Timing.** 3 weeks. | **a.** *See* Careplan 49: Toxic Epidermal Necrolysis (Ritter's Disease).<br>**b.** Consult dermatologist about specific skin therapy.<br>**c.** Monitor TPR q1h until stable, then q4h.<br>**d.** Plan patient's care to provide adequate rest. |
| **2.** Photophobia due to conjunctivitis, and potential corneal ulceration leading to scarring and/or blindness.<br>**Objectives.** Patient appears comfortable; no corneal damage.<br>**Timing.** 3 weeks. | **a.** Ensure that an ophthalmologist has been consulted.<br>**b.** Cleanse patient's eyelids with N saline q4h.<br>**c.** If eyes are hypersensitive to light, darken room.<br>**d.** Assess level of pain and sensitivity; record progress q8h. |
| **3.** Potential anorexia and dehydration due to stomatitis.<br>**Objective.** Adequate nutritional intake.<br>**Timing.** 3 weeks. | **a.** *See* Careplan 128: Stomatitis.<br>**b.** Report to dr if child is coughing. (Mucous membrane involvement can be extensive and life threatening.)<br>**c.** Offer high-protein, high-calorie fluids frequently (e.g, ice cream, jello, milk shakes).<br>**d.** Record intake and notify dr if it is inadequate. (Fluids may have to be given by i.v. if child cannot drink.) |
| **4.** Potential dysuria or urinary retention due to pain caused by meatal and urethral involvement.<br>**Objective.** Adequate urinary output.<br>**Timing.** 3 weeks. | **a.** Remain with patient when he is trying to void.<br>**b.** If child cannot void easily, place in sitz bath or tub for voiding, if appropriate.<br>**c.** Record output and notify dr if patient has dysuria or urinary retention. Observe for hematuria. |
| **5.** Patient anxious and concerned about altered appearance.<br>**Objective.** Patient discusses concerns and fears.<br>**Timing.** Before discharge. | **a.** Stay with patient when he needs comforting and reassurance.<br>**b.** Encourage the patient to talk about his concerns. Reassure him that the skin lesions will not leave permanent scars.<br>**c.** Show patient the skin areas where healing is occurring.<br>**d.** If appropriate, encourage patient to help in his care. |
| **6.** Potential recurrence of disease.<br>**Objective.** No recurrence.<br>**Timing.** Until discharge. | **a.** If etiology is known to be drug-related, advise parents that their child should not be given the drug(s).<br>  –Ensure that this is recorded appropriately in patient's records.<br>  –Recommend that the child wear a Medic Alert bracelet.<br>**b.** Ensure that parents have appropriate follow-up appointments. |

**Goal for Discharge or Maintenance**
Skin lesions are healed.

| Usual Problems/Objectives/Timing | Nursing Orders |
|---|---|
| 1. *Isolation.* | *See* Careplan 12: Isolation: Psychological Aspects. |
| 2. Potential secondary infection due to denudation of skin.<br>**Objective.** No secondary infection.<br>**Timing.** 10 days. | **a.** Follow hospital procedure for protective technique.<br>**b.** Limit visitors and exclude those with colds or other infections.<br>**c.** Use sterile water for bathing the patient.<br>**d.** Follow dermatologist's instructions for skin care.<br>**e.** Apply compresses of N saline as ordered. Do not cover more than 25% of the body at any one time (avoid temperature drop).<br>**f.** Protective technique may be modified when open lesions are healing. |
| 3. Potential pain from blisters and denudation of skin.<br>**Objective.** Pain minimized.<br>**Timing.** 10 days. | **a.** Avoid unnecessary disturbances and handling of patient (e.g., take temperature in axilla).<br>**b.** Place infant on plastic-bubble sheeting or PUF. (Lubricate bubbled plastic with sterile liquid paraffin if necessary.)<br>**c.** Use a bed-cradle to keep covers off patient's skin.<br>**d.** Trim hair away from patient's face p.r.n. |
| 4. Potential fluid and electrolyte imbalance and loss of body protein due to seepage of fluid through denuded areas.<br>**Objective.** Adequate hydration.<br>**Timing.** 5 days. | **a.** Record weight daily. Notify dr if it is fluctuating.<br>**b.** Record fluid intake and output. Record color of urine. Establish best method of estimating output (e.g., weigh diapers or catch urine in plastic-bubble sheeting). *Do not use* collectors with adhesive attachments.<br>**c.** Ensure that patient receives adequate protein in diet.<br>**d.** Record size of skin lesions and amount of discharge.<br>**e.** Record patient's level of responsiveness (alert or lethargic). |
| 5. Potential hypothermia due to exposure.<br>**Objective.** Normal temperature.<br>**Timing.** 5 days. | **a.** Record patient's temperature q1-2h until stable, then q4h.<br>**b.** Check room temperature; increase p.r.n.<br>**c.** Place additional covers over bed-cradle.<br>**d.** **Infant.** Nurse him in an incubator. |
| 6. Parents/child anxious and concerned about altered appearance.<br>**Objective.** Patient/family members discuss concerns and feelings and are reassured.<br>**Timing.** Before discharge. | **a.** Encourage child and family to discuss their concerns.<br>**b.** Encourage parents to participate in care of their child.<br>**c.** Show parents the skin areas where healing is occurring.<br>**d.** Reassure child and parents that the skin lesions will not leave permanent scars. |

139

continued

| Usual Problems/Objectives/Timing | Nursing Orders |
|---|---|
| **6. (Continued).** | **e.** Refer parents' concerns about medical problems to designated dr. |
| | **f.** Ensure that parents know their child's skin will be dry for a few months after the lesions heal. Teach them about colloidal oatmeal baths (oilated Aveeno) and how to apply cream or lotion as ordered. |

**Goals for Discharge or Maintenance**
Parents understand the condition and demonstrate ability to cope with home care and follow-up.

| Usual Problems/Objectives/Timing | Nursing Orders |
|---|---|
| **1.** Potential mismanagement of diet at home due to lack of understanding of condition and its treatment.<br><br>**Objectives.** Parents demonstrate their understanding of a well-balanced diet and are willing to follow the prescribed food guidelines.<br><br>**Timing.** By end of first clinic visit. | **a.** Reinforce dr's explanation of child's anemia and why changes in the child's diet are necessary.<br><br>**b.** Dietitian or designated nurse:<br><br>–Discuss child's usual eating habits at home.<br><br>–Explain the importance of giving the child a well-balanced diet.<br><br>–Suggest ways of changing child's eating habits (e.g., reduce amount of milk when solids are being introduced into diet; if child fills up on milk, he will not have the interest in or appetite for other foods).<br><br>–Explain which foods are rich in iron.<br><br>–Give parents specific written instructions about diet, and appropriate printed materials (e.g., *A Simple Guide to Anemia.* Ministry of Health, Ontario). |
| **2.** Potential continuing anemia due to incorrect administration of medication.<br><br>**Objectives.** Parents understand the need to give medication as instructed. They demonstrate correct administration.<br><br>**Timing.** By end of first clinic visit. | **a.** Provide *written* instructions about times and amount of medication to be given.<br><br>**b.** Teach parents:<br><br>–If patient is taking a liquid form of iron: the medicine must be diluted with water or orange juice (not milk) and the dose followed by a drink of water or juice. This increases absorption of iron and prevents staining of teeth.<br><br>–If patient is taking the tablet form of iron: the tablet must be swallowed whole (not crushed, broken, or chewed).<br><br>–The medication should be given between meals. (If this causes stomach upset, it may be given with meals or a snack, but not with dairy products.)<br><br>**c.** Explain to parents that:<br><br>–The medicine may cause darkening of the stools. This is harmless.<br><br>–Iron has a constipating effect, so the child should be encouraged to eat more roughage (e.g. bran products, prunes) to counteract this.<br><br>**d.** Ensure that parents understand the importance of giving iron as prescribed. Give appropriate explanations to illustrate this (e.g., iron forms part of the red blood cells that carry oxygen to all parts of the body).<br><br>**e.** Explain importance of regular follow-up for blood tests (to determine need for continuing medication). |
| **3.** Potential ingestion of overdose of iron.<br><br>**Objectives.** Parents understand the need to keep iron stored in a safe place; they can recognize symptoms | **a.** Emphasize the need to store iron in a place that is not accessible to children.<br><br>**b.** Explain the importance of getting medical assistance |

| Usual Problems/Objectives/Timing | Nursing Orders |
|---|---|
| **3. (Continued).**<br><br>of overdose, and know what to do if child ingests an accidental overdose of iron.<br><br>**Timing.** By end of first clinic visit. | *stat*, if the child accidentally ingests an overdose of the iron medication **(give emergency phone numbers).**<br>**c.** Teach parents how to recognize signs of an overdose of iron:<br>  –Vomiting.<br>  –Diarrhea.<br>  –Hematemesis.<br>  –Melena.<br>  –Rapid and weak pulse.<br>  –Lethargy.<br>  –Convulsions.<br>  –Coma. |
| **4.** Potential recurrence of anemia or continuing anemia, due to misunderstanding or noncompliance with treatment regimen.<br><br>**Objectives.** Parents state their understanding of treatment regimen and the importance of continuing with the medication and diet.<br><br>**Timing.** Ongoing, at each clinic visit. | **Designated nurse** (preferably the one who did the initial teaching):<br>**a.** Explore parents' understanding of treatment.<br>**b.** Reinforce instructions/information.<br>**c.** Ensure that family's usual life-style is taken into consideration when establishing medication times, etc.<br>**d.** Provide further written information as appropriate.<br>**e.** Ensure that follow-up is arranged. |

# Hemophilia (Factor VIII Deficiency; Factor IX Deficiency): Post-Emergency Ward Care

**Goals for Discharge or Maintenance**
Family members understand the disease and treatment and express realistic plans for home care.

| Usual Problems/Objectives/Timing | Nursing Orders |
|---|---|
| **1.** Hemarthrosis: pain and potential fixation of joints.<br>**Objective.** Joints are mobile.<br>**Timing.** Until discharge. | **a.** Give analgesics as ordered. *(Do not give ASA.)*<br>**b.** Apply ice-packs to affected joints.<br>**c.** Support affected limb in proper alignment.<br>**d.** If patient is in traction, *see* Careplan 158: Traction.<br>**e.** Apply the exercise program devised by physical therapist. |
| **2.** Potential bleeding.<br>**Objective.** No bleeding or its early detection.<br>**Timing.** Until discharge. | **a.** *Do not give medication i.m.*<br>**b.** After venipuncture, apply firm pressure to site until oozing ceases.<br>**c.** Observe precautions, and instruct the child, to avoid injury.<br>**d.** Check frequently (as appropriate to age and general condition) for bleeding. |
| **3.** Potential hematuria.<br>**Objective.** No hematuria or its early recognition.<br>**Timing.** Until discharge. | **a.** If hematuria occurs:<br>  –Report to dr *stat*.<br>  –Enforce bed rest.<br>**b.** Encourage child to drink a lot.<br>**c.** Reassure him that although the problem is troublesome it is not usually serious. |
| **4.** Patient's potential anxiety about:<br>**a.** Therapy, especially if having transfusions.<br>**b.** Outcome, especially if another family member is affected.<br>**Objective.** Patient appears relaxed.<br>**Timing.** As soon as possible. | **a.** Be present when dr explains the condition.<br>**b.** Reassure child, reinforcing the dr's explanations.<br>**Note:** Few of these children require transfusion after the emergency has been dealt with. |
| **5.** Potential parental overprotection.<br>**Objective.** Parents express realistic plans for home care.<br>**Timing.** By discharge. | **a.** Assess child–family relationships.<br>**b.** Designated nurse to spend time with parents to:<br>  –Discuss their concerns.<br>  –Discuss precautions to avoid trauma (e.g., pad infant's crib and playpen; supervise closely when child is learning to walk; ensure that child avoids contact sports).<br>  –Stress need for as much normal activity as possible.<br>**c.** Refer parents to Hemophilia Society and see that patient has Medic Alert bracelet. |
| **6.** Potential intracranial hemorrhage. | **a.** Be alert for signs of increased intracranial pressure.<br>**b.** *See* Careplan 71: Increased Intracranial Pressure. |

| Usual Problems/Objectives/Timing | Nursing Orders |
|---|---|
| **7.** Potential mismanagement at home, due to insufficient knowledge of the disorder. Also (even if no other family members are known to be affected), parents may have guilt feelings relating to the heritable nature of the disorder.<br><br>**Objectives.**<br>**a.** Parents state an understanding of the disease and treatment.<br>**b.** They have access to counseling whenever they require it.<br><br>**Timing.**<br>**a.** Before discharge.<br>**b.** Continuing. | **a.** Reinforce dr's teaching.<br>**b.** Stress precautions needed during dental work.<br>**c.** If this is the child's first hospitalization, arrange for hematology clinic orientation.<br>**d.** If appropriate, arrange for hematology clinic staff to teach parents and child to give cryoprecipitate when necessary.<br>**e.** If appropriate, refer parents to genetics department for counseling. |

# Careplan 52 Idiopathic Thrombocytopenic Purpura

**Goal for Discharge or Maintenance**
Family members understand the disease, treatment, and medication.

| Usual Problems/Objectives/Timing | Nursing Orders |
|---|---|
| **1.** Potential intracranial hemorrhage. | **a.** Be alert for signs of increased intracranial hemorrhage.<br><br>**b.** *See* Careplan 71: Increased Intracranial Pressure. |
| **2.** Potential spontaneous bleeding from mucous membranes, epistaxis, and/or petechial hemorrhages.<br><br>**Objective.** No trauma.<br><br>**Timing.** 2 weeks. | **a.** To prevent or minimize trauma to child:<br>  –Pad child's bed-sides and chair.<br>  –Ensure that toys are smooth-edged.<br>  –Avoid constricting garments.<br>  –Perform as few venipunctures as possible.<br>  –Use mouthwash, or lemon and glycerin swabs, rather than toothbrush.<br>  –*Do not give medication i.m.*<br><br>**b.** Maintain bed rest if ordered; provide quiet diversions, especially soft music.<br><br>**c.** When patient is allowed to get up, supervise activity to prevent falls and trauma.<br><br>**d.** Record distribution of petechiae.<br><br>**e.** Report to dr if active bleeding occurs.<br><br>**f.** If epistaxis occurs:<br>  –Apply pressure by pinching nostrils.<br>  –Notify dr *stat* if bleeding continues longer than 10 min. |
| **3.** Potential gastrointestinal irritation by steroid medication.<br><br>**Objective.** No gastrointestinal bleeding.<br><br>**Timing.** Until discharge. | **a.** Give milk routinely with each dose of steroid and teach parents to continue this at home.<br><br>**b.** Report to dr promptly if vomitus or stool contains frank blood or stool is darker than usual. |

# Careplan **53** Leukemia

**Goals for Discharge or Maintenance**
Parents understand and are willing to carry out home care, including medication and follow-up.

| Usual Problems/Objectives/Timing | Nursing Orders |
|---|---|
| **1.** Potential bleeding due to low platelet count. <br><br> **Objective.** Early detection of bleeding. <br><br> **Timing.** Until discharge. | **a.** Do not give injections i.m. <br><br> **b.** If platelet count is low, apply pressure to any injection site for at least 5 min. <br><br> **c.** If epistaxis occurs: <br>   –Apply pressure by pinching bridge of patient's nose. <br>   –Notify dr *stat* if bleeding continues longer than 10 min. <br><br> **d.** If platelet count is low or gums are bleeding, use lemon and glycerine swabs instead of toothbrush. <br><br> **e.** Observe urine, stools, and emesis; report evidence of an increase in bleeding. <br><br> **f.** If patient's abdomen is distended, notify dr. <br><br> **g.** Look for and record any increase in petechiae or purpura. <br><br> **h.** If bleeding occurs, take away soiled linen, tissues, etc., as soon as possible. Record estimated blood loss. <br><br> **i.** Do not give ASA. |
| **2.** Pyrexia. | *See* Careplan 10: Pyrexia |
| **3.** Nausea, vomiting, and anorexia due to disease or medication. <br><br> **Objectives.** Nausea and vomiting lessened. Patient is eating part of each meal. <br><br> **Timing.** By discharge. | **a.** Request antiemetic if necessary and give as ordered. <br><br> **b.** Cater as much as possible to patient's likes and dislikes. <br><br> **c.** Allow parents to bring favorite foods if unavailable in hospital. <br><br> **d.** If appropriate, have dietitian arrange menus with patient. |
| **4.** Weakness and fatigue due to disease or medication. <br><br> **Objective.** Patient appears less fatigued. <br><br> **Timing.** Until discharge. | **a.** Plan for undisturbed rest periods. <br><br> **b.** Assist in daily activities p.r.n. <br><br> **c.** If patient is fatigued, restrict visitors to short periods or quiet sitting. <br><br> **d.** Modify or omit procedures (e.g., bed-making) if not essential to patient's comfort. |
| **5.** Potential infection. <br><br> **Objective.** No infection. <br><br> **Timing.** Until discharge. | **a.** Daily, at bath times: <br>   –Check all skin punctures for redness and/or swelling. <br>   –Check anal region for fissures or signs of infection. <br>   –Check mouth for signs of infection. |

continued

| Usual Problems/Objectives/Timing | Nursing Orders |
|---|---|
| **5. (Continued).** | **b.** Check temperature q4h for 48 hr or until he is afebrile, then t.i.d.<br><br>**c.** Record and report to dr:<br>—Sudden changes in respiratory rate or depth.<br>—Dysuria or cloudy urine.<br>—Perineal pruritis.<br><br>**d.** If WBC count is low, ensure that patient's roommates are infection-free. |
| **6.** Potential stomatitis due to infection or medication. | *See* Careplan 128: Stomatitis. |
| **7.** Constipation due to chemotherapy (vinblastine sulfate).<br><br>**Objective.** Regular, soft stools.<br><br>**Timing.** Until discharge. | **a.** Record frequency and consistency of stools.<br><br>**b.** Notify dr if abdomen becomes distended or passage of stool is difficult. |
| **8.** Patient is emotional, anxious, or angry because of separation from family members, pets, etc., and/or has fears of mutilation or death.<br><br>**Objectives.** Patient appears comforted and satisfied with information. Contact is maintained between child, family members, and friends.<br><br>**Timing.** Until discharge. | **a.** Encourage child to discuss fears and concerns and help him cope with them.<br><br>**b.** Avoid medical discussion in vicinity of patient.<br><br>**c.** Clarify with dr and parents what the child has been told. If parents do not want their child to know prognosis, tell them that their wishes will be respected but that if he asks questions he will be answered truthfully and they will be informed.<br><br>**d.** Encourage and help family to participate in care. Include siblings in visiting plans (make special arrangements for young ones).<br><br>**e.** Provide child with suitable age-appropriate toys or activities to give an outlet for emotions, fears, and concerns.<br><br>**f.** Allow time to listen to patient other than when doing treatments, if appropriate.<br><br>**g.** Assess and record best method of preparing child for procedures and tests.<br><br>**h.** If child becomes very irritable and demanding, remain calm and try to anticipate his needs, but be firm about carrying out necessary procedures.<br><br>**i.** If another child dies on the ward and the patient asks about it, tell him the truth; take time to answer his questions to his satisfaction, and ensure that he has settled reasonably well before you leave him. |
| **9.** Family anxious and concerned.<br><br>**Objectives.** Family members display their feelings and talk about their concerns and fears.<br><br>**Timing.** Until discharge. | **a.** Encourage the parents to discuss their fears and concerns and help them to start planning realistically for the future.<br><br>**b.** Plan with the dr to be present when he talks to the parents.<br><br>**c.** Establish supportive rapport with family; spend time daily with parents listening to their concerns and wishes (away from patient's room), if appropriate. |

| Usual Problems/Objectives/Timing | Nursing Orders |
|---|---|
| **9.** (Continued). | **d.** Explain all procedures and tests carefully, and try to anticipate needs (e.g., for information on condition), to avoid frustration and misunderstanding. |
| | **e.** Recognize that family may channel anger toward staff. Avoid retaliation. |
| | **f.** Ensure that the parents understand the dr's plan for follow-up care and that appropriate clinics and agencies are contacted. |
| **10.** Potential concern or embarrassment about alopecia due to chemotherapy or irradiation.<br><br>**Objective.** Patient accepts hair-loss or alternative head-coverings (hat, scarf, or wig).<br><br>**Timing.** Before discharge. | **a.** Reassure patient that hair-loss is temporary.<br><br>**b.** For children, contact the public health nurse for assistance in purchasing wigs. |

# Careplan 54    Sickle-Cell Crisis

## Goal for Discharge or Maintenance
Parents and child have some understanding of the condition and the acute state.

| Usual Problems/Objectives/Timing | Nursing Orders |
|---|---|
| **1.** Pain due to occlusion of small blood vessels.<br>**Objective.** Relief from pain.<br>**Timing.** 5 days. | **a.** Provide a quiet environment.<br>**b.** Give analgesics as ordered. Record and report to dr the adequacy of analgesia.<br>**c.** Reassure the child by remaining with him during episodes of severe pain. |
| **2.** Potentially inadequate hydration due to insufficient fluid intake.<br>**Objective.** Adequate hydration.<br>**Timing.** 3–4 days. | **a.** Encourage child to drink.<br>**b.** Record intake and output accurately.<br>**c.** Explain to patient and family the importance of hydration in reducing sickling and thus reducing pain. |
| **3.** Anxiety about the pain and recurring crises, especially if patient is aware of other person(s) severely affected.<br>**Objective.** Patient appears relaxed.<br>**Timing.** As soon as possible. | **a.** Assure child that he will receive medication to relieve the pain during crises.<br>**b.** Provide continuity of nursing care.<br>**c.** Provide gentle diversions, particularly soft music.<br>**d.** Encourage child to resume normal activities when ready. |
| **4.** Potential mismanagement at home, due to lack of understanding.<br>**Objective.** Parents understand the condition and how to prevent or lessen crises.<br>**Timing.** Before discharge. | **a.** Spend time with the parents discussing their concerns.<br>**b.** Be present when dr discusses the condition with patient/parents; reinforce dr's explanations.<br>**c.** Stress importance of avoiding infections and undue or sudden physical exertion.<br>**d.** Ensure that parents know how to lessen the severity of the crisis (e.g., bed rest, extra fluids, analgesics).<br>**e.** Recommend that patient wear a Medic Alert bracelet and ensure that family knows about the Sickle Cell Association. |
| **5.** Parents' potential guilt feelings about inherited disease.<br>**Objective.** Parents have access to counseling whenever required.<br>**Timing.** As soon as possible and continuing. | **a.** Notify public health or community nurse.<br>**b.** If appropriate, refer parents for genetic counseling. |

# Careplan 55 Thalassemia Major

**Goals for Discharge or Maintenance**
Family members have some understanding of the disorder, understand the treatment plan, and can cope with home care and follow-up.

| Usual Problems/Objectives/Timing | Nursing Orders |
|---|---|
| 1. Potential reactions to the numerous blood transfusions.<br><br>**Objective.** Early detection of transfusion-related complications.<br>**Timing.** Until transfusions are discontinued. | **a.** Administer blood transfusions slowly and carefully. (The potential for allergic reaction increases with repeated transfusions.)<br>**b.** Report *stat* to dr any signs of blood reaction (e.g., urticaria, chills, or fever). |
| 2. Potential congestive heart failure. | *See* Careplan 111: Congestive Heart Failure. |
| 3. Psychological stress due to the chronic and debilitating nature of the disease and the need for continuing treatment. (Many patients, particularly adolescents, become chronically depressed.)<br><br>**Objective.** Reduction of stress whenever possible.<br>**Timing.** Until discharge. | **a.** Consistent assignment of nursing staff when possible.<br>**b.** Provide quiet diversions (e.g., soft music, reading).<br>**c.** Refer to appropriate services p.r.n. (e.g., public health nurse, social services, psychiatrist, schoolteacher).<br>**d.** If patient's depression is severe, *see* Careplan 35: Depression in Adolescence. |
| 4. Potential mismanagement at home, due to lack of knowledge of the disorder, and parents' potential guilt feelings relating to inherited disease.<br><br>**Objectives.** Family members understand the treatment plan, and parents have access to counseling whenever required.<br>**Timing.** Before discharge. | **a.** Arrange for an interpreter if necessary to ensure that all explanations and instructions are understood.<br>**b.** If home supervision is necessary, notify public health nurse.<br>**c.** Be present when dr discusses the condition with patient/parents; reinforce dr's instructions to parents.<br>**d.** Spend time with family members discussing their concerns, their understanding of the disorder, and plans for follow-up. Refer parents to genetics department if appropriate.<br>**e.** Suggest that patient wear a Medic Alert bracelet. |

# Metabolic Disorders

(Excluding Structural Defects: *see* Skeletal and Connective-tissue Disorders)

# Careplan 56 Cystinuria

## Goals for Discharge or Maintenance
**I.** Renal calculi are prevented through compliance with fluid and medication regimen.
**II.** Patient/parents understand disorder and express willingness and ability to cope with home care and follow-up.

| Usual Problems/Objectives/Timing | Nursing Orders |
|---|---|
| **1.** Potential renal calculi due to high concentration of cystine in urine.<br><br>**Objective.** Renal calculi are prevented or detected early in formation.<br><br>**Timing.** Until discharge. | **a.** Maintain high fluid intake as ordered. Night fluids to be given h.s. and at 0200–0300 hr. If patient is not drinking well, give smaller amounts more frequently (q1–2h).<br><br>**b.** Encourage patient to drink water and sugarless fluids rather than high-calorie, cariogenic fluids.<br><br>**c.** Administer Na bicarbonate and/or penicillamine as ordered.<br><br>**d.** Observe patient for signs and symptoms of renal calculi:<br>– Pain.<br>– Fever.<br>– Hematuria.<br>– Stones or gravel in urine.<br>If stones are suspected, sieve urine through gauze.<br><br>**e.** Check urine pH and specific gravity (SG) q12h. Notify dr if pH is less than 8 or if SG increases. |
| **2.** Potential hypertension in Na bicarbonate-sensitive patients due to high sodium load.<br><br>**Objective.** Patient's BP is in range appropriate for age.<br><br>**Timing.** Until discharge. | **a.** Monitor BP q12h.<br><br>**b.** Notify dr if BP is elevated. |
| **3.** Parents' potential guilt feelings relating to heritable nature of the disorder.<br><br>**Objective.** Parents have access to genetic counseling.<br><br>**Timing.** Before discharge. | **a.** Ensure that genetic counseling has been provided by the metabolic service.<br><br>**b.** Allow family time and opportunity to express concerns and ask questions.<br><br>**c.** Refer to social services as necessary. |
| **4.** Potential mismanagement at home due to lack of understanding of disorder and/or failure to comply with treatment regimen.<br><br>**Objectives.** Patient/parents state understanding of the disorder and are willing to comply with treatment regimen.<br><br>**Timing.** Before discharge. | **a.** Reinforce dr's explanations of disorder and its management.<br><br>**b.** Emphasize to parents the importance of establishing a routine for the child that will ensure intake of prescribed amount of fluid every 24 hr and regular medication times (e.g., set alarm for 0200 hr, use a timer during the day, keep a daily diary).<br><br>**c.** Refer to the public health nurse. The nurse and the teacher must be aware of the child's need for increased fluids (particularly during hot weather or illness, especially if child has vomiting or diarrhea).<br><br>**d.** Teach patient/parent to test urine for pH. Ensure they have necessary equipment to do test at home.<br><br>**e.** Teach patient/parents the danger signals of the disorder (e.g., pain, fever, hematuria, stones in urine). |

*continued*

| Usual Problems/Objectives/Timing | Nursing Orders |
|---|---|
| **4. (Continued).** | **f.** Ensure that parents are aware of potential side effects of: <br><br> –Na bicarbonate (hypertension). <br><br> –Penicillamine (rash, fever, joint pain, bleeding tendency, and infections). <br><br> Instruct parents to contact dr if any of these side effects occur. Ensure that they know how to contact dr. <br><br> **g.** Ensure that a follow-up appointment is arranged for metabolic clinic. |

# Careplan **57**   Diabetes Mellitus: Ketoacidosis

## Goals for Discharge or Maintenance
I. Patient and parents show some insight into reasons for ketoacidosis.
II. They state willingness to take action to prevent further episodes.

| Usual Problems/Objectives/Timing | Nursing Orders |
|---|---|
| **1.** Dehydration due to polyuria caused by increased osmotic pressure of glucose in renal tubules. Potential nausea and vomiting secondary to ketoacidosis and/or underlying illness.<br><br>**Objectives.** Patient is well hydrated. No nausea or vomiting.<br><br>**Timing.** 24 hr. | **a.** Maintain i.v. fluids as ordered.<br>**b.** Check i.v. q1/2h. Notify dr *stat* if ordered amount is not being delivered.<br>**c.** Record accurate intake and output. Notify dr if patient is in negative fluid balance (i.e., if output is greater than intake).<br>**d.** Assess level of hydration q1h for 8 hr then q2h for 16 hr. Notify dr if patient's hydration is not improving or if patient is exhibiting signs/symptoms of overhydration.<br>**e.** Keep patient n.p.o. unless ordered otherwise.<br>**f.** When oral fluids are allowed, offer clear fluids (regular, *not sugar-free).*<br>**g.** When patient is tolerating clear fluids, gradually increase to full fluids as ordered.<br>**h.** Give mouth care q1–2h while patient is n.p.o. |
| **2.** Ketoacidosis due to acute insulin deficiency caused by:<br>–Onset of diabetes mellitus.<br>–Illness.<br>–Failure to administer prescribed insulin.<br><br>**Objectives.** No ketoacidosis; patient is awake and alert; vital signs are within normal limits.<br><br>**Timing.** 24 hr. | **a.** Observe and record:<br>–Respiratory rate, rhythm, and depth [i.e., presence of Kussmaul (panting) respirations], q1h for 8 hr, then q2h for 16 hr.<br>–Level of consciousness.<br>–Orientation to place, time, etc.<br>–Pulse rate and BP q1h for 8 hr, then q2h for 16 hr; temperature q4h for 24 hr.<br>*Notify dr stat if patient's level of consciousness deteriorates.*<br>**b.** Administer insulin, Na bicarbonate, and i.v. fluids as ordered.<br>**c.** Test *each* void for glucose and ketones and record results. |
| **3.** Potential complications of treatment: Hypoglycemia and cerebral edema.<br><br>**Objective.** Early detection and prompt reporting of problems.<br><br>**Timing.** Until patient's condition is stabilized. | **a.** Be aware that the combination of rehydration and insulin therapy can result in hypoglycemia. If patient exhibits signs/symptoms of hypoglycemia (e.g., deterioration in level of consciousness):<br>–Do blood-glucose (Chemstrip bG) test *stat and* send capillary specimen of blood to laboratory for *stat* blood-glucose estimation.<br>–Record time that each blood sample was drawn. At the same time total the patient's fluid intake and output on the diabetes flow sheet.<br>**b.** When results of blood tests are received, record on flow sheet beside time blood sample was drawn and notify dr *stat.* |

continued

| Usual Problems/Objectives/Timing | Nursing Orders |
|---|---|
| **3. (Continued).** | **c.** If patient's level of consciousness is deteriorating and hypoglycemia has been ruled out, cerebral edema must be considered. *See* Careplan 63: Cerebral Edema. Initiate q15 min head injury routine. |
| **4.** Potential recurrence due to:<br>–Failure to administer prescribed insulin.<br>–Poor understanding of illness management.<br>**Objectives.** Patient/parent state their understanding of:<br>–The significance of high urine/blood glucose plus ketones in urine.<br>–The importance of contacting the dr at the onset of an illness or infection.<br>–The necessity of coming to hospital immediately if child vomits more than once in 24 hr.<br>–The importance of having Regular (Toronto) insulin on hand even when the child is not on it routinely.<br>–The importance of continued supervision of the entire insulin injection routine.<br>**Timing.** Before discharge. | **a.** Review family's testing technique (blood and urine) and the equipment being used for testing.<br>**b.** Reinforce significance of high blood- and urine-glucose levels when ketones are present.<br>**c.** Emphasize importance of contacting dr at onset of illness/infection or if child vomits more than once in 24 hr.<br>**d.** Review the action of Regular insulin and its use in illness management.<br>**e.** Reinforce the necessity for supervision of the *entire* injection routine, particularly in patients with unexplained recurrent acidosis.<br>**f.** Refer to public health nurse as necessary. |

# 58

## Diabetes Mellitus: Newly Diagnosed Patient

**Goals for Discharge or Maintenance**
Patient/parents demonstrate ability to comply with instructions for home care and follow-up.

**Note.** Family members of a newly diagnosed diabetic child have a planned teaching program conducted by the diabetes team (doctor, teaching nurse, and dietitian). Both parents and older siblings attend several 2-hr sessions with practice in class and at home. A designated ward nurse is responsible for teaching the patient on the ward (older patients may also attend the formal program). The parents and the patient receive teaching manuals. The newly diagnosed diabetic patient is usually in hospital for 10–14 days.

| Usual Problems/Objectives/Timing | Nursing Orders |
|---|---|
| **1.** Potential failure to accept diabetes and/or potential uncontrolled diabetes, due to lack of understanding of the disease.<br><br>**Objectives.** Parents/patient state their understanding of the basic pathophysiology of diabetes mellitus, and importance of food, insulin, and activity balance.<br><br>**Timing.** Before discharge. | **a.** On admission, notify the diabetes teaching nurse.<br><br>**b.** Designated ward nurse to explain her role in the teaching program:<br><br>–To plan a teaching program for the patient (appropriate to patient's age and level of understanding).<br><br>–To establish routines that fit in with patient's usual activities of daily living.<br><br>–To consult the diabetes teaching nurse about suitable teaching aids and whether patient should be included in the family's formal teaching program (as well as ward teaching).<br><br>–To include parents in routines such as urine testing, blood-glucose testing, and giving insulin injections, as appropriate. |
| **2.** Potential misunderstanding of home care plan due to lack of knowledge about assessment and treatment measures:<br><br>  **i.** *Urine and blood-glucose testing.*<br><br>**Objective.** Parents/patient state understanding of and demonstrate compliance with urine and blood-glucose testing routines.<br><br>**Timing.** Before discharge. | **a.** Teach:<br><br>–Reasons for urine and blood testing.<br><br>–Times the tests are to be done, and the importance of adhering to these times.<br><br>–Interpretation of results.<br><br>–Double void routine and reasons for the routine.<br><br>–Testing techniques.<br><br>–Correct handling, cleaning, and storage of equipment.<br><br>–Recording of results.<br><br>**b.** If patient is not capable of giving double voided sample, test each sample.<br><br>**c. Infant.** Place cotton fluffs in diaper. When infant voids, squeeze urine from fluffs into a cup and then do test. |
|   **ii.** *Insulin injections.*<br><br>**Objective.** Parents/patient state understanding of and demonstrate compliance with insulin injection routine.<br><br>**Timing:** Before discharge. | **a.** Teach:<br><br>–Importance of insulin injection (e.g., time, amount, action).<br><br>–How to withdraw, mix, and inject insulin using aseptic technique. |

continued

| Usual Problems/Objectives/Timing | Nursing Orders |
|---|---|
| **2. (Continued).** | –Importance and method of rotating the injection sites.<br><br>–Correct handling and storage of insulin and equipment. |
| **iii.** *Diet.*<br>**Objectives.** Parents/patient understand and demonstrate compliance with diet therapy.<br>**Timing.** Before discharge. | **a.** Consult dr and dietitian for specific orders about diet. Dietitian to assess the patient's dietary habits (e.g., food preferences).<br>**b.** Teach:<br>–Reason for diet.<br>–Importance of adhering to the diet schedule (e.g., times of meals and snacks, eating all food offered).<br>**c.** Check meal trays and snacks before they are given to patient and check afterwards to see if food has been eaten. Give food replacements if there is more than 1/3 of the meal left or if less than 1/3 is left and patient is still hungry. Request solid replacements for solids refused. *Notify dr and dietitian if patient complains of hunger or is consistently unable to complete meals.* |
| **iv.** *Exercise.*<br>**Objective.** Parents/patient state understanding of relationship between exercise and blood-glucose balance.<br>**Timing.** Before discharge. | **a.** Teach:<br>–Effect of activity on blood glucose.<br>–Benefits of activity.<br>–How to plan for prolonged or strenuous activity with extra food intake.<br>**b.** Encourage parents to take child out on excursions during the hospitalization. |
| **v.** *Hypoglycemia (insulin reaction).*<br>**Objective.** Parents/patient state understanding of hypoglycemia, its cause, treatment, and prevention.<br>**Timing.** Before discharge. | **a.** Teach:<br>–Signs and symptoms of hypoglycemia.<br>–Cause, treatment, and prevention of hypoglycemia.<br>**b.** Reinforce use of Medic Alert bracelet. |
| **vi.** *Hyperglycemia and ketoacidosis.*<br>**Objective.** Parents/patient state understanding of hyperglycemia and ketoacidosis.<br>**Timing:** Before discharge. | **a.** Teach:<br>–Signs and symptoms of hyperglycemia and ketoacidosis.<br>–Causes, treatment, and prevention of hyperglycemia and ketoacidosis.<br>**b.** Emphasize the significance of ketonuria, illness as a precipitating factor, and the importance of notifying dr when illness or ketonuria occurs. |
| **3.** Emotional impact of diabetes mellitus on child and family.<br>**Objectives.** Family is getting over shock of diagnosis and is able to assimilate information given.<br>**Timing.** As soon as possible. | **a.** Recognize that families react in a variety of ways.<br>**b.** Provide consistent assignment of nurses.<br>**c.** Do not overload parents with information for the first few days (even though they may request it). They will be able to assimilate information more easily when they see their child responding to treatment. |

| Usual Problems/Objectives/Timing | Nursing Orders |
|---|---|
| **3.** (Continued). | **d.** Reinforce the information that diabetes does not go away; treatment will be lifelong; child can live normally otherwise.<br><br>**e.** Record information given and teaching progress.<br><br>**f.** Be prepared to repeat information as often as necessary. |
| **4.** Potential mismanagement at home due to lack of knowledge about the disease and its treatment and because of emotional upset over diagnosis.<br><br>**Objectives.** Parents/patient understand reasons for treatment. They demonstrate confidence in doing prescribed tests and in following the insulin and diet regimen.<br><br>**Timing.** By discharge. | **a.** Ensure that parents/patient:<br><br>–Demonstrate correct procedure for doing urine and blood tests and can keep an accurate record.<br><br>–Can describe the different types of insulin and how to store and handle it correctly; can give injections accurately and safely.<br><br>–Can state the differing signs/symptoms of insulin reaction and ketoacidosis, and know what to do for each situation.<br><br>–Understand and accept dietary instructions, and plan well-balanced meals consistent with the needs for growth, activity, and family life-style.<br><br>–Understand the importance of good health habits, including exercise; care of teeth, feet and skin; and adequate rest.<br><br>**b.** Ensure that parents/patient have equipment and supplies at home and know how to obtain further supplies.<br><br>**c.** Emphasize that patient must wear diabetes identification, such as Medic Alert bracelet.<br><br>**d.** Ensure that child's teacher and school nurse (and others, as appropriate) know about the diabetes and how it is managed (but that child should be treated as normal in other respects).<br><br>**e.** Ensure that parents/patient have their manuals and other printed instructions for home care and follow-up, and know whom to contact if they are concerned. |

# 59

## Rickets, Vitamin-D Resistant (Refractory)

### Goals for Discharge or Maintenance
I. Parents express understanding of the disease and treatment, and are willing to comply with home care and follow-up.
II. Parents can recognize signs/symptoms of hypocalcemia.

| Usual Problems/Objectives/Timing | Nursing Orders |
|---|---|
| **1.** Potential convulsions and tetany due to decreased serum calcium.<br><br>**Objective.** Early detection of convulsions or tetany.<br><br>**Timing.** Ongoing. | **a.** Observe for signs/symptoms of tetany or convulsions.<br><br>**b.** Check serum calcium results. If calcium is below 7 mg, do Trousseau's and Chvostek's tests. *Notify dr stat if either test is positive.*<br><br>**c.** Explain to parents importance of a well-balanced diet. Consult dietitian if necessary.<br><br>**d.** Teach family how to recognize convulsions and tetany. |
| **2.** Potential bone pain and pathological fracture.<br><br>**Objectives.** Patient appears comfortable. Early detection of possible fracture.<br><br>**Timing.** By discharge. | **a.** Handle patient carefully, support extremities, and avoid sudden movements.<br><br>**b.** Change patient's position at least q2h.<br><br>**c.** Assess and record degree and location of any pain.<br><br>**d.** If any fracture has occurred, protect site. |
| **3.** Parents' anxiety and guilt feelings about the heritable nature of the disease, the child's deformities, and (possibly) lengthy hospitalization.<br><br>**Objectives.** Parents state some understanding of the disease and are making realistic plans for home care.<br><br>**Timing.** Before discharge. | **a.** Reinforce dr's explanation of disease and treatment progress.<br><br>**b.** Designated nurse to spend time when parents visit, listening to concerns.<br><br>**c.** Arrange for genetic counseling, as ordered.<br><br>**d.** Explain all procedures and treatments. Encourage parents to participate in care, giving medications etc. |
| **4.** Potential mismanagement of medication at home.<br><br>**Objective.** Parents demonstrate knowledge and skill in giving medication.<br><br>**Timing.** By discharge. | **a.** Designated nurse to assess parents' capabilities and adjust teaching.<br><br>**b.** Teach parents the effects of hypervitaminosis:<br>–Polyuria.<br>–Nocturnal enuresis.<br>–Polydipsia.<br>–Anorexia, with weight loss.<br><br>**c.** For patients on phosphate therapy, explain that:<br>–They will have a bad taste in their mouth and may have diarrhea. (Both are temporary conditions.)<br>–Time intervals between doses must be adhered to, even at school.<br><br>**d.** For patients on small amounts of medication, use a 1 ml syringe to measure doses.<br><br>**e.** Teach and have parents demonstrate giving of the medication.<br><br>**f.** Give parents instructions in writing. |

| Usual Problems/Objectives/Timing | Nursing Orders |
|---|---|
| 4. (Continued). | **g.** Notify public health nurse if parents need help with medication or patient needs supervision at school. |
| | **h.** Ensure that parents have follow-up appointment(s) and have name and number of person to call if problems arise. |

## Goals for Discharge or Maintenance
**I.** Parents and patient express understanding of the condition and treatment.
**II.** They are able to cope with the medication and prescribed diet.

| Usual Problems/Objectives/Timing | Nursing Orders |
|---|---|
| **1.** Potential discomfort, pain, or injury due to hypertonia, tremors, dysarthria, and rigidity caused by accumulation of copper deposits in basal ganglia.<br><br>**Objective.** Patient displays fewer spasms and tremors, less rigidity, and no injury.<br><br>**Timing.** Ongoing. | **a.** When patient is in bed, keep bed-sides up; when in wheelchair, restrain firmly.<br>**b.** Reassure patient that symptoms will decrease as treatment takes effect.<br>**c.** Use warm baths and warmed towels to promote relaxation.<br>**d.** Involve physical therapist p.r.n.<br>**e.** Document in detail any changes in the patient's condition. |
| **2.** Patient's potential frustration about inability to perform activities of daily living, due to tremors, dysarthria, and hypertonia.<br><br>**Objective.** Patient is able to feed himself and perform personal care.<br><br>**Timing.** Before discharge. | **a.** Assess patient's ability to perform daily activities (e.g., bathing).<br>**b.** Encourage patient to retain as much independence as possible. Place objects so he can reach them.<br>**c.** Help with activities that patient finds difficult. Involve family in helping patient.<br>**d.** If patient drools, be sure he has tissues or a towel available; apply cream to lips and chin.<br>**e.** Involve occupational therapist as necessary. |
| **3.** Potential frustration due to communication difficulties. | *See* Careplan 67: Dysphasia (Expressive), Acute. |
| **4.** Potential emotional lability or behavior problems due to copper deposits and/or reaction to illness.<br><br>**Objective.** Normal affect.<br><br>**Timing.** By discharge. | **a.** Encourage patient to maintain previous level of independence.<br>**b.** Designated nurse to establish a structured program with the patient for daily activities.<br>**c.** Establish limits and enforce them consistently.<br>**d.** Involve family in plans to manage behavior. |
| **5.** Potential jaundice and/or hemolysis due to accumulation of copper in the liver.<br><br>**Objective.** Early detection of jaundice, petechiae, or melena.<br><br>**Timing.** Ongoing. | **a.** Observe for and record presence of jaundice, petechiae, or other signs of bleeding. Notify dr if any of these occur.<br>**b.** If prothrombin time and partial thromboplastin time are elevated, use mouthwash or lemon and glycerin swabs rather than a toothbrush. |
| **6.** Potential esophageal varices due to hepatic cirrhosis.<br><br>**Objective.** Early detection of gastrointestinal bleeding.<br><br>**Timing.** Ongoing | **a.** Observe for signs of esophageal bleeding (vomiting fresh blood, melena, shock).<br>**b.** Report *stat* to dr any signs of bleeding.<br>**c.** *If varices are present:* adjust patient's diet to soft, bland foods. |
| **7.** Potential seizures. | *See* Careplan 11: Seizures. |

| Usual Problems/Objectives/Timing | Nursing Orders |
|---|---|
| **8.** Potential hypersensitivity to penicillamine.<br><br>**Objective.** Early detection of signs of hypersensitivity.<br><br>**Timing.** Until discharge. | **a.** Observe for rash and fever.<br><br>**b.** Check laboratory results (e.g., complete blood count, urinalysis) for signs of bone marrow suppression and/or proteinuria. Notify dr if there are any changes in results. |
| **9.** Parental anxiety and/or guilt feelings due to symptoms, prognosis, or genetic cause of disease.<br><br>**Objectives.** Family discuss feelings about the disease. They understand genetic basis of disease. All family members have been tested.<br><br>**Timing.** By discharge. | **a.** Reinforce dr's explanation about symptoms and prognosis.<br><br>**b.** Designated nurse to provide opportunities for family to air feelings, *away from patient*, especially when patient's progress is slow.<br><br>**c.** Check that testing of parents, siblings, and close relatives and that genetic counseling are arranged. |
| **10.** Potential mismanagement at home, due to lack of understanding of the disease and the necessity for continuing treatment.<br><br>**Objectives.** Parents/patient are able to give medication correctly and can cope with the prescribed diet.<br><br>**Timing.** Before discharge. | **a.** Reinforce information and teaching given by dr and geneticist. Emphasize the importance of patient adhering to diet and chemotherapy.<br><br>**b.** Ensure that dietitian has spoken to parents and patient about the low copper diet.<br><br>**c.** Allow parents and patient to select foods from the menu. Supervise their choices and reinforce information about foods to avoid (e.g., chocolate, shellfish, nuts, organ meats).<br><br>**d.** Teach and supervise parents in giving medication. Explain about possible side effects of medication.<br><br>**e.** Make arrangements with pharmacy department to have an adequate supply of medication for the parents to take home.<br><br>**f.** Refer parents to appropriate social agency if problems arise with expenses, transportation, schooling, etc.<br><br>**g.** Ensure that parents have written instructions for:<br>–Medication.<br>–Diet.<br>–Follow-up appointment(s).<br>–Contact person if there are problems. |

# Careplan 61

## Maple-Syrup-Urine Disease (MSUD) (Branched-Chain Ketonuria)

### Goals for Discharge or Maintenance
Parents have some understanding of the disease, understand the diet, and can cope with home care.

| Usual Problems/Objectives/Timing | Nursing Orders |
|---|---|
| **1.** Potential coma and death due to inability to metabolize leucine, isoleucine, and valine.<br><br>**Objective.** Prevention of coma and death.<br><br>**Timing.** Continuing. | **a.** *Notify clinical investigation unit nutritionist* immediately when the patient is admitted. *Patient must remain on special semisynthetic formula and diet or on i.v. fluids.*<br><br>**b.** All formula and solids must come from the clinical investigation unit (CIU) kitchen. However, if parent brings formula to hospital, use it until a supply is prepared.<br><br>**c.** Patient must consume all of prescribed diet every 24 hr.<br><br>**d.** Report any missed formula/diet or vomiting to dr and nutritionist *stat.*<br><br>**e.** Observe for changes in symptoms from baseline assessment on admission. *See* nursing order 2(a).<br><br>**f.** If patient requires dialysis, *see* Careplan 144: Peritoneal Dialysis.<br><br>**g.** If serum amino acid test is requested, check with laboratory before taking blood sample. |
| **2.** Potential precipitation of amino acid imbalance by the stresses of normal development (e.g., teething) or infections.<br><br>**Objective.** Early recognition of signs and symptoms of metabolic imbalance (i.e., rash, stomatitis, regression in developmental tasks, changes in behavior, poor weight gain).<br><br>**Timing.** Until discharge. | **a.** Assess and record:<br>  –Level of consciousness.<br>  –Vomiting.<br>  –Ability to suck.<br>  –Changes in muscle tone (e.g., gait).<br>  –Level of irritability.<br>  –Respirations.<br>  –Changes in behavior.<br>  –Odor of urine. (Maple syrup odor indicates elevation of serum leucine level.)<br><br>**b.** Be particularly alert to observations made by parents.<br><br>**c.** Record dietary intake (include note of any formula not taken at home on the day of admission).<br><br>**d.** Give formula p.o. or by NG tube, as ordered. Observe closely for any signs of aspiration and notify dr *stat.*<br><br>**e.** If patient is on n.p.o., hypoglycemia may develop; give 10% dextrose in water i.v. as ordered.<br><br>**f.** Be alert to any possible stresses the child may be exposed to. Ensure that patient's roommates are free of infection.<br><br>**g.** Document any rash or stomatitis. (Neither will resolve until the amino acid balance is restored to the normal level for that patient.) |

continued

| Usual Problems/Objectives/Timing | Nursing Orders |
|---|---|
| **2. (Continued).** | **h.** If rash is present, keep skin clean and dry (to prevent infection). |
| | **i.** Test each voided urine for ketones. |
| **3.** Parents' potential guilt feelings about the heritable nature of the disease and its effects on their child and their concern about their child's actual or potential mental retardation and probable early death.<br><br>**Objectives.** Parents express their concerns and state realistic understanding of the short- and long-term implications of disease.<br><br>**Timing.** As soon as possible. | **a.** Ensure that dr has referred parents for genetic counseling.<br><br>**b.** Provide opportunities for questions and expression of concerns.<br><br>**c.** Reinforce dr's and nutritionist's information and instructions.<br><br>**d.** Refer to social services if necessary.<br><br>**e.** Refer family to the MSUD Club. |
| **4.** Potential mismanagement at home due to lack of understanding of the disease and its management.<br><br>**Objectives.** Parents demonstrate understanding of the disease and its dietary management, and ability to prepare the diet; they are willing to maintain close contact with dr and nutritionist.<br><br>**Timing.** By discharge. | **a.** Assess and record the family's understanding of the patient's progress. (Dr and nutritionist will instruct parents. They will maintain contact with the family by phone and/or clinic visits.)<br><br>**b.** Teach parents how to test urine for ketones, and ensure that they have the equipment to do the test at home.<br><br>**c.** Ensure that parents understand and can recognize danger signs and know when and how to contact the dr.<br><br>**d.** Ensure that parents have written instructions about diet, testing, and follow-up.<br><br>**e.** Refer the family to public health nurse as necessary. |

### Goals for Discharge or Maintenance

Parents understand the condition, are willing to keep their infant on the prescribed diet, and will adhere to instructions for follow-up.

**Note:** Infants in whom phenylketonuria (PKU) has just been diagnosed are usually admitted to a pediatric unit for 1 to 2 weeks. The condition is explained to the parents, who are given instructions about their infant's diet and are taught how to do the Guthrie test. They are also informed that follow-up will be long term and will be carried out in the PKU center nearest to them.

After the initial stay in the pediatric unit, the patient is followed-up at the clinic and by the family doctor. Developmental assessment is continuous: height, weight, and head circumference are measured at every clinic visit. Behavior, personality, social achievement, coordi-

nation, language development, and school records are checked when appropriate. Psychological assessment is done once a year unless otherwise indicated.

During the first year the parents will be asked to do the Guthrie test twice weekly. The test results will be assessed by the PKU clinic staff who will then contact the parents by telephone to adjust the child's diet according to the blood level of phenylalanine. The child will be seen in the PKU clinic every 4–6 weeks during the first year. As the child grows older, the blood testing and clinic visits will be less frequent.

| Usual Problems/Objectives/Timing | Nursing Orders |
|---|---|
| 1. Potential mismanagement of diet and failure to comply with follow-up and to attend clinic, due to parents' lack of understanding of the condition and its treatment.<br><br>**Objectives.** Parents state an accurate understanding of the condition and are willing to follow the prescribed diet and attend clinic(s).<br><br>**Timing.** By the end of the first clinic visit. | **a.** Determine what the parents understand about the condition, the prescribed diet, and the follow-up program.<br><br>**b.** Reinforce the dr's explanations about PKU.<br><br>**c.** Give the parents an appropriate booklet or other printed information (e.g., National Society for Mentally Handicapped Children, *The Child with Phenylketonuria*. London: Millbrook Press, 1974).<br><br>**d.** Stress the importance of adhering to the prescribed diet. (The child's inability to metabolize protein, specifically phenylalanine, can result in mental retardation.)<br><br>**e.** Ensure that the dietitian has explained key points to parents:<br>–Infants need special formula.<br>–Family members, friends, etc., must not feed treats to the child.<br>–It is important to read food labels.<br>–Food and fluids must be measured.<br>–Clarify what is meant by choices and equivalents (e.g., one choice or equivalent contains 15 mg of phenylalanine).<br><br>**f.** Give parents printed dietary instructions, including equivalent phenylalanine values of foods. Ask them to read this at home and bring it to the clinic at each visit.<br><br>**g.** Ensure that the parents know:<br>–The type and amount of formula/food to be given.<br>–How and when to do the Guthrie test and where to send the blood specimen. (If they cannot do this test, make arrangements for a public health nurse to do it.)<br>–They must take a supply of the infant's formula with |

continued

| Usual Problems/Objectives/Timing | Nursing Orders |
|---|---|
| **1. (Continued).** | them if he will be fed away from home.<br><br>–Whom to call in the event of problems.<br><br>–Date and location of next appointment.<br><br>**h.** Ensure that the family dr knows of the patient's progress. |
| **2.** Potential delay in assessment, because the child's parents are reluctant to do the Guthrie test.<br><br>**Objective.** Blood specimens are received regularly for determination of child's serum phenylalanine level.<br><br>**Timing.** As long as testing is necessary. | **At each clinic visit:**<br><br>**a.** Remind parents of the need to continue the Guthrie test for regular assessment of phenylalanine in their child's blood.<br><br>**b.** If necessary:<br><br>–Explain again that regular testing is necessary so the dr can assess their child's condition and adjust the diet accordingly.<br><br>–Teach parents again how to do Guthrie test: demonstrate the procedure, and observe them doing it.<br><br>**c.** Ascertain from the parents whether the Guthrie test causes them undue anxiety. (It may be necessary to contact a public health nurse to do or supervise this in the home.)<br><br>**d.** Ensure that the parents have the supplies to do test and to send the blood samples, and that they know when to do it and where to send the specimen. |
| **3.** Potential mismanagement of the diet by parents, especially when the diet is being adjusted.<br><br>**Objectives.** Parents follow the instructions for the prescribed diet, are aware that there may be problems, and know how to deal with them.<br><br>**Timing.** As long as the diet is necessary. | **General Nursing Order**<br><br>Help the parents establish an attitude toward the diet that permits some flexibility, to reduce emphasis on the child's diet within the family. |
| **a.** During the neonatal period and early infancy. | **a.** *The infant must consume the prescribed quantity of formula each day.* If infant is ill and is refusing the formula, parents can substitute "free" fluids; but if this illness persists for 24 hr, especially if he is febrile, they must notify the child's dr and/or the PKU clinic.<br><br>**b.** Ensure that parents know where and how to obtain the formula and how to prepare it.<br><br>**c.** Help parents establish a routine for feeding.<br><br>**d.** Ensure parents' understanding that a supply of the formula must accompany the infant if he is to be fed away from home. |
| **b.** During the transition to solid foods. | **a.** At a suitable time the dietitian will advise the parents of commercially prepared low-protein foods, such as bread, pasta, cookies and biscuits, and fruit gelatin.<br><br>**b.** Using the printed instructions as a guide, reinforce the dietitian's instructions. Explain appropriate choices or equivalents that can be given and how to alter the amount of formula. |

| Usual Problems/Objectives/Timing | Nursing Orders |
|---|---|
| **3. (Continued).** | **c.** Ensure that parents have the address and phone number of the specialty foods store. |
| **c.** During the transition to finger foods and table foods. | **a.** Ask parents to explain the instructions to relatives, neighbors, etc., to ensure that their child is *not* given snacks, etc. <br><br> **b.** Check that parents are reading food labels, measuring foods correctly, and giving a reasonable selection of allowed foods. <br><br> **c.** Ensure that the family's food is stored where the patient cannot reach it. |
| **d.** When child must eat away from home. | **a.** Ensure that the parents know to take/send foods for their child if suitable foods will not be available (friends' homes, school, when traveling, etc.). <br><br> **b.** Ensure that child's schoolteacher knows he is on the diet but that he should be treated as normal. <br><br> **c.** Help parents plan snacks of "free" foods for their child. <br><br> **d.** Instruct child not to eat any snacks, etc., unless his parents have given permission. |
| **e.** Refusal of food during childhood. | **a.** If child is refusing food (e.g., when he has a cold), instruct parents to give him fruit gelatin and "free" fluids. <br><br> **b.** If he refuses food for more than 1 day, instruct them to notify the child's dr or the PKU Clinic nurse. |
| **4.** Potential lack of dietary control, due to the child's normal expression of independence. (This is most likely in young schoolchildren.) <br><br> **Objective.** The child achieves normal independence with minimal loss of dietary control. <br><br> **Timing.** As long as the diet is necessary. | **a.** Ensure that parents are aware that it is normal for children to express independence through eating habits. <br><br> **b.** Help parents make arrangements that provide their child with some independence through control of his own diet. <br><br> **c.** Help parents devise ways to lessen the emphasis on diet by increasing the child's feeling of responsibility in other activities (e.g., suggest that he be given money to buy the newspapers each day). <br><br> **d.** Advise parents that their child may use the diet to try to manipulate them and other family members, and discuss how to prevent this. (If the diet does interfere with family relationships, it may be necessary to discontinue the rigid diet and substitute one that is simply free of high-protein foods.) |
| **Note:** If a patient with PKU is likely to become pregnant, she must revert to the low-protein diet and be under the care of her dr. | |

Careplan

# 63

Cerebral Edema

**Goals for Discharge or Maintenance**
See Objectives.

| Usual Problems/Objectives/Timing | Nursing Orders |
|---|---|
| | **General Nursing Order**<br>*See* Careplan 71: Increased Intracranial Pressure. |
| **1.** Hypoxia due to the tissue response to a lesion, infection, surgery or other trauma, or an autoimmune reaction.<br><br>**Objective.** Prevention or early detection of factors that aggravate edema and hypoxia.<br><br>**Timing.** Until discharge. | **a.** Position patient as ordered by dr (usually semi-prone).<br><br>**b.** Administer steroids as ordered. Consult dr about giving antacids (to reduce possibility of gastric ulcer); give steroids with food whenever possible.<br><br>**c.** Avoid unnecessary strain and agitation, which increase intracranial pressure. |
| **Factors that aggravate edema and hypoxia:**<br><br>**a.** *Pyrexia:* Increases cerebral $O_2$ requirement and blood flow.<br><br>**Objective.** Temperature in normal range.<br><br>**Timing.** Until discharge. | **a.** *See* Careplan 10: Pyrexia; but record temperature at least q2h as long as it is elevated.<br><br>**b.** Give antipyretics as ordered.<br><br>**c.** Notify dr if difficult to control temperature; additional cooling measures may be ordered.<br><br>**d.** If cooling blanket, ice, etc., applied, use continuous temperature monitoring device. |
| **b.** *Hypoventilation:* Leads to respiratory acidosis and cerebral vasodilation. *Upper or lower airway obstruction:* Increases intrathoracic pressure and impedes cerebral venous return.<br><br>**Objectives.** Airway not obstructed; other respiratory problems detected early.<br><br>**Timing.** Until discharge. | **a.** Maintain clear airway:<br>–Position patient semiprone—*never on back* (prevent neck flexion).<br>–Turn at least q2h.<br>–Encourage deep-breathing if patient is able.<br>–Suction p.r.n. to clear the nasopharynx.<br>–If patient is hypoventilating, apply mild stimulation to help promote deeper breathing (e.g., stroke limbs, change patient's position).<br><br>**b.** Assess respiratory status at least q1h. Check:<br>–Movement of chest.<br>–Air entry and breath sounds.<br>–Respiratory rate and volume.<br>–Patient's color and behavior.<br><br>**c.** Report significant changes to dr *stat* (chest films and blood-gas tests may be ordered). |
| **c.** *Fluid overload and electrolyte imbalance.*<br><br>**Objective.** Fluid balance.<br><br>**Timing.** Until discharge. | **a.** Regulate *all* fluid intake carefully (via i.v. and nasogastric tubes, orally, and by transfusion). Adjust as necessary to meet prescribed total intake.<br><br>**b.** Record intake and output. (For infants it may be necessary to weigh diapers.)<br><br>**c.** Note whether urine is concentrated or dilute: determine SG as ordered by dr and when you consider it necessary.<br><br>**d.** If patient has signs of overhydration, report to dr *stat*: |

171

continued

| Usual Problems/Objectives/Timing | Nursing Orders |
|---|---|
| 1. (Continued). | –Input > output. |
| | –Sudden weight gain. |
| | –Irritability, confusion. |
| | –Respiratory distress. |
| | –Pitting edema. |
| | e. If abnormal serum electrolyte values are obtained, report to dr *stat*. |
| | f. If mannitol is given: |
| | –Assess efficacy (increased urine output, improved general status). |
| | –Be aware of correct dosage and concentration. |
| | –Consult dr about duration of infusion, particularly if patient is a young child or infant. |

**Goals for Discharge or Maintenance**
See Objectives

| Usual Problems/Objectives/Timing | Nursing Orders |
|---|---|
| **1.** *Postoperatively.* | *See* Careplan 76: Neurosurgery, Major: General Care. |
| **2.** If patient has a tracheotomy or wired jaws. | *See* Careplan 104: Tracheotomy: Acute *and* Careplan 160: Wired Jaw. |
| **3.** Potential airway obstruction due to thick, sanguinous secretions blocking the ET tube and/or tracheotomy tube.<br><br>**Objective.** Patent airway.<br><br>**Timing.** Until extubated. | **a.** *See* Careplan 101: Older Infants and Children on a Ventilator.<br><br>**b.** Suction naso- and oropharynx and ET or tracheotomy tube, q1h and p.r.n.<br>  –Use a small catheter for nasopharyngeal suctioning (because of gingival swelling).<br>  –Guide catheter carefully along side of mouth, taking care not to dislodge wires.<br><br>**c.** Ensure that patient's inspired gases are humidified (usually by Puritan nebulizer and T-piece extension).<br>  –Insert heating rod into the Puritan nebulizer, as ordered by dr.<br>  –If heating device is being used, check temperature and misting q1h.<br><br>**d.** If secretions are thick and difficult to remove, consult dr about instilling N saline into ET tube before and during suctioning procedure.<br><br>**e.** Encourage patient to deep breathe and *cough* q1–2h. |
| **4.** Potential hypoxia due to:<br>  –Airway obstruction.<br>  –Hypoventilation.<br>  –Oversedation.<br>  –Anemia.<br><br>**Objective.** Adequate oxygenation.<br><br>**Timing.** Until extubated and/or swelling subsides. | **a.** Ensure continuous administration of humidified gases via T-piece or tracheotomy collar. Analyze $O_2$ concentration of inspired gases q2-4h. Do blood gas sampling as ordered.<br><br>**b.** Monitor vital signs (apical heart rate, respiratory rate, BP), quality of respirations, air entry, and color of nail beds and lips, q1–2h.<br><br>**c.** Notify dr if signs of respiratory distress are present.<br><br>**d.** Administer analgesic as ordered (usually a continuous morphine infusion for 48 hr) but *do not oversedate* (may cause respiratory and neurological depression).<br><br>**e.** Report excessive bleeding from operative site. Check Hb and administer blood products as ordered. |
| **5.** Potential aspiration due to:<br>  –Excessive amounts of mucus, blood, and saliva in airway.<br>  –Inability to swallow for first 48–72 hr. | **a.** *Ensure that wire cutters are available at all times* (taped to head of bed, or attached to stretcher, wheelchair, or patient's clothing).<br><br>**b.** Keep head of bed elevated at least 45 degrees. |

**173**

continued

| Usual Problems/Objectives/Timing | Nursing Orders |
|---|---|
| **5. (Continued).**<br><br>–Nausea and vomiting.<br>–Jaws being wired.<br>**Objective.** No aspiration.<br>**Timing.** Until swelling subsides and patient can swallow (usually 3–5 days). | **c.** Sit patient in chair t.i.d., and ambulate as soon as appropriate, even when ET tube is in place.<br>**d.** Suction q1-2h and p.r.n.<br>–Teach patient (if appropriate) how to use a tonsil suction tip and to suction mouth as needed.<br>**e.** Keep tracheotomy/ET cuff inflated during first postoperative night; then follow cuff deflation routine as ordered by dr (being careful to suction airway thoroughly before deflation).<br>**f.** Maintain patency of NG tube:<br>–Irrigate NG tube q2h with 5–10 ml N saline. (Check position of NG tube before irrigating.)<br>–If intermittent suction is being used, check at least q1h to ensure that it is working.<br>–Consult dr before attempting to insert or adjust NG tube.<br>**g.** Administer antiemetic p.r.n., as ordered.<br>**h.** If patient vomits, sit him up with head tilted forward. Suction around the wires (and nasally, if not contraindicated). If patient cannot cope with the emesis and is in distress, cut the "up" and "down" wires using the wire cutters (to free the jaw). Support patient's jaw to minimize movement. Have someone notify dr *stat*. |
| **6.** Potential respiratory distress after extubation due to upper airway swelling and/or obstruction. (May occur almost instantly or a few hours later.)<br>**Objective.** Early detection of respiratory distress.<br>**Timing.** 24 hr. | **a.** *Before extubation:*<br>–Explain procedure, as appropriate.<br>–Ensure the patient is not heavily sedated. (Sedation is usually discontinued 48 hr postoperatively.)<br>–Withhold feedings (oral and NG) for at least 4 hr.<br>**b.** *At time of extubation:*<br>–Have O₂, suction, and reintubation equipment ready at bedside.<br>–Prepare patient for a feeling of shortness of breath immediately on extubation, and encourage him to take slow, deep breaths at this time.<br>–Aspirate and remove NG tube as ordered.<br>–Suction ET tube and nasopharynx thoroughly.<br>–Assist dr with the extubation.<br>–Keep patient in head-up position.<br>–Assess patient's respiratory rate, heart rate, and color throughout procedure.<br>–Support and reassure patient constantly.<br>**c.** *After extubation:*<br>–Observe patient closely for several hours for signs of respiratory distress.<br>–Suction nasopharynx and mouth p.r.n. |

| Usual Problems/Objectives/Timing | Nursing Orders |
|---|---|
| **6. (Continued).** | −Report to dr *stat* any signs of dyspnea.<br>−Keep intubation equipment at bedside for 24 hr.<br>**Note:** *Racemic epinephrine inhalations may be ordered to reduce swelling.* |
| **7.** Potential hypovolemia and dehydration due to excessive loss of body fluid from surgical area.<br><br>**Objective.** No hypovolemia or dehydration.<br><br>**Timing.** Until oozing stops and patient is able to swallow saliva. | **a.** Monitor vital signs q1h and report significant changes.<br>**b.** Maintain i.v. fluids as ordered.<br>**c.** Measure intake and output.<br>**d.** Estimate sanguinous losses from nasopharynx and measure NG tube losses q4h.<br>**e.** Interpret laboratory results.<br>**f.** If patient hemorrhages:<br>−Place in shock position.<br>−Suction to keep airway clear.<br>−Monitor BP.<br>−Have someone notify dr *stat*. |
| **8.** Potential cerebral edema when intracranial surgical approach is used.<br><br>**Objective.** Control and/or prevention of further cerebral edema.<br><br>**Timing.** Until discharge. | **a.** *See* Careplan 63: Cerebral Edema.<br>**b.** Keep head of bed elevated 30 degrees-45 degrees.<br>**c.** Follow fluid intake orders meticulously to avoid overload.<br>**d.** Do neurological assessment q1h until patient is fully recovered from anesthesia, then q4h. (Level of consciousness may be difficult to assess since the patient's eyes may be swollen or sutured shut and teeth are wired.)<br>**e.** Administer steroids as ordered.<br>**f.** Turn patient q2h, ambulate early, and do deep-breathing and coughing exercises q2h to maintain normal blood gases. |
| **9.** Pain due to extensive surgery of head and face, and at donor site(s).<br><br>**Objective.** Patient is able to cope with the pain/discomfort and is able to rest.<br><br>**Timing.** As soon as possible. | **a.** Administer analgesic as ordered.<br>**b.** Ensure that the head of the bed is elevated 30 degrees-45 degrees (to promote reduction of facial edema). Turn patient from side to side q2h.<br>**c.** Have tracheotomy and ET tube tapes readjusted as facial swelling increases.<br>**d.** **Iliac bone graft:** Patient may lie on side, sit, or stand (if not contraindicated). Move and position patient carefully.<br>**e.** **Rib bone graft:** Support affected area during deep-breathing and coughing. Ensure patency of chest drain. |
| **10.** Potential infection in various surgical sites:<br>−Chest.<br>−Eyes. | **a.** Use aseptic suctioning technique (sterile gloves and catheters).<br>**b.** Encourage early ambulation and deep-breathing and coughing q2h. |

continued

| Usual Problems/Objectives/Timing | Nursing Orders |
|---|---|
| **10. (Continued).**<br>– Sinuses.<br>– Gums.<br>– Meninges.<br>– Bones.<br>– Skin.<br>  **Objective.** No infection or its early detection.<br>  **Timing.** Continuing until surgical areas healed. | **c.** If patient's eyes are swollen or sutured, cleanse q2h with N saline and apply ointment or drops as ordered.<br>**d.** Unless contraindicated, suction nose frequently and keep nasal area clean.<br>**e.** Ensure diligent mouth care q4h and p.r.n.<br>  – Sit patient up and have suction on hand (patient may prefer doing own mouth care).<br>  – For mouth care, use a Water Pik® with half-strength hydrogen peroxide. (*Do not rinse patient's mouth with water after using peroxide.*)<br>  – Keep lips moist with petrolatum.<br>  – Check frequently for any protruding wires and coat them with bone wax.<br>**f.** Keep donor sites clean and dry.<br>**g.** Administer antibiotics as ordered.<br>**h.** Report prolonged fever or any discharge from incision, nares, or ears suggesting infection or CSF leak. |
| **11.** Patient unable to swallow due to persistent swelling, fear, and/or pain.<br>  **Objective.** Patient is able to swallow adequately.<br>  **Timing.** Before transfer from ICU. | **a.** Encourage patient to attempt swallowing as much as possible.<br>**b.** Assess patient's ability to swallow by giving water by mouth, using a catheter attached to the end of a syringe.<br>**c.** When patient is able to swallow, start feeding by mouth. Give *water* only (not juices, etc.) for the first 5 postoperative days.<br>  – Sit patient upright for feedings.<br>**d.** If intubation is prolonged (and bowel function has resumed), administer NG feedings as ordered. |
| **12.** Patient is upset, frustrated, and possibly depressed, because of difficulty in breathing and swallowing, inability to communicate verbally, and own physical appearance.<br>  **Objectives.** Patient is less anxious and able to communicate verbally or in writing, can cope with his appearance, and is showing interest in general ward activities.<br>  **Timing.** Before discharge. | **a.** Organize care to allow patient as much rest as possible.<br>**b.** Reassure patient that a nurse is close by. Provide aids to communicate (e.g., clipboard, paper and pencil).<br>**c.** When speaking to patient, use sentences that require only short answers.<br>**d.** Encourage patient to dress in own clothes (if appropriate) and attend to own personal hygiene.<br>**e.** Shampoo patient's hair as soon as condition allows.<br>**f.** Provide patient with a mirror as soon as he is able to cope with this (and if appropriate). Stay with the patient the first time until you feel that he is settled (the swelling is usually worse than patient expected it would be). |

| Usual Problems/Objectives/Timing | Nursing Orders |
|---|---|
| **13.** Parents anxious due to feelings of guilt about having surgery done, helplessness in comforting their child, and/or rejection of their child's postoperative appearance.<br><br>**Objectives.** Parents are able to express their feelings, can cope with information given to them about their child's appearance, and are able to participate in their child's care.<br><br>**Timing.** As soon as possible. | **a.** Reassure parents that their child's appearance will improve as swelling decreases.<br><br>**b.** Reassure parents that analgesics will be given to alleviate pain as much as possible.<br><br>**c.** Encourage parents to visit whenever possible. Assist and support them in participating in child's care (ambulation, mouth care, feeding, recreation, etc.).<br><br>**d.** Encourage parents to express their feelings, away from their child's bedside. Arrange for additional supportive services as necessary (e.g., social worker).<br><br>**e.** Keep parents informed of their child's daily progress; arrange for them to speak with dr as necessary. |

# Careplan 65

## Craniofacial Surgery: Pre-operative and Postoperative Ward Care

### Goals for Discharge or Maintenance
**I.** Patient develops or maintains social relationships.
**II.** Parents/patient demonstrate competence in all aspects of home care.

| Usual Problems/Objectives/Timing | Nursing Orders |
|---|---|
| **1.** *Pre-operatively.* | **a.** *See* Careplan 17: Pre-operative Care, General *and* Careplan 76: Neurosurgery, Major: General Care.<br><br>**b.** Notify physical therapist, social worker, and/or dietitian, as appropriate.<br><br>**c.** Explain to parents/patient:<br>–There will be facial swelling and discoloration, especially around the eyes.<br>–Mouth and suture line care.<br>–i.v. therapy.<br>–NG suction.<br>–Chest physical therapy.<br>–Diet. |
| **2.** *Postoperatively.* | **a.** *See* Careplan 21: Postoperative Care, General *and* Careplan 76: Neurosurgery, Major: General Care.<br><br>**b.** If patient has wired jaws, *see* Careplan 160: Wired Jaw.<br><br>**c.** If patient has a tracheotomy, *see* Careplan 104: Tracheotomy, Acute. |
| **3.** Potential meningitis due to contamination of exposed dura.<br><br>**Objective.** Early detection of signs of meningitis.<br><br>**Timing.** Until discharge. | **a.** *See* Careplan 73: Meningitis, Purulent: Acute Phase.<br><br>**b.** Observe for and report to dr any CSF leakage from nose, ears, or incision. |
| **4.** Patient unable to see, due to swelling caused by extensive manipulation of orbital region.<br><br>**Objectives.** Swelling is reduced. Patient reports clearing vision.<br><br>**Timing.** Day 5. | **a.** Reassure patient and parents that swelling will gradually subside, and that vision problems are temporary.<br><br>**b.** *See* Careplan 85: Vision Defects. |
| **5.** Patient's fear of rejection because of facial appearance.<br><br>**Objectives.** Patient is able to talk about his appearance and learns to cope with others' reactions.<br><br>**Timing.** By discharge. | **a.** Be aware that patient may have had problems coping with his appearance before the operation.<br><br>**b.** Be careful of *your* facial expressions and comments while in patient's and parents' presence.<br><br>**c.** Encourage patient to talk about his appearance. Show patient where there is some improvement day by day (e.g., swelling going down, bruises fading).<br><br>**d.** Help patient with personal grooming, selection of clothes, etc.<br><br>**e.** Explain to parents, siblings, and any others having contact with the patient (e.g., other parents) the importance of treating the child as normal. |

| Usual Problems/Objectives/Timing | Nursing Orders |
|---|---|
| 6. Potential mismanagement at home, particularly if patient's jaws are wired, due to lack of knowledge.<br><br>**Objective.** Parents/patient demonstrate ability to carry out home care.<br><br>**Timing.** Before discharge. | a. Reinforce all instructions and information relating to the child's surgery.<br><br>b. Explain that it takes about 2 weeks for swelling to completely subside and that bruising may take longer to fade.<br><br>c. Ensure that parents/patient have demonstrated skill in doing procedures (e.g., mouth care).<br><br>d. Ensure that parents have supplies and equipment ready at home.<br><br>e. Explain and give specific written instructions.<br><br>f. Give names and numbers of persons to call in an emergency, also the date and location of follow-up appointments. (The patient may have to attend several clinics.) |

## Goals for Discharge or Maintenance

Family members express understanding of the disease and treatment, signs of dehydration, and need for regular medical follow-up.

| Usual Problems/Objectives/Timing | Nursing Orders |
|---|---|
| **1.** Potential dehydration due to polyuria caused by insufficiency of antidiuretic hormone (ADH).<br><br>**Objective.** Adequate hydration.<br><br>**Timing.** Until discharge. | **a.** Record TPR and BP q4h until polyuria is stabilized by medication regimen.<br><br>**b.** Provide premeasured fluids at bedside. For infants and young children, give extra fluids as ordered.<br><br>**c.** Provide privacy for frequent urination. Ensure that bedpan/urinal is readily available.<br><br>**d.** Measure specific gravity (SG) at every void. Notify dr if SG is 1.005 or less on 2 consecutive voids.<br><br>**e.** Maintain accurate intake and output record. Notify dr if hourly output exceeds hourly intake for 2 hr or more.<br><br>**f.** Explain to patient/parents the importance of reporting all intake and output.<br><br>**g.** Weigh patient daily, before breakfast. Notify dr if there is excessive loss/gain (3% of body weight).<br><br>**h.** Observe and report to dr any signs/symptoms of dehydration:<br>–Increased heart rate.<br>–Decreased BP.<br>–Sunken eyes or fontanelle.<br>–Loss of skin turgor.<br>–Elevated temperature.<br>–Dry mucous membranes.<br><br>**i.** Administer medication as ordered and record effects. Notify dr if there is no decrease in urination, or if SG has not increased within 1 hr.<br><br>**j.** If the patient must fast for a prolonged period of time (e.g., for a test), check with dr about method to be used to maintain hydration (e.g., water p.o. or i.v. fluids).<br><br>**k.** Record stools (number, color, consistency). Notify dr if patient is constipated. |
| **2.** Anorexia and poor nutrition due to polydipsia.<br><br>**Objectives.** Patient is offered a diet appropriate for age and eats at least ¾ of solids.<br><br>**Timing.** Until discharge. | **a.** Offer frequent, small, nutritious meals. Encourage patient to eat solids before drinking fluids.<br><br>**b.** If patient is overweight, provide low-calorie fluids (e.g., water, sugar-free Kool-Aid, or soft drinks).<br><br>**c.** If patient is underweight, provide high-protein, high-calorie fluids (e.g., milkshakes).<br><br>**d.** Record and report concerns about patient's intake. |
| **3.** Potential diaper rash in child who is not toilet trained, due to frequent urination.<br><br>**Objective.** Skin clear and intact. | **a.** Check diapers q½–1h and change p.r.n.<br><br>**b.** Place cotton fluffs in diapers. When patient voids, squeeze urine into a cup then test SG. |

180

| Usual Problems/Objectives/Timing | Nursing Orders |
|---|---|
| **3. (Continued).**<br>**Timing.** Until discharge. | **c.** If rash occurs, *see* Careplan 41: Diaper Rash.<br><br>**Note:** Urine collectors may be used for occasional collections but if they are used routinely skin breakdown will occur. |
| **4.** Potential water toxicity if fluid intake exceeds output in a nondehydrated patient.<br>**Objectives.** Patient is adequately hydrated. Frequency and dosage of medication has been determined.<br>**Timing.** Before discharge. | **a.** Observe and report:<br>–High SG with decreased urine output.<br>–Edema (location, degree).<br>–Weight gain.<br>–Confusion. |
| **5.** Potential disruption in patient's activities (sleep, play, school) due to polyuria and polydipsia.<br>**Objective.** Minimal disruption in activities of daily living.<br>**Timing.** By discharge. | **a.** If patient's sleep is disturbed frequently, allow for rest periods during day.<br>**b.** Encourage parents to discuss their child's condition with the school teacher.<br>**c.** Assure patient/parents that problems will decrease when the child's condition is stabilized on a medication schedule. |
| **6.** Potential recurrence of symptoms due to patient's and family's lack of knowledge about the disease and treatment.<br>**Objectives.** Symptoms are controlled. Family members state understanding of the disease and treatment and demonstrate correct administration of medications.<br>**Timing.** Before discharge. | **a.** Designated nurse to teach patient/family:<br>–Signs and symptoms of ADH insufficiency.<br>–Importance of adequate hydration.<br>–Administration of medication:<br>  –Dose.<br>  –Time or indications (drug may be ordered to be given p.r.n.).<br>  –Technique.<br>**b.** Allow time for family members to express concerns and ask questions.<br>**c.** Ensure that patient/parents have:<br>–Equipment to measure SG (and can demonstrate correct technique).<br>–Written instructions about when to call the dr, whom to call, and how dr can be reached (e.g., if child begins to vomit).<br>–Follow-up appointment in writing.<br>**d.** Refer to public health nurse. |

# Careplan 67    Dysphasia (Expressive), Acute

**Goals for Discharge or Maintenance**
See Objectives.

| Usual Problems/Objectives/Timing | Nursing Orders |
|---|---|
| | **Special Nursing Order**<br><br>Limit the number of personnel having direct contact with the patient. Record in detail the various approaches used and their effectiveness. |
| **1.** Patient exhibits frustration and anxiety about his sudden inability to express himself clearly.<br><br>**Objectives.** Gestures of frustration less frequent; child appears relaxed.<br><br>**Timing.** By discharge. | **a.** Treat patient as a normal child.<br><br>**b.** Provide quiet, calm atmosphere, with limited distractions.<br><br>**c.** Allow adequate rest periods (fatigue aggravates the condition). Listening to soft music will help the child to relax; ensure that he is positioned comfortably, and schedule the periods according to his physical condition.<br><br>**d.** Provide materials to aid communication (e.g., paper and pencil, picture board).<br><br>**e.** Remain calm; give the child ample time and the means to express himself; accept mood swings as part of the condition.<br><br>**f.** Select activities that will not challenge the patient too much or frustrate him.<br><br>**g.** Frame questions so they can be answered in one word. Avoid talking too fast or too loudly.<br><br>**h.** Recognize that the patient has high and low tides of energy. Spend time with him when he is most responsive (e.g., after breakfast, after resting).<br><br>**i.** Reassure child, and instruct family to be patient, understanding, and reassuring. |
| **2.** Patient's potential loss of independence, due to underestimation of his capabilities.<br><br>**Objective.** Patient maintains independence to the level of his capabilities.<br><br>**Timing.** Check daily. | **a.** Obtain information from parents about their child's capabilities, interests, etc., before his illness.<br><br>**b.** With the family's help, establish a routine for their child's daily activities.<br><br>**c.** Each day, set aside time to work with the patient and family.<br><br>**d.** Discuss with parents approaches that will help to reduce the family's frustration and, consequently, that of the patient.<br><br>**e.** Contact rehabilitation department, speech therapist, and others for advice about special aids or personnel who can assist.<br><br>**f.** Help patient to maintain his independence. Provide time and materials to aid communication.<br><br>**g.** Encourage patient to do his own care, but be available in case of need. Arrange his belongings within reach.<br><br>**h.** Encourage patient with his efforts, but be aware of his limits. Praise all signs of progress and encourage family members to do this. |

**Goals for Discharge or Maintenance**
See Objectives.

| Usual Problems/Objectives/Timing | Nursing Orders |
|---|---|
| **1.** *Isolation.* | **a.** Follow hospital procedure for aseptic technique. |
|  | **b.** *See* Careplan 12: Isolation: Psychological Aspects. |
| **2.** Potential pyrexia. | *See* Careplan 10: Pyrexia. |
| **3.** Headache and irritability.<br>**Objective.** Patient appears more comfortable.<br>**Timing.** Before discharge. | **a.** Observe for symptoms of headache (restlessness, irritability, screaming spells). |
|  | **b.** If patient can speak, ask him to describe the headaches (frequency, location, severity, duration). |
|  | **c.** Provide aids to patient's comfort (e.g., cold cloth to forehead; cool, quiet, darkened room). Plan care to minimize interruptions. Avoid use of overhead lights. |
|  | **d.** Restrict visitors. |
|  | **e.** Give analgesics as ordered. If analgesics are not ordered, explain to parents/patient the importance of not masking symptoms. |
|  | **f.** Explain reasons for procedures and treatment. |
| **4.** Potential neurological deterioration due to cerebral inflammation.<br>**Objective.** Early detection of deterioration.<br>**Timing.** Ongoing. | **a.** On admission assess and record:<br>  –Level of consciousness.<br>  –Muscular coordination and control (speech and swallowing).<br>  –Patient's orientation to time and place.<br>  –Inappropriate behavior for age. |
|  | **b.** Assess level of consciousness and behavior each time vital signs are checked. Report significant change to dr *stat* (e.g., apathy, mental confusion, speech difficulties, hyperexcitability, unprovoked outbursts, stupor, or coma). Deterioration of condition may necessitate constant observation. |
|  | **c.** During uncontrolled outbursts or severe restlessness remain calm; ask for assistance to handle the patient if necessary. Padded bed-sides and/or restraints may be needed to prevent injury. |
|  | **d.** If patient becomes unconscious, *see* Careplan 15: Unconscious Patient. |
|  | **e.** Have emergency resuscitation equipment readily available (condition may deteriorate rapidly). |
| **5.** Potential seizures. | *See* Careplan 11: Seizures. |
| **6.** Potential cerebral edema. | *See* Careplan 63: Cerebral Edema. |
| **7.** Parents anxious and fearful about the disease and uncertain prognosis. | **a.** Preferably, designate a nurse to stay with parents when they need comforting and reassurance. |

continued

| Usual Problems/Objectives/Timing | Nursing Orders |
|---|---|
| **7. (Continued).**<br><br>**Objective.** Parents discuss their fears and concerns.<br><br>**Timing.** As soon as possible. | **b.** Encourage parents to be with their child; explain need for a quiet environment.<br><br>**c.** Arrange for dr to talk to parents often (at least once a day).<br><br>**d.** Allow parents to express fear, guilt, and anger away from the child's bedside or room.<br><br>**e.** Reinforce dr's explanation and allow opportunities for questions.<br><br>**f.** Explain reasons for procedures and treatment.<br><br>**g.** Encourage parents to leave the room for meals and sleep (inquire tactfully about parents' ability to get home, cope with family routines, etc.). |

# Careplan 69     Encephalopathy

**Goals for Discharge or Maintenance**
I. Parents have some understanding of the causal disease and present condition.
II. They understand and can cope with home care and follow-up.

| Usual Problems/Objectives/Timing | Nursing Orders |
|---|---|
| **1.** Patient exhibits frustration and anxiety about the neurologic and pathologic disturbances.<br><br>**Objective.** Decreased frustration and anxiety as communication, coordination, and memory improve.<br><br>**Timing.** Before discharge. | **a.** Determine patient's capabilities before the pre-encephalopathy illness.<br><br>**b.** Anticipate patient's needs and assist him as necessary.<br><br>**c.** Consult rehabilitation department about plans for routine activities, physical therapy, occupational therapy, and speech therapy.<br><br>**d.** Encourage patient's attempts and praise his accomplishment of each task, however simple.<br><br>**e.** Provide thick pencil or crayon and paper.<br><br>**f.** Document patient's progress. |
| **a.** Difficulty communicating. | **a.** *Assume that patient understands more than he appears to.*<br><br>**b.** Speak slowly, precisely, and not too loudly to patient.<br><br>**c.** Maintain a calm, unhurried manner; allow patient to finish words and/or sentences.<br><br>**d.** Explain procedures, routines, etc., in simple terms, just before they are to be done.<br><br>**e.** Try to interpret patient's body movements, grimaces, and sounds. Record information that will assist communication between patient and others. |
| **b.** Poor hand–eye coordination, with or without decrease in visual perception. | **a.** Provide patient with opportunities for practicing hand–eye activities (e.g., catching a ball).<br><br>**b.** Identify objects; state size, shape, position, etc. |
| **c.** Memory lapses or loss. | **a.** Daily, assess extent of patient's memory.<br><br>**b.** Encourage family members to talk about familiar experiences and places (e.g., school, friends, and pets).<br><br>**c.** Assign daily tasks to improve patient's recall. Start with simple examples (e.g., names, numbers, letters, and dates). |
| **2.** Potential injuries while patient is restless or during seizures or ataxia.<br><br>**Objective.** No injuries.<br><br>**Timing.** Until discharge. | **a.** Pad side-rails.<br><br>**b.** Use restraints—with discretion (they *can* provoke increased restlessness).<br><br>**c.** Supervise patient closely, especially when he is restless.<br><br>**d.** Assess ataxia and determine patient's progress. Consult physical therapist about patient's ambulation (how long he should be up, need for walking aids, etc.).<br><br>**e.** Assist patient as necessary: do not allow him to become fatigued. |

continued

| Usual Problems/Objectives/Timing | Nursing Orders |
|---|---|
| **3.** Disorientation.<br><br>**Objective.** Patient's speech and/or actions indicate awareness of time, place, and people.<br><br>**Timing.** By discharge. | **a.** Introduce yourself on entering patient's room; repeat each time.<br>**b.** Use calendars, clocks, and/or posters, to orient patient to time and place.<br>**c.** Try to change patient's environment as little as possible; keep familiar objects around him.<br>**d.** Help family members to participate in patient's reorientation.<br>**e.** Daily, assess patient's recall. |
| **4.** Potential seizures. | *See* Careplan 11: Seizures. |
| **5.** Potential poor self-image, due to debility and depression.<br><br>**Objectives.** Patient participates in daily activities, shows interest in physical appearance, and/or expresses positive feelings.<br><br>**Timing.** By discharge. | **a.** Spend time with patient, allowing him time to express his feelings.<br>**b.** Encourage patient to dress appropriately, join in ward activities, and socialize.<br>**c.** Give praise for the smallest improvements (compliment him about hairstyle, etc., and accomplishments).<br>**d.** Explain to patient that progress is expected to be slow, but assure him that he is progressing well. |
| **6.** Potential gastrointestinal disturbances due to inactivity and change in diet.<br><br>**Objective.** No constipation or diarrhea.<br><br>**Timing.** By discharge. | **a.** Get patient up as soon as possible.<br>**b.** Provide foods that promote normal fecal excretion.<br>**c.** Assist patient to use commode/toilet as soon as he is able.<br>**d.** If necessary, give laxative or enema as ordered by dr. |
| **7.** Potential malnutrition due to poor appetite and difficulty feeding himself.<br><br>**Objectives.** Patient maintains weight, is eating a well-balanced diet, and can feed himself adequately.<br><br>**Timing.** By discharge. | **a.** Ask parents about child's likes and dislikes, and try to include his favorite foods in his diet.<br>**b.** Consult dietitian p.r.n.<br>**c.** Select foods the patient can handle on his own.<br>**d.** Provide utensils that will help patient to feed himself.<br>**e.** Encourage patient to feed himself. |
| **8.** Potential skin breakdown due to inactivity or poor nutrition. | *See* Careplan 13: Prolonged Immobilization. |
| **9.** Parents anxious and frustrated, not knowing duration of symptoms and prognosis.<br><br>**Objective.** Parents express their anxiety and have some understanding of the disease process.<br><br>**Timing.** As soon as possible. | **a.** Designated nurse to spend time with parents each day, without distractions and away from the child's room. Encourage questions and discussion of parents' concerns; keep them informed of planned activities, procedures, etc.<br>**b.** Encourage parents to participate in the care and activities that have been planned for their child.<br>**c.** Ensure that their dr speaks to them at regular, frequent intervals.<br>**d.** Teach parents any special care that will have to be continued at home. |

| Usual Problems/Objectives/Timing | Nursing Orders |
|---|---|
| 9. (Continued). | e. If the child requires additional care/rehabilitation: before discharge, ensure that the requisite departments/authorities have made arrangements to meet the child's needs. |
| | f. Ensure that parents have written instructions for home care and follow-up. |

### Goals for Discharge or Maintenance
Parents/patient understand the condition and can cope with home care and follow-up.

| Usual Problems/Objectives/Timing | Nursing Orders |
|---|---|
| **1.** Potential skin breakdown and/or contractures due to decreased innervation of limbs and immobility.<br><br>**Objectives.** Skin intact; full range of movement of all joints.<br><br>**Timing.** Until recovery or discharge. | **a.** Support affected limbs to avoid strain and trauma.<br><br>**b.** Ensure that good body alignment is maintained.<br><br>**c. Bed patients.** Turn q2h and gently massage bony prominences with cocoa butter.<br><br>**d.** Perform full range of passive movements q4h. Help child progress to active exercises as outlined by the physical therapist. Use age-appropriate toys to stimulate exercise (e.g., have him squeeze a ball, kick a balloon).<br><br>**e.** Give patient a daily tub bath unless contraindicated.<br><br>**f.** Change soiled bed linen promptly. |
| **2.** Patient's frustration over increased dependence because of paresis, and potentially because of aphasia/dysphasia and/or impairment of thought and memory.<br><br>**Objective.** Patient displays less frustration and appears reasonably satisfied with explanations.<br><br>**Timing.** Until recovery or discharge. | **a.** Anticipate patient's needs.<br><br>**b.** Arrange patient's belongings within his reach.<br><br>**c.** Even if patient is not dysphasic, *see* Careplan 67: Dysphasia. (The frustration and lack of independence experienced by these patients are very similar.)<br><br>**d.** Ask rehabilitation department to assist with devices, exercises, etc., that patient can use or do with unaffected hand.<br><br>**e.** Encourage patient to participate in activities and/or his care within the limits of his disability, but ensure he rests frequently. (Fatigue lessens ability and increases frustration.)<br><br>**f.** Allow patient ample time for physical tasks, but interrupt him when frustration is impending.<br><br>**g.** Repeat quietly any information the patient has forgotten.<br><br>**h.** Praise patient for his attempts as well as accomplishments.<br><br>**i.** Record patient's attempts and progress. |
| **3.** Potential injury or unilateral self-neglect because of perceptual loss (with or without visual field defect).<br><br>**Objective.** No injury or self-neglect.<br><br>**Timing.** Until discharge. | **a.** Remind and reassure patient frequently that the affected limbs (especially the arm) are still there, particularly if he has a visual field defect. *See* Careplan 85: Vision Defects, if appropriate.<br><br>**b.** Ensure that the affected limbs are well-supported and protected when patient is being moved in bed or in and out of bed. (Hemiplegic limbs are flaccid initially: their dead weight can pull patient out of a bed or chair.)<br><br>**c.** Check patient daily for undetected injury.<br><br>**d.** Instruct patient/parents how to avoid injury.<br><br>**e.** During personal hygiene, physical therapy, and dressing, refer specifically to affected limbs (name them). *See also* nursing order 5(e). |

| Usual Problems/Objectives/Timing | Nursing Orders |
|---|---|
| **4.** Potential constipation and lack of appetite, due to decreased activity.<br><br>**Objectives.** Usual defecation pattern maintained or regained. Adequate nutrition.<br><br>**Timing.** By discharge. | **a.** Encourage increased roughage in diet; increase fluid intake.<br>**b.** Arrange for small, frequent meals (they may be less tiring) and make the meal tray look attractive.<br>**c.** Have dietitian see patient/parents to determine likes and dislikes.<br>**d.** If patient is feeding himself, make sure he has time to eat his meals and can cope.<br>**e.** Report to dr if abdominal distention develops.<br>**f.** Give laxative or suppository, as ordered. |
| **5.** Patient/parents fearful and anxious about the disabilities and whether others will accept them.<br><br>**Objectives.** Patient/parents discuss their fears and concerns. Parents are making plans to help others accept the disabilities (e.g., at school).<br><br>**Timing.** Before discharge. | **a.** Ensure a consistent assignment of nurses, to establish trust.<br>**b.** Spend time with parents away from their child's bedside.<br>**c.** Encourage patient to socialize with others on the ward.<br>**d.** Teach parents how to give care that will be required at home (e.g., physical therapy, speech therapy).<br>**e.** Encourage and help patient to dress in clothes that will improve his appearance and are easily put on and removed. Supervise or help with patient's personal grooming. |
| **6.** *If hemiplegia is prolonged or irreversible.* | **a.** *See* Careplan 13: Prolonged Immobilization.<br>**b.** Contact appropriate authorities (e.g., public health nurse, crippled children's society).<br>**c.** Help parents arrange child's schooling. |

**Goals for Discharge or Maintenance**
See Objectives.

| Usual Problems/Objectives/Timing | Nursing Orders |
|---|---|
| **1.** Potential brain damage (destruction of brain-cell function) due to increased intracranial pressure (ICP).<br><br>**Objective.** Early detection of increased ICP.<br><br>**Timing.** Until discharge. | **a.** Each time vital signs are checked, assess patient's level of consciousness: *rouse him fully, especially at night.*<br><br>**b.** Check TPR, BP, and pupil size and reaction at least q4h, and more frequently if indications of change in status.<br><br>**c.** Compare with baseline signs or signs normal for patient's age. Be aware of other factors that may affect signs (e.g., pain, infection, or crying).<br><br>**d.** If vital signs change (BP ↑, change in temperature or pupil reaction, respiratory rate ↓, pulse rate ↓), recheck in 15 min. If vital signs are still cause for concern, report to dr.<br><br>**e.** Look for other signs of increased ICP:<br>–Vomiting.<br>–Headache.<br>–Irritability.<br>–Ataxia.<br>–Limb weakness.<br>–Sensory loss.<br>–Bowel or bladder dysfunction.<br>–Bulging of burr holes or fontanelles.<br>–Head circumference increasing.<br>–Disturbed vision. |
| **2.** Potential respiratory arrest due to severe depression of respiratory center.<br><br>**Objective.** Respiration maintained.<br><br>**Timing.** Until discharge. | **a.** Ensure that suction and O₂ are at bedside.<br><br>**b.** Observe patient closely for respiratory depression.<br><br>**c.** If patient is difficult to rouse and/or vital signs change, have ventricular tap equipment ready at bedside. |
| **3.** Headache and irritability.<br><br>**Objectives.** Patient appears comfortable and/or expresses increased comfort. Rests during day and sleeps at night.<br><br>**Timing.** Until discharge. | **a.** Record nature of headache, site, severity, and time of onset.<br><br>**b.** Give analgesics if ordered. If not ordered, explain to patient and parents the importance of not masking symptoms with medication.<br><br>**c.** Provide aids to patient's comfort (e.g., cold facecloth to forehead; cool, quiet, darkened room). Plan care to minimize interruptions. |
| **4.** Parents' potential anxiety and frustration over personality changes in their child.<br><br>**Objective.** Parents express understanding of personality changes.<br><br>**Timing.** By discharge. | **a.** Obtain from parents a description of their child's usual behavior. Record differences.<br><br>**b.** Be patient and understanding with child: this is *not* a discipline problem.<br><br>**c.** Explain to parents what is happening; tell them how they can help, and support their attempts. |
| **5.** Potential aspiration and/or fluid and electrolyte imbalance due to vomiting.<br><br>**Objectives.** No aspiration; adequate hydration. | If patient is vomiting:<br><br>**a.** Record intake and output.<br><br>**b.** Record signs of dehydration. |

| Usual Problems/Objectives/Timing | Nursing Orders |
|---|---|
| **5. (Continued).**<br>**Timing.** Until discharge. | **c.** If antiemetic ordered p.r.n., give when patient is nauseated or shows signs of impending vomiting.<br>**d.** If antiemetic to be given regularly, give ½ hr before meals.<br>**e.** Position patient on side or abdomen for sleep and if level of consciousness is decreased.<br>**f.** Feed slowly and carefully.<br>**g.** Have suction apparatus ready at bedside. |
| **6.** Potential injury during decreased consciousness or because of motor and sensory dysfunction.<br>**Objective.** No injury.<br>**Timing.** Until discharge. | **a.** Keep side-rails up when patient is unattended.<br>**b.** Take temperature rectally or in axilla—not orally.<br>**c.** Supervise patient closely or constantly, depending on level of consciousness. |
| **7.** Parents anxious, fearing diagnosis and prognosis.<br>**Objective.** Parents discuss their fears and concerns.<br>**Timing.** Before discharge. | **a.** Provide opportunities for parents to express feelings, away from vicinity of patient.<br>**b.** Reinforce dr's explanations and allow opportunities for questions. |
| **8.** Cerebral edema and hypoxia due to tissue response to a lesion, infection, or surgical manipulation. | *See* Careplan 63: Cerebral Edema. |

# Careplan 72  Laminectomy, Lumbar or Thoracic

## Goal for Discharge or Maintenance
Parents/patient able to cope with home care and follow-up.

| Usual Problems/Objectives/Timing | Nursing Orders |
|---|---|
| **1.** *Pre-operatively.* | **a.** *See* Careplan 17: Pre-operative Care, General.<br><br>**b.** Provide patient's bed with a firm mattress, and a bed board if appropriate.<br><br>**c.** *See* Careplan 76: Neurosurgery, Major: Pre-operative Checklist and Teaching Guide.<br><br>**d.** *See* Pre-operative Teaching Guide for Post-Laminectomy Physical Therapy (page 194).<br><br>**e.** Bathe and scrub patient with antibacterial cleanser the evening before and day of surgery. |
| **2.** Parents/child anxious about surgery and (depending on disease) potentially poor outcome.<br><br>**Objectives.** Parents/patient know pre-operative procedures and usual postoperative care and discuss their concerns openly.<br><br>**Timing.** As soon as possible. | **a.** Designated nurse to do pre-operative teaching. *(See* nursing orders for **problem 1.**)<br><br>**b.** Reinforce dr's explanations.<br><br>**c.** *See* especially nursing orders for problems 2 and 4 in the patient's Stresses of Hospitalization careplan. |
| **3.** *Postoperatively.* | **a.** *See* Careplan 21: Postoperative Care, General.<br><br>**b.** *See* Spinal-Cord Testing (page 195).<br><br>**c.** Record TPR, BP, and spinal-cord testing, q1h for 4–6 hr, then q2–4h.<br><br>**d.** Ensure that patient does deep-breathing and coughing exercises q1–2h for 24 hr, then p.r.n. |
| **4.** Potential strain on incision, due to back flexion.<br><br>**Objective.** Incision healed.<br><br>**Timing.** Day 8–10. | **a.** Ensure good body alignment: back straight (prone or supine); minimal knee flexion.<br><br>**b.** When turning patient, use log-roll method. Support patient's legs with pillow between knees, bend knees *slightly* (avoid flexion), support back with pillows and, if necessary, place a small, firm pad under his head.<br><br>**c. Small child.** Restrain p.r.n.<br><br>**d.** Turn patient and do skin care q2h. Avoid sudden jerks or twisting. |
| **5.** Potential bowel and bladder problems due to nerve injury and/or edema.<br><br>**Objective.** Early detection of bowel and bladder problems.<br><br>**Timing.** Day 1–2. | **a.** Record intake and output.<br><br>**b.** If patient has difficulty voiding, provide assistance:<br>–Use slipper bedpan or kidney basin.<br>–Leave a tap running within the patient's hearing.<br>–Apply warm compresses to patient's abdomen.<br>–Trickle warm water over patient's abdomen.<br>–Have patient move his hands in warm water.<br><br>**c.** Report to dr: |

| Usual Problems/Objectives/Timing | Nursing Orders |
|---|---|
| **5. (Continued).** | –Abdominal distention.<br>–Dribbling of urine.<br>–Urinary frequency or retention.<br>–Absence of bowel sounds. |
| **6.** Potential leakage of cerebrospinal fluid (CSF).<br>**Objective.** Early detection of CSF leakage.<br>**Timing.** Day 8–10. | **a.** Check for leakage q1–2h. Report signs of leakage to dr (e.g., dressings wet, unexplained moisture on clothing or bedding). |
| **7.** Patient reluctant to ambulate because he fears pain.<br>**Objective.** Patient able to ambulate without undue discomfort.<br>**Timing.** Day 2–3 after ambulation started. | **a.** Ensure that patient uses methods of moving taught by physical therapist. Assure him that these methods will minimize pain. Dr orders when ambulation is to start—usually 5–10 days postoperatively.<br>**b.** Give analgesic p.r.n. *before* getting patient up.<br>**c.** Help patient to get out of bed (follow physical therapist's instructions; see Pre-operative Teaching Guide, page 194).<br>**d.** Stay with patient while he is walking. Ensure that he wears well-fitting shoes (*not slippers*). *Patient must not sit* unless ordered by dr.<br>**e.** Record patient's gait. |
| **8.** Potential mismanagement of home care, due to lack of knowledge.<br>**Objective.** Parents/patient know care to be done at home.<br>**Timing.** By discharge. | **a.** Reinforce dr's instructions:<br>–Activities patient is allowed.<br>–Correct body mechanics (how to walk and sit).<br>–No stooping; he must keep back straight and bend knees.<br>–Exercises.<br>–Firm mattress and/or bed board.<br>–Avoid constipation (strain).<br>–Care of incision line.<br>–Patient must keep return appointment(s). |

# Pre-operative Teaching Guide for Post-Laminectomy Physical Therapy

1. Explain to the patient the necessity for deep-breathing and coughing, to prevent pneumonia, atelectasis, etc.
   a. Mucus production is increased after a patient has had an anesthetic.
   b. Patient will be relatively immobile for a few days postoperatively.
   c. He will be reluctant to breathe deeply and cough, because of fear of pain.
2. Teach, and have the patient demonstrate, deep-breathing and effective coughing.
3. Explain the importance of doing foot and ankle exercises (e.g., to help the "muscle pump" circulate blood through the legs and back to the heart).
4. Teach, and have the patient demonstrate, foot and ankle exercises: pull the foot up and down; make circles with the feet—in one direction, then the other. Each exercise should be done 10 times and should be repeated as often as necessary for the patient to be able to do this well.
5. Teach, and have patient demonstrate, methods of moving to a sitting position and/or getting in and out of bed.
   a. If patient is allowed to sit, teach him to turn onto his side, then use his arms to push himself up into the sitting position.
   b. If patient is not allowed to sit, teach him:
      – To get out of bed by rolling into prone position, diagonally across the bed, then pushing with his arms until his feet touch the floor.
      – To get into bed by facing diagonally across the bed, then lying face down on the bed and simultaneously raising the leg nearer the bed backward onto the bed. Support the patient's other leg and help him to roll into bed, onto his back.

# Spinal Cord Testing: A Guide for Nursing Care (Pre-operative and Postoperative Observations of Patients with Spinal Lesions)

Spinal cord testing includes vital signs, movement of limbs, sensation in response to touch, bladder function, bowel function, and other observations and symptoms.

The frequency and extent of testing will be ordered by the doctor, according to the level and type of lesion.

**A. Vital signs (frequency as ordered)**
1. **Blood pressure:** Decrease indicates
   a. Surgical shock
   b. Orthostatic/postural hypotension (when a recumbent patient stands up)
2. **Pulse:** Increase indicates
   a. Surgical shock
   b. Respiratory distress
3. **Respirations** (rate, rhythm, type): Respiratory distress indicates
   a. High cord lesion
   b. Chest complications (pneumonia, cardiac failure)
4. **Temperature**
   a. Elevated in infection of chest, bladder, wound, etc.
   b. Poikilothermy
      –In normal or cool weather: Failure to keep body temperature up to normal, because of sympathetic-nerve interference (inappropriate shivering)
      –In hot weather: Failure to keep body temperature down to normal, because of lack of sweating

**B. Limbs**
1. **Movement**
   The ability to move relates to the level of spinal cord injury. Any change should be reported at once; decreased ability indicates the possibility of cord compression.
2. **Sensation in response to light touch and squeeze**
   This testing is done with the hand and a fairly sharp object (e.g., an orange-stick; do *not* use a pin). The nurse should be aware of any change in sensory response and should report anything unusual to the doctor. (For young children, make a game of the testing—do it first with the child watching, then ask him to close his eyes while you repeat it.)

**C. Bladder function**
1. **Without catheter**
   a. Voiding: Time, amount
      –Retention
      –Overflow incontinence (frequent passage of small amounts of urine)
   b. Visible or palpable swelling of lower abdomen suggests retention of urine
   c. Bladder and urethral sensation: Does the patient have the sensation that the bladder feels full? Is the patient aware of the passage of urine?
2. **With catheter**
   a. Is the catheter felt? Is the need to void felt?
   b. Quantity of urine collected

**D. Bowel function**
1. Continence/incontinence (beyond age of toilet-training)
2. Abdominal distention
3. Bowel sounds
4. Flatus

**E. Other observations and symptoms**
1. Chest complications (especially with high lesions): cyanosis, increased pulse rate, shallow rapid breathing, facial sweating, fever
2. Pain: location, type
3. Operation site: Appearance, discharge
4. Skin surfaces: Condition, color, temperature. Pay particular attention to heels and sacrum, and to elbows in cases of cervical lesion
5. Leg veins: Phlebitis, swelling, redness, local heat, tenderness (if sensation is present)
6. Record medication ordered for a specific symptom (e.g., carbachol for retention of urine)
7. Mental state and attitude: Apprehension, depression; euphoria

**Goals for Discharge or Maintenance**
See Objectives.

| Usual Problems/Objectives/Timing | Nursing Orders |
|---|---|
| **1.** *Isolation.* | **a.** Follow hospital procedure for asepsis.<br>**b.** Follow hospital protocol for therapy.<br>**c.** *See* Careplan 12: Isolation: Psychological Aspects. |
| **2.** Potential aspiration of vomitus due to depression of central nervous system.<br><br>**Objectives.** No aspiration of vomitus. Early detection of significant changes.<br><br>**Timing.** 24 hr. | **a.** **Infant.** Position *at all times* on side or abdomen.<br>**b.** Keep patient n.p.o. for 24 hr or until awake and alert. |
| **3.** Potential cerebral edema due to inflammation, over-hydration, and/or inappropriate excretion of ADH.<br><br>**Objective.** Early detection of cerebral edema.<br><br>**Timing.** 48 hr. | **a.** Provide constant observation if patient not fully conscious or has had seizure(s) within past 24 hr.<br>**b.** Check vital signs (TPR, BP, and pupil reaction) q1h until temperature stable; then q4h.<br>**c.** Report to dr *stat:*<br>  – Increased BP.<br>  – Decreased pulse rate.<br>  – Pupil changes.<br>  – Respiratory distress; apnea.<br>  – Twitching or seizures.<br>  – Change in level of consciousness.<br>**d.** Record intake and output and total balances q8h. (If necessary, apply urine collector or place cotton balls in perineum and squeeze out urine.)<br>**e.** Test each urine specimen for specific gravity. Notify dr if not 1.005–1.015.<br>**f.** Weigh patient daily or b.i.d. if there are signs of fluid retention.<br>**g.** **Children under 2 years.** Chart head circumference daily.<br>**h.** Report to dr *stat:*<br>  – No urinary output for 4 to 8 hr (depending on age of patient).<br>  – Edema of eyelids or extremities. |
| **4.** Pyrexia. | **a.** *See* Careplan 10: Pyrexia.<br>**b.** Use continuous temperature monitoring device to minimize disturbance to patient.<br>**c.** Give antipyretics as ordered. *Do not give ASA if disseminated intravascular coagulation (DIC) is present.* |
| **5.** Potential seizures. | *See* Careplan 11: Seizures. |

| Usual Problems/Objectives/Timing | Nursing Orders |
|---|---|
| **6.** Irritability, hyperesthesia, lethargy, headache, stiffness of neck and back, and photophobia, due to cerebral irritation.<br><br>**Objectives.** Patient rests quietly, tolerates daylight, can flex neck, and allows diaper/bed linen change without crying.<br><br>**Timing.** 72 hr. | **a.** Provide a dark, quiet, nonstimulating environment. Lower blinds in room or turn child away from sunlight.<br><br>**b.** Disturb patient as seldom as possible.<br><br>**c.** Position patient to support neck.<br><br>**d.** Speak softly, move quietly, and lower side-rails carefully.<br><br>**e.** Restrict visitors.<br><br>**f. For children 2 years old and over.** If severe headache and irritability persist after 24 hr, consult dr about giving analgesics. |
| **7.** Potential shock, coma, and death, due to overwhelming infection, bleeding, and brain-stem damage.<br><br>**Objective.** Vital signs stable and within normal limits.<br><br>**Timing.** 24 hr. | **a.** *See* nursing order 3(b) and 3(c).<br><br>**b.** Report to dr *stat:*<br>  –Pallor.<br>  –Increased petechiae or purpura.<br>  –Abnormal bleeding from injection sites. |
| **8.** Parental anxiety (fear of death or brain damage) and guilt feelings due to rapid onset of serious illness.<br><br>**Objectives.** Parents express concerns; their facial expressions are more relaxed; they state realistic observations about their child's condition and the disease; and they comfort him when he arouses.<br><br>**Timing.** 48 hr. | **a.** Preferably, designate a nurse to stay with parents when they need comforting and reassurance.<br><br>**b.** Encourage parents to visit; explain need for a quiet environment.<br><br>**c.** Arrange for dr to talk with them often (at least q24h).<br><br>**d.** Give concise, factual information about child's condition. Do not be too pessimistic or optimistic when trying to reassure parents, especially concerning the prognosis.<br><br>**e.** Allow parents to express fear, guilt, and anger away from child's bedside or room.<br><br>**f.** Explain reasons for procedures and treatment, incorporating information about the disease process.<br><br>**g.** Encourage parents to leave the room for meals and sleep (inquire tactfully about parents' ability to get home, cope with family routines, etc.). |

# Careplan 74    Meningitis, Purulent: Convalescent Phase

**Goals for Discharge or Maintenance**
Parents can cope with home care and follow-up.

| Usual Problems/Objectives/Timing | Nursing Orders |
|---|---|
| 1. Irritability due to continued cerebral irritation and restricted movement.<br><br>**Objective.** Patient plays quietly for short periods, appears generally content.<br><br>**Timing.** Until discharge. | **a.** Provide toys that patient can appreciate while restricted by i.v. system (e.g., mobiles, balloons).<br>**b.** Remove restraints for supervised periods (e.g., mealtimes, bath times, and play), at least q4h.<br>**c.** Show parents how to hold and play quietly with child without dislodging i.v. cannula. |
| 2. Potential phlebitis due to prolonged i.v. therapy.<br><br>**Objectives.** Temperature normal (37°C ± 1°); i.v. site and vein not swollen, inflamed, or painful.<br><br>**Timing.** Until i.v. discontinued. | **a.** Check temperature q4h.<br>**b.** Observe for and report swelling, redness, or tenderness of i.v. site or vein above it.<br>**c.** Ensure that antibiotics are diluted appropriately before infusion. |
| 3. Potential anorexia.<br><br>**Objective.** Patient takes diet appropriate for age.<br><br>**Timing.** Until discharge. | **a.** Gradually increase diet as tolerated, starting with small portions.<br>**b.** Encourage parents to participate in mealtime if appropriate.<br>**c.** Provide preferred foods when possible. |
| 4. Potential interruption of i.v. therapy or displacement of needle or cannula as child becomes more active.<br><br>**Objective.** Child's i.v. lines remain patent and in place.<br><br>**Timing.** Until i.v. discontinued. | **a.** Restrain child if necessary.<br>**b.** Emphasize the importance of keeping i.v. tubing and needle in place. Explain to parents and/or patient that medication is given this way for 7–10 days.<br>**c.** Teach parents how to pick up and hold child without disturbing the i.v. |
| 5. **For toddler or older child.** Potential weakness, dizziness, and/or ataxia, due to immobility.<br><br>**Objective.** Child is able to walk short distances unassisted.<br><br>**Timing.** By discharge. | **a.** Increase child's mobility; encourage movement in bed:<br>**Day 5.** Begin dangling feet over side of bed q4h.<br>**Day 6.** Sit child in chair q8h.<br>**Day 7.** Encourage child to walk with assistance between bed and chair q8h.<br>**Day 8.** Allow child up and about in room without assistance.<br>**b.** Involve parents in plan. |
| 6. Potential sequelae of meningeal infection (e.g., subdural effusion, cerebral abscess, deafness, septic arthritis).<br><br>**Objectives.** Patient is afebrile, fontanelle is level, and irritability is decreased. Vital signs stable. Patient moves joints freely.<br><br>**Timing.** By discharge. | **a.** Observe for increased blood pressure, irritability, or temperature.<br>**b.** Record whether responses to sights and sounds are appropriate for age.<br>**c. Infant.** Continue daily recording of head circumference.<br>**d.** Report to dr any signs of swelling, pain in joints, or reluctance to move limbs.<br>**e.** On discharge from hospital, make appointments for meningitis clinic and audiology clinic for 2 weeks after discharge. Give parents written note of appointments. |

## Goals for Discharge or Maintenance

I. Patient's capabilities are maximized and deficits are minimized.

II. Parents understand child's immediate and long-term treatment and demonstrate competence and confidence in all aspects of care.

| Usual Problems/Objectives/Timing | Nursing Orders |
|---|---|
| 1. Paralysis caused by abnormal development of spinal cord or spinal nerve roots.<br><br>**Objective.** Full range of passive joint movement.<br><br>**Timing.** By discharge. | **a.** Record movement of hips, knees, and ankles. Note if movement is voluntary or reflex (e.g., does movement occur while child is awake or asleep? in response to stimuli?).<br><br>**b.** Provide passive range of exercises q3–4h to legs and arms as instructed by physical therapist.<br><br>**c.** If infant is being nursed prone on a Bradford frame, turn his head from side to side q2h.<br><br>**d.** Stimulate use of infant's hands and arms with age-appropriate toys.<br><br>**e.** When diapering, dressing, etc., lift infant with palm of hand under buttocks. *Do not lift his body by pulling on legs:* this could further dislocate hips.<br><br>**f.** Enroll patient in rehabilitation department's spina bifida program. |
| 2. Potential meningitis and further loss of function due to contamination of exposed neural tissue.<br><br>**Objective.** Defect is clean, with no redness or discharge. Early detection of possible meningitis.<br><br>**Timing.** Until discharge. | **a.** Ensure that infant's buttocks and genitalia are kept scrupulously clean.<br><br>**b.** Report:<br>–Any CSF leakage.<br>–Signs of infection (e.g., elevated TPR).<br>–Signs of meningitis (e.g., lethargy, fever, vomiting, or poor color).<br><br>**c.** Nurse infant on a Bradford frame, appropriately restrained. Do not pick up unless ordered.<br><br>**d.** Keep defect moist at all times (e.g., with N saline dressings *(defect must not become dry and cracked).* Consult dr if dressing is ineffective.<br><br>**e.** If infant can be picked up, protect defect with a well-fitting donut-shaped pad secured by a binder. |
| 3. Potential increased intracranial pressure due to obstruction of CSF flow.<br><br>**Objective.** Early detection of increased intracranial pressure.<br><br>**Timing.** Ongoing. | **a.** *See* Careplan 71: Increased Intracranial Pressure.<br><br>**b.** Measure head circumference daily and report any increase. |
| 4. *If surgery for repair of meningocele is necessary.* | *See* Careplan 17: Pre-operative Care, General *and* Careplan 21: Postoperative Care, General. |
| 5. Potential urinary tract infection and reflux, and constipation with overflow, due to innervation of bladder and bowel. | **a.** Follow dr's orders for estimating residual urine and for intermittent catheterization.<br><br>**b.** Check infant at least q1h and change wet/soiled linen |

continued

| Usual Problems/Objectives/Timing | Nursing Orders |
|---|---|
| **5. (Continued).**<br><br>**Objectives.** Urine is clear and free of infection; bladder is emptied regularly. No constipation.<br><br>**Timing.** Until discharge. | promptly. (There will be frequent dribbling of urine and feces because of the lax ureteral and anal sphincters.)<br><br>**c.** Report any signs of infection: fever, vomiting, irritability, foul urine, or excoriation of perineum.<br><br>**d.** Increase fluid intake if infection is suspected.<br><br>**e.** For older infants, initiate dietary measures to prevent constipation:<br><br>  –Give extra fruit (especially prunes) and fluids.<br><br>  –Delete rice cereals.<br><br>**f.** If no stools for 2 days, give laxative, glycerine suppository, or enema, as ordered.<br><br>**g.** Disimpact feces as ordered.<br><br>**h.** When Bradford frame is discontinued (usually 2–3 weeks after surgery), ensure that the urology service is notified to do urological work-up (e.g., IVP, urodynamic testing, urine cultures, blood tests). |
| **6.** Potential skin breakdown due to loss of sensation, enforced immobility on Bradford frame, and/or poor circulation.<br><br>**Objective.** Skin is clear and intact.<br><br>**Timing.** Until discharge. | **a.** If infant is on frame:<br><br>  –Observe for redness of all areas in contact with frame.<br><br>  –Keep frame covering dry and wrinkle-free.<br><br>**b.** If infant is not on frame:<br><br>  –Turn him q2–3h.<br><br>  –Change wet or soiled diapers promptly.<br><br>  –Bathe him in tub daily.<br><br>**c.** Use extra care with bed-cradles, safety pins, restraints, temperature of bath water, etc. |
| **7.** Delayed developmental milestones, due to lack of usual stimulation or enforced immobility.<br><br>**Objectives.**<br><br>*Neonate reaches the following milestones with minimal delay:*<br><br>**a.** Hand-to-mouth contact (at birth).<br><br>**b.** Recognition of voices within a few days. Visual attention at 2–4 weeks includes focusing, following objects (to 30 degrees from midline), and waving hands at objects and faces (random responses to stimuli).<br><br>**c.** Demonstration of head control in sitting position (at birth, 2–3 sec; at 4 weeks, good control).<br><br>**d.** Gradual response to stimuli (Moro reflex, increasing alertness, etc.).<br><br>*Older child. Each milestone depends on attainment of the previous one.*<br><br>**Timing.** As appropriate; continuing. | **a.** When feeding and bathing baby, apply visual, tactile, and auditory stimulation.<br><br>**b.** Attach toys and brightly colored objects at eye level on side of crib (mirrors are excellent stimuli). Move objects in front of infant's eyes (horizontal following occurs first, then vertical). When feeding baby, look at him, smile, talk, and show him the bottle.<br><br>**c.** Put within infant's reach toys that produce sounds (e.g., bracelets with bells), to stimulate hand movement. Whenever possible, position child so that hands are free for exploration.<br><br>**d.** Place in infant's hands objects of varied texture (soft, hard, furry, etc.).<br><br>**e.** When dr orders (usually after sutures are removed), lift infant from frame, support trunk in sitting position, and move him slowly from side to side, backward and forward, to improve head control.<br><br>**f.** While baby is on frame, encourage parents to remove restraints, touch him, rub baby's hands, move his hands to their faces or his mouth, etc. Encourage |

| Usual Problems/Objectives/Timing | Nursing Orders |
|---|---|
| **7. (Continued).** | them, especially the mother, to get into a face-to-face position, to facilitate bonding.<br><br>**g.** Record child's level of alertness and strength of reflex reaction to various stimuli (sound, touch, etc.).<br><br>**h.** Patient should be assessed for level of habilitation, so that a specific program can be developed. |
| **8.** Potential feeding problems, respiratory distress, and quadriplegia, due to Arnold-Chiari syndrome.<br><br>**Objectives.** Child sucks and swallows easily; chest is clear and respiration is normal; child uses hands and arms appropriately and has head control.<br><br>**Timing.** Continuing. | **a.** Report to dr *stat* any nasal regurgitation, stridor, cyanosis, apneic spells, and loss of gag reflex and swallowing.<br><br>**b.** For feeding, move infant from bed to stretcher, maintaining prone position. Lift infant's head slightly and support it with the palm of your hand. Feed slowly and carefully. (Burping is increased in this position).<br><br>**c.** Have $O_2$ and suction equipment at hand.<br><br>**d.** Advise dr *stat* if infant loses arm function or head control. |
| **9.** Parental anxiety stemming from guilt feelings, fear of child's condition, and/or feeling of inability to cope with home management.<br><br>**Objectives.** Parents understand and discuss spina bifida defect accurately and have been advised of follow-up care and facilities.<br><br>**Timing.** By discharge. | **a.** Provide numerous opportunities for questions and discussion.<br><br>**b.** Explain spina bifida to parents:<br>–Cause is not known.<br>–The disorder occurs during fourth week of gestation, usually before mother is aware of pregnancy.<br>–Discuss availability of genetic counseling for future pregnancies.<br><br>**c.** Teach parents the program devised for their infant:<br>–Exercises and stimulation.<br>–Care of unrepaired myelomeningocele.<br>–Care of shunt; signs of blocked shunt.<br>–Care of bowel and bladder; signs of infection.<br>–Skin care and safety precautions.<br>–Medication, if appropriate.<br><br>**d.** Provide supervised practice for feeding, bathing, intermittent catheterization, and disimpaction of feces if ordered.<br><br>**e.** Encourage attendance at spina bifida classes.<br><br>**f.** Inform parents about local crippled children's center and the Spina Bifida and Hydrocephalus Association. |

**Goal for Discharge or Maintenance**
Patient/family members express understanding of usual course after neurosurgery.

| Usual Problems/Objectives/Timing | Nursing Orders |
|---|---|
| **1.** *Pre-operatively.* | *See* Careplan 17: Pre-operative Care, General, *and* Pre-operative Checklist and Teaching Guide for Major Neurosurgery (page 204). |
| **2.** *Postoperatively.* | **a.** *See* Careplan 21: Postoperative Care, General.<br>**b.** Perform HIR q1h for 12 hr, and longer if indicated. |
| **3.** Potential increase in intracranial pressure. | *See* Careplan 71: Increased Intracranial Pressure. |
| **4.** Pyrexia due to blood and/or chemicals in CSF, and possibly infection.<br>**Objectives.** Temperature gradually returns to 37°C ± 1°. Patient/parents express understanding of reason for pyrexia.<br>**Timing.** Day 7. | **a.** *See* Careplan 10: Pyrexia.<br>**b.** *See* Careplan 71: Increased Intracranial Pressure.<br>**c.** Explain to family that fever is usual after neurosurgery and may last 1–2 weeks (usually less, although sometimes longer).<br>**d.** Ask dr to explain to family the reason for the fever.<br>**e.** Reinforce dr's explanations p.r.n. |
| **5.** Discomfort due to external swelling and ecchymoses of eyes and scalp, caused by tissue-response to surgery, CSF leakage, and/or bleeding.<br>**Objectives.** Gradual reduction in swelling; patient/parents express understanding of usual course of swelling.<br>**Timing.** 2–3 days. | **a.** Cleanse patient's eyes with N saline q2h.<br>**b.** Elevate head of bed 30–45 degrees unless contraindicated.<br>**c.** After day 2, apply warm compress to eyes q2–3h.<br>**d.** If swelling is severe, consult dr about need to check pupils.<br>**e.** Inform parents and patient that swelling and bruising usually peak in 1–2 days and then recede. |
| **6.** Discomfort due to pain of incision, tightness of turban, and itching under turban.<br>**Objectives.** Patient appears comfortable; turban remains intact.<br>**Timing.** Until turban is removed. | **a.** If analgesics not ordered, explain to patient/parents that drugs may mask important changes.<br>**b.** If posterior fossa decompression has been done:<br>–Turn patient's head and shoulders as one unit, to avoid pull on incision.<br>–When lifting or sitting patient up, support head to prevent head lag.<br>–When patient is lying flat, insert small, flat pillow to support head.<br>**c.** As external swelling increases, check tightness of turban (it should allow entry of one finger on side opposite to incision). If ordered, slit turban 2–3 inches (5–7 cm) at back; bridge the slit with wide adhesive tape.<br>**d.** Explain to patient/parents importance of their not pushing fingers up under turban.<br>**e.** Restrain child's arms with elbow splints if necessary.<br>**f.** When initial dressing is taken off, remove adhesive residue to reduce itching (a dry shampooing may |

| Usual Problems/Objectives/Timing | Nursing Orders |
|---|---|
| **6. (Continued).** | help). Cover incision with gauze; attach to skin with light adhesive tape. Change dressing daily until stitches are removed. |
| **7.** Potential neck stiffness, headache, fever, irritability, photophobia, due to meningeal irritation and/or cerebral edema.<br><br>**Objectives.** Patient appears comfortable and parents accept behavior changes, such as irritability.<br><br>**Timing.** Until discharge. | **a.** Accept patient's irritability as part of the illness.<br>**b.** Explain to parents the reason for his irritability.<br>**c.** Allow child to assume comfortable position (within the limits ordered), and then support body appropriately.<br>**d.** Explain to parents that cerebral edema peaks by the fifth day, by which time all symptoms may be exaggerated. |
| **8.** Potential seizures due to cerebral edema and pyrexia. | *See* Careplan 10: Pyrexia *and* Careplan 11: Seizures. |
| **9.** Potential embarrassment, depression, and withdrawal, because of altered appearance (loss of hair, bruising, and/or swelling).<br><br>**Objectives.** Patient socializes with other patients and visitors; he visits other parts of ward or hospital.<br><br>**Timing.** Before discharge. | **a.** Explain that swelling recedes in a few days.<br>**b.** If remaining hair is long enough, arrange it to hide a small dressing.<br>**c.** Ask parents to bring scarves or loose-fitting sunhats. (Boys like to wear adjustable baseball caps.)<br>**d.** Patient can wear a wig when sutures are out and incision is well healed.<br>**e.** Adolescents can wear makeup (not close to incision) to cover facial bruises. |
| **10.** Potential injury if large skull defect is present.<br><br>**Objective.** No injury.<br><br>**Timing.** Until defect is closed. | **a.** Prevent pressure on defect.<br>**b.** Dr will recommend type of helmet to be used if necessary [e.g., ordinary hockey helmet or special adaptations (orthotics department)].<br>**c.** Until a helmet is available, supervise child closely and restrict potentially hazardous activities. |
| **11.** Parents anxious about surgery and have potential guilt feelings (e.g., about delay in seeking advice, surgery necessitated by preventable injury).<br><br>**Objective.** Parents express their concerns and channel their feelings constructively.<br><br>**Timing.** As soon as possible. | **Designated nurse:**<br>**a.** Be available when the parents need to talk (be supportive, not judgmental).<br>**b.** Apply relevant orders in patient's Stresses of Hospitalization careplan and for specific aspects (preoperative care, etc.). |

# Pre-operative Checklist and Teaching Guide for Major Neurosurgery

**Check off when done**

| Parents | Patient |
|---------|---------|

1. Ensure that patient/parents have spoken to neurosurgeon and anesthesiologist.
2. Evaluate:
   a. What is the parents' interpretation of their child's condition or surgery?
   b. What is the child's interpretation?
   *Record this information on the patient's careplan.*
3. Help clarify the surgical procedure:
   a. Reinforce what the doctor has told the parents about the operation.
   b. Show the parents (on a demonstration board) the types of shunts that may be used.
4. Explain:
   –Hairwashes and scrubs with antibacterial cleanser.
   –The importance of n.p.o.
   –Enemas.
   –Deep-breathing, coughing, turning, and walking.
   –Hair-shaves.
   –Bandages (types, location), sutures, color of skin-preparation solution.
   –Facial swelling and/or discoloration postoperatively.
5. Explain that:
   –A nurse or other escort (identify) will take the child, in his bed, to the OR playroom 30–40 min *before* the scheduled OR time.
   –There will be toys, TV, other children, and a recreationist to keep him company.
   –A nurse or doctor, or both, will take him to the OR.
6. Explain that, in the OR:
   –A doctor will help to transfer him onto the special table.
   –There will be 5 or 6 people wearing caps, masks, and green gowns.
   –There will be big lights shining.
   –He will feel a prick on his hand and then will go to sleep. (Some children can choose to have a mask to induce anesthesia themselves.)
7. Explain that:
   –The child will wake up in the Recovery Room/PAR; it can be very busy and noisy there.
   –He will stay there until the doctor allows him to return to the ward. Check with the surgeon; this period is usually 2–4 hr, but the child may stay overnight.
   –HIR will be done q15–60 min (TPR, BP, pupil reaction, and level of consciousness).
8. Explain to parents that:
   –They can see their child on the ward pre-operatively. Then they should wait in the parents' postoperative waiting room, where the surgeon will come to see them immediately after the operation.
   –Transfer from the OR to the PAR or the ICU may take more than an hour after the surgeon has spoken to them, so prepare the parents for another wait.
   –Ward staff will probably visit them in the waiting room. (*This practice is much appreciated by parents.*)
   –If parents visit their child in the PAR, he may have an i.v. line in place, a drain, and oxygen by mask.
9. Explain to the parents that:
   –Their child may return not to the same room but to a room closer to the nursing station.
   –Bed rest will be maintained according to the extent of surgery and the doctor's orders.
   –(Unless contraindicated) Usually the child can drink as soon as he feels like it and can eat in a day or two.
10. *Remember to ask for parents' questions*; answer them if you can or refer them to the surgeon.

Reference: Petrillo, M., and Sanger, S. *Emotional Care of Hospitalized Children: An Environmental Approach* (2nd ed.) Philadelphia: Lippincott, 1980, chap. 6.

**Goals for Discharge or Maintenance**
Parents understand reason for shunt insertion and can cope with home care and follow-up.

| Usual Problems/Objectives/Timing | Nursing Orders |
|---|---|
| **1.** Increased intracranial pressure. | **a.** *See* Careplan 71: Increased Intracranial Pressure. <br> **b.** Elevate head of bed 30 degrees unless ordered otherwise by dr. |
| **2.** *Pre-operatively.* | **a.** *See* Careplan 17: Pre-operative Care, General. <br> **b.** Bathe and shampoo patient b.i.d. the evening before and day of surgery. <br> –**Infant.** Use ordinary soap unless ordered otherwise. <br> –**Older child.** Use antibacterial cleanser. <br> **c. If this is the patient's first shunt.** Designated nurse to ensure that parents/patient have some understanding of the disease and treatment. <br> –Be present when dr explains the operation. <br> –Reinforce dr's explanations. <br> –Encourage questions. (At this time, some parents wish to start discussing home care and follow-up.) <br> –Use diagrams or actual shunts, and teaching doll, to demonstrate the procedure. |
| **3.** *Postoperatively.* | **a.** *See* Careplan 21: Postoperative Care, General. Follow HIR q1h until patient's condition is stable, then q2h, then q4h. <br> **b. First or new shunt.** Bed rest as ordered. <br> **c. Shunt revision.** Patient usually can be up as tolerated (unless ordered otherwise by dr). Elevate head of bed. <br> **d. Ventriculopleural shunt.** Listen to chest sounds each time you record vital signs (q1–4h); encourage deep-breathing and coughing (*but no clapping*) q1–4h. <br> **e. Ventriculoperitoneal shunt.** Before increasing diet (usually 24 hr), check that bowel sounds are present. |
| **4.** *Ventriculoatrial shunt*: Potential cardiac overload, septicemia, or pulmonary embolism. <br> **Objective.** Early detection of complications. <br> **Timing.** 5 days (cardiac overload); continuing. | **a.** Check apical rate (not radial pulse rate). <br> **b. New shunts.** Keep patient flat in bed for *at least* 24 hr. <br> –Raise head of bed gradually as ordered by dr. <br> **c. If shunt is revised.** Head of bed can be elevated immediately after return from PAR. <br> **d.** Observe for continually and report to dr *stat*: <br> –Shortness of breath. <br> –Tachycardia. <br> –Sudden rise in temperature. <br> –Chest pains. <br> –Pulmonary edema. <br> –Cardiac arrhythmia. |

continued

| Usual Problems/Objectives/Timing | Nursing Orders |
|---|---|
| **5.** *Infants* (occasionally evident in older children also): Potential lethargy, irritability, and vomiting, and severely depressed fontanelle, due to too-rapid decrease in CSF pressure.<br><br>**Objective.** Early detection of severe drop in CSF pressure.<br><br>**Timing.** 3–4 days. | **a.** Check level of fontanelle each time you record vital signs and before feeding.<br><br>**b.** If fontanelle is markedly depressed, lower the head of the bed (quietly) and place infant flat. Notify dr (danger of subdural hemorrhage if sudden change in pressure).<br><br>**c.** As fontanelle becomes less depressed, raise head of bed gradually as ordered.<br><br>**d.** Pick up the infant for feeding, but *do not hold him upright*. |
| **6.** Potential increased intracranial pressure postoperatively due to blockage of shunt.<br><br>**Objective.** No increase in intracranial pressure.<br><br>**Timing.** Until discharge. | **a.** Be alert for signs/symptoms of blockage.<br><br>**b.** Elevate head of bed 30 degrees unless otherwise ordered.<br><br>**c.** *See* Careplan 71: Increased Intracranial Pressure. |
| **7.** Potential blockage of shunt.<br><br>**Objective.** Shunt is patent.<br><br>**Timing.** Until discharge. | **a.** Record parents' observations when their child's shunt appears to be blocking. (Each child reacts differently.) Keep these records available for subsequent admissions: attach them to nursing records in chart.<br><br>**b.** Be alert to the signs/symptoms of impending blockage, in general (*see* Careplan 71: Increased Intracranial Pressure) and in this particular patient.<br><br>**c.** If you think blockage might be impending, record vital signs more frequently.<br><br>**d.** If incision or pump site is swelling, report to dr.<br><br>**e.** Pump the shunt only if ordered by dr:<br><br>–Depress pump with forefinger firmly and quickly. Leave finger on pump to feel refilling. (If shunt is working well, pump refills within seconds.)<br><br>–If pump is difficult to depress, do not force it; notify dr. |
| **8.** *Ventriculoperitoneal shunt*: Potential blockage by pressure of impacted feces.<br><br>**Objective.** Regular defecation.<br><br>**Timing.** Until discharge. | **a.** If it is still effective, institute child's usual routine for preventing constipation.<br><br>**b.** Record type and frequency of stools.<br><br>**c.** If the routine is not preventing constipation, devise a new one:<br><br>–Increase roughage in diet (if tolerated).<br><br>–Try different laxatives.<br><br>**d.** If child has passed no stool for 2 days, insert glycerin suppository.<br><br>**e.** If a suppository is not effective, give enema as ordered.<br><br>**f.** If enema is not effective, notify dr. |
| **9.** Potential wound infection.<br><br>**Objective.** No infection. | **a.** Do not give tub baths or shampoo hair until sutures are removed.<br><br>**b.** Do not change the first dressing until ordered (usual- |

| Usual Problems/Objectives/Timing | Nursing Orders |
|---|---|
| **9. (Continued).**<br><br>**Timing.** Until discharge. | ly day 5); then, change gauze dressings daily as ordered.<br><br>**c.** When changing dressings, do not cleanse incision (this would increase risk of wound dehiscence and infection). Attach dry gauze with tape that leaves no sticky residue (e.g., Blenderm, Scotch Tape/Sellotape).<br><br>**d.** Check incision(s) frequently. If swelling or discharging occurs, report to dr. |
| **10.** Possible concomitant illness.<br><br>**Objective.** Early differentiation from impending blockage of shunt.<br><br>**Timing.** Until discharge. | *See* nursing order 7(a). |
| **11.** Parents'/patient's concern about management of home care and follow-up.<br><br>**Objectives.** Parents/patient voice concerns. Patient making plans to take part in age-appropriate activities (within limits imposed by disease). Parents/patient demonstrate ability to perform care required at home.<br><br>**Timing.** Before discharge. | **a.** Designated nurse to explain discharge instructions. Give parents/patient Information for Parents of Children with Neurosurgical Shunts (p. 208) and reinforce dr's explanations about treatment, etc.<br><br>**b.** Parents must display understanding of key points in home care:<br><br>–Recognition of signs of increased intracranial pressure.<br><br>–Prevention or management of constipation (ventriculoperitoneal shunts).<br><br>–How and when to contact dr.<br><br>–How to pump the shunt (if this has been ordered by dr). |
| **12.** Potential discouragement of parents/patient, because of frequent admissions to hospital.<br><br>**Objectives.** Parents/patient understand reason for admissions, voice concerns, and are willing to make any necessary changes in home-care routines.<br><br>**Timing.** By discharge. | **a.** Whenever possible, assign patient to same ward each time and assign nurses who know family members from previous admissions.<br><br>**b.** Explore patient's/parents' understanding of reason for this admission.<br><br>**c.** *Listen to patient's/parents' concerns.* Show interest.<br><br>**d.** Ensure that the dr speaks to patient/parents regularly and frequently.<br><br>**e.** If there are nonmedical problems, confer with a social worker, public health nurse, etc., and/or notify appropriate community agencies (e.g., school), p.r.n.<br><br>**f.** Reinforce explanations/instructions for home care.<br><br>**g.** Stress even the slightest progress and encourage patient's independence. |

# Information for Parents of Children with Neurosurgical Shunts

A small tube has been placed in your child's brain to drain off excess fluid to another part of the body. This is called a shunt.

### Pump

If your child's shunt has a pump, this is apparent as a small lump under the scalp. (It does not show when the hair has grown back.) The lump should be handled gently, and only during washing unless otherwise instructed by your doctor. Teach your child not to touch the lump.

### Activity

Your child can resume normal activities, unless otherwise advised by your doctor. He should be treated as any other child, emotionally and physically.

### Signs that the shunt may not be working:

Increasing drowsiness (most important sign).
Vomiting. Headache. Irritability. Restlessness.
Swelling around the pump or tubing, or persistent bulging of the fontanelle (the soft area of a baby's head).

If your child is drowsy and vomiting, keep him lying on his side. *If the signs persist*, notify your family dr, or telephone the hospital and ask for the neurosurgical resident on call.

The commonest reasons for malfunction of a shunt are tiny particles of tissue clogging the tube, kinking of the tube, or pressure on the tube (for example, when constipation expands the bowel).

Also, as your child grows taller, the tube may be pulled out of place; this is another reason why he should have regular appointments for follow-up care.

### Positioning

Your doctor may want you to elevate your child's head about 30 degrees (on pillows) for sleeping. Check with the charge nurse on the ward or with your doctor.

### Sutures

There are three common types of sutures: silk, wire, and clips.

These sutures will be removed before your child returns home. It is safe to wash over the suture line 1 week after removal of the sutures.

**If your child has a peritoneal shunt,** *you must not allow him to become constipated.* The dilation (expansion) of the bowel may squeeze off the shunt tubing.

### Diet

Add plenty of fruit (e.g., rhubarb, prunes, or apples), vegetables, and bran cereals to your child's diet to help ensure regularity. Avoid white rice, rice cereals, and pasta.

### Laxatives

Give your child a mild laxative (e.g., milk of magnesia) if he has not passed a stool for 2 days.

### Enema

If the laxative is not effective, and your child has not passed a stool for 3 days, give him an enema. (You can buy disposable pediatric Fleet® enemas at drug stores.)

**Goals for Discharge or Maintenance**
See Objectives.

| Usual Problems/Objectives/Timing | Nursing Orders |
|---|---|
| **1.** Potential asphyxia due to paralysis of breathing muscles.<br><br>**Objective.** Adequate artificial ventilation is maintained.<br><br>**Timing.** Until normal breathing is restored. | **a.** *See* Careplan 101: Older Infants and Children on a Ventilator.<br><br>**b.** Ensure that low-pressure alarm is connected to the ventilator and that hand ventilation equipment is at bedside.<br><br>**c.** Place sign on patient's bed, *clearly visible*, indicating that paralyzing drugs are in use.<br><br>**d.** Ensure that patient's respiration is maintained by ventilator or manually *at all times*. |
| **2.** Potential aggravation of underlying respiratory problem, due to immobility and inability to cough.<br><br>**Objective.** No further respiratory problems.<br><br>**Timing.** Until effects of blocking agent wear off. | **a.** Turn patient at least every 2 hr (side, back, side) using log-roll method.<br><br>**b.** Do deep endotracheal and nasopharyngeal suctioning q1h and p.r.n. |
| **3.** Urinary retention and constipation due to lack of voluntary muscle control.<br><br>**Objectives.** Patient's bladder is emptied completely every 2–3 hr. Regular evacuation of stool is established and maintained.<br><br>**Timing.** Until effects of blocking agent wear off. | **a.** Maintain urinary catheter drainage. (*See* Careplan 148: Urinary Catheter, Indwelling.)<br><br>**b.** If no catheter is in place, manually express patient's bladder every 2–3 hr. Care must be taken not to use too much pressure (patient cannot complain of pain).<br><br>**c.** If paralyzing drugs are to be in use for several days, obtain order for suppository or laxative to be given p.r.n. |
| **4.** Potential damage to spinal cord, muscles, tissues, and joints due to lack of muscle tone.<br><br>**Objectives.** No spinal cord deficit or injury. Skin is healthy and intact.<br><br>**Timing.** Until patient is fully mobile. | **a.** Use log-rolling technique when moving patient.<br><br>**b.** *Do not pick infant up by heels when changing diapers or bed linen.*<br><br>**c.** Consult the physical therapist about positioning patient.<br><br>**d.** Consult dr about a suitable program of exercises. (These may be contraindicated if patient has increased intracranial pressure.) |
| **5.** Potential pressure sores and/or skin breakdown due to unrelieved pressure on skin and underlying tissues.<br><br>**Objective.** Skin clear and intact.<br><br>**Timing.** Until patient is fully mobile. | **a.** Turn patient q2h (side-back-side) unless contraindicated.<br><br>**b.** Nurse on alternating-pressure mattress, plastic bubble-sheeting, or sheepskin, together with flannelette sheets.<br><br>**c.** Keep skin clear and dry.<br><br>**d.** Observe pressure points closely for redness. |
| **6.** Potential dryness of eyes and corneal abrasions due to decreased or no tearing.<br><br>**Objective.** No corneal abrasions.<br><br>**Timing.** Until normal tearing resumes. | **a.** Use ocular lubricant (drops or ointment) as ordered.<br><br>**b.** Keep patient's eyes closed. Use transparent tape to keep eyelids positioned together. |

**209**

continued

| Usual Problems/Objectives/Timing | Nursing Orders |
|---|---|
| **7.** Patient anxious and frightened by inability to move and breathe on own, and frustrated by inability to communicate.<br><br>**Objectives.** Patient appears less anxious and is able to rest. Patient's needs are communicated effectively.<br><br>**Timing.** Until effects of blocking agent wear off. | **a.** Explain to patient that:<br>–This condition is temporary.<br>–The machine will do the "breathing" for him.<br>–A nurse or dr will always be at his side.<br>–The drug will not affect his consciousness or thinking.<br><br>**b.** Explain all procedures and orient patient to time and place at regular intervals.<br><br>**c.** When speaking to the patient, open his eyes so he can see who is talking to him, then close them again.<br><br>**d.** Provide diversions (e.g., soft music, reading a story), if not contraindicated (e.g., by increased intracranial pressure).<br><br>**e.** Ensure that only appropriate conversation is made within patient's hearing. (Always assume that the patient is awake.)<br><br>**f.** Assess level of patient's anxiety and discomfort (increased heart rate and BP, skin flushing, sweating). Consult dr about giving sedation (usually a continuous morphine infusion, with diazepam p.r.n.). Be aware that, although the patient is paralyzed, he is able to feel pain and has discomfort due to not being able to change position, stretch, or relax muscles. |
| **8.** Parental anxiety.<br><br>**Objectives.** Parents are able to cope with explanations of the treatment and can support their child.<br><br>**Timing.** Until effects of blocking agent wear off and patient's normal breathing restored. | **a.** Explain to parents about the drug (why it is being given, how it works, how it will help their child). Reassure them that the paralysis will be only temporary.<br><br>**b.** Reassure parents frequently that their child may be conscious and fully aware of their presence.<br><br>**c.** Encourage parents to speak to their child in a normal manner, hold his hand, stroke his head, and read stories to him. |
| **9.** Potential ineffectiveness of therapy due to inappropriate level of drug.<br><br>**Objective.** Ordered drug level is maintained.<br><br>**Timing.** Until treatment is completed. | **a.** Administer drug as ordered (usually i.v., pushed slowly). Dr gives the initial dose.<br><br>**b.** Be aware of side effects of drugs in use. Examples include:<br>–Pancuronium bromide—slight tachycardia and increased BP for a few minutes after injection.<br>–Succinylcholine—bradycardia, tachycardia, cardiac arrhythmia.<br><br>**c.** Observe patient closely. If patient's own breathing efforts interfere with the ventilator before the next scheduled dose, notify dr (patient may need an increase in dose or frequency). |

**Goals for Discharge or Maintenance**
See Objectives.

| Usual Problems/Objectives/Timing | Nursing Orders |
|---|---|
| **1.** Raised intracranial pressure (ICP) and low cerebral perfusion pressure (CPP) secondary to cerebral edema.<br><br>**Objective.** ICP below 20 mm Hg or as ordered.<br><br>**Timing.** Until cerebral edema subsides and subarachnoid (Richmond) bolt is discontinued. | **a.** Maintain patient on controlled ventilation as ordered. (*See* Careplan 101: Older Infants and Children on a Ventilator.)<br><br>**b.** Do minimal suctioning of endotracheal (ET) tube q1–2h. Maintain ordered ICP with hand ventilation equipment while suctioning.<br><br>**c.** Hyperventilate patient with hand ventilation equipment during rises in ICP.<br><br>**d.** Monitor arterial blood-gases q4h and p.r.n.<br><br>**e.** Monitor end tidal $CO_2$.<br><br>**f.** Monitor ventilator settings, fractional concentration of inspired gases, and respirations, q1h.<br><br>**g.** Administer Na bicarbonate as ordered if acidosis is present.<br><br>**h.** Check calibration and balance transducer to atmospheric pressure q8h and p.r.n. Set alarms as ordered.<br><br>**i.** Raise head of bed 30 degrees and position patient's head and neck in good alignment (to promote venous drainage from the head).<br><br>**j.** Monitor ICP closely:<br>– Observe for elevated ICP readings and waveforms (spikes and plateaus).<br>– If spikes are above 15 mm Hg (normal range is 0–10 mm Hg), notify dr *stat*, hand ventilate patient, and monitor $pCO_2$.<br><br>**k.** *If ICP is unstable*, do not turn or disturb patient. Avoid activities that may increase ICP.<br><br>**l.** Organize care to allow periods of rest between treatments and consider effect of treatment on ICP.<br><br>**m.** Administer drugs as ordered; monitor levels and side effects. For example:<br>– Barbiturates (hypotension).<br>– Steroids (GI bleeding).<br>– Sedatives (hypotension).<br>– Diuretics (rebound phenomenon).<br><br>**n.** If decompression has been done to control ICP, observe head dressing for tightness.<br><br>**o.** Maintain normothermia. Monitor rectal temperature continuously if patient is on hypothermia. |
| **2.** Potential respiratory problems (e.g., aspiration, asphyxia) due to paralysis of breathing muscles by neuromuscular blocking agents. | **a.** *See* Careplan 78: Paralysis, by Neuromuscular Blocking Agents.<br><br>**b.** If secretions are thick and difficult to suction, consult dr about: |

211

continued

| Usual Problems/Objectives/Timing | Nursing Orders |
|---|---|
| **2. (Continued).**<br><br>**Objectives.** No respiratory problems or their early detection.<br><br>**Timing.** Until effects of blocking agent wear off. | −Instilling N saline into ET tube before suctioning.<br>−Sending specimen of secretions for bacterial and virology cultures.<br>**c.** Inflate and deflate ET cuff as ordered by dr. |
| **3.** Potential fluid and electrolyte imbalance due to use of diuretics, hypoglycemia, and fluid restrictions.<br><br>**Objective.** Fluid and electrolyte balance is maintained.<br><br>**Timing.** Ongoing. | **a.** Assist dr with insertion of arterial and CVP lines.<br>**b.** Monitor heart rate, BP, CVP, and CPP, q1h.<br>**c.** Maintain strict intake and output record. (Minimum urine output expected = 0.5–1.0 ml/kg/hr.)<br>**d.** Observe for signs/symptoms of dehydration. If hypovolemia is present, give fresh frozen plasma as ordered.<br>**e.** Maintain electrolyte and blood-glucose levels as ordered. |
| **4.** Potential bleeding disorders and hypoglycemia due to liver dysfunction.<br><br>**Objective.** Normal PT, PTT, and blood-glucose levels maintained.<br><br>**Timing.** Ongoing. | **a.** Assist dr with liver biopsy. Observe for bleeding at the site and for evidence of internal bleeding.<br>**b.** Monitor blood chemistry and hematology as ordered, i.e.:<br>−Ammonia, SGOT, albumin, bilirubin (total and direct) levels.<br>−Alkaline phosphotase, glucose electrolytes.<br>−Drug screening for ASA.<br>−CBC, PT, PTT, and platelet count.<br>**c.** Give fresh frozen plasma and vitamin K (to correct clotting disorders).<br>−Observe puncture sites for prolonged bleeding.<br>−Check NG tube drainage for presence of blood and give NG antacids as ordered by dr.<br>**d.** Maintain glucose at 8–11 mmol/l. Give extra dextrose as ordered.<br>**e.** Give neomycin by NG tube or by enema q6h, as ordered. |
| **5.** Patient anxious and fearful because of strange environment and loss of control.<br><br>**Objective.** Patient appears less anxious.<br><br>**Timing.** As soon as possible. | **a.** Always assume that patient is awake and understands what is being said.<br>**b.** Reassure patient that someone will be at the bedside at all times.<br>**c.** Orient patient to time and place, etc.<br>**d.** Explain all procedures while they are being done.<br>**e.** Have parents bring in favorite toy or security object.<br>**f.** Provide soft music as appropriate. |
| **6.** Parental anxiety due to the severity of their child's illness and possibly poor prognosis.<br><br>**Objectives.** Parents express their concerns and are able to cope with information given.<br><br>**Timing.** As soon as possible. | **a.** Keep parents well informed of child's progress.<br>**b.** Ensure that dr speaks to parents at least once daily. Reinforce dr's explanations.<br>**c.** Encourage parents to talk to their child and assist in procedures such as mouth care and bathing. |

| Usual Problems/Objectives/Timing | Nursing Orders |
|---|---|
| 6. (Continued). | **d.** Involve other members of the health team as appropriate (e.g., social worker, chaplain). |
| | **e.** Explain usual routines (as appropriate) for weaning child off the ventilator, paralyzing drugs, and other therapy. |
| | **f.** Ensure that parents know when plans are made to transfer patient from ICU to a ward. |

Spina Bifida, Paraplegic
(Preschoolers and Older Children)

## Goals for Discharge or Maintenance

**I.** Patient and family members understand the condition and will continue necessary adaptations to or follow prescribed changes in their life-style.

**II.** Patient maintains or increases his prehospitalization degree of independence.

**III.** Patient develops or maintains social relationships.

| Usual Problems/Objectives/Timing | Nursing Orders |
|---|---|
| **1.** *If patient has a shunt.* | **a.** *See* Careplan 77: Neurosurgical Shunt.<br><br>**b.** Be alert to the signs/symptoms of increase in intra-cranial pressure, induced by blockage of the shunt. |
| **2.** *When exercise and mobility are unusually restricted (e.g., after surgery):* Potential decrease in muscle tone of upper limbs and torso; potential decrease in muscle tone of lower limbs, and contractures.<br><br>**Objectives.** Usual muscle tone maintained; no contractures.<br><br>**Timing.** Throughout hospital stay. | **a.** *See* Careplan 13: Prolonged Immobilization.<br><br>**b.** Notify rehabilitation department.<br><br>**c.** Follow the individual exercise program set up by the physical therapist.<br><br>**d.** Encourage mobilization and resumption of activities *as soon as possible* after surgery or illness. |
| **3.** Potential skin problems and/or obesity due to inappropriate diet. (Wrong foods, treats, or extra food given to a patient to compensate for the handicap aggravate skin problems, such as acne, delay healing of pressure sores, and induce obesity.)<br><br>**Objectives.** Patient/parents understand the need for restricted diet and patient adheres to it. Patient's skin clear and weight controlled.<br><br>**Timing.** Continuing. | **a.** Ensure that patient/parents understand why the diet is necessary and can follow the instructions. Consult dietitian if necessary.<br><br>**b.** Push fluid intake:<br><br>2–5 yr, at least 1000 ml/24 hr.<br>6–12 yr, at least 1500 ml/24 hr.<br>13 yr and over, 2000 ml/24 hr.<br><br>**c.** Encourage patient to eat greater proportion of bulk foods (fresh fruit, vegetables, and bran cereals).<br><br>**d.** Limit amount of milk or substitute skimmed milk. *See* nursing order 4(b).<br><br>**e.** Restrict foods high in calories, sugar, or salt (chocolate, candies, chips, etc.). |
| **4.** Potential renal calculi resulting from the restricted diet and prolonged immobilization.<br><br>**Objective.** No renal calculi.<br><br>**Timing.** Continuing. | **a.** Observe and report signs/symptoms of renal calculi:<br><br>–Cloudy urine.<br>–Hematuria.<br>–Pyuria.<br>–Fever and chills.<br>–Skin gray and sweaty.<br>–Nausea and vomiting.<br><br>**b.** Restrict dairy products in diet (they precipitate formation of calcium or phosphorus stones).<br><br>**c.** If patient passes a stone, save it for laboratory examination.<br><br>**d.** If patient experiences pain, check with dr about analgesic. |
| **5.** Potential urinary infection due to abnormal or absent innervation of bladder.<br><br>**Objectives.** Bladder emptied regularly; urine clear, with normal odor. | **a.** Continue home methods to empty bladder (e.g., manual expression of urine by patient while sitting on toilet), unless ordered otherwise by dr.<br><br>**b.** Express urine or catheterize at stated intervals, whether patient is wet or dry. |

| Usual Problems/Objectives/Timing | Nursing Orders |
|---|---|
| **5. (Continued).**<br>**Timing.** Continuing. | **c.** If intermittent catheterization is being ordered for the first time, teach parents/patient and observe them during procedure.<br>**d.** If urine is cloudy or foul-smelling or difficult to express, notify dr. |
| **6.** Potential constipation due to decreased peristalsis and poor muscle tone.<br>**Objective.** Patient **(a)** establishes or **(b)** maintains regular evacuation of stool.<br>**Timing.**<br>**a.** By discharge.<br>**b.** Continuing. | **a.** Institute child's usual routine for preventing constipation, if it is still effective, or devise a new one (e.g., more roughage in diet, different laxative).<br>**b.** If necessary, disimpact bowel or give enema as ordered by dr. |
| **7.** Problems related to lack of sensation.<br>**Objective.** No problems.<br>**Timing.** Continuing. | **a.** Examine the child carefully and regularly, looking for these potential problems. |
| **a.** Potential skin excoriation due to dribbling of urine, fecal soiling, and/or poor circulation.<br>**Objective.** Skin clear and intact. | **a.** Change patient promptly when wet or soiled. Check at least q2h.<br>**b.** Give daily tub baths.<br>**c.** If skin is breaking down:<br>–Give patient sitz baths t.i.d.<br>–Expose buttocks to air whenever possible (usually during rest periods and at night).<br>–Instruct patient to avoid sitting for longer than 1 hr.<br>–Use a Bradford frame with aperture p.r.n. |
| **b.** Potential skin breakdown due to friction from braces or to peripheral ischemia.<br>**Objectives.** No pressure sores; early detection of ischemia. | **a.** *See* Careplan 152: Braces.<br>**b.** Throughout day, q4h: remove braces and inspect skin (especially toes and feet) for ischemia.<br>**c.** If skin breakdown occurs, remove brace until skin has healed.<br>**d.** If ischemia develops, notify dr. |
| **c.** Potential injuries.<br>**Objective.** No injuries. | Teach patient/family to avoid hazards:<br>**a.** Check temperature of bath water.<br>**b.** Do not use safety pins or heating pads; use caution when radiators are in use.<br>**c.** Avoid constricting clothing and tight-fitting shoes.<br>**d.** Soak toes before cutting nails; cut toenails *straight across*.<br>**e.** Reinforce these instructions before patient is discharged. |
| **8.** Patient is dependent on others, due to handicap and/or lack of motivation or stimulation. | **a.** On admission, obtain information about child's usual activities at home. Incorporate these activities into plan of care. |

continued

| Usual Problems/Objectives/Timing | Nursing Orders |
|---|---|
| **8. (Continued).**<br><br>**Objective.** Patient is independent within limit set by disability.<br><br>**Timing.** Before discharge. | **b.** Encourage patient to maintain independence (e.g., by dressing himself, getting into and out of wheelchair and tub) and praise his efforts (e.g., in doing self-catheterization).<br><br>**c.** Allow sufficient time for patient to perform tasks; praise his achievements.<br><br>**d.** Plan activities appropriate for age (school work, recreation, and socializing with peers). |
| **9.** If patient is not on intermittent catheterization, potential embarrassment about incontinence, urine-smell of clothes and appliances, etc.<br><br>**Objective.** Patient can manage satisfactory personal hygiene.<br><br>**Timing.** Before discharge. | **a.** Consult other nurses who have looked after similarly handicapped patients.<br><br>**b.** Discuss problems with patient and family, and help them to devise a routine to keep him dry. (It may be necessary to try several methods.)<br><br>**c.** Stress the need for washable, loose-fitting clothes.<br><br>**d.** Instruct patient/parents to wash appliances and rinse clothes in vinegar, to reduce odor.<br><br>**e.** Incorporate drinks in diet that reduce odor of urine (e.g., cranberry juice). |
| **10.** Depression due to low self-esteem and fancied or real social unacceptability. | *See* Careplan 35: Depression in Adolescence. |
| **11.** Parents/patient concerned about home care and follow-up (e.g., costly brace adjustments, transportation).<br><br>**Objective.** Parents/patient express concerns, are helped to overcome them, and are making plans for home care.<br><br>**Timing.** Before discharge. | **Designated nurse:**<br><br>**a.** Consult dr about follow-up.<br><br>**b.** Listen to parents'/patient's concerns.<br><br>**c.** Ensure that parents/patient have written instructions and understand them.<br><br>**d.** Ensure that parents are referred to appropriate agencies for assistance with braces, transportation, schooling, etc. |

**Goals for Discharge or Maintenance**
See Objectives.

| Usual Problems/Objectives/Timing | Nursing Orders |
|---|---|
| **1.** Potential additional hemorrhage.<br><br>**Objective.** Risk of further hemorrhage minimized, or early detection if it does occur.<br><br>**Timing.** Until surgery. | **a.** Observe patient constantly.<br><br>**b.** Place child in quiet room, free of distractions, and darkened, if required or if he requests this. Restrict visiting to parents only.<br><br>**c.** Place child flat or in low semi-Fowler's position (elevate head of bed further only if ordered by dr).<br><br>**d.** Assess neurologic status and vital signs, q1h or as ordered by dr (TPR, BP, state of consciousness, pupil reactions, and movement of extremities).<br><br>**e.** Report any sudden increase in headache, neck stiffness, and/or photophobia.<br><br>**f.** Keep child inactive in bed and as quiet as possible, even if he appears well.<br><br>**g.** If child is restless, try to determine the reason (e.g., headache, photophobia) and ask dr about sedation order.<br><br>**h.** Increase child's activities only on dr's orders (these may include TV or radio in room, books or puzzles).<br><br>**i.** Discuss diet with dr (i.v., clear fluids, or soft foods).<br><br>**j.** Avoid suctioning if possible.<br><br>**k.** Prevent gagging, choking, or straining with cough. Prevent straining with bowel movements: ask dr about laxative to prevent constipation. |
| **2.** Headache, neck stiffness, and photophobia.<br><br>**Objective.** Minimal pain and discomfort.<br><br>**Timing.** Until surgery. | **a.** Ensure that child has as much rest as possible.<br><br>**b.** Speak softly.<br><br>**c.** Inform child before turning up lights. Explain about light before checking pupils.<br><br>**d.** Give age-appropriate explanations of discomfort. |
| **3.** Parents/child anxious about child's present condition and impending surgery.<br><br>**Objectives.** Parents express their concerns to the staff and communicate positively with the child. Child evidences minimal fear and anxiety.<br><br>**Timing.** Until surgery. | **a.** Reinforce explanations given by dr and explain all procedures and tests to patient/parents.<br><br>**b.** Reassure patient and parents that a nurse will be present at all times.<br><br>**c.** Encourage parents to help in child's care and participate in diversions (reading stories, doing puzzles). |
| **4.** Boredom and frustration due to restriction of activity.<br><br>**Objective.** Patient demonstrates minimal boredom and frustration.<br><br>**Timing.** Until surgery. | **a.** Reinforce explanations of need for quiet.<br><br>**b.** Provide diversions with gentle activities (e.g., read stories, play quiet games, provide soft music).<br><br>**c.** Provide a radio; if patient is allowed TV, ask about favorite programs. |
| **5.** Potential hemiplegia, increased intracranial pressure, dysphasia, vision defects, and/or seizures. | *See* appropriate careplans. |
| **6.** *Pre-operatively and postoperatively.* | *See* Careplan 76: Neurosurgery, Major: General Care. |

# Careplan 82    Eye Surgery

**Goals for Discharge or Maintenance**
Parents describe home care accurately and agree to comply with instructions.

| Usual Problems/Objectives/Timing | Nursing Orders |
|---|---|
| **1.** *Pre-operatively.* | **a.** *See* Careplan 17: Pre-operative Care, General.<br><br>**b.** Explain to parents/child:<br>  –There may be some bloody discharge from the eye(s) postoperatively.<br>  –Splint jackets (elbow restraints) may be used to prevent patient from touching eyes.<br>  –The eye(s) may be covered with a dressing or patch.<br><br>**c.** If eye(s) to be covered, have patient practice wearing patch(es) and learn to identify designated nurse by voice.<br><br>**d.** **Young child.** Demonstrate eye-patching on a doll or teddy bear. |
| **2.** Parents/patient worried about possible change in vision, eye movements, etc., postoperatively.<br><br>**Objectives.** Parents/patient are aware of the expected outcome and seem able to cope with the information.<br><br>**Timing.** As soon as possible. | **a.** Ensure that parents/child understand the ophthalmologist's explanation of the surgery and expected outcome.<br><br>**b.** Explain:<br>  –Swelling, bruising, red sclera.<br>  –Potential blood-stained tears.<br><br>**c.** Be available when they want to talk about their concerns. Be supportive (not judgmental), particularly if injury or delay in seeking advice necessitated the surgery.<br><br>**d.** Ensure that supportive services (social worker, etc.) are available to parents if required.<br><br>**e.** If relevant, *see* Careplan 85: Vision Defects. |
| **3.** *Postoperatively.* | *See* Careplan 21: Postoperative Care, General.<br>  –Follow dr's orders for eye medication, removal of patch(es), and cleansing of eye. |
| **4.** Potential injury.<br><br>**Objective.** No injury.<br><br>**Timing.** Until discharge. | **a.** Use splint jackets to restrain young patients (to prevent them from rubbing their eyes) until child is aware of surroundings and is cooperative.<br><br>**b.** If both eyes are patched, side-rails must remain up when no one is supervising the patient. These periods should be as brief as possible. Provide assistance with ambulation. Have call-bell *within reach.* |
| **5.** Apprehension and potential boredom while bilateral eye-patches are in place. | *See* Careplan 83: Hyphema, nursing orders for problems 2 and 3. |
| **6.** Potential mismanagement at home, due to lack of knowledge of treatment.<br><br>**Objectives.** Parents state willingness to continue prescribed care and demonstrate it correctly. | **a.** Teach parents the importance of handwashing and the correct technique for instilling eye drops or ointment and cleansing eye(s).<br><br>**b.** If child must wear eye-patch or shield, teach correct application. |

**219**

continued

| Usual Problems/Objectives/Timing | Nursing Orders |
|---|---|
| **6. (Continued).**<br>　**Timing.** Before discharge. | **c.** Reinforce dr's instructions about activity limitations (e.g., when child can return to school, avoidance of contact sports and swimming until seen by dr).<br>**d.** Ensure that parents/patient have written instructions for home care and follow-up appointments. |

**Goals for Discharge or Maintenance**
See Objectives.

| Usual Problems/Objectives/Timing | Nursing Orders |
|---|---|
| **1.** Potential recurrent bleeding due to restlessness or overactivity.<br><br>**Objective.** No recurrence of bleeding.<br><br>**Timing.** 7 days. | **a.** Maintain patient on bed rest as ordered by dr.<br>  –Head can be raised on pillow unless contraindicated.<br>  –Patient can participate in quiet activities and watch TV *only* if approved by dr.<br>  –Patient can sit up to eat. Identify tray contents and position (e.g., milk is at 2 o'clock).<br>**b.** Place call-bell within easy reach.<br>**c.** If patient is restless, try to determine cause (e.g., fear of dark or pain). *See also* the nursing orders for problem 2. If necessary, ask dr about order for sedative/analgesic.<br>**d.** Notify dr *stat* if patient has severe pain. This may indicate raised intraorbital pressure due to another hemorrhage.<br>**e.** *Do not give ASA.* |
| *If both eyes are patched*<br>**2.** Apprehension due to bilateral patching, increased dependency, and injury.<br><br>**Objectives.** Patient appears to be comfortable. Patient and family members express fears and concerns.<br><br>**Timing.** 3 days. | **a.** Announce yourself when approaching patient.<br>**b.** Explain activities involving him or occurring around him.<br>**c.** Anticipate his needs.<br>**d.** Spend time with patient and family to allow them to express their concerns.<br>**e.** Reassure patient/parents that eye-patching is only temporary, and that dr will be checking the affected eye frequently.<br>**f.** Depending on patient's level of anxiety, consult dr about removing one of the eye-patches at mealtimes (this may help to calm and reassure patient). |
| **3.** Potential boredom due to lack of stimulation.<br><br>**Objective.** Patient is involved in organized program of stimulation.<br><br>**Timing.** 7 days. | **a.** Plan each day to provide stimulation centered on routine activities (what the patient can do for himself during feeding, bathing, bed-changing etc.).<br>**b.** Praise patient's involvement and accomplishments.<br>**c.** Plan diversions to stimulate patient to use his unaffected senses.<br>**Hearing.** For example, provide patient with a tape-recorder or radio; read or tell stories to patient.<br>**Touch.** For example, provide modeling clay or toys of various materials; touch or stroke patient when talking to him.<br>**Speech.** For example, provide puppet play or encourage him to talk to staff and other patients.<br>**Intellect.** For example, play guessing games or memory quizzes. |

221

continued

| Usual Problems/Objectives/Timing | Nursing Orders |
|---|---|
| **7. (Continued).** | **d.** Encourage parents to participate as much as possible. Child may be held for cuddles. |
| | **e.** Ask playroom volunteers to spend time with the child. |

# Careplan 84 — Retinal Detachment: Pre-operative and Postoperative Care for Vitrectomy

## Goals for Discharge or Maintenance
Parents/patient can cope with home care, including instillation of eye drops, and understand the importance of follow-up.

| Usual Problems/Objectives/Timing | Nursing Orders |
|---|---|
| **1.** *Pre-operatively.* | *See* Careplan 17: Pre-operative Care, General. |
| **2.** Anxiety about vision loss and outcome of surgery.<br><br>**Objectives.** Parents/patient express concerns and are able to cope with information given.<br><br>**Timing.** Before surgery. | **a.** Reinforce dr's explanations about surgery and usual postoperative care (e.g., unilateral or bilateral eye-patches, reduction in activity).<br><br>**b.** As appropriate, reassure about return of vision.<br><br>**c.** Orient patient to surroundings (room and people).<br><br>**d.** Keep bed-sides up (to offer security) and have call-bell within reach. |
| **3.** *Postoperatively.* | *See* Careplan 21: Postoperative Care, General. |
| **4.** Pain, especially if cryotherapy has been used.<br><br>**Objective.** Patient expresses reasonable comfort.<br><br>**Timing.** 2–3 weeks. | **a.** Assess patient's level of discomfort and give analgesic as ordered.<br><br>**b.** Maintain a quiet environment.<br><br>**c.** Instruct patient not to bend from the waist, lift heavy objects, make sudden movements, or sneeze or cough forcefully (if possible).<br><br>**d.** Instill eyedrops as ordered. Explain that there will be some discomfort; reassure patient.<br><br>**e.** Encourage patient to participate in quiet activities that are within limits of vision such as coloring, listening to stories/music. |
| **5.** Swelling of eyelids due to manipulation during surgery.<br><br>**Objective.** Some reduction in swelling.<br><br>**Timing.** By discharge. | **a.** Elevate head of bed 30 degrees.<br><br>**b.** Instruct patient to lie on unaffected side.<br><br>**c.** Consult dr about applying cold compresses to the affected eye.<br><br>**d.** Observe and record degree of swelling. Explain to parents/patient that some swelling of eyelids is to be expected for 10–12 days. |
| **6.** Photophobia due to dilation of pupil by atropine and swelling of the eye.<br><br>**Objective.** Gradually decreasing sensitivity to light.<br><br>**Timing.** By discharge. | **a.** Regulate lights so that they are dimmed. Increase exposure to light as tolerated.<br><br>**b.** Instruct patient to wear dark glasses as necessary if sensitivity persists. (Photophobia will remain to some extent for 2–3 weeks due to effect of atropine drops.) |
| **7.** Potential mismanagement of home care due to lack of knowledge.<br><br>**Objectives.** Parents/patient demonstrate confidence in doing eye care. They are willing to comply with home care and follow-up.<br><br>**Timing.** Before discharge. | **a.** Reinforce dr's instructions for home care and follow-up.<br><br>**b.** Explain to parents:<br><br>–Child may return to school but must not engage in gym or any rough activities for 3–4 weeks.<br><br>–Child may watch TV. |

223

continued

| Usual Problems/Objectives/Timing | Nursing Orders |
|---|---|
| **7. (Continued).** | **c.** Teach parents how to instill eye drops:<br>    –Wash hands thoroughly before starting.<br>    –Have child sit or lie down with head tilted back.<br>    –Retract the lower eyelid and have child look up (to inhibit the blinking reflex).<br>    –Drop the ordered amount of medication into the lower middle part of the eyelid (taking care not to contaminate the dropper by touching the eyelids).<br>    –Replace the eyedropper directly into bottle without touching the sides.<br>    –Close the child's eyelid gently (do not squeeze).<br>    –Use thumb to apply pressure to the inner canthus of the eye to prevent medication entering the lacrimal (tear) duct.<br>    –Use cotton fluff or tissue to wipe excess fluid from face.<br>**d.** If patient still has sensitivity to light, dark eye glasses may be used for a few days. *Eye shields should not be used.*<br>**e.** Ensure that parents have instructions for home care and follow-up appointments in writing and that they know whom to contact if they are concerned. |

## Goals for Discharge or Maintenance
**I.** Patient and family understand the type of defect, how it will be treated, etc.
**II.** Patient is independent in daily activities.

| Usual Problems/Objectives/Timing | Nursing Orders |
|---|---|
| **1.** Discomfort due to photophobia, blurred vision, and/ or diplopia.<br><br>**Obectives.** Patient appears comfortable, with relaxed facial expression; he reports clearing vision.<br><br>**Timing.** Before discharge. | **a.** Dim the lighting in patient's room.<br><br>**b.** Consult dr about use of sunglasses.<br><br>**c.** Cleanse patient's eyes with N saline p.r.n.<br><br>**d.** Patch eyes as ordered by dr.<br><br>**e.** Observe and report abnormal head posturing. (This may indicate that the patient is accommodating for visual field defects.)<br><br>**f.** Provide listening diversions (e.g., radio, records, reading to patient) and encourage him to explore his sense of touch. |
| **2.** Potential corneal ulceration due to decreased sensation and loss of corneal reflex.<br><br>**Objective.** No corneal ulceration.<br><br>**Timing.** Return of corneal reflex; or, by discharge. | **a.** Prevent patient from rubbing eyes. Restrain him p.r.n. If rubbing persists, notify dr: eye-patching may be ordered.<br><br>**b.** Apply eye lubricant as ordered by dr.<br><br>**c.** Assess patient's level of discomfort. Consult dr about giving analgesic, p.r.n. |
| **3.** Fear and anxiety over visual field defects and loss of vision.<br><br>**Objectives.** Patient is reasonably independent, sustains no injuries, socializes with other patients, and (when appropriate) visits other areas of hospital.<br><br>**Timing.** By discharge. | **a.** Designated nurses to establish teaching of patient and family and to discuss their feelings and concerns with them.<br><br>**b.** Assess child's capabilities and anticipate his needs.<br><br>**c.** Announce yourself when approaching child.<br><br>**d.** Explain all procedures fully to patient/parents.<br><br>**e.** Orient child to his surroundings and do not rearrange furniture.<br><br>**f.** Encourage child to participate in normal activities.<br><br>**g.** Instruct child to wear shoes or firm slippers when up.<br><br>**h.** When walking with a blind patient, let him hold your elbow so he is slightly behind you and can sense your movements.<br><br>**i.** At meals, identify tray contents and location (e.g., milk is at 2 o'clock).<br><br>**j.** **Bitemporal hemianopia** *(tunnel vision).* Arrange belongings, food, etc., in center of child's vision. When child is up, teach him to turn head from side to side frequently so he can scan environment.<br><br>**k.** **Homonymous hemianopia** *(one-sided vision in both eyes).* Arrange belongings to side of child's vision. Avoid approaching child from blind side. When child is up, teach him to turn head slightly to blind side, to increase visual field and so he can scan environment.<br><br>**l.** Contact rehabilitation medicine or neuroophthalmology department for information about special aids for blind children. |

**Goals for Discharge or Maintenance**
Parents understand instructions and can cope with home care.

| Usual Problems/Objectives/Timing | Nursing Orders |
|---|---|
| **1.** *Pre-operatively.* | *See* Careplan 17: Pre-operative Care, General.<br>**a.** Be aware of possible hearing defect: speak *en face* or to the patient's "good" side.<br>**b.** Explain to patient/parents that:<br>  –Some hair will be removed from around the ear.<br>  –A dressing will be placed over the ear, and a bandage around the head will hold it in place.<br>  –Patient may be dizzy and/or nauseated for a few days.<br>**c.** Shampoo patient's hair; then use elastic bands to secure it on top of head or, if hair is long, braid it.<br>**d.** *If patient has not had an audiogram within the past week,* notify dr. |
| **2.** *Postoperatively.* | *See* Careplan 21: Postoperative Care, General. |
| **3.** Potential infection if dressing too loose; potential pain if dressing too tight.<br><br>**Objective.** Dressing is intact and not creating pain from pressure.<br><br>**Timing.** Until dressing is removed. | **a.** Notify dr if dressing is too loose or too tight (dr will adjust it).<br>**b.** Instruct patient not to touch or remove the dressing, drain, or packing. Use restraint jacket with splinted elbows p.r.n. |
| **4.** Potential facial paralysis resulting from damage to seventh cranial nerve.<br><br>**Objective.** Early detection of damage to seventh cranial nerve.<br><br>**Timing.** By discharge. | **a.** Observe for facial weakness on same side as operation. (Ask child to smile, clench teeth, and blink.) If present, notify dr.<br>**b.** Report increasing facial edema; dressing may need to be loosened by dr. |
| **5.** Potential mismanagement of home care, due to parents' lack of understanding.<br><br>**Objective.** Parents describe discharge instructions correctly.<br><br>**Timing.** By discharge. | **a.** Reinforce dr's instructions for home care and follow-up appointment(s):<br>  –If patient is discharged with dressing and bandage over ear, these must be left on until dr removes them.<br>  –If no dressings are in place, the ear and the area surrounding the incision must be kept clean and dry.<br>  –The patient must not shower or shampoo his hair until this is approved by dr (usually 10–14 days postoperatively).<br>  –Before shower or shampoo, the child's ear must be plugged with petrolatum-coated cotton-wool.<br>  –When patient shampoos hair, his ear must be plugged (see above) and his head tilted so water cannot enter the affected ear.<br>  –If incision is red, swollen, painful, or discharging, notify dr.<br>**b.** Be supportive when child/parents discuss concerns about hearing (dr will have talked to them about this; reinforce the information). |

**Goal for Discharge or Maintenance**
Patient/parents express understanding of home care regimen.

| Usual Problems/Objectives/Timing | Nursing Orders |
|---|---|
| 1. *Pre-operatively.* | *See* Careplan 17: Pre-operative Care, General. |
| 2. *Postoperatively.* | *See* Careplan 21: Postoperative Care, General. |
| 3. Potential bleeding from ears.<br>**Objective.** No bleeding from ears.<br>**Timing.** Day 1. | **a.** Use wash cloth and warm water to cleanse the **external** part of the ear.<br>**b.** If much drainage, put dry cotton fluff over ear orifice and change p.r.n.<br>**c.** Notify dr if any fresh bleeding occurs. |
| 4. Potential mismanagement of ear care at home, due to lack of understanding or experience.<br>**Objective.** Patient/parents understand home care.<br>**Timing.** Before discharge. | **a. Instruct parents:**<br>–Keep water out of child's ears. When bathing or washing, insert cotton fluff dipped in petrolatum into outer part of ear.<br>–If purulent ear discharge develops, notify dr.<br>–Do not allow patient to swim until dr gives permission.<br>**b.** Provide Instructions to Parents (*see* next page).<br>**c. Optional.** Discuss with dr about custom-made earmolds from hearing-aid dealers. |

# Instructions to Parents on Home Care of Child with Ear Drainage Tubes in Place

## Purpose of the Tubes

To ventilate (air) the middle ear and prevent fluid build up. The tubes drain the fluid away from the ear drum and equalize the air pressure in the middle part of the ear. This helps improve your child's hearing and reduce the incidence of infection.

## What to Expect

The tubes are left in place for 5 to 12 months, possibly longer. Your child should not experience any discomfort while the tubes are in place.

There might be some blood-tinged discharge from the affected ear(s) for 2 to 3 days; then a pale grayish discharge for 1 to 2 days; and then the area should be dry.

After this time, a grayish brown discharge, occasionally with some blood, indicates an acute infection in the ear. Do not be alarmed, but if the discharge persists for longer than 4 to 5 days, *or* if it becomes thick and yellow and has a strong odor, notify your doctor.

## Instructions

1. Do not try to remove the tubes.
2. Do not allow water to get into your child's ear(s). This could cause infection.
3. Clean only the outer part of the ear. Wipe drainage away with a cotton swab moistened with water.
4. Before your child has a bath or his hair is washed, put a plug of absorbent cotton (cotton-wool, cotton batting) dipped in petrolatum into the outer part of his ears. Afterward, remove the plug and dry the outer part of the ear.
5. If swimming is allowed by your child's dr, ensure that your child's ears are plugged (as when bathing), a bathing cap is worn, and the head is not ducked under water. Children under 3 years need only the cap if they are not going under water. Boys may prefer a cap with the top cut off so it looks like a headband. Supervise your child's swimming and prevent ducking.

# 88

## Otitis Media: Outpatient Care

**Goals for Discharge or Maintenance**
Parents describe home care accurately and know that they must keep the return appointment.

| Usual Problems/Objectives/Timing | Nursing Orders |
|---|---|
| 1. Potential mismanagement due to lack of understanding of home care.<br><br>**Objectives.** Parents understand:<br>(a) need to give *complete* course of medication as instructed;<br>(b) ways to provide reasonable comfort;<br>(c) reason for cleaning only the outer part of the ear.<br><br>**Timing.** By end of first clinic visit. | **a.** Provide written instructions for timing medication, including during school time. Explain that *the course of medication must be completed*.<br><br>**b.** Reinforce dr's instructions about analgesia. Suggest other appropriate comfort measures (e.g., hot-water bottle, holding nose and blowing out with mouth closed).<br><br>**c.** Emphasize instruction to clean *only* the outer part of the ear, p.r.n.<br><br>**d.** Stress to parents/patient that:<br>  –It is essential to keep return appointment, even if child is symptom-free.<br>  –They must return to clinic sooner if ear is discharging.<br>  –They should notify clinic if no improvement in 24–48 hr.<br><br>Give parents/patient a written list of names and telephone extensions of dr and nurse. |

# Careplan 89    Tympanoplasty

## Goals for Discharge or Maintenance
See Objectives.

| Usual Problems/Objectives/Timing | Nursing Orders |
|---|---|
| **1.** *Pre-operatively.* | **a.** *See* Careplan 17: Pre-operative Care, General.<br>**b.** Explain to the child's parents that:<br>–Some hair around ear will be removed.<br>–The ear will be covered with a dressing.<br>–Patient may feel dizzy for a few days.<br>**c.** Shampoo patient's hair. Braid long hair or secure it on top of the head with elastic bands.<br>**d.** *If patient has not had an audiogram in the past week, notify dr.* |
| **2.** *Postoperatively.* | *See* Careplan 21: Postoperative Care, General. |
| **3.** Potential pain if dressing is too tight; potential infection if dressing is too loose.<br>**Objective.** Dressing dry, clean, and intact.<br>**Timing.** Until dressing is removed. | **a.** Notify dr if dressing is too loose or too tight. (Dr may loosen dressing or secure it.)<br>**b.** Instruct patient not to remove dressing.<br>**c.** If drainage seeps through, outline area using a pen (mark clearly). If perimeters increase significantly, notify dr.<br>**d.** Reinforce dressing as ordered by dr. |
| **4.** Potential facial paralysis resulting from damage to seventh cranial nerve.<br>**Objective.** No obvious facial paralysis.<br>**Timing.** 48 hr. | **a.** Observe patient for eyelid ptosis or mouth-drooping on affected side. (Ask patient to smile, blink, and/or clench teeth.)<br>**b.** Notify dr if any facial asymmetry or weakness is noted. |
| **5.** Potential mismanagement at home due to lack of knowledge of home care.<br>**Objective.** Parents understand discharge instructions.<br>**Timing.** By discharge. | **a.** Instruct patient/parents:<br>–Do not get water in ears. (Put petrolatum-coated cotton [cotton-wool] into outer part of ear before shampooing or shower.)<br>–Do not blow nose.<br>–Do not swim or travel by air unless approved by dr.<br>–Do not shampoo hair for 10 days postoperatively. Then, plug ear (*see above*) and shampoo with head tilted so water cannot enter the affected ear.<br>–Importance of keeping follow-up appointment (usually, 2–3 wk). |

**Goals for Discharge or Maintenance**
**I.** Patient/parents state specific, correct knowledge of home care.
**II.** Patient/parents are willing and able to comply with dr's follow-up routine.

| Usual Problems/Objectives/Timing | Nursing Orders |
|---|---|
| | **Note:** |
| | **a.** *Do not take temperature orally.* |
| | **b.** For patients with cystic fibrosis, obtain special mouthpiece for inhalations while packing is in place. |
| **1.** *Pre-operatively.* | **a.** *See* Careplan 17: Pre-operative Care, General. |
| | **b.** Instruct patient: |
| |   –Not to blow nose or sneeze after surgery (if absolutely necessary to sneeze, do so with mouth open). |
| |   –That packing will create a sensation of inability to breathe. |
| |   –To expect swelling and discoloration (particularly if the surgery involves bone). |
| | **c.** If patient is having a septorhinoplasty, ensure that pre-operative photographs have been taken. |
| **2.** *Postoperatively.* | **a.** *See* Careplan 21: Postoperative Care, General. |
| | **b.** Remind patient not to blow nose or sneeze as long as packing is in place. |
| | **c.** Check dressing for bleeding when checking TPR. |
| **3.** Swelling and discoloration around eyes, due to surgery.<br><br>**Objective.** Swelling and discoloration gradually decreasing.<br><br>**Timing.** Until discharge. | **a.** Apply ice compresses to bridge of patient's nose, as ordered by dr (e.g., partly fill rubber glove with crushed ice, and seal with elastic band; place glove so the fingers are across the bridge of the nose and the hand is on the forehead).<br><br>**b.** Elevate head of bed 45–60 degrees. |
| **4.** Copious nasal drainage, especially after eating (due to mastication).<br><br>**Objectives.** Gradual decrease in drainage. Patient appears comfortable and less concerned over drainage.<br><br>**Timing.** By discharge. | **a.** Change "mustache-dressing" p.r.n.<br><br>**b.** Facilitate drainage by elevating head of bed 45–60 degrees.<br><br>**c.** Encourage patient to spit out drainage rather than swallow it.<br><br>**d.** Do mouth care at least q2h during day (to decrease halitosis and freshen mouth).<br><br>**e.** Give clear fluids p.o. as tolerated; increase intake to include soft, warm (not hot), easily chewed food.<br><br>**f.** Ensure that patient has sufficient supplies to deal with drainage (e.g., tissues, towel, K basin, paper bag). |
| **5.** Pain and discomfort due to pressure of nasal packing.<br><br>**Objective.** Patient states increasing comfort.<br><br>**Timing.** Until packing is removed (usually 48 hr). | **a.** Keep patient medicated, per dr's order, for reasonable comfort. |

continued

| Usual Problems/Objectives/Timing | Nursing Orders |
|---|---|
| **6.** Potential gagging and/or bleeding if nasal packing is dislodged.<br><br>**Objective.** Packing not dislodged.<br><br>**Timing.** Until packing is removed. | **a.** Check packing at least q2h. Strings are taped to cheek, with gauze pad in place under nose. *Report excessive bleeding to dr*, even if pack appears to be in place.<br><br>**b.** If packing appears dislodged, check oropharynx. *Do not try to remove packing.* Call dr and stay with patient. |
| **7.** Potential anxiety due to feeling of inability to breathe.<br><br>**Objective.** Patient visibly less anxious.<br><br>**Timing.** Until packing is removed. | **a.** Reassure patient of ability to breathe.<br><br>**b.** Elevate head of bed 30 degrees.<br><br>**c.** Place patient in room with other patients, or in room near nursing station. |
| **8.** Potential irritation and/or infection of eye due to close proximity of surgical area.<br><br>**Objective.** Early detection of eye problems.<br><br>**Timing.** 48 hr. | **a.** Observe and report to dr:<br>– Excessively reddened sclera.<br>– Complaints of itchiness or burning sensation in eyes.<br>– Excessive tearing.<br><br>**b.** Encourage patient not to touch or rub eyes. |
| **9.** Potential mismanagement due to lack of understanding of home care.<br><br>**Objective.** Parents/patient understand home care.<br><br>**Timing.** Before discharge. | **a.** Explain that nasal discharge will be profuse for the first 3–4 days after the nasal packing is removed, then will gradually decrease.<br><br>**b.** Instruct patient to blow nose gently.<br><br>**c.** Explain that discoloration and swelling will gradually subside.<br><br>**d.** Ensure that parents/patient have the surgeon's specific discharge instructions and follow-up appointment. |

**Goals for Discharge or Maintenance**
Parents understand follow-up care, have a copy of instruction sheet, and describe accurately how to cope with any problems.

| Usual Problems/Objectives/Timing | Nursing Orders |
|---|---|
| **1.** *Pre-operatively.* | **a.** *See* Careplan 17: Pre-operative Care, General. |
| | **b.** Explain to patient: |
| | –Discomfort on swallowing. <br>–Medication for sore throat. <br>–Need to drink frequently. |
| **2.** *Postoperatively.* | *See* Careplan 21: Postoperative Care, General. |
| **3.** Potential hemorrhage. <br>**Objective.** Early detection of hemorrhage. <br>**Timing.** 16 hr. | **a.** Monitor pulse and respiration: q1h for 4 hr; then q4h. If pulse rate is increasing, check more frequently; notify dr if not decreasing after 20–30 min. |
| | **b.** Record temperature q4h. Notify dr if low-grade fever persists longer than 8 hr. |
| | **c.** Observe patient closely for signs/symptoms of fresh bleeding: |
| | –Rapid pulse. <br>–Frequent swallowing. <br>–Vomiting fresh blood. <br>–Fresh blood oozing from nares. <br>–Restlessness. <br>–Pallor. |
| | Notify dr *stat* if any of these occur. |
| | **d.** Have emergency equipment available. |
| **4.** Potential clot formation on tonsil bed (likely if fluid intake low). <br>**Objectives.** No clot formation. Patient says he is feeling better and/or appears comfortable. Adequate oral intake: minimum, 600 ml/24 hr. <br>**Timing.** 24 hr. | **a.** Explain need for extra fluids and that drinking will be painful at first. (Good swallows rather than sips help to clear mucus and dried blood from the mouth and throat.) |
| | **b.** Encourage family to give fluids; demonstrate persistence. |
| | **c.** Avoid acidic drinks, such as orange or lemon juice. |
| | **d.** Give cold, fruit-flavored drinks (e.g., Kool-Aid), diluted apple juice, or popsicles—or, if the parents do not object, "flat" or bubbly cola or ginger ale. |
| | **e.** Patient may have ice cream when taking clear fluids well and when little or no mucus is inside mouth or throat. |
| | **f.** Do not allow patient to use straws. |
| | **g.** If patient's throat is very painful, give analgesic per dr's order; wait 20 min, then try fluids again. <br>–Do *not* give ASA. |
| | **h.** Offer fluids at least q1h until bedtime, and at least twice during the night. |
| **5.** Potential mismanagement at home due to lack of understanding and/or parents' fear of hurting their child by making him drink. | **a.** Explain importance of oral fluids (to clean mouth and throat, promote healing, prevent infection, etc.). |

continued

| Usual Problems/Objectives/Timing | Nursing Orders |
|---|---|
| **5. (Continued).**<br><br>**Objectives.** Parents understand the importance of getting their child to drink. They demonstrate ability in doing this.<br><br>**Timing.** Before discharge. | **b.** Encourage parents to stay (at least during the day) and participate in their child's care.<br><br>**c.** Demonstrate methods of encouraging child to drink, and support parents in their attempts (gentle persistence may be required).<br><br>**d.** Explain that it is usual for some old (stale) blood to be present in mucus. This will clear up soon.<br><br>**e.** Ensure that parents have the surgeon's printed instructions and follow-up appointment, and that they know whom to contact in an emergency. |

# Careplan 92   Cleft-Lip Correction (Infants)

## Goals for Discharge or Maintenance
I. Parents understand follow-up regimen.
II. There is no evidence of suture-line breakdown.
III. Patient is receiving adequate nutrition.

| Usual Problems/Objectives/Timing | Nursing Orders |
|---|---|
| 1. *Pre-operatively.* | a. *See* Careplan 17: Pre-operative Care, General. <br> b. Explain to family: <br> –Use of elbow restraints. <br> –Feeding routine. <br> –Routine protective isolation for infants. |
| 2. *Postoperatively.* | *See* Careplan 21: Postoperative Care, General. |
| 3. Potential aspiration due to type of surgery, feeding difficulties, or positioning. <br> **Objective.** No aspiration. <br> **Timing.** Continuing. | a. Nurse infant in supine position; keep head of bed elevated 30 degrees. <br> b. Check infant frequently to ensure that he has not slipped down in bed or turned onto stomach. <br> c. Have infant in upright sitting position for feeding; give feeds slowly, with frequent rest periods and frequent burping. <br> d. If infant needs to be suctioned (rarely required), do not exceed 10 mm Hg; suction *away from* suture line. |
| 4. Potential scar formation due to crusting. <br> **Objective.** No crusting on suture line. <br> **Timing.** Until discharge. | a. Do lip and nostril care after each feeding using cotton-tipped swabs (Q-tips): <br> **Lip Care.** Cleanse with rolling motion along suture line, *not across it.* Wash with sterile N saline and rinse with sterile water. Lubricate with ointment as ordered. <br> **Nostril Care.** Cleanse outer part of nostrils only using rolling motion. *Do not insert Q-tip into nostril.* |
| 5. Potential breakdown of suture line, due to picking or rubbing face on bed linen; excessive sucking or crying; and/or injury while feeding. <br> **Objective.** Suture line is intact. <br> **Timing.** Until discharge. | a. Prevent infant from picking at or rubbing suture line: <br> –Use elbow restraints. <br> –Do not allow infant to lie on abdomen. <br> –Ensure that infant's nails are short. <br> b. *Do not use spoon for feeding.* <br> c. Feed by pipette for 3 days, giving clear fluids for 2 days and formula for third day. <br> d. Bottle-feed from fourth day until sutures are removed; use a long, soft nipple. Additions (e.g., rice cereal) may be put in formula from day 5. |
| 6. Potential excessive crying because of discomfort, inability to satisfy sucking needs, and restriction of movement. <br> **Objective.** Crying does not exceed 2-3 min. | a. If infant is restless or crying, check for warmth and dryness. <br> b. Encourage a family member to hold and cuddle the infant. |

continued

| Usual Problems/Objectives/Timing | Nursing Orders |
|---|---|
| **6. (Continued).**<br><br>**Timing.** Until discharge. | **c.** Provide diversions, such as mobiles and music.<br><br>**d.** Plan periods of *supervised* exercising and play at least t.i.d.<br><br>**e.** Remove elbow restraints for supervised meals and play. |
| **7.** Potential mismanagement at home due to lack of knowledge.<br><br>**Objective.** Parents demonstrate ability in following instructions for home care.<br><br>**Timing.** Before discharge. | **a.** Reinforce dr's instructions for home care and follow-up.<br><br>**b.** Teach parents:<br><br>   –To clean lip and nostril area using soap, water, and washcloth. (They should not use Q-tips or attempt to insert anything into a nostril.)<br><br>   –To apply polysporin ointment/petrolatum as ordered by dr (for 2–6 weeks).<br><br>   –Importance of keeping infant's nails short and clean.<br><br>**c.** Explain that child is to wear elbow restraints for 2 weeks after discharge. These can be removed when child is being supervised.<br><br>**d.** If appropriate, ensure that parents know that infant is to be weaned from bottle-feeding before admission for cleft palate repair.<br><br>**e.** Ensure that parents have elbow restraints and written instructions for home care and follow-up, and know whom to call if they have concerns. |

**Goals for Discharge or Maintenance**
Parents describe outpatient regimen correctly, including speech therapy and dentistry if appropriate.

| Usual Problems/Objectives/Timing | Nursing Orders |
|---|---|
| **1.** *Pre-operatively.* | **a.** *See* Careplan 17: Pre-operative Care, General.<br>**b.** Explain:<br>  –Need to drink a lot.<br>  –Mouth care.<br>  –Purpose of elbow restraints and child's need for extra TLC while restrained.<br>  –Need to rest voice for five days postoperatively. |
| **2.** *Postoperatively.* | *See* Careplan 21: Postoperative Care, General. |
| **3.** Potential airway obstruction leading to atelectasis, due to swelling, and/or vomitus.<br>**Objective.** Patent airway.<br>**Timing.** Until discharge. | **a.** Keep head of bed elevated 45 degrees at all times.<br>**b.** Monitor respirations at least q1h for 12 hr.<br>**c.** Notify dr *stat* if signs of respiratory distress (increased respiratory rate, coughing, choking, restlessness, or cyanosis) occur.<br>**d.** Keep nasal suction apparatus at bedside, but use only per dr's order.<br>**e.** Position patient on side, with tongue forward (a tongue suture may be inserted).<br>**f.** Provide extra humidity (e.g., vaporizer at bedside). |
| **4.** Potential dehydration due to inadequate oral intake.<br>**Objectives.** Adequate oral intake; no dehydration.<br>**Timing.** Day 3-4. | **a.** Administer fluids i.v. until oral intake is adequate.<br>**b.** Follow oral feeding schedule as ordered, using a plastic spoon, or cup, as appropriate for age.<br>**Infant (under 2 years old).** Sterile, clear fluids for 24 hr, clear fluids for 24 hr, full fluids for 48 hr, then diluted baby foods and regular formula (by pipette or cup).<br>**Older child.** Clear fluids for 24 hr, fluids for 48 hr, then soft diet that requires minimal chewing. |
| **5.** Potential coating of mouth and tongue, and halitosis, because of reluctance to swallow or to allow anyone to touch mouth.<br>**Objective.** Clean mouth and tongue.<br>**Timing.** Until discharge. | **a.** Give patient water to drink after each oral intake.<br>**b. Older child.** Use diluted mouthwashes (e.g., 1/2 strength hydrogen peroxide).<br>**c.** Apply petrolatum or ointment, per dr's order, to corners of mouth.<br>**d. Nurse or parent:**<br>  –Brush patient's tongue with sponge swabs or toothbrush.<br>  –Brush patient's teeth. |
| **6.** Potential trauma to suture line.<br>**Objective.** Suture line is intact. | **a.** Remove injurious objects from patient's reach (e.g., spoons, pacifiers, or sharp toys). |

237

continued

| Usual Problems/Objectives/Timing | Nursing Orders |
|---|---|
| **6. (Continued).**<br><br>**Timing.** Until suture removal (usually 10 days postoperatively). | **b. Infant or toddler.** Apply elbow restraints. Remove for meals and for supervised play or exercise.<br><br>**c.** Do not use straws or give patient popsicles on a stick.<br><br>**d. Older child.** Encourage patient to rest voice for 5–6 days; provide pad and pencil, etc., and call-bell. Use elbow restraints at night. |
| **7.** Potential anxiety about effect of surgery on speech, etc.; potential mismanagement at home, due to lack of understanding or failure to comply with follow-up program.<br><br>**Objectives.** Parents express understanding of follow-up program and have access to all necessary habilitation services.<br><br>**Timing.** Before discharge. | **a.** Discuss follow-up with parents, stressing the desirability of habilitation. (Bear in mind that they are almost certainly hoping for faster improvement in speech than is possible.)<br><br>**b.** Check that any necessary appointments have been made for speech therapy, dentistry, social worker, etc. (coordinate appointments).<br><br>**c.** Explain:<br>–Child to have only soft foods for next 2 weeks (no sticky foods).<br>–Parents to give mouth care after meals/snacks and at bedtime.<br>–Child to wear elbow restraints for 2 weeks (remove when child is being supervised).<br><br>**d.** Ensure that parents have written instructions about home care and follow-up appointments, and know whom to contact if problems arise. |

# Careplan 94 — Lip Surgery (Older Children)

**Goals for Discharge or Maintenance**
Parents and patient can cope with home care and follow-up.

| Usual Problems/Objectives/Timing | Nursing Orders |
|---|---|
| **1.** *Pre-operatively.* | **a.** *See* Careplan 17: Pre-operative Care, General.<br><br>**b.** Explain that lip and nose will be swollen and tender for a while. |
| **2.** *Postoperatively.* | *See* Careplan 21: Postoperative Care, General. |
| **3.** Potential scar formation due to crusting.<br><br>**Objectives.** No crusting on suture line; no scar formation.<br><br>**Timing.** Until discharge. | **a.** Do lip and nostril care p.c. and h.s. using cotton-tipped swabs.<br><br>**Lip care.** Cleanse with sterile N saline and rinse with sterile water. Use rolling motion along suture line, *not across it*. Lubricate with ointment as ordered.<br><br>**Nostril Care.** Cleanse outer part of nostrils with rolling motion. *Do not insert swab into nostril.* |
| **4.** Potential breakdown of suture line due to picking, rubbing face on bedclothes, or accidental trauma.<br><br>**Objective.** Suture line is intact.<br><br>**Timing.** Until discharge. | **a.** Keep head of bed elevated 45 degrees.<br><br>**b.** Explain importance of protecting surgical area (e.g., not touching mouth or rubbing mouth on bedclothes).<br><br>**c.** Provide extra humidity, especially at night.<br><br>**d.** Give fluids by cup or glass:<br>  –Clear fluids for 1 day.<br>  –Full fluids for 2 days.<br>  –Soft or pureed diet thereafter.<br><br>**e.** Allow patient to use spoon, but instruct him to keep edge of spoon away from suture line.<br><br>**f.** If appropriate, allow patient to see his mouth in a mirror.<br><br>**g.** Provide diversions, such as music, TV, books, and quiet games. (Patient is allowed to get up but should be restricted to quiet activities.) |
| **5.** Potential mismanagement at home due to lack of knowledge.<br><br>**Objective.** Patient/parents state willingness to follow instructions for home care.<br><br>**Timing.** Before discharge. | **a.** Reinforce dr's instructions for home care.<br><br>**b.** Explain importance of protecting lip while it is healing.<br>  –Do lip and nostril care as instructed.<br>  –Avoid foods that are hard to bite on or chew.<br>  –Avoid contact sports and gym.<br>  Follow this regimen for 2 weeks or as ordered by dr.<br><br>**c.** Ensure that parents/patient have written instructions for home care and follow-up appointment(s). |

### Goals for Discharge or Maintenance
Family members state their understanding of the disease and can cope with continuing care.

| Usual Problems/Objectives/Timing | Nursing Orders |
|---|---|
| **1.** Respiratory distress due to bronchospasm.<br><br>**Objective.** Normal respiration.<br><br>**Timing.** 24 hr. | **a.** Position patient in semi- or high Fowler's position.<br><br>**b.** Ensure that $O_2$ is set up at bedside.<br><br>**c.** Administer humidified $O_2$ by mask, nasal prongs, or hood, as ordered.<br><br>**d.** Administer inhalation as ordered. Ensure the child is sitting in upright position during the inhalation. Notify dr if wheezing occurs before next inhalation is due.<br><br>**e.** Auscultate the patient's lungs before and after each inhalation; q4h if patient is not on inhalations.<br><br>**f.** Measure patient's peak flow rate as ordered by dr.<br><br>Usual routine:<br><br>–On admission (for baseline).<br><br>–Three times a day, if inhalations are being done frequently (immediately before and 15 min after an inhalation).<br><br>–Once a day (in early a.m.) if patient is on inhalations p.r.n.<br><br>**g.** Carry out chest routine and relaxed breathing methods as instructed by physical therapist. |
| **2.** Potential exhaustion due to frequent coughing and dyspnea.<br><br>**Objective.** Patient carries out normal activities without undue fatigue.<br><br>**Timing.** 48 hr. | **a.** Provide for uninterrupted rest between treatments.<br><br>**b.** For older child, keep frequently used objects within easy reach.<br><br>**c.** Observe for respiratory fatigue; if present notify dr *stat*. |
| **3.** Potential dehydration due to loss of fluids from respiratory tract and difficulty drinking.<br><br>**Objective.** Adequate hydration.<br><br>**Timing.** 24 hr. | **a.** Maintain i.v. fluids as ordered.<br><br>**b.** Assess level of hydration q4h.<br><br>**c.** Record intake and output.<br><br>**d.** Offer clear fluids at least q2h when patient is awake. |
| **4.** Parents and child apprehensive.<br><br>**Objectives.** Relaxed facial expression. Parents provide verbal and nonverbal support to child.<br><br>**Timing.** 24 hr. | **a.** Stay with child during periods of acute distress.<br><br>**b.** Allow patient to discuss fears and concerns.<br><br>**c.** Assist and encourage parents to support child when he is apprehensive.<br><br>**d.** Explain all procedures and treatments.<br><br>**e.** Encourage parents to rest if they appear fatigued. |
| **5.** Potential complication: status asthmaticus.<br><br>**Objective.** No increase in severity of attack.<br><br>**Timing.** 24 hr. | **a.** Report to dr *stat* any deterioration in patient's respiratory status:<br><br>–Increasing level of exhaustion, anxiety, or apprehension. |

continued

| Usual Problems/Objectives/Timing | Nursing Orders |
|---|---|
| **5. (Continued).** | –Cyanosis.<br>–Decreased air entry.<br>–Increased or decreased respiratory rate.<br>–Increase in frequency of coughing spasms.<br>–Increased restlessness or lethargy. |
| **6.** Potential mismanagement at home, due to lack of understanding of disease and treatment.<br><br>**Objective.** Parents state accurate knowledge of disease and treatment.<br><br>**Timing.** Before discharge. | **a.** Designated nurse to explain/teach:<br>–Amounts, times, and side effects of medications to be given at home. (To promote compliance with the treatment regimen, it is important to arrange medication times that fit in with the patient's usual home routines.)<br>–How to identify factors that precipitate an attack (and know the steps to avoid these factors).<br>–What steps to take at signs of an impending attack.<br>–Need to avoid exposure to cold, sudden exertion, and emotional upsets.<br>–How to recognize signs and symptoms of respiratory infection.<br>**b.** Document progress.<br>**c.** Request referral from dr to asthma program at a local crippled children's center, if appropriate. |

# 96

## Goals for Discharge or Maintenance
Parents have some understanding of the disease and can cope with home care and follow-up.

| Usual Problems/Objectives/Timing | Nursing Orders |
|---|---|
| **1.** Respiratory distress due to narrowing of the bronchiolar lumen (by mucosal thickening, mucous plugs, cellular debris), and in severe cases, air trapping in the alveoli.<br><br>**Objective.** Decreased respiratory distress.<br><br>**Timing.** 24 hr. | **a.** Place patient in semi- or high Fowler's position (e.g., use infant seat in crib).<br><br>**b.** Dress patient so that chest area can be easily observed (e.g., gown on back to front and loosely tied).<br><br>**c.** Administer humidified air or $O_2$ by croup tent, hood, or mask, as ordered by dr.<br><br>**d.** Keep patient's nasal airway open and clear of mucus to decrease respiratory difficulty (infants are obligatory nose breathers).<br><br>**e.** Check apical pulse and respiratory rate q1h. Report signs of increasing respiratory distress *stat.*<br><br>**f.** Auscultate chest for breath sounds q1h until respiratory rate drops to within normal limits.<br><br>**g.** Have patient in upright position for inhalations. |
| **2.** Potential exhaustion due to frequent coughing and dyspnea.<br><br>**Objectives.** Patient appears less anxious and is getting adequate ventilation and rest.<br><br>**Timing.** 48 hr. | **a.** Plan patient's care to provide uninterrupted rest between treatments.<br><br>**b.** Restrict visitors to those essential for care; avoid excessive handling of patient.<br><br>**c.** When feeding patient or doing other care, leave patient in croup tent or hold $O_2$ mask (40% $O_2$) close to his face. |
| **3.** Potential dehydration due to loss of fluid from respiratory tract, difficulty in drinking, and/or fever.<br><br>**Objective.** Adequate hydration.<br><br>**Timing.** Ongoing. | **a.** Administer parenteral fluids as ordered.<br><br>**b.** Offer patient small amounts of clear fluid. If feeding precipitates severe hacking cough, allow patient to rest; plan feedings in smaller, more frequent amounts. (It may be necessary to have patient on n.p.o. until respiratory distress lessens.)<br><br>**c.** Record intake and output.<br><br>**d.** Assess patient's level of hydration q2h.<br><br>**e.** *See* Careplan 10: Pyrexia. |
| **4.** *Potential complications:*<br><br>–Exhaustion and anoxia.<br><br>–Secondary bacterial infection.<br><br>–Apnea spells.<br><br>–Circulatory collapse.<br><br>**Objective.** Early detection of complications.<br><br>**Timing.** Until discharge. | **a.** Maintain close direct observation of patient, and report to dr any increase in:<br><br>–Respiratory rate and depth.<br><br>–Frequency of coughing spasms.<br><br>–Exhaustion.<br><br>–Cyanosis.<br><br>–Fatigue.<br><br>**b.** Have all necessary equipment ready for emergency tests/treatment (e.g., to do blood-gas determinations). |

continued

| Usual Problems/Objectives/Timing | Nursing Orders |
|---|---|
| **5.** Parents anxious and fearful about their child's condition.<br><br>**Objectives.** Parents express their concerns, have some understanding of the condition, and are able to support their child.<br><br>**Timing.** As soon as possible. | **a.** Reinforce dr's explanations of child's condition.<br>**b.** Explain equipment and procedures.<br>**c.** Stay in room while patient is in acute distress.<br>**d.** Maintain a calm, unhurried appearance.<br>**e.** Allow parents time to discuss their fears and concerns.<br>**f.** Encourage parents to rest if they appear fatigued. |
| **6.** Potential mismanagement at home due to lack of understanding.<br><br>**Objective.** Parents demonstrate understanding of the condition and are willing to carry out home care and follow-up.<br><br>**Timing.** Before discharge. | **a.** Ensure that parents have been taught any procedures that are to be carried out at home (e.g., medications, humidification).<br>**b.** Explain importance of avoiding exposure to infection, especially upper respiratory tract infection.<br>**c.** Ensure that parents have follow-up appointment(s) and know whom to contact if problems arise. |

**Goals for Discharge or Maintenance**
See Objectives.

| Usual Problems/Objectives/Timing | Nursing Orders |
|---|---|
| **1.** *Pre-operatively.* | **a.** *See* Careplan 17: Pre-operative Care, General.<br><br>**b.** Explain to parents that a croup tent may be used postoperatively. |
| **2.** *Postoperatively.* | *See* Careplan 21: Postoperative Care, General. |
| **3.** Potential respiratory distress due to swelling, trauma, or mucous plug.<br><br>**Objectives.** No respiratory distress. No blood in mucus.<br><br>**Timing.** 24 hr. | **a.** Place patient in croup tent if respirations are noisy.<br><br>**b.** Check respirations q15 min for 1 hr, or until stable; then q4h.<br><br>**c.** Observe for and report to dr *stat:*<br>  –Difficulty in swallowing or breathing.<br>  –Laryngeal stridor or unusual hoarseness.<br>  –Nasal flaring or substernal indrawing.<br>  –Tachycardia, tachypnea.<br>  –Cyanosis.<br>  –Subcutaneous crepitus around patient's face and neck.<br>  –Hemoptysis.<br>  –Chest pain.<br>  –Elevated temperature.<br>  –Unusual irritability or restlessness.<br><br>**d.** Encourage coughing and deep breathing q2h. Check for expectoration of blood.<br><br>**e.** Maintain patient on n.p.o. for 4 hr postoperatively, then give clear fluids as tolerated until next morning unless dr orders otherwise.<br><br>**f.** If patient has difficulty breathing, try tipping him over your lap or the edge of bed, and slapping him sharply on back unless contraindicated (if there is a plug of mucus, this may help to dislodge it). *Notify dr stat.* Administer $O_2$ (by mask or croup tent). Stay with patient. |
| *If patient has a tracheotomy*<br><br>**4.** Potential asphyxiation due to occlusion of the tracheotomy tube and edema of the tracheal tissue.<br><br>**Objective.** Patent cannula.<br><br>**Timing.** 24–36 hr. | **a.** *See* Careplan 104: Tracheotomy, Acute.<br><br>**b.** Institute constant, direct observation of patient for 24–36 hr postanesthetic, or as ordered by dr. (The patient is dependent on tracheotomy for his airway. Any space between the tube and the wall of the trachea—allowing some air to pass should the tube become plugged—may be occluded by edematous tissue.)<br><br>**c.** Suction frequently (q5–10 min) for first few hours, then reduce as mucus lessens. Record consistency and color of mucus, and frequency of suctioning.<br><br>**d.** Check patient's respiratory status at least q20 min: |

continued

| Usual Problems/Objectives/Timing | Nursing Orders |
|---|---|
| **4. (Continued).** | –Go to bedside and observe for rise and fall of chest. |
| | –Place hand over tracheotomy to feel air passing through. |
| | –Observe patient's color (if child has naturally dark skin, check nail beds for cyanosis). |
| | **e.** Ensure that patient wears clothing that allows for observation of breathing (e.g., place child's gown on with ties in front). |

## Goals for Discharge or Maintenance
I. Adequate air entry and oral intake.
II. Parents/patient express understanding of illness and describe home care accurately.

| Usual Problems/Objectives/Timing | Nursing Orders |
|---|---|
| **1.** Respiratory distress.<br><br>**Objective.** Normal respirations.<br><br>**Timing.** Day 2. | **a.** Monitor TPR q1h until patient's condition is stable, then q4h.<br><br>**b.** If apical rate exceeds 160/min, or respirations are over 40/min, notify dr *stat*.<br><br>**c.** Observe for signs of increasing distress that may indicate need for transfer to ICU:<br>–Restlessness.<br>–Cough.<br>–Stridor.<br>–Suprasternal, substernal, or intercostal indrawing.<br>–Tracheal tugging.<br>–Nasal flaring.<br>–Drooling.<br>–Circumoral cyanosis.<br><br>If any of these are present, notify dr and do not leave child until dr arrives. If patient is drooling or has circumoral cyanosis, notify dr *stat* (indications of epiglottitis).<br><br>**d.** Dress child so that chest area can be observed easily (e.g., gown on back to front and tied loosely).<br><br>**e.** Maintain maximal humidification with croup tent.<br><br>**f.** Keep intubation equipment at hand. |
| **2.** Pyrexia. | *See* Careplan 10: Pyrexia. |
| **3.** Potential dehydration due to sore throat, vomiting, and/or diarrhea.<br><br>**Objective.** Adequate hydration.<br><br>**Timing.** Day 2. | **a.** Offer fluids that patient prefers, frequently.<br><br>**b.** Get parents to encourage their child to drink.<br><br>**c.** Maintain record of fluid intake and output, and observe type of bowel movement. Report low intake or diarrhea to dr. |
| **4.** Patient anxious about unfamiliar environment, tent noise, confinement, and respiratory distress.<br><br>**Objectives.** Patient stays in tent and shows interest in diversional material.<br><br>**Timing.** Day 2. | **a.** Explain use of the croup tent; make it a game (e.g., a house).<br><br>**b.** Allow patient to discuss fears and concerns; reassure him constantly.<br><br>**c.** Allow favorite blanket (not wool) or nonfriction toy in the croup tent.<br><br>**d.** Keep patient dry and comfortable. |
| **5.** Parents anxious at seeing their child in distress because of lack of knowledge about illness.<br><br>**Objective.** Parents understand illness and treatment.<br><br>**Timing.** As soon as possible. | **a.** Explain the function of the tent, the need for adequate fluid intake, and the usual course of the illness.<br><br>**b.** Give parents printed Information for Parents of a Child with Croup (*See* page 250). |

247

continued

| Usual Problems/Objectives/Timing | Nursing Orders |
|---|---|
| **5. (Continued).** | **c.** Encourage parents to participate in their child's care even though he is in the croup tent.<br><br>**d.** If the parents have been up all night, suggest they go away for a rest and return later. |
| **6.** If respiratory distress is not relieved, extreme restlessness and anxiety due to hypoxia.<br><br>**Objective.** Decreased restlessness and anxiety as ventilation improves.<br><br>**Timing.** ½ hr after start of treatment. | **a.** Have equipment ready for epinephrine inhalation.<br><br>**b.** Explain the procedure of inhalation by mask, appropriate to child's understanding.<br><br>**c.** Reassure the child constantly.<br><br>**d.** Wrap child in blanket to restrain arms if necessary.<br><br>**e.** Unless ordered otherwise by dr, hold child upright on your lap, or position him upright.<br><br>**f.** Ensure that the mask is held firmly against the child's face during inhalation.<br><br>**g.** Observe child's breathing closely. |
| **7.** Increasing tachycardia due to medication (epinephrine), increasing hypoxia, and/or restlessness.<br><br>**Objective:** Decreasing tachycardia and restlessness.<br><br>**Timing.** ½ hr after start of treatment. | **a.** Monitor heart rate at least once during each inhalation treatment.<br><br>**b.** Remain with patient after treatment is completed. Continue monitoring q½h; disturb patient as little as possible.<br><br>**c.** Notify dr *stat* if tachycardia persists. |
| **8.** Potential continuance of respiratory distress despite treatment, or its recurrence.<br><br>**Objective.** Respirations within normal limits.<br><br>**Timing.** ½ hr after start of treatment. | **a.** Observe rate and character of respirations q¼–1h.<br><br>**b.** Notify dr *stat* if respiratory rate unchanged ½ hr after start of treatment, or if it decreases then increases.<br><br>**Note:** If respiratory distress is not relieved, the dr may order transfer to ICU. |
| **9.** Parental anxiety about possible recurrence of croup.<br><br>**Objectives.** Parents express their concerns. They know what to do if child develops croup at home.<br><br>**Timing.** Before discharge. | **a.** Reinforce dr's instructions for home care.<br><br>**b.** Instruct parents that if child develops hoarseness and a croupy cough, or if he wakes up in the middle of the night with a croup attack they should:<br><br>–Take child into bathroom and close door.<br><br>–Turn on the hot water in the shower or tub, and let the room fill up with steam.<br><br>–Sit with child in the bathroom, with the water still running, for 10–15 min. (Sitting on a mat on the floor may be more comfortable than sitting on a chair.)<br><br>–Remain calm. Talk to child quietly; read him a story.<br><br>–If there is no improvement in the child's condition, notify dr.<br><br>**c.** Tell parents that if child's breathing is improved the steps above they should:<br><br>–Set up a cold-air vaporizer in child's room.<br><br>–Place child back in bed. Let him choose the position |

| Usual Problems/Objectives/Timing | Nursing Orders |
|---|---|
| 9. (Continued). | most comfortable for him (do not make him lie down). |
| | –Cool the temperature of the room. |
| | –Give child popsicle and/or clear fluids to drink. |
| | **d.** Notify dr if child's symptoms increase (e.g., noisier breathing, difficulty in swallowing, drooling, increased restlessness). |
| | **e.** Ensure that parents have written instructions for home care and know what to do and whom to call if they are concerned. |

# Information for Parents of a Child with Croup

Croup is an inflammation of the upper respiratory passages. It is caused by a virus, and the type of virus is diagnosed by special studies. Croup usually affects infants and children 1 to 4 years old, especially boys. The time of year seems to have some effect (in Canada, the incidence of croup is highest during October through May).

### Why does the croup attack come on so fast, especially at night?

The course of croup is usually quite rapid. Your child probably had a mild cough with slight laryngitis. When he awoke, he probably had a croupy cough, was very restless, had a hoarse voice, and had difficulty breathing. This breathing was a bit better when he was sitting up. These symptoms were enough to frighten you.

### Why must he be in a tent?

This tent, which is called a croup tent, is useful for treatment. It provides high humidity, with air or oxygen, at a comfortable temperature for the child. The croup tent aids the child's breathing by providing high moisture content, making coughing less distressing and secretions less thick.

### Why do the nurses want my child to drink extra fluids?

The nurses emphasize extra fluids because fluid helps to liquefy mucus. As your child's condition improves, his diet will be changed to soft foods suitable for his age.

### Can we take our child out of the tent when we visit?

Your child remains in bed in a croup tent for the first 24 hours. If his condition has improved by then, he may be allowed to come out of the tent while you are here. An ideal time to come is lunch or supper time, so that you have a chance to see your child, and also to help him eat and drink. During the acute stage of his illness, the most important care is rest and moisture; therefore, we may ask you not to enter his room for a few hours. Never hesitate to telephone the ward.

### What should I do for my child when he comes home?

First of all, your child should stay indoors for 1 week. A vaporizer or humidifier is ideal if he has a troublesome cough or lingering hoarseness (these may persist for a week or two after discharge). Your child can have a regular diet but should have extra fluids for a few days. He should not be in contact with people who have infections. A checkup with your family doctor or the clinic is advisable.

## Goals for Discharge or Maintenance
Family members describe home care and medication accurately and agree to comply with instructions.

| Usual Problems/Objectives/Timing | Nursing Orders |
|---|---|
| **1.** Poor nutritional status due to impaired digestion. (Viscous mucus reduces or prevents pancreatic enzymes from reaching small intestine.)<br><br>**Objectives.** Adequate nutrition is established/maintained. Patient is taking enzymes and vitamins as ordered.<br><br>**Timing.** By discharge. | **a.** Give enzymes as ordered:<br>– Give enzymes throughout meal (e.g., ⅓ at beginning, ⅓ half-way through, and ⅓ at end).<br>– Mix enzymes with a small amount of food (e.g., applesauce, mashed banana).<br>– Always mix enzymes in same food. (Child will associate only that food with medication.)<br>– Do not mix enzymes in formula (they coat the bottle and begin to digest the formula).<br>– Give food immediately after mixing in the enzymes.<br><br>**Note.** Enzymes are unnecessary if patient is having special predigested formula or clear fluid snacks.<br><br>**b.** Encourage patient to eat foods high in calories and protein and low to moderate in fat.<br><br>**c.** Avoid giving meals/formula immediately after treatment (when coughing and vomiting are more likely to occur).<br><br>**d.** Give vitamins as ordered (be aware that higher doses than usual of water-soluble vitamins are given because patient has absorption problems).<br><br>**e.** Record eating habits (food refused/taken, appetite, etc.).<br><br>**f.** Observe and record bulk and consistency of stools. Check for diarrhea and abdominal cramps (these may indicate inadequate oral enzymes), constipation, distention, and rectal prolapse.<br><br>**g.** Weigh infants daily, and older children at least twice a week.<br><br>**h.** If necessary, *see* Careplan 129: Total Parenteral Nutrition. |
| **2.** Potential chest infection due to retention of excessively thick mucus and decreased resistance to infection.<br><br>**Objectives.** Chest is clear; rib cage is normally mobile; patient is coughing up mucus.<br><br>**Timing.** Ongoing. | **a.** Give inhalations by compressed air for 15–20 min (just before postural drainage). Ensure that mask is close to patient's face. Encourage deep breaths through mouth.<br><br>**b.** Supervise inhalations, diverting child with play as necessary.<br><br>**c.** Keep patient away from others with respiratory infection.<br><br>**d.** Give antibiotics, expectorants, and/or bronchodilators as ordered.<br><br>**e.** Record TPR q4h while febrile, then q8h. Record BP daily, in p.m. Note character of respirations; describe cough and secretions produced. |

continued

| Usual Problems/Objectives/Timing | Nursing Orders |
|---|---|
| **3.** Potential heat prostration due to excessive loss of salt in sweat during fever, hot weather, and/or strenuous exercise.<br><br>**Objective.** No signs or symptoms of heat prostration.<br><br>**Timing.** Until discharge. | **a.** Select the child's room carefully; it should be cool and have an even temperature.<br><br>**b.** Provide extra salt with meals in hot weather or when patient is febrile.<br><br>**c.** Dress patient in light, preferably cotton, clothing; change clothing frequently.<br><br>**d.** Plan patient's day to allow for periods of rest and quiet activity, as appropriate.<br><br>**e.** Observe for muscle cramps, listlessness, abdominal pain, and vomiting. |
| **4.** Potential skin breakdown, especially in infants, due to enzymatic irritation and frequent stooling.<br><br>**Objective.** Clear skin.<br><br>**Timing.** Until discharge. | **a.** Provide good skin care and frequent position changes.<br><br>**b.** Change clothing and bedding as often as necessary to keep patient dry.<br><br>**c.** **Infants** (especially during first few weeks after beginning to take enzymes):<br>–Apply vaseline to mouth before feeding.<br>–Give a little more food/formula to "rinse" mouth after the enzymes are given.<br>–After feeding, wipe out mouth with a wet sponge or cloth.<br>–Change diapers promptly; apply vaseline to buttocks.<br><br>**d.** If perineal area becomes excoriated, *see* Careplan 41: Diaper Rash. |
| **5.** Potential resistance to treatment regimen due to chronicity of condition and need for daily, time-consuming therapy.<br><br>**Objective.** Patient complies with treatment regimen.<br><br>**Timing.** Until discharge. | **a.** Provide for continuity in repeated admissions (e.g., same unit, same nurses).<br><br>**b.** Encourage expression of feelings. Spend time listening. Correct any misinformation.<br><br>**c.** Explain each procedure, medications, etc., as appropriate for age.<br><br>**d.** Plan day's activities with patient; try to follow home routine whenever possible.<br><br>**e.** Encourage grooming and social activity. Emphasize patient's good points and give praise for accomplishments, however small.<br><br>**f.** Introduce patient to other children with cystic fibrosis having similar treatment regimen.<br><br>**g.** Keep other members of the cystic fibrosis team informed of patient's progress and measures that have been successful. |
| **6.** Potential mismanagement at home due to lack of knowledge about the disease and its treatment and because of emotional upset over diagnosis.<br><br>**Objectives.** Family members understand reasons for treatment and demonstrate correct administration of medication, inhalation, and postural drainage. Par- | **a.** Reinforce teaching given about the disease by cystic fibrosis team.<br><br>**b.** Have patient and parents participate in giving medication and treatment under supervision.<br><br>**c.** Organize timing of treatments to fit in with family's normal home routines. |

| Usual Problems/Objectives/Timing | Nursing Orders |
|---|---|
| **6. (Continued).**<br>ents and child express feelings about the diagnosis and treatment.<br>**Timing.** By discharge. | **d.** Encourage parents and patient to express their concerns and feelings about the diagnosis, change in family routines, etc.<br>**e.** Provide information about the Cystic Fibrosis Foundation and other support groups in the community.<br>**f.** Ensure that parents/patient have written instructions for home care and follow-up and know whom to contact if they are having problems.<br>**g.** Notify public health nurse and school as necessary. |
| **7.** Potential depression due to chronicity or advanced stage of disease, and knowledge of prognosis, especially if other(s) in family have the disease and when another patient with cystic fibrosis dies.<br>**Objectives.** Patient is able to express feelings and can cope with information given. Patient is able to rest and states a reasonable level of comfort.<br>**Timing.** Ongoing. | **a.** As appropriate, *see* Careplan 35: Depression in Adolescence, and Careplan 14: Terminally Ill Patient.<br>**b.** Provide opportunities for patient to vent feelings either in group with other cystic fibrosis patients or on own.<br>**c.** Ensure that dr speaks to patient and family regularly and that they have access to other members of the cystic fibrosis team as needed.<br>**d.** Assess need for analgesic or sedative. (Be aware that pain, anxiety, and restlessness are more likely to be increased at night. Morphine infusion supplemented by i.v. diazepam may be ordered.)<br>**e.** Administer $O_2$ as ordered.<br>**f.** Provide support when another patient dies. Explain in simple terms, as appropriate, what has happened. Stay with patient until you feel he is able to cope with the information given. |

**Goals for Discharge or Maintenance**
Patient has adequate spontaneous respiration after extubation.

| Usual Problems/Objectives/Timing | Nursing Orders |
|---|---|
| **1.** Potential asphyxia due to accidental dislodging of ET tube.<br><br>**Objective.** ET tube remains in correct position in trachea.<br><br>**Timing.** Until planned extubation. | **a.** Monitor patient continuously.<br>**b.** Observe for signs of dislodged ET tube (sudden cyanosis, audible cry, restlessness, retraction).<br>**c.** If ET tube tapes are loose or wet, ensure they are changed or reinforced *immediately* by ICU dr.<br>**d.** Ensure that patient cannot reach the tube. Use elbow restraints on patient *at all* times.<br>**e.** *Only* if assisted ventilation is necessary, attach $O_2$ equipment to ET tube.<br>**f.** If patient is restless or anxious, give sedation as ordered by dr. |
| **2.** Potential asphyxia due to obstruction of ET tube.<br><br>**Objective.** No obstruction of ET tube.<br><br>**Timing.** Until planned extubation. | **a.** Observe patient closely for restlessness, indrawing, cyanosis.<br>**b.** If secretions are thick (usually the first 24 hr), instill N saline into the ET tube as ordered and suction ET tube q½-1h, p.r.n. As secretions become thinner, suction less frequently.<br>**c.** Record amount and consistency of secretions.<br>**d.** Provide $O_2$ (usually 40%) in hood with 2 heated Puritan nebulizers for maximum humidity. |
| **3.** Patient unable to swallow or handle secretions due to sore throat and swelling.<br><br>**Objective.** Patient able to swallow.<br><br>**Timing.** 2–3 days. | **a.** Suction mouth and nasopharynx gently, p.r.n.<br>**b.** Position patient comfortably: sitting upright or lying flat on side.<br>**c.** Do not give oral fluids until about 4 hr after extubation.<br>**d.** Reassure child (and parents) that as swelling goes down and secretions become thinner, swallowing will become easier. |
| **4.** Patient anxious and frustrated due to strange environment, restrictions, fear of tube, suctioning, sore throat.<br><br>**Objectives.** Patient has relaxed facial expression, is able to rest, and is participating in diversional activities.<br><br>**Timing.** 2–3 days. | **a.** Reassure child that tube will be removed when his throat is better.<br>**b.** Provide quiet diversional activity (e.g., story reading, TV, talking, or by 3rd day, a walk). Encourage parents to participate in diversion.<br>**c.** If child is very anxious:<br>–Give sedation as ordered.<br>–Cuddle child or allow him to sit on parent's lap (only if child cannot settle otherwise). |
| **5.** Pyrexia.<br><br>**Objective.** Normal temperature.<br><br>**Timing.** 2–3 days. | **a.** *See* Careplan 10: Pyrexia.<br>**b.** Record rectal temperature q2h. *Do not take temperature orally.* |

| Usual Problems/Objectives/Timing | Nursing Orders |
|---|---|
| **6.** Parents' anxiety due to their child's sudden illness and distress.<br><br>**Objectives.** Parents express concerns and are able to relate to child in a positive manner.<br><br>**Timing.** 2–3 days. | **a.** Ensure that a nurse accompanies parents on their first visit to ICU.<br><br>**b.** Explain ICU routines, procedures, and equipment being used.<br><br>**c.** Reinforce dr's explanations of illness and treatment.<br><br>**d.** Explain usual course of events (e.g., use of ET tube until child can swallow, secretions becoming thinner, fever abating, extubation, transfer from ICU to a ward). |

## Goals for Discharge or Maintenance
Adequate spontaneous respiration.

| Usual Problems/Objectives/Timing | Nursing Orders |
|---|---|
| | **General Nursing Orders** |
| | **a.** *A nurse must be in the child's room at all times.* |
| | **b.** In the event of mechanical problems that you cannot rectify at once: |
| |   –Start manual ventilation *stat.* |
| |   –Call respiratory technology department. |
| **1.** Problems relating to the condition that has necessitated mechanical ventilation. | *See* appropriate careplans. |
| **2.** Potential hypoxia due to:<br>  **a.** Accidental disconnection from ventilator.<br><br>  **Objective.** No interruption in ventilator support.<br><br>  **Timing.** Until patient is weaned off ventilator. | **a.** Ensure that all alarms on ventilator are set as ordered.<br>**b.** If alarm sounds:<br>  –Check that no water has collected in the pressure tubing.<br>  –Look for disconnection or leak in the system.<br>  –If there is a disconnection, reconnect tubing and ensure that it is secure.<br>  –If there is a leak, hand ventilate patient until leak is repaired.<br>**c.** Position ventilator close to the patient's bedside. Leave enough slack in lines to the patient so he can move his head without disconnecting them from the tube. (Add extra tubing if necessary.)<br>**d.** Position the child comfortably:<br>  –Restrain hands p.r.n.<br>  –If necessary, place a rolled towel to prevent infant from moving his head too much.<br>  –Keep towel under lines to prevent tubing from becoming obstructed.<br>  –Give sedation as ordered.<br>**e.** Monitor vital signs q1–2h (apical heart rate, respiratory rate, BP), quality of respirations, air entry, and skin color.<br>**f.** Obtain samples for blood-gas determinations as ordered. Report significant results. |
|   **b.** Mechanical failure.<br><br>  **Objective.** No interruption in ventilator support.<br>  **Timing.** Until patient is weaned off ventilator. | **At beginning of each tour of duty:**<br>**a.** Check ventilator settings with dr's orders.<br>**b.** Ensure that all connections are tight.<br>**c.** Test alarm systems.<br>**d.** Check that hand ventilation equipment is connected to $O_2$ supply and is ready for emergency use. |

| Usual Problems/Objectives/Timing | Nursing Orders |
|---|---|
| **2. (Continued).** | **e.** Check that the ventilator's $O_2$ supply is safely connected.<br><br>**f.** Record the $O_2$ concentration of the ventilator and the spontaneous-breathing circuit, at least q4h and each time that:<br>    −Blood is sampled for gases.<br>    −Respiratory settings are altered.<br>    −The child's condition changes.<br><br>**g.** Record inspiratory and expiratory pressure readings q1h. (Read the pressure dial that is closer to the child's airway.) Notify dr if positive end-expiratory pressure (PEEP) is not at correct level. |
| **c.** Accidental extubation.<br>**Objective.** Tube remains in correct position in airway.<br>**Timing.** Until planned extubation. | **a.** Ensure that tapes of ET tube, or ties of tracheotomy tube, are secure:<br>    −Keep tapes as dry as possible.<br>    −Call dr to retape p.r.n.<br><br>**b.** Move child carefully and slowly.<br><br>**c.** Disconnect ventilator briefly when turning or moving child some distance (get assistance if child is large).<br><br>**d.** Stabilize ET or tracheotomy tube connector with one hand while disconnecting any equipment.<br><br>**e.** *See* nursing orders 2a (b) & (c). |
| **d.** Airway obstruction.<br>**Objective.** Patent ET or tracheotomy tube.<br>**Timing.** Until extubation. | **a.** Suction tube at least q2h.<br>    −During suctioning, hand ventilate with 100% $O_2$.<br>    −If secretions are thick and difficult to remove, check that the humidification system is functioning well. Ask dr for permission to instill sterile N saline into the tube during suctioning to loosen secretions.<br><br>**b.** Prevent kinking of ET tube or displacement of tracheotomy tube.<br><br>**c.** Keep the humidifier filled with sterile water.<br><br>**d.** Check that there are beads of moisture in the inspiratory line (indicating adequate humidity). Empty excess water p.r.n.<br><br>**e.** Check that the spontaneous-breathing circuit is adequately humidified.<br><br>**f.** If a heated humidifier is in use:<br>    −Record the temperature of inspiratory gases q1h.<br>    −Adjust the heater p.r.n. to keep gases at $36^0$–$37^0$C.<br><br>**g.** If $O_2$ hood is being used, consult dr about use of heating rod to maintain humidity. |
| **3.** Patient fearful and frustrated because of inability to speak, attachment to equipment, and strange surroundings. | **a.** Hold child's hand, and explain, as appropriate for age:<br>    −Necessity for the tube and respirator. |

continued

| Usual Problems/Objectives/Timing | Nursing Orders |
|---|---|
| **3. (Continued).**<br>**Objective.** Patient appears less fearful.<br>**Timing.** Until extubated. | –All procedures and equipment used for him.<br>–Other ICU aspects that cause him concern.<br>**b.** Anticipate child's needs. Include his parents in identifying and meeting his needs; if appropriate, ask them to bring a favorite toy. (Not a friction toy.)<br>**c.** Try to read the child's lips. Encourage him to mouth words slowly.<br>**d.** Provide:<br>–For older child, a writing board (avoid placing the i.v. needle in his writing hand).<br>–For young child, a picture board.<br>–A call-bell, if suitable.<br>**e. Infant.** Talk to him, hold him, and cuddle him as much as possible. (Remember to support the ET or tracheotomy tube and the respirator lines.)<br>**Older child.**<br>-If patient's condition is stable, sit him in a chair at least t.i.d. (Support the tube and respirator lines.)<br>-If patient's condition is not yet stabilized, spend extra time sitting with him, reading to him, etc. If appropriate, ask the occupational therapist to help. |
| **4.** Parents anxious about intubation and use of ventilator.<br>**Objective.** Parents display no undue anxiety about equipment.<br>**Timing.** Until extubated. | **a.** Explain equipment and procedures, including alarm sounds.<br>**b.** Reassure parents that a nurse is present at all times and that manual ventilation equipment is always ready as an alternative.<br>**c.** Encourage parents' participation in their child's care. |
| **5.** Potential skin breakdown due to unrelieved pressure on skin and underlying tissues, friction from tapes/tubes, or pressure of air from ventilator.<br>**Objective.** No skin breakdown.<br>**Timing.** Until patient is weaned off ventilator and is ambulatory. | **a.** Turn patient q2h. Encourage him to move on own (within limits imposed by ventilator system).<br>**b.** Bathe patient daily. Keep skin lubricated with skin lotion.<br>**c.** Change ET and tracheotomy tube tapes p.r.n. (to prevent friction burn and skin breakdown).<br>**d.** Ensure that lines are not lying directly on patient.<br>**e. Long-term intubation.** Use alternate nostrils when changing ET tube.<br>**f.** When taking patient off ventilator, ensure that the high pressure of the heated air in ventilator is not directed at patient (this may cause a burn). |
| **6.** Potential hypoxia while patient is being weaned from ventilator.<br>**Objectives.** Adequate blood-gas levels maintained without mechanical ventilation. Patient is breathing spontaneously for gradually increasing lengths of time.<br>**Timing.** Until patient is able to breathe entirely on own. | **a.** Ensure that detailed orders for weaning from ventilator have been written.<br>**b.** Explain the procedure to child, as appropriate for age.<br>**c.** When connecting the spontaneous-breathing circuit to the ventilator set it at the same $O_2$ concentration and ensure adequate humidification.<br>**d.** Withhold sedation before starting to wean. |

| Usual Problems/Objectives/Timing | Nursing Orders |
|---|---|
| 6. (Continued). | **e.** Be aware that crying and anxiety may cause child to have respiratory difficulty. Stay with child; reassure him and encourage him to take deep breaths. |
| | **f.** Record the ventilator rate, and the frequency of the child's own respirations. |
| | **g.** Note the depth and quality of the child's own respirations. |
| | **h.** Monitor vital signs and arterial gases. |
| | **i. Report:** |
| |     —Extremes in the child's respiratory rate, and significant changes in other vital signs and/or arterial gases. |
| |     —Increasing dyspnea and/or decreased air entry. |
| |     —Deterioration in skin color and/or level of response. |
| | **j.** If the child is not tolerating weaning, stop the procedure, reinstitute controlled ventilation, and notify dr. |
| | **k.** Consult dr about restarting weaning procedure. |

# Careplan **102** Pneumonia

**Goals for Discharge or Maintenance**
See Objectives.

| Usual Problems/Objectives/Timing | Nursing Orders |
|---|---|
| **1.** Dyspnea due to decreased gas exchange.<br><br>**Objectives.** Normal respiration; no cyanosis.<br><br>**Timing.** Day 3. | **a.** Place patient in position most conducive to easy respiration.<br><br>**b.** Turn and position patient q2h. Each time, encourage him to do breathing exercises (deep-breathing and coughing).<br><br>**c.** Administer humidified $O_2$ by croup tent, mask, or nasal prongs, as ordered.<br><br>**d.** Observe and record respiratory rate, indrawing, air entry, and color, q2h while child is distressed.<br><br>**e.** At mealtimes or feeding times, assess patient's ability to remain out of $O_2$ without distress. If $O_2$ is necessary, give by nasal prongs, unless contraindicated. |
| **2.** Pyrexia. | *See* Careplan 10: Pyrexia. |
| **3.** Anxiety, irritability, and fatigue, due to respiratory distress and unfamiliar equipment and surroundings.<br><br>**Objectives.** Patient is resting comfortably, plays quietly, and understands treatment.<br><br>**Timing.** Day 2. | **a.** Provide quiet, restful environment.<br><br>**b.** Combine nursing procedures to maximize rest periods.<br><br>**c.** Remain with patient during periods of acute distress.<br><br>**d.** Provide quiet, age-appropriate diversions.<br><br>**e.** When appropriate, explain procedures, treatment, and equipment. |
| **4.** Potential dehydration due to increased fluid loss and anorexia.<br><br>**Objective.** Adequate oral intake.<br><br>**Timing.** Day 2. | **a.** Offer fluids at least q2h when patient is awake.<br><br>**b.** Involve parents in encouraging child to drink.<br><br>**c.** Observe for signs of dehydration. |
| **5.** Parents anxious because of child's distress and unfamiliar procedures.<br><br>**Objectives.** Parents discuss concerns and fears, appear relaxed with child, and participate in care.<br><br>**Timing.** Day 2. | **a.** Take time to talk to parents; encourage expression of feelings.<br><br>**b.** Explain treatments, especially if $O_2$ inhalations, physical therapy, antibiotics, and i.v. lines are used.<br><br>**c.** Encourage parents' participation in care and play.<br><br>**d.** Explain importance of rest for the patient; seek parents' cooperation in limiting visitors. |

**Goals for Discharge or Maintenance**
See Objectives.

| Usual Problems/Objectives/Timing | Nursing Orders |
|---|---|
| **1.** Severe respiratory distress due to bronchospasm.<br>**Objective.** Decreased distress.<br>**Timing.** As soon as possible. | **a.** Keep patient in semi-Fowler's position. If older child, have him lean forward on pillows placed on over-bed table.<br>**b.** Report to dr if distress increasing (e.g., increased agitation, respiratory rate, or diaphoresis; confusion; increasing drowsiness; or cyanosis).<br>**c.** Auscultate the chest at least q1h; report improvement or deterioration.<br>**d.** Administer inhalations as ordered by dr.<br>**e. Blood-gas determinations.** Take blood samples from arterial line, as ordered.<br>**f.** If patient has to be intubated, *see* Careplan 101: Older Infants and Children on a Ventilator.<br>**g.** Report to dr if extreme restlessness causes difficulties with ventilation. (Curare may be required.) |
| **2.** Exhaustion due to prolonged respiratory distress and frequent disturbances for essential care.<br>**Objective.** Provision made for rest.<br>**Timing.** Until discharge from ICU. | **a.** Position patient comfortably with pillows.<br>**b.** Organize nursing care to allow for rest periods.<br>**c.** Ensure that environment is as quiet and nonstimulating as possible.<br>**d.** Disturb as infrequently as possible and restrict the number of personnel in contact with child. |
| **3.** Potential cardiac complications due to administration of high concentrations of i.v. drugs (isoproterenol, salbutamol, and aminophylline).<br>**Objective.** Minimal complications.<br>**Timing.** Until bronchospasm is relieved. | **a.** Prepare the infusions as ordered. A separate line will be needed for each drug (Harvard pumps for isoproterenol and salbutamol; regular i.v. setup for aminophylline).<br>**b.** Ensure that dr orders rate of each infusion.<br>**c.** Each infusion must be checked and recorded by 2 nurses when solution is first prepared and at each change of shift.<br>**d.** Label each line:<br>–On bag of solution or pump.<br>–On tubing near insertion site.<br>**e.** Ensure that medications are not given or blood samples taken via these lines and that lines are not flushed.<br>**f.** Institute ECG monitoring:<br>–Cleanse skin well and apply electrodes carefully.<br>–Check that electrodes do not slip (profuse diaphoresis may detach them).<br>–Check that the monitor's rate alarms are functioning.<br>**g.** If tachycardia or cardiac arrhythmia develops, report to dr *stat*. |

261

continued

| Usual Problems/Objectives/Timing | Nursing Orders |
|---|---|
| **3. (Continued).** | **h.** Frequently, check the written orders for the infusions (concentration and rate). Notify dr *stat* if there is any discrepancy. |
| **4.** *If patient is on neuromuscular blocking drugs.* | *See* Careplan 78: Paralysis, by Neuromuscular Blocking Agents. |
| **5.** Fearfulness about the respiratory distress and the stressful environment.<br><br>**Objective.** Patient understands what is happening and becomes less fearful.<br><br>**Timing.** As soon as possible. | **a.** Stay with child as much as possible.<br><br>**b.** Speak calmly and quietly; allay his fears and assure him that the episode is temporary.<br><br>**c.** Explain the need for ICU care and that it will help him to get well; explain procedures and equipment. |
| **6.** Potential dehydration due to loss of fluids from respiratory tract and difficulty drinking.<br><br>**Objective.** Adequate hydration.<br><br>**Timing.** 24 hr. | **a.** Maintain i.v. fluids as ordered.<br><br>**b.** Assess level of hydration q2h.<br><br>**c.** Record intake and output.<br><br>**d.** When patient's distress lessens, offer small amounts of clear fluid (do not force). |
| **7.** Parents anxious about the severity of their child's condition.<br><br>**Objective.** Parents are reassured and less anxious.<br><br>**Timing.** Before discharge from ICU. | **a.** Explain to parents all procedures and equipment.<br><br>**b.** Reassure them that a nurse will be with their child at all times.<br><br>**c.** Explain that their child should be disturbed as little as possible; thus it is preferable for them to spend only brief periods with him—unless the child settles better when they are present. |

**Goals for Discharge or Maintenance**
I. Parents understand and can cope with follow-up care.
II. Parents describe how to recognize respiratory difficulty and know what to do if this develops.

| Usual Problems/Objectives/Timing | Nursing Orders |
|---|---|
| **1.** *Pre-operatively.* | **a.** *See* Careplan 17: Pre-operative Care, General. <br><br> **b.** Ensure that $O_2$ and suctioning equipment are at bedside. |
| **2.** Parents/patient anxious and fearful about acute respiratory distress and/or insertion of tracheotomy tube. <br><br> **Objectives.** Parents/patient have had procedures/equipment explained to them and appear able to cope with information given. <br><br> **Timing.** As soon as possible. | **a.** If patient is in respiratory distress: <br> –Stay with patient. <br> –Constantly reassure patient/parents. <br> –Explain procedures. <br> Notify dr *stat* if there is any deterioration in patient's respiratory status. <br><br> **b.** Reinforce dr's explanation of condition and its treatment. Show parents/patient a tracheotomy tube (use tracheotomy teaching doll) and explain how it acts as the new airway. <br><br> **c.** Explain what to expect postoperatively: <br> –Tracheotomy collar and nebulizer (to supply humidity). <br> –Suctioning procedure. <br> –Bloodstained mucus. <br> –$O_2$ and i.v. therapy. <br> –Temporary loss of voice. <br> –Monitoring equipment. <br><br> **d.** Provide opportunity to see another child who has adjusted well to having a tracheotomy and to talk with the parents of a tracheotomized child if appropriate. |
| **3.** *Postoperatively.* | **a.** *See* Careplan 21: Postoperative Care, General. <br><br> **b.** Designated nurse(s) trained in tracheotomy procedures to provide constant direct observation of the patient as per dr's orders (length of time depending on patient's age, reason for tracheotomy, and general condition). <br><br> **c.** Ensure that $O_2$, suction apparatus, hand ventilation equipment, ET tube (with lumen smaller than tracheotomy tube), scissors, and duplicate tracheotomy set are at bedside. <br><br> **d.** Follow hospital procedure for suctioning through tracheotomy. |
| **4.** Potential respiratory distress due to incorrect size or placement of tracheotomy tube and/or obstruction of cannula by thick mucus. <br><br> **Objectives.** Cannula patent; early detection of problems. | **a.** Place patient on a cardiac monitor for 24 hr or as ordered by dr. (*See* Careplan 107: Cardiac Monitoring.) <br><br> **b.** Record pulse and respiratory rate q15 min for 1 hr, then q30 min for 1 hr, then decrease frequency as |

continued

| Usual Problems/Objectives/Timing | Nursing Orders |
|---|---|
| **4. (Continued).**<br><br>**Timing.** Until extubation. | patient's condition stabilizes.<br><br>**c.** Observe closely for signs of respiratory distress:<br>–Increasing restlessness.<br>–Extreme fatigue.<br>–Dyspnea.<br>–Tachypnea or tachycardia.<br>–Retractions.<br>–Noisy respirations.<br>–Cyanosis or pallor.<br>–Diaphoresis.<br><br>**d.** Suction tracheotomy q20-30 min until no blood staining; then suction q1h for 12–16 hr, then q2h until patient coughs up secretions easily. (Eventually suctioning is done early in morning, before each feeding/meal, at bedtime, and p.r.n.).<br><br>**e.** Maintain humidity with tracheal mist collar and nebulizer for 24 hr, then:<br><br>**Older children.** If secretions are loose and easily coughed out, decrease period of time on mist as tolerated except during rest periods and at night.<br><br>**Infants and younger children.** Take off mist for short periods only as tolerated. (Any crusting will occlude smaller tube.)<br><br>**f.** If secretions are thick and difficult to remove, instill N saline drops before suctioning. Use heating rod in nebulizer, as ordered, to further loosen secretions.<br><br>**g.** Provide constant reassurance during suctioning procedure. Encourage patient to cough up own secretions, as appropriate.<br><br>**h.** Check frequently that the tracheotomy tube is held in place securely by ties with a triple knot. (One finger should fit between the tie and the patient's neck.)<br><br>**i.** Notify dr *stat* if patient is continuously coughing, air entry is diminished, or it is repeatedly difficult to insert catheter past the end of the tracheotomy tube (if tube is too long it may be resting on the carina or slipping into the main stem of the bronchus, usually the R).<br><br>**j.** If patient is in respiratory distress:<br>–Instill N saline into tracheotomy tube and suction; repeat if necessary.<br>–Sit patient upright.<br>–If distress is not relieved within a few seconds, notify dr *stat*.<br>–Stay with patient, hand ventilate, and/or administer $O_2$.<br>–Prepare for emergency resuscitation and/or change |

| Usual Problems/Objectives/Timing | Nursing Orders |
|---|---|
| **4. (Continued).** | of outer cannula by dr. *Do not attempt to change the outer cannula.*<br><br>**Note:** The dr does first tube change(s) and will order when the procedure can be done by designated nurses trained in the procedure. |
| **5.** Potential subcutaneous emphysema, pneumothorax, or bleeding due to surgical trauma and/or displacement of the tracheotomy tube.<br><br>**Objective.** Early detection of emphysema, pneumothorax, or bleeding.<br><br>**Timing.** 24 hr. | **a.** Immediately after patient's arrival on ward:<br>–Examine for excessive swelling or crepitus, and fresh bleeding around tracheotomy.<br>–Assess respiratory status.<br>–Auscultate chest to ascertain adequate air entry.<br>–Ensure that tracheotomy tube is in position and that the ties are not too tight.<br>–Observe for blood in tracheal secretions.<br>Check again when taking vital signs.<br>**b.** If swelling, crepitus, or respiratory difficulty occurs:<br>–Have someone call dr *stat.*<br>–Stay with patient; provide assisted breathing as necessary.<br>**c.** If bleeding occurs:<br>–Notify dr *stat.*<br>–Apply pressure at site.<br>–If there is bleeding into trachea, instill N saline and suction frequently (to keep airway clear).<br>–Constantly reassure patient.<br>–Monitor vital signs closely. |
| **6.** Potential aspiration of fluids due to depressed cough reflex or patient's difficulty in swallowing because of presence of tube in throat.<br><br>**Objective.** No aspiration.<br><br>**Timing.** Day 5. | **a.** Maintain patient on i.v. fluids and n.p.o. as ordered.<br>**b.** When patient's condition has stabilized and he is fully alert, offer sips of water to drink.<br>**c.** If patient is swallowing without difficulty, give small amounts of clear fluid, then increase to full fluids and diet as tolerated.<br>**d.** Instill N saline and suction *stat* if fluids/food come through tracheotomy. Observe for respiratory distress. Consult dr before giving further feeds.<br>**e.** If aspiration is a problem:<br>–Thicken feeds as ordered by dr.<br>–Suction tracheotomy before feeding. (Suctioning during or just after feeding may cause vomiting and aspiration.)<br>–Burp infant well after feeding and position him upright on R side.<br>–*Never leave feeding bottle with patient.* |
| **7.** Potential obstruction of tube by foreign body.<br><br>**Objective.** No obstruction. | **a.** Ensure that tracheotomy is not occluded by patient's chin or neck. |

continued

| Usual Problems/Objectives/Timing | Nursing Orders |
|---|---|
| **7. (Continued).**<br>**Timing.** Until extubation. | **b.** When removing inner cannula for suctioning, place a roll under patient's neck; replace inner cannula immediately.<br>**c.** Keep clothing away from tube.<br>**d.** Ensure that no crumbs or fluid enter the tube and that child does not have access to beans, beads, or toys with small parts. |
| **8.** Potential chest infection or infection of stoma due to skin contaminants or retention of secretions.<br>**Objective.** Early detection of infection.<br>**Timing.** Until extubation. | **a.** Use aseptic technique when suctioning and ensure replacement inner cannula has been sterilized.<br>**b.** Do deep suctioning as necessary to remove mucus p.r.n.<br>**c.** Change patient's position q2h until he is ambulant.<br>**d.** Follow dr's order for physical therapy.<br>**e.** If dressing is in place around stoma, do not change. If there is no dressing, cleanse area with ½ strength hydrogen peroxide followed by N saline.<br>**f.** Observe and report signs of infection:<br>–Pyrexia.<br>–Purulent discharge and erythema around tracheotomy site.<br>–Increased amounts of thick yellow or green blood-tinged mucus.<br>–Noisy respirations.<br>**g.** Give antibiotics as ordered by dr. |
| **9.** Potential injury to mucosa, due to dryness, forceful suctioning, or irritants.<br>**Objective.** No mucosal injury.<br>**Timing.** Until extubation. | **a.** Ensure that satisfactory humidity is maintained per tracheal mist collar. Use heating rod in nebulizer, as ordered by dr.<br>**b.** Instill drops of N saline when suctioning.<br>**c.** Suction gently using intermittent suction, only as necessary.<br>**d.** Maintain adequate hydration.<br>**e.** Avoid using powders, aerosols, and agents with irritating fumes near patient. |
| **10.** Patient/parents are anxious and afraid because of the tube in neck, absence of voice, and (usually) urgency of surgery.<br>**Objectives.** Patient appears less anxious and apprehensive. Parents are able to participate in their child's care.<br>**Timing.** As soon as possible. | **a.** Reassure patient/parents and explain usual course of events.<br>**b.** Reinforce purpose of tracheotomy, suctioning, etc. (Use the tracheotomy doll to show the child what the tube looks like and exactly how you use the catheter.)<br>**c.** Always tell patient when you are going to suction the tube:<br>**Older child.** Have patient assist with procedure as appropriate.<br>**Young child.** Have assistant *gently* restrain him. Give simple explanations in a soothing tone of voice. (Child may not understand what is being said but |

| Usual Problems/Objectives/Timing | Nursing Orders |
|---|---|
| 10. (Continued). | will learn from experience that he feels better afterward.) |
| | **d.** Reassure parents/patient that voice will come back once the tube is removed. Demonstrate how patient can say a few words by covering the tracheotomy. |
| | **e.** Provide pad and pencil, magic slate, or picture cards for communication. |
| | **f.** Encourage parents to participate in their child's care. |
| | **g.** Encourage child to resume normal activities as condition permits. |

# Careplan **105** Cardiac Arrhythmia

**Goals for Discharge or Maintenance**
See Objectives.

| Usual Problems/Objectives/Timing | Nursing Orders |
|---|---|
| **1.** Potential delay in treatment due to undocumented episodes of arrhythmia.<br><br>**Objective.** Episodes of arrhythmia are documented.<br><br>**Timing.** Ongoing. | **a.** *See* Careplan 107: Cardiac Monitoring.<br><br>**b.** Obtain a cardiac monitor with a rhythm strip recorder.<br><br>**c.** Check that ECG tracing paper is in the recorder and that recorder is on automatic. (If the alarm is activated, a 10–15 sec recording is made.)<br><br>**d.** If arrhythmia is noted on oscilloscope:<br><br>–Take a 10–15 sec tracing (if this was not done automatically).<br><br>–Label the tracing with the date, time, and patient's name.<br><br>–Notify dr and charge nurse.<br><br>–Count patient's apical heart rate; record regularity and rate. |
| **2.** Potential cardiac arrest if arrhythmia produces symptoms in patient.<br><br>**Objective.** Early detection of complications.<br><br>**Timing.** Until arrhythmia controlled. | **a.** Observe patient for chest pain, dizziness, sudden drop in BP, or diaphoresis. If they are present, stay with the patient and have someone report symptoms *stat.*<br><br>**b.** Ensure that all necessary equipment is ready for emergency treatment. |

**Goals for Discharge or Maintenance**
See Objectives.

| Usual Problems/Objectives/Timing | Nursing Orders |
|---|---|
| **1.** *Precatheterization.* | **a.** Follow hospital procedure for preparing patient for cardiac catheterization.<br><br>**b. Infant weighing less than 10 kg.** Ensure that blood typing and cross-match are done.<br><br>**c.** If Hb is >18 g/dl or Hct >55%, maintain i.v. fluids as ordered (because of potential problem of a cerebrovascular accident in polycythemic patients).<br><br>**d. Adolescent.** Do shave prep of both groins and upper thigh, if appropriate.<br><br>**e.** Check pedal pulse and mark site *before* cardiac catheterization (to provide comparison with post-test pedal pulse if groin is used as access for test).<br><br>**f.** Morning of catheterization, give patient a bath using an antibacterial cleanser; dress patient in gown.<br><br>**g.** Follow dr's orders for n.p.o. (usually from midnight except for a clear fluid drink 4 hr before booked catheterization time). |
| **2.** Parents/patient anxious about procedure done on the heart.<br><br>**Objectives.** Parents/patient have had the procedure explained to them (and have given informed consent), expressed their concerns, and appear able to cope with information given to them.<br><br>**Timing.** As soon as possible. | **a.** Reinforce information given to parents/child by dr, and explain steps of procedure. Use visual aids (e.g., diagrams or model of heart).<br><br>**b. Parents and older children.** Show slide tape presentation about heart tests.<br><br>**c.** Reassure parents that a nurse or nursing aide will be with their child throughout the procedure to hold his hand and comfort him.<br><br>**d.** Ensure that parents are advised of their child's progress and his return to his room. |
| **3.** Potential cardiac arrhythmia from introduction of foreign body into heart.<br><br>**Objective.** Apical rate within patient's usual range.<br><br>**Timing.** 24 hr. | **a.** Monitor heart rate and rhythm and BP: q¼h for 1 hr, q½h for 4 hr, q4h for 12 hr, and then b.i.d. if stable by the next morning.<br><br>**b.** If heart rate is irregular:<br>–Use cardiac monitor (*see* Careplan 107: Cardiac Monitoring).<br>–Place patient on bed rest.<br>–Notify dr. |
| **4.** Potential hemorrhage at incision site(s).<br><br>**Objective.** Early detection of hemorrhage.<br><br>**Timing.** 24 hr. | **a.** Check catheterization site(s) q1h.<br><br>**b.** If hemorrhage occurs:<br>–Apply direct pressure with fingers for 5–10 min.<br>–Institute complete bed rest for 8–12 hr.<br>–Apply or reinforce pressure dressing.<br>–Notify dr *stat*.<br>–Monitor apical rate and BP q15–30 min. |

| Usual Problems/Objectives/Timing | Nursing Orders |
|---|---|
| **4. (Continued).** | –Check dressings p.r.n. |
| **5.** Potential blood vessel blockage by clot formation.<br>**Objective.** Limb warm and of normal color.<br>**Timing.** 8 hr. | **a.** Check pedal pulse (radial pulse if arm has been used for test) when monitoring heart rate.<br>**b.** Check limb for warmth, color, sensation, and capillary filling.<br>**c.** Report abnormalities immediately to dr. |
| **6.** Potential nausea and vomiting (side effects of premedication or procedure).<br>**Objective.** No nausea or vomiting.<br>**Timing.** 24 hr. | **a.** Keep patient n.p.o. per dr's orders (usually 1–2 hr).<br>**b.** Start patient on sips of clear fluid; increase as tolerated to full fluids, then normal diet.<br>**c.** Record intake and output.<br>**d.** Observe for dehydration.<br>**e.** Give medication per dr's order. |
| **7.** Potential pyrexia: reaction to test dye. | *See* Careplan 10: Pyrexia. |
| **8.** Potential infection of cutdown site by pathogens introduced during or after catheterization.<br>**Objective.** No infection.<br>**Timing.** Until discharge. | **a.** Change cutdown site dressing daily and p.r.n. for 5 days, then leave site exposed.<br>**b.** Keep site clean and dry for 5 days; no tub baths or showers.<br>**c.** Observe for redness, swelling, or discharge.<br>**d.** If patient is discharged soon after catheterization, instruct parents about dressings and observation. |
| **9.** In cyanotic patients, potential blue spells due to sedation.<br>**Objective.** Color and respirations return to those usual for patient.<br>**Timing.** 24 hr. | If patient has a blue spell:<br>**a.** Notify dr *stat.*<br>**b.** Place patient in knee-chest position.<br>**c.** Administer $O_2$.<br>**d.** Stay with patient.<br>**e.** Give medication per dr's order. |
| **10.** Potential mismanagement of home care due to lack of understanding, or possibly parental overprotection.<br>**Objective.** Parents/patient are able to cope with home care and follow-up.<br>**Timing.** Before discharge. | **a.** Reinforce dr's instructions for home care and follow-up.<br>**b.** If patient is discharged soon after catheterization, instruct parents to:<br>–Change bandage over incision every day until 6 days post-catheterization (explain that sutures are a dissolving type).<br>–Give child sponge baths until final dressing is removed.<br>–Notify dr if there is any redness or swelling around incision line.<br>–Encourage child to resume regular diet and activity. (Child may have a sore leg for a few days and be reluctant to move; he should be up and moving around.)<br>–Ensure that parents have written discharge instructions, appointment(s) for follow-up, and prescription for medication if ordered. |

# Careplan **107** Cardiac Monitoring

## Goals for Discharge or Maintenance
See Objectives.

| Usual Problems/Objectives/Timing | Nursing Orders |
|---|---|
| **1.** Anxiety due to restricted activity and noise of monitor.<br><br>**Objectives.** Patient expresses feelings; he participates in his own care and diversional activities.<br><br>**Timing.** Until monitoring is discontinued. | **a.** Explain monitoring equipment (what it is, how it works, the reason for its use, the length of time it can be used, and the alarm bell).<br><br>**b.** Involve patient in his own care. When appropriate, allow him to take off his monitor leads.<br><br>**c.** Provide diversions and activities appropriate for his age. (Recreation department may help with materials and/or personnel.) |
| **2.** Potential skin breakdown due to frequent (or too infrequent) removal of monitor electrodes.<br><br>**Objective.** Skin at lead sites intact.<br><br>**Timing.** Until monitoring discontinued. | **a.** Change electrodes q3 days (neonatal electrodes q7-10 days), or when an electrode has become dislodged:<br><br>–Remove lead, clean off old tape marks, dry skin, and expose skin to air for a few minutes.<br><br>–Select new site and cleanse it with alcohol (to remove dead skin cells and improve conductivity). |
| **3.** Potential undetected changes in heart rate or rhythm, due to malfunction of monitor.<br><br>**Objective.** Early detection of monitor malfunction.<br><br>**Timing.** Until monitoring is discontinued. | **a.** Count the apical beat q1h, using a stethoscope, for a full minute; observe monitor simultaneously.<br><br>**b.** If ECG tracing or digital (heart rate) number on the monitor is not within 10–15 beats either way of the apical beat, check the leads and connections.<br><br>**c.** If monitor is still malfunctioning, obtain another monitor and notify the medical engineering department.<br><br>**d.** Check monitor and leads more frequently if the child is very restless or diaphoretic. |
|  | **Note.** The apical rate will be difficult to hear if electrodes are placed on small infant's chest. |

**Goals for Discharge or Maintenance**
See Objectives.

| Usual Problems/Objectives/Timing | Nursing Orders |
|---|---|
| **1.** Potential decrease in cardiac output, due to malfunctioning pacemaker, lack of contact between pacing catheter and heart wall, and/or myocardial failure.<br><br>**Objectives.** Adequate cardiac output. Early detection of malfunctioning pacemaker.<br><br>**Timing.** Until pacemaker is removed. | **a.** Place patient on cardiac monitor (*see* Careplan 107: Cardiac Monitoring).<br><br>**b.** Record on patient's careplan:<br>  –Date and time pacemaker was initiated.<br>  –Date when battery is due to be changed (every 5 days for A–V sequential pacemaker).<br><br>**c.** Note whether pacemaker is set on demand pacing or fixed pacing. Record rate set and voltage:<br>  –On progress notes at beginning of each shift.<br>  –On patient's careplan.<br>  –Whenever settings are changed.<br><br>**d.** Observe for early indications of battery failure:<br>  –Slight decrease in pacing rate (5–10 beats).<br>  –Altered or absent pacing stimulus on ECG.<br><br>**e.** Ensure that another functioning pacemaker is available on the ward.<br><br>**f.** Notify dr when pacemaker battery is due to be changed or is malfunctioning. (Note that charge nurses on the cardiology unit or ICU may change the battery in an emergency.)<br><br>**g.** Ensure that wire-insertion sites are labeled "ventricular" and "atrial," as appropriate.<br><br>**h.** Ensure that wires and pacemaker connections are kept dry and intact, and screwed tightly into terminals. Check connections q1h and p.r.n. (especially after patient has been moved or turned). Change gauze over insertion site daily (*remove with extreme caution*), and check connections to patient. Bathe patient in bed, not bathtub.<br><br>**i.** Record apical rate q1h (count 1 full minute), and note whether heart is sensing or pacing.<br><br>**j.** Observe for any heart rhythm disturbances by comparing apical rate with pacemaker reading.<br><br>**k.** Observe for signs of cardiac insufficiency (e.g., hypotension, cyanosis, decreased urinary output, poor peripheral perfusion). In an emergency, and as ordered by dr, a nurse may adjust the milliamperes (MA/OUTPUT) control to a higher rate to increase the patient's cardiac output.<br><br>**l.** Ensure that patient does not tamper with equipment:<br>  –Protect all dial settings and connections with plastic covers or clear adhesive tape.<br>  –Provide adequate supervision. |

continued

| Usual Problems/Objectives/Timing | Nursing Orders |
|---|---|
| **1. (Continued).** | –If patient is ambulatory, use safety pins and adhesive tape to secure the pacemaker to clothing.<br><br>–If patient is in bed, use safety pin to secure pacemaker to bed clothes.<br><br>**m.** If the patient leaves the ward, ensure he is accompanied by a nurse.<br><br>**n.** Provide activities that are suitable to the patient's level of tolerance and condition. |
| **2.** Potential infection due to contaminated wire-insertion site.<br><br>**Objective.** Early detection of infection.<br><br>**Timing.** Until pacemaker is removed. | **a.** Change gauze over the insertion site daily and secure dressing well with adhesive tape.<br><br>**b.** Notify dr if there are any signs of infection. |
| **3.** Parents' and patient's anxiety due to the added complication of cardiac arrhythmia following surgery.<br><br>**Objective.** Parents/patient express fears and concerns about pacemaker.<br><br>**Timing.** Until pacemaker is removed. | **a.** Reinforce dr's explanation about the cause of the arrhythmia and the purpose of the pacemaker.<br><br>**b.** Demonstrate to the patient/parents how they can protect the pacemaker.<br><br>**c.** Explain why the cardiac monitor is being used, (e.g., to observe the heart beat in relation to the pacemaker rate).<br><br>**d.** Provide diversional activities for the patient.<br><br>**e.** Explain procedures involving the pacemaker.<br><br>**f.** Provide opportunities for parents to discuss their concerns away from child's bedside. |

### Goals for Discharge or Maintenance
**I.** Patient is allowed to lead as normal a life as possible.
**II.** Patient/parents are able to cope in a positive way with the pacemaker and the limitations that it sets on some activities.

| Usual Problems/Objectives/Timing | Nursing Orders |
|---|---|
| **1.** *Pre-operatively.* | *See* Careplan 17: Pre-operative Care, General. |
| **2.** *Postoperatively.* | *See* Careplan 21: Postoperative Care, General.<br><br>**Notes.** The internal pacemaker wires may already have been inserted during previous cardiac surgery.<br><br>The external transvenous wires are left in place until the internal pacemaker is judged to be stable. |
| **3.** Potential decrease in cardiac output, due to:<br>–Displacement of wires.<br>–Malfunctioning pacemaker.<br>**Objective.** Early detection of problems.<br>**Timing.** Until discharge. | **a.** Place patient on bed rest.<br>**b.** *See* Careplan 107: Cardiac Monitoring. (Patient is routinely monitored for 24–48 hr postoperatively.)<br>**c.** Ensure that an external pacemaker is available.<br>**d.** Record rate that pacemaker has been set at on patient's careplan (see dr's order on the anesthetic record sheet—rate is usually set at 70–100/min).<br>**e.** Count the apical rate for 1 full minute, q1h. Note rate, rhythm, and regularity. Record on flowsheet.<br>**f.** If the apical rate and rhythm are not within the established parameters for the patient, notify charge nurse and dr *stat*. |
| **4.** Potential infection (wound and skin, infective endocarditis, and/or septicemia), due to contamination of incision or wires.<br>**Objective.** No infection or its early detection.<br>**Timing.** 7 days. | **a.** Observe incision sites for redness, swelling, and drainage.<br>**b.** Report any temperature elevation to dr.<br>**c.** Wrap dry, clean gauze dressing loosely around wire-insertion sites. Change dressing p.r.n. and remove dressing when patient has a bath. |
| **5.** Pain at site of insertion.<br>**Objective.** Patient appears comfortable and is not complaining of pain.<br>**Timing.** 24–48 hr. | **a.** Position patient comfortably.<br>**b.** Dress patient in clothes that are loose-fitting, especially at waist band.<br>**c.** Give analgesic as ordered by dr. |
| **6.** Parents' and patient's anxiety due to:<br>–Lack of knowledge about the heart's conducting system and the function of a pacemaker.<br>–Further hospitalizations (e.g., for battery changes: in children, the life span of a battery is 18–24 months).<br>–The responsibility for a life-sustaining device.<br>**Timing.** Before discharge. | **a.** Set aside time for daily teaching sessions for patient/parents:<br>–Basic anatomy and physiology of the heart.<br>–Patient's specific cardiac problem.<br>–Function of a pacemaker.<br>–How to take the radial pulse for 1 full minute.<br>**b.** Instruct parents in the importance of good hygiene and nutrition to prevent infection.<br>**c.** Explain what the limitations in activities will be (e.g., no contact sports, gradual build up of exercise |

continued

| Usual Problems/Objectives/Timing | Nursing Orders |
|---|---|
| **6. (Continued).** | tolerance), but emphasize the importance of treating their child as normal within these limits. |
| | **d.** Provide information and help parents contact the pacemaker clinic and other support services. |
| | **e.** Give patient/parents appropriate printed booklets (e.g., *Jeff's New Pacemaker.* Medtronic 1974, *Pacing Your Heart.* Medtronic, 1979). |
| | **f.** Encourage patient to wear a Medic Alert bracelet or necklace. Help parents complete the form. |
| | **g.** Ensure that parents have written instructions about home care, management of the pacemaker, whom to contact if there are problems, and follow-up appointments. |

# 110

## Coarctation of the Aorta

**Goals for Discharge or Maintenance**
Parents have realistic expectations of outcome of surgery and understand importance of follow-up.

| Usual Problems/Objectives/Timing | Nursing Orders |
|---|---|
| | **Note.** The patient is admitted 2 days before surgery to allow time for tests, consultations, and teaching. |
| **1.** *Pre-operatively.* | **a.** *See* Careplan 17: Pre-operative Care, General. |
| | **b.** Explain usual routines: |
| | – Patient is seen by cardiologist, anesthesiologist, and surgeon. |
| | – Assessment is done by physical therapist and program of exercises started (e.g., deep-breathing and coughing). |
| | – A dental consultation may be arranged. |
| | – Blood tests and x-rays will be done. |
| | – Family will see a slide tape presentation about ICU and meet with ICU nurse. |
| | **c.** Explain that the day of admission is usually very busy but there will be time the next day to talk about what they have learned and what they still need to know. |
| | **d.** Obtain baseline BP measurements on all four limbs and record on flowsheet and functional enquiry sheet. (BP will be elevated in arms and decreased in legs.) |
| | – Use a slightly larger cuff to take leg BP. |
| | – Use a Doppler apparatus only if necessary (an accurate diastolic pressure is important.) |
| **2.** *Postoperatively.* | *See* Careplan 21: Postoperative Care, General. |
| **3.** Potential tension on suture line and breakdown of repair due to elevated BP postop. **Objective.** Early detection of complications. **Timing.** 10 days. | **a.** Take BP in the R arm and L leg as ordered (at least q4h), using appropriate size cuff. Compare with preoperative BP. |
| | **b.** Check dr's order for the reference BP (the arm BP level at which the dr is to be notified or antihypertensive drug administered). |
| | **c.** Check femoral pulses at least q4h. Notify dr if they are very weak or not palpable. |
| | **d.** Gradually increase the patient's activity as ordered. Record date of activity on the patient's care plan. |
| | **Usual routine:** |
| | **First 48 hr.** Keep patient flat in bed. Turn him from side to side without elevating his head and do not tip him for physical therapy. |
| | **Day 3.** Elevate head of bed 30–45 degrees. Patient may sit up in bed or in wheelchair. |
| | **Day 4.** Ambulate patient (check with dr before initiating ambulation). |

continued

| Usual Problems/Objectives/Timing | Nursing Orders |
|---|---|
| **4.** Potential hemorrhage from repair site due to tension on suture line, elevated BP, or endocarditis.<br><br>**Objective.** Early detection of hemorrhage.<br><br>**Timing.** 10 days. | **a.** Report persistently elevated BP (usually, greater than 150/100).<br><br>**b.** Report *stat* any of the following signs and symptoms:<br>–Sudden drop in BP not associated with antihypertensive drugs.<br>–Complaint of sudden chest pain.<br>–Chest suddenly very noisy on auscultation.<br>–Increased chest tube drainage.<br>–Restlessness, lethargy, apprehension.<br>–Signs of shock: tachypnea or tachycardia; pale, cool, or clammy skin.<br><br>**c.** If these symptoms occur, prepare for emergency treatment. |
| **5.** Potential abdominal pain due to paralytic ileus or increased blood flow.<br><br>**Objective.** Early detection of abdominal pain or ileus.<br><br>**Timing.** 24–48 hr. | **a.** Keep patient n.p.o. as ordered.<br><br>**b.** Assess for bowel sounds. Do not start oral feedings until bowel sounds are heard.<br><br>**c.** After bowel sounds return start patient on clear fluids; give frequent small amounts (e.g., 30-50 ml q1-2h).<br><br>**d.** Gradually introduce regular diet as ordered (e.g., clear fluids × 24 hr, full fluids × 24 hr, then soft to regular diet).<br><br>**e.** Observe and report:<br>–If bowel sounds are absent beyond 48 hr.<br>–Severe abdominal pain.<br>–Abdominal distention.<br>–Persistent vomiting when oral fluids started. |
| **6.** *If correction is done in infancy.* Potential lack of understanding that coarctation may recur.<br><br>**Objectives.** Parents state understanding of condition and are able to cope with information given.<br><br>**Timing.** Before discharge. | **a.** Ensure that dr speaks with parents about prognosis and management. Reinforce explanations (do not be overly optimistic).<br><br>**b.** If parents seem to have an unrealistic attitude, have the dr speak with them again. Involve support services (e.g., social worker, public health nurse, family dr) p.r.n.<br><br>**c.** Emphasize importance of keeping follow-up clinic appointments.<br><br>**d.** Encourage parents to treat the child as normal once he has recuperated from surgery. |

**Goals for Discharge or Maintenance**
Parents/patient recognize signs/symptoms of heart failure and know importance of continuing medication and attending for follow-up.

| Usual Problems/Objectives/Timing | Nursing Orders |
|---|---|
| **1.** Respiratory distress due to body's attempts to supply $O_2$ to vital organs, pulmonary edema, and hepatomegaly.<br><br>**Objective.** Decreased respiratory distress.<br><br>**Timing.** 24 hr after start of treatment. | **a.** Elevate patient's head and chest. (For infants, use an infants' seat or special cardiac chair.)<br><br>**b.** Administer humidified $O_2$ as ordered by dr.<br><br>**c.** Observe at least q1h for:<br>  –Tachypnea.<br>  –Dyspnea.<br>  –Grunting or labored respiration.<br>  –Nasal flaring.<br>  –Pallor or cyanosis.<br>  –Pyrexia or subnormal temperature (skin or core).<br>  –Decreased peripheral perfusion.<br>  –Distended scalp and neck veins.<br>  –Increased irritability.<br>  If symptoms increase or persist, notify dr *stat.*<br><br>**d.** Listen to chest sounds q1h. If air entry is diminished and/or patient is wheezing, notify dr *stat.*<br><br>**e. Infant.** Avoid gastric distention; do not overfeed. A full stomach will impede lung expansion. Burp thoroughly. Feeds may be withheld while respirations are very rapid or labored.<br><br>**f. Infant weighing less than 5 kg.** Nurse in incubator. |
| **2.** Tachycardia.<br><br>**Objective.** Heart rate within patient's normal limits.<br><br>**Timing.** 24 hr after start of treatment. | **a.** Use cardiac monitor (*see* Careplan 107: Cardiac Monitoring).<br><br>**b.** Record apical heart rate: q1h during acute phase, then q2–4h as ordered.<br><br>**c.** Give medication as ordered. If signs/symptoms of toxicity develop, report to dr *stat.*<br><br>**d.** Do not overdress the patient and avoid constricting clothing. Use light bedcovers.<br><br>**e. Infant:**<br>  –Adjust amounts and times of feedings, to avoid overfatigue.<br>  –Limit handling immediately before feedings.<br>  –*See* nursing order 6(a). |
| **3.** Potential respiratory/cardiac arrest due to acute pulmonary edema.<br><br>**Objective.** Early detection of problems.<br><br>**Timing.** Until pulmonary edema is resolved. | **a. Notify dr *stat*** if these signs/symptoms occur:<br>  –Tachycardia above 180/min.<br>  –Tachypnea above 90/min.<br>  –Temperature increasing.<br>  –Extreme irritability/restlessness. |

279

continued

| Usual Problems/Objectives/Timing | Nursing Orders |
|---|---|
| **3. (Continued).** | **b.** If any of these develop, place the patient in *high* Fowler's position and hyperextend the neck (and trachea) by placing a rolled diaper or towel under it. Give $O_2$ by hood or mask.<br><br>*–Stay with patient.*<br><br>–Have all necessary equipment ready for emergency treatment (e.g., blood-gas concentrations will be determined; sodium bicarbonate will be given).<br><br>**c.** Monitor electrolytes closely. |
| **4.** Diminished urinary output and edema due to retention of sodium and water.<br><br>**Objectives.** Intake and urinary output balanced; blood electrolytes within normal range.<br><br>**Timing.** As soon as possible. | **a.** Weigh patient daily (at the same time, on the same scale):<br><br>**Infant.**  Naked.<br><br>**Older child.**   In nightwear, no footwear, on standing scales.<br><br>Notify dr or charge nurse if weight increase exceeds 0.3 kg.<br><br>**b.** Regulate fluid restrictions; distribute fluid intake evenly over the day.<br><br>**c.** Record intake and output in detail (for infants: weigh diapers). Notify dr if output is diminished.<br><br>**d.** If diuretic is given, record this (time and dose) on the intake/output chart. Notify dr if the diuretic is not effective. (If the patient is placed on a diuretic routine, electrolytes are to be done twice weekly.)<br><br>**e.** Record excessive diaphoresis (source of fluid loss) and/or edema of eyelids, abdomen, scrotum, sacral area, and ankles (fluid retention).<br><br>**f.** While edema is present, avoid constricting clothes and examine pressure areas for potential breakdown of skin. |
| **5.** Patient anxious, irritable, and readily fatigued due to increased cardiac workload.<br><br>**Objective.** Patient appears less anxious and is getting adequate rest.<br><br>**Timing.** Continuing. | **a.** Plan care to provide frequent rest periods; ensure that patient *does* rest.<br><br>**b.** Anticipate the child's needs.<br><br>**c.** Respond promptly to any signs of distress (e.g., crying).<br><br>**d.** Support patient emotionally.<br><br>**Infant.**  Pick up and cuddle frequently; if no contraindications use a pacifier.<br><br>**e.** Assist patient with bathing, feeding, etc.<br><br>**f.** If patient becomes increasingly irritable or restless, notify dr *stat*. |
| **6.** Potential malnutrition due to increased caloric requirements.<br><br>**Objective.** Body weight maintained.<br><br>**Timing.** Continuing. | **a. Infant**<br><br>–Give frequent small feedings. Use a soft, short nipple; feed infant slowly, and burp him frequently. Supplement with NG feedings p.r.n.<br><br>–Hold $O_2$ mask over infant's face during feeding. |

| Usual Problems/Objectives/Timing | Nursing Orders |
|---|---|
| **6.** (Continued). | **b. Older child.** Present high-calorie foods served attractively.<br><br>**c.** If there are fluid restrictions, consult the dietitian about adding concentrated calories to the diet.<br><br>**d.** If fatigue is severe (infant/child very slow to feed; cyanosis and respiratory distress increasing), notify dr.<br><br>**e.** Do mouth care q4h and p.r.n. |
| **7.** Increased susceptibility to infection.<br>**Objective.** No infection.<br>**Timing.** Continuing. | **a.** Try to ensure that the patient's roommates are free of infection.<br><br>**b.** Adults who have contact with the patient should be free of colds or other infection.<br><br>**c.** Pay careful attention to hand-washing, etc.<br><br>**d. Child under 2 years.** Wear a gown. |
| **8.** Parents anxious about their child's distress and their own ability to cope with home care.<br>**Objectives.** Parents express concerns and are making plans for home care.<br>**Timing.** Before discharge. | **a.** Encourage parents to participate (under supervision) in their child's care.<br><br>**b.** Teach parents:<br>    –The signs and symptoms of heart failure.<br>    –What to do when they occur.<br>    –Importance of medication.<br>    –Side effects of medication.<br>    –If the patient is an infant, methods of feeding and giving other infant care.<br><br>**c.** Refer to the appropriate agency for follow-up at home (usually a public health nurse).<br><br>**d.** Ensure that the parents know whom to contact when problems arise at home. |

**Goals for Discharge or Maintenance**

I. Parents understand the condition.

II. They recognize the warning signs and can prevent a severe attack.

| Usual Problems/Objectives/Timing | Nursing Orders |
|---|---|
| 1. Potential cyanotic attack due to lack of anticipation or prevention.<br><br>**Objective.** Measures instituted to prevent attacks.<br><br>**Timing.** Before discharge. | a. Teach parents and other adults caring for and in contact with the child how to recognize the signs of an impending attack.<br><br>b. **Infant or toddler**<br><br>–Change diaper promptly.<br><br>–Feed as soon as he is ready.<br><br>–Pick up and cuddle when he is upset.<br><br>c. **Older child**<br><br>–Allow moderate exercise only.<br><br>–Prevent overexertion.<br><br>–Recognize that some routine activities are stressful for the child (e.g., weighing, having blood taken for tests).<br><br>d. If crying persists, hold child in knee-chest position and soothe him until he feels better. |
| 2. Potential respiratory difficulty, deep cyanosis, and eventual loss of consciousness, due to pulmonary infundibular spasm.<br><br>**Objectives.** Improvement in color and respiration; patient is conscious.<br><br>**Timing.** By end of attack. | a. **Infant or toddler.** Pick child up; hold him in knee-chest position, and cuddle him.<br><br>b. **Older child.** Place in knee-chest position; stay with child.<br><br>c. Give medication as ordered (usually morphine i.m.).<br><br>d. When medication has taken effect, give $O_2$ by mask. ($O_2$ will not be effective until spasm has lessened.) |
| 3. Parents are fearful and feel inadequate during child's attack.<br><br>**Objectives.** Parents understand what a cyanotic attack is and can cope with measures to prevent severe ones.<br><br>**Timing.** Before discharge. | a. Designated nurse to explain:<br><br>–Anatomy of heart defect (in appropriate terms).<br><br>–What is believed to be causing the attacks.<br><br>–How to anticipate and/or prevent attacks.<br><br>b. Help parents to cope with attacks. Emphasize to them that a severe attack can occur even if thorough preventive measures are taken; i.e., some attacks cannot be prevented.<br><br>c. Reinforce dr's plan for home care and follow-up. |

# Careplan 113   Endocarditis, Infective

**Goals for Discharge or Maintenance**
I. Parents understand the importance of prophylaxis.
II. They can cope with home care and follow-up.

| Usual Problems/Objectives/Timing | Nursing Orders |
|---|---|
| **1.** Prolonged bed rest. | *See* Careplan 13: Prolonged Immobilization. |
| **2.** Lethargy and malaise due to pyrexia.<br><br>**Objective.** Patient appears comfortable.<br><br>**Timing.** Continuing. | **a.** *See* Careplan 10: Pyrexia.<br>**b.** Give patient antipyretics as ordered.<br>**c.** Change his clothes and bed linen frequently.<br>**d.** Provide quiet diversions. |
| **3.** Potential phlebitis due to prolonged antibiotic therapy, and pain or emotional upset caused by frequent i.v. stabs.<br><br>**Objectives.** No phlebitis; minimal number of i.v. infusions started; patient tolerates i.v. therapy reasonably well.<br><br>**Timing.** Until i.v. therapy is discontinued (usually 6 weeks). | **a.** Immobilize the affected limb.<br>**b.** Whenever possible, have the same person start the i.v. infusions.<br>**c.** Ensure that antibiotics are appropriately diluted before infusion.<br>**d.** Check the i.v. rate and site q1h: at the first sign of redness, change the site of the needle.<br>**e.** Notify dr if there is swelling, redness, or tenderness of the i.v. site or the vein above. |
| **4.** Parents/patient concerned about the disruption of family life by the prolonged hospitalization.<br><br>**Objective:** Parents and other family members maintain contact with the child.<br><br>**Timing.** Before discharge. | **Designated nurse:**<br>**a.** Spend time listening to concerns, answering questions, and reinforcing information.<br>**b.** Encourage family contacts by visitors, letters, and telephone calls. Allow younger siblings and friends to visit when possible. |
| **5.** Potential mismanagement of home care due to lack of understanding.<br><br>**Objective.** Parents understand the importance of prophylaxis.<br><br>**Timing.** Before discharge. | **a.** Ascertain what the parents/patient know about the prophylactic treatment.<br>**b.** Explain the need for its accurate maintenance.<br>**c.** Ensure that parents understand the information. Reinforce instructions (orally and in writing).<br>**d.** Arrange supervision by a public health nurse p.r.n. |

## Goals for Discharge or Maintenance
**I.** Parents and patient state understanding of the condition and importance of follow-up.
**II.** Parents are reassured and will allow child to be treated as normal.

| Usual Problems/Objectives/Timing | Nursing Orders |
|---|---|
| **1.** Parents/patient anxious about heart murmur because of preconceived ideas about heart conditions.<br><br>**Objective:** Parents/patient express concerns and appear reassured by explanations.<br><br>**Timing.** As soon as possible. | **a.** Explain usual routines for the clinic visit:<br>  –Height and weight.<br>  –ECG and roentgenogram.<br>  –Consultation with cardiologist.<br>  –Echocardiogram (possibly).<br>**b.** Explain that heart murmur is not necessarily associated with heart disease; some murmurs disappear when the child reaches adolescence.<br>**c.** Explain that heart murmur is produced by the circulation of blood through the valves and chambers of the heart. (Use diagrams, anatomical drawing, or model to demonstrate.)<br>**d.** Encourage parents/patient to ask questions and voice concerns.<br>**e.** Provide written information when indicated (e.g., Ontario Heart Foundation leaflet *Innocent Heart Murmurs in Children*). |
| **2.** Potential mismanagement of home care and follow-up due to lack of understanding.<br><br>**Objectives.** Parents understand the importance of follow-up and state willingness to allow child to be treated as normal.<br><br>**Timing.** By end of first visit. | **a.** Reinforce dr's explanation about the heart murmur.<br>**b.** Explain that child can lead a normal life and that activities, including sports, need not be restricted.<br>**c.** Reassure parents and patient that it is the usual routine for all children with functional heart murmur to be examined by a cardiologist at stated intervals (to confirm original diagnosis).<br>**d.** Give parents name and telephone number of person to be contacted if they are worried. |

**Goals for Discharge or Maintenance**

**I.** Parents are willing to follow dr's outpatient regimen.
**II.** Patient is allowed to return to normal activity.

| Usual Problems/Objectives/Timing | Nursing Orders |
|---|---|
| **1.** *Pre-operatively.* | **a.** *See* Careplan 17: Pre-operative Care, General. |
| | **b.** Explain to parents: |
| | –i.v. therapy. |
| | –Chest physical therapy. |
| | –Incision (location, size). |
| | **c.** Explain to the parents the *usual* course of events after the operation: |
| | –The child stays in the PAR for 4–5 hr. (Arrangements can be made to visit children in the PAR.) |
| | –If there are no complications, their child will return to the ward the same day. |
| | –If there are complications, their child will stay in the PAR overnight or will be admitted to the ICU. |
| | **d.** If the child can cooperate, teach him and have him demonstrate deep-breathing, coughing, and arm exercises. |
| | **e.** Give child a shampoo and bath, and scrub with antibacterial cleanser, the evening before and the day of surgery. |
| **2.** *Postoperatively.* | **a.** *See* Careplan 21: Postoperative Care, General. |
| | **b.** Keep child n.p.o. until bowel sounds audible (check q2–4h); then, allow sips of fluids as tolerated. Increase diet as ordered. |
| **3.** Potential elevation of BP, due to altered circulation.<br>**Objective.** BP within normal range.<br>**Timing.** 2–3 days. | **a.** Record BP q4h, unless otherwise ordered. (BP may be elevated for 1–2 days postoperatively, until the heart has compensated for the ligated ductus.)<br>**b.** Notify dr if BP is higher than 150/100 mm Hg. |
| **4.** Discomfort, pain, and reluctance to move left side.<br>**Objectives.** Minimal discomfort. Full range of movement.<br>**Timing.** 3–4 days. | **a.** Give sedation as ordered.<br>**b.** Follow program of passive and active exercises set by the physical therapist, q2–4h.<br>**c.** Encourage patient to move his left arm and shoulders, by placing books, toys, or mobiles just within or slightly beyond his reach. |
| **5.** Potential pneumonia or atelectasis because of patient's reluctance to cough up secretions.<br>**Objective.** Prevention or early detection of respiratory problems.<br>**Timing.** 5 days. | **a.** Record respiratory rate: q1h for 24 hr, then as ordered (usually q4h, along with other vital signs).<br>**b.** Encourage child to cough and deep-breathe: q1h for 12 hr, q2h for 12 hr, then q4h. (Splint the thoracotomy incision with a pillow or towel.)<br>**c.** Turn the child at least q2h (side to side and semi-Fowler's position). |

continued

| Usual Problems/Objectives/Timing | Nursing Orders |
|---|---|
| **5. (Continued).** | **d. Infant.** Gentle suctioning may be necessary to stimulate coughing. |
| **6.** Potential parental overprotection of their child.<br>**Objective.** Parents treating child as normal.<br>**Timing.** Before discharge. | **a.** Listen to parents' concerns and answer all their questions.<br>**b.** Encourage parents to participate in their child's care, so they will see the change in his condition.<br>**c.** Reassure parents that their child will be able to live a normal life (unless contraindicated by other disease or defects).<br>**d.** If they require further reassurance, ask the dr to speak to them. Reinforce this information.<br>**e.** Ensure that parents have a follow-up appointment and know whom to contact if they are having problems. |

**Goals for Discharge or Maintenance**
**I.** Patient resumes normal activities within limitations of heart disease.
**II.** Parents understand importance of penicillin prophylaxis.
**III.** Parents can cope with home care and follow-up.

| Usual Problems/Objectives/Timing | Nursing Orders |
|---|---|
| **1.** Potential progressive heart damage.<br><br>**Objective.** Prevention of further heart damage.<br><br>**Timing.** Until discharge. | **a.** Maintain bed rest (usually for a minimum of 2–4 weeks). Patient may feed himself unless contraindicated by extreme illness or restlessness.<br><br>**b.** Plan patient's care to provide adequate rest.<br><br>**c.** Instruct parents to spend only brief periods with their child (unless he rests better when they are there). Ask them to limit visitors. Explain to patient and parents the reason for restriction and importance of rest.<br><br>**d.** Record fluid intake and output.<br><br>**e.** If edema develops, notify dr.<br><br>**f.** Weigh patient at least twice a week (same clothing, same time of day, same scales).<br><br>**g.** Record apical heart rate resting and sleeping. (Take for a full minute.) |
| **2.** Pyrexia. | *See* Careplan 10: Pyrexia. (Do not give patient additional ASA.) |
| **3.** General malaise, profuse sweating, and (possibly) painful joints.<br><br>**Objectives.** Patient is comfortable and is able to participate in quiet activities.<br><br>**Timing.** 1 week. | **a.** Position patient comfortably.<br><br>**b.** Use bed-cradle to keep weight off affected joints.<br><br>**c.** Use light, absorbent, nonrestrictive clothing and bedcovers.<br><br>**d.** Encourage appetite: offer small meals served attractively.<br><br>**e.** Increase fluid intake unless ordered otherwise.<br><br>**f.** Give mouth care p.r.n.<br><br>**g.** Provide quiet diversions (e.g., roommates, music, TV). |
| **4.** Prolonged immobilization. | *See* Careplan 13: Prolonged Immobilization. (Do not allow active exercises until joint pains have subsided.) |
| **5.** Potential excessive weight gain due to steroid therapy.<br><br>**Objective.** Weight gain is within normal limits.<br><br>**Timing.** Throughout steroid therapy. | **a.** Record intake of solids (as well as fluids).<br><br>**b.** Reduce salt in diet, as ordered.<br><br>**c.** Limit both the number of snacks and their caloric value.<br><br>**d.** Consult dietitian p.r.n.<br><br>**e.** Ask parents to bring toys or books instead of food as gifts.<br><br>**f.** Instruct parents/patient about diet to be followed at home. |

287

continued

| Usual Problems/Objectives/Timing | Nursing Orders |
|---|---|
| **6.** Potential loss of contact with family and friends, due to lengthy hospitalization. <br><br> **Objective.** Contact maintained with family and friends. <br><br> **Timing.** Until discharge. | **a.** Encourage family members to visit (for short periods at first, then longer as patient's condition improves). <br><br> **b.** If family cannot visit, encourage contact by telephone or letters. <br><br> **c.** Encourage visits by siblings (including young ones whenever possible). <br><br> **d.** Help patient maintain contact with school friends and interests. <br><br> *(All would-be visitors must be screened for infection.)* |
| **7.** Potential concern about changed self-image, due to the heart disease. <br><br> **Objective.** Patient has some understanding of his condition and accepts limitations. <br><br> **Timing.** By discharge. | **a.** Encourage patient to discuss concerns and ask questions. <br><br> **b.** Ask dr to explain to patient, in appropriate terms, the condition and the anatomy of the heart. <br><br> **c.** Reinforce dr's explanations; illustrate with diagrams. <br><br> **d.** Explain to parents the importance of treating their child normally. Ask them to explain the child's condition and appropriate treatment to his schoolteacher, friends, etc. <br><br> **e.** Particularly if patient was previously a sports enthusiast, check that consultation has been arranged with a psychologist, career-guidance counselor, etc. |
| **8.** Parents are concerned about home care and have fears about child's heart damage. <br><br> **Objective.** Parents have some understanding of their child's condition and can relate this to the planned home care and follow-up. <br><br> **Timing.** Before discharge. | **a.** Ask dr to speak to parents frequently about their child's progress. <br><br> **b.** If degree of heart damage has been established, reinforce dr's explanations about future tests and/or surgery (e.g., cardiac catheterization, valvar surgery). <br><br> **c.** If possible, arrange for parents/patient to meet a patient who has undergone surgery for the same condition. <br><br> **d.** Teach parents/patient: <br> –Penicillin prophylaxis. <br> –Medication. <br> –Dietary restrictions (if any). <br> –Physical restrictions (if any). <br> –Symptoms of recurrence or progression of heart disease (including chorea). <br> –Importance of outpatient care. <br><br> **e.** Ensure that home schooling has been arranged. |

**Goals for Discharge or Maintenance**
I. Parents understand that the stridor may persist for about 2 years postoperatively.
II. Patient is performing activities that are normal for his age.

| Usual Problems/Objectives/Timing | Nursing Orders |
|---|---|
| **1.** *Pre-operatively.* | **a.** *See* Careplan 17: Pre-operative Care, General. |
| | **b.** Explain to parents that their child will be transferred to the ICU for special care after the operation and that a nurse will take them there to visit him. Designated nurse to show parents slide tape presentation about ICU. |
| | **c.** Explain to the parents: |
| |    –i.v. therapy. |
| |    –Chest physical therapy. |
| |    –That the stridor will probably persist after the operation. |
| |    –If vomiting is present, the operation will probably cure it. |
| | **d.** Follow the physical therapist's plan for deep-breathing and coughing. |
| | **e.** Give child a shampoo and bath, and scrub with antibacterial cleanser, the evening before and the day of surgery. |
| **2.** *Postoperatively.* | **a.** *See* Careplan 21: Postoperative Care, General. |
| | **b.** Keep child n.p.o. until bowel sounds are audible (check q2–4h); then, allow sips of fluid as tolerated. Increase the diet as ordered. |
| **3.** Discomfort, pain, and reluctance to move the affected side.<br>**Objectives.** Minimal discomfort. Full range of movement.<br>**Timing.** 3–4 days. | **a.** Give analgesics as ordered.<br>**b.** Follow the program of passive and active exercises set by the physical therapist, q2–4h.<br>**c.** Encourage patient to move his arms and shoulders, by placing playthings or mobiles just within or slightly beyond his reach. |
| **4.** Potential pneumonia or atelectasis because of patient's reluctance to cough up secretions.<br>**Objective.** Prevention or early detection of respiratory problems.<br>**Timing.** 5 days. | **a.** Record the respiratory rate q1h for 24 hr, then q4h.<br>**b.** Encourage patient to deep-breathe and cough: q1h for 12 hr, q2h for 12 hr, then q4h. (Splint the thoracotomy incision with a pillow or towel.)<br>**c.** Turn patient at least q2h (side to side and semi-Fowler's position).<br>**d.** **Infant.** Gentle suctioning may be necessary to stimulate coughing. |
| **5.** Parents are concerned about continuing stridor.<br>**Objective.** Parents understand why stridor is still present and accept it.<br>**Timing.** Before discharge. | **a.** Reinforce dr's explanations about the stridor and its possible duration. (It can last up to 2 years postoperatively.)<br>**b.** Ensure that parents understand and accept this information. |

continued

| Usual Problems/Objectives/Timing | Nursing Orders |
|---|---|
| 5. (Continued). | c. Reassure parents frequently:<br>   –Point out immediate positive effects of operation (e.g., their child has stopped vomiting).<br>   –Reassure them that their child will be able to take part in activities normal for his age after his return home.<br>d. Ensure that parents have a follow-up appointment and know whom to contact if they are concerned. |

| Usual Problems/Objectives/Timing | Nursing Orders |
|---|---|
| **5. (Continued).**<br>**Timing.** Until discharge. | **d.** Reassure patient/parents that odor will become less offensive as patient responds to dietary regimen. |
| **6.** Potential edema due to hypoproteinemia.<br>**Objective.** No edema, or its early detection.<br>**Timing.** Until discharge. | **a.** Check for edema daily. If present, notify dr.<br>**b.** If patient has edema:<br>   –Institute bed rest.<br>   –Change patient's position at least q2h.<br>   –Record and report any skin changes to dr. |
| **7.** Potential recurrence of symptoms due to noncompliance with diet.<br>**Objectives.** Family members state their understanding of the disease and treatment and the importance of life-long adherence to the diet.<br>**Timing.** Before discharge. | **a.** Reinforce dietary and medical teaching.<br>**b.** Provide opportunities for questions and expression of concerns by patient and family.<br>**c.** Refer to public health nurse as necessary.<br>**d.** Ensure that parents have written instructions about diet, information about specialty food shops, and follow-up appointments. |

# Careplan 120    Constipation, Chronic

## Goals for Discharge or Maintenance
**I.** Bowel has been emptied and bowel training initiated.
**II.** Parents/patient express understanding of the cause and treatment of chronic constipation and are willing to comply with preventive measures.

| Usual Problems/Objectives/Timing | Nursing Orders |
|---|---|
| **1.** Constipation and/or fecal soiling caused by overflow of retained stool. <br><br> **Objectives.** Patient's bowel is emptied and bowel routine has been initiated. <br><br> **Timing.** By discharge. | **a.** Designated nurse to obtain nursing history, including: <br> –Previous bowel training attempts. <br> –Present defecation pattern. <br> –Usual dietary intake (quality, quantity). <br><br> **b.** Administer enemas/laxative to empty bowel, as ordered by dr. (Care *must* be taken to prepare the child in an age-appropriate manner before an enema is given.) <br><br> **c.** Establish a toileting routine. Have patient sit on toilet/potty (with feet flat on floor or footstool) for 5–10 minutes after each meal. <br><br> **d.** Maximize opportunities for success: <br> –As soon as possible, try to establish when in the day this routine is most successful (e.g., after breakfast). <br> –When time has been established, eliminate routine for rest of day. <br><br> **e.** Instruct child not to strain excessively. <br><br> **f.** Direct child not to flush toilet until contents have been checked. <br><br> **g.** Record number, consistency, and size of stools; soiling; and reaction to training. <br><br> **h.** Praise patient when he defecates into toilet. <br><br> **i.** If soiling occurs, be matter of fact about it. <br><br> **j. Older child.** Reassure him that this problem will cease once a regular pattern is established. <br><br> **k.** Ensure that patient receives a balanced diet; document food intake. <br><br> **l.** Encourage and help child join in physical activities. |
| **2.** Potential conflict between parent and child about the persistent constipation and/or fecal soiling. <br><br> **Objectives:** Conflict recognized and measures implemented to help family resolve it. <br><br> **Timing.** By discharge. | **a.** Nursing staff to act as role models for parents by reinforcing positive behavior and calmly accepting accidents. <br><br> **b.** Document interactions between parents and child. <br><br> **c.** Consult dr about referral to psychiatric and/or social services p.r.n. <br><br> **d.** Provide opportunities for parents to express their feelings, in private, away from their child's room. |
| **3.** Potential recurrence of constipation at home due to family's lack of adherence to regimen. | **a.** Spend time with parents discussing importance of regular bowel training and suitable diet. Get dietitian's help if necessary. |

| Usual Problems/Objectives/Timing | Nursing Orders |
|---|---|
| **3. (Continued).**<br><br>**Objective.** Parents/patient state their understanding of the cause, treatment, and prevention of chronic constipation.<br><br>**Timing.** Before discharge. | **b.** Give parents written instructions for bowel routine for their child.<br><br>**c.** Refer to public health nurse as necessary.<br><br>**d.** Ensure that parents/patient have follow-up appointment(s) and know whom to contact if there are problems. |

## Goals for Discharge or Maintenance
Parents describe home care accurately and agree to comply with instructions.

| Usual Problems/Objectives/Timing | Nursing Orders |
|---|---|
| 1. Nonpersistence in carrying out instructions at home due to misunderstanding of plan of care.<br><br>**Objective.** Parents understand the need for medication and for carrying out treatment as instructed, for as long as instructed.<br><br>**Timing.** By end of first clinic visit. | a. Provide written instructions for timing of medication.<br><br>b. Demonstrate insertion of suppository or giving enema, if necessary.<br><br>c. Teach correct positioning to promote evacuation. |
| 2. Potential mismanagement due to lack of knowledge and understanding of diet required for proper bowel function.<br><br>**Objective.** Parents know the kinds of food to include in diet, daily and otherwise.<br><br>**Timing.** By end of first clinic visit. | a. Emphasize the importance of providing foods that aid elimination. Give written list if indicated. |
| 3. Need for consistent, understanding approach to management at home.<br><br>**Objective.** Parents state willingness to help child establish healthy bowel habits.<br><br>**Timing.** By end of first clinic visit. | a. Discuss with parents the need to be positive, but not obsessive, in helping child attain normal bowel routine.<br><br>–Instruct parents to return to clinic if behavioral conflicts arise.<br><br>–Give parents a written list of names and telephone extensions of dr and nurse. Instruct parents to telephone p.r.n. |

# Careplan **122** Crohn's Disease

**Goals for Discharge or Maintenance**
 **I.** Family members state an understanding of the disease, treatment, and medication.
**II.** They are willing to comply with home care and follow-up regimen.

| Usual Problems/Objectives/Timing | Nursing Orders |
|---|---|
| **1.** Abdominal pain and cramping due to inflammation of the bowel.<br><br>**Objective.** Abdomen relaxed.<br>**Timing.** Before discharge. | **a.** Position patient comfortably. (Some patients prefer to lie on their side, supported by pillows, others on their stomach.)<br>**b.** Apply dry heat to patient's abdomen p.r.n. (e.g., warmed towels or, if ordered by dr, a hot-water bottle filled with *warm* water).<br>**c.** Notify dr when patient has pain. Record precipitating factors, location, duration, type, and severity.<br>**d.** Provide a quiet environment.<br>**e.** Administer analgesics if ordered (rarely used). |
| **2.** Potential mouth ulcers due to inflammatory process.<br><br>**Objective.** Early detection of mouth ulcers.<br>**Timing.** Until discharge. | **a.** Encourage patient to rinse his mouth with mouthwash after meals, snacks, and p.r.n.<br>**b.** Observe for mouth ulcers daily. If lesions are present, record location and description; notify dr.<br>**c.** Clean lesions with diluted mouthwash q4h during waking hours.<br>**d.** Apply petrolatum to the lips to prevent cracking.<br>**e.** Reassure patient that lesions will heal as condition of bowel improves. |
| **3.** Potential perianal lesions due to inflammatory process.<br><br>**Objective.** Early detection of lesions.<br>**Timing.** Until discharge. | **a.** Observe for perianal lesions daily. If lesions are present, record location and description; notify dr.<br>**b.** Keep perineal area clean and dry. Use soft tissue for wiping.<br>**c.** Lubricate area well to protect it from fecal irritation.<br>**d.** Provide sitz baths, t.i.d. |
| **4.** Potential dehydration and weight loss due to poor intake and diarrhea.<br><br>**Objective.** Nutritional status and hydration maintained/improved.<br>**Timing.** Before discharge. | **a.** Place patient on bed rest during acute phase of illness.<br>**b.** Assess level of hydration b.i.d.<br>**c.** Weigh patient daily, before breakfast.<br>**d.** Record all intake and output.<br>**e.** Record:<br>  –Number, consistency, color, and amount of stools.<br>  –Presence of blood.<br>  –Degree of urgency.<br>  –Passage of flatus.<br>**f.** Keep fluids available at bedside unless contraindicated.<br>**g.** Establish diet in collaboration with patient, dietitian, and dr. Encourage high protein, high-calorie |

continued

| Usual Problems/Objectives/Timing | Nursing Orders |
|---|---|
| **4. (Continued).** | choices (patient will avoid food that causes him distress).<br><br>h. Administer elemental diet via NG tube or TPN according to protocol, if ordered. If patient is on TPN, *see* Careplan 129: Total Parenteral Nutrition. |
| **5.** Potential bowel obstruction, fistulae, and abscesses (rectal or intraabdominal) due to inflammation.<br><br>**Objective.** Early detection of bowel obstruction, fistulae, or abscesses.<br><br>**Timing.** Until discharge. | a. Notify doctor *stat* if patient has severe abdominal or rectal pain, vomiting, or rectal bleeding.<br><br>b. Record TPR and BP q4h, and report significant changes to dr.<br><br>c. Report to dr any complaints of dysuria, air in urinary stream, or fecal material in urine. |
| **6.** Fatigue and malaise due to:<br>  –Rectal bleeding.<br>  –Iron deficiency anemia.<br>  –Sleep deprivation.<br>  –Inflammatory process.<br><br>**Objective.** Patient appears rested and comfortable.<br><br>**Timing.** 2-3 weeks. | a. Record amount of blood and number and size of clots in stools.<br><br>b. Limit patient's activity during acute phase of illness (bed rest or patient up in his room). Provide a quiet environment and appropriate recreation.<br><br>c. Limit nonfamily visitors if necessary. |
| **7.** Embarrassment over frequent, foul-smelling stools and urgency.<br><br>**Objective.** Embarrassment limited by privacy and consideration of patient's feelings.<br><br>**Timing.** Throughout hospital stay. | a. Keep room well ventilated and free of odor.<br><br>b. Place patient in a single room, if possible.<br><br>c. During acute phase, keep a *covered* bedpan or commode within patient's reach.<br><br>d. Empty and return bedpan promptly.<br><br>e. Check patient frequently at night because of increase in stooling at this time. |
| **8.** Frustration and anxiety due to:<br>  –Difficulty adjusting to acute and chronic implications of the disease.<br>  –Delayed physical and sexual development.<br>  –Possibility of surgery (bowel resection or colectomy).<br><br>**Objectives.** Patient/parents express fears and frustration, and state realistic understanding of short- and long-term implications.<br><br>**Timing.** Before discharge. | a. Ensure a consistent assignment of nurses. Designate one nurse to establish rapport with patient and parents.<br><br>b. Provide opportunities for questions and the expression of expectations and concerns. Keep dr informed. (Be aware that surgery may be necessary in the future.)<br><br>c. Encourage family involvement in planning and providing care.<br><br>d. Provide information about support groups (e.g., Canadian Foundation for Ileitis and Colitis). |
| **9.** Potential regression due to illness and hospitalization.<br><br>**Objective.** Patient regains independence as condition improves.<br><br>**Timing.** Before discharge. | a. Encourage patient's independence in daily routines. Set short-term goals (e.g., choosing diet, getting dressed).<br><br>b. Record, daily, patient's level of activity and family's involvement. Encourage appropriate diversional activity.<br><br>c. Emphasize to family members that they should treat patient as normal, especially as condition improves. |

| Usual Problems/Objectives/Timing | Nursing Orders |
|---|---|
| **9. (Continued).** | **d.** Coordinate activities of health-team members (e.g., social worker, dietitian, and psychiatrist) and confer with them p.r.n.<br><br>**e.** Refer patient to the school teacher as soon as he is able to return to school work. |
| **10.** Potential joint pains and/or skin lesions associated with acute inflammation.<br><br>**Objective.** Early detection of symptoms.<br><br>**Timing.** Until discharge. | **a.** Notify dr if patient complains of joint pain or joints appear swollen.<br><br>**b.** To reduce stiffness, bathe patient in warm water. Allow time to soak, adding water periodically to maintain temperature.<br><br>**c.** Reassure patient and parents that the joint pain will subside as the bowel condition improves.<br><br>**d.** Check skin daily for skin lesions; report unusual findings to dr.<br><br>**e.** If skin is dry, initiate use of a bath lubricant and/or skin cream. |
| **11.** Potential difficulties in management at home due to lack of understanding of treatment and long-term implications of the disease.<br><br>**Objective.** Patient and parents express realistic understanding of the disease process, treatment, and home care.<br><br>**Timing.** Before discharge. | **a.** Establish a teaching program for the patient and family based on his treatment regimen.<br><br>**b.** Encourage patient and parents to participate in giving medications in hospital. Reinforce teaching by questioning and by supervising repeated demonstrations.<br><br>**c.** Reinforce dr's encouragement to resume normal activities (e.g., school, social events).<br><br>**d.** Reinforce teaching about steroid medication:<br>  –The common side effects (e.g., moon face, increased appetite, weight gain, and acne) and that these will resolve once the medication is discontinued.<br>  –Taking the medication with milk, food, or an antacid to prevent gastric irritation.<br>  –Taking the medication *ONLY* as ordered. Altering dosage or discontinuing drug must not be done without dr's advice.<br>  –Notify dr if patient develops polyuria, polydipsia, or an infection; is exposed to chickenpox; or has recurrence of early symptoms of the disease.<br>  –Referral to Medic Alert organization.<br><br>**e.** Encourage patient to avoid situations that may contribute to relapse (e.g., emotional upsets, fatigue, irregular pattern of daily living, and failure to comply with the medication regimen).<br><br>**f.** Ensure parent/patient has follow-up appointment.<br><br>**g.** Refer to public health nurse p.r.n. |

# Careplan 123    Diarrhea: Outpatient Care

**Goals for Discharge or Maintenance**
Parents can cope with home care and will comply with follow-up instructions.

| Usual Problems/Objectives/Timing | Nursing Orders |
|---|---|
| **1.** Potential dehydration due to fluid and electrolyte loss.<br><br>**Objective.** Adequate hydration.<br><br>**Timing.** By end of first clinic visit. | **a.** Assess patient q15–30 min (depending on patient's condition) for signs/symptoms of dehydration. If these develop, *notify dr stat.*<br><br>**b.** Offer patient small amounts of clear fluid at least q30 min.<br><br>**c.** Collect stools as instructed by dr.<br><br>**d.** Obtain urine specimen for routine analysis, culture, and sensitivities.<br><br>**e.** Record intake, stools (amount, color, and consistency), and urine output.<br><br>**Note:** Dr will decide whether (and when) the child can go home or should be admitted to hospital. |
| **2.** Potential mismanagement at home, due to parents' lack of understanding of the necessary care.<br><br>**Objectives.** Parents understand the need for the prescribed fluid intake, and the reason for diet restrictions.<br><br>**Timing.** By end of first clinic visit. | **a.** Teach parents:<br>  –How to recognize signs/symptoms of dehydration.<br>  –Significance of dehydration in children, especially infants.<br>  –Management of diaper rash, if this is present; *see* Careplan 41: Diaper Rash.<br>  –To give only medication ordered by clinic dr.<br><br>**b.** Explain importance of giving extra fluids to replace fluid being lost by diarrhea.<br><br>**c.** Instruct parents about feeding routine:<br>**First 24 hr.** Give clear fluids only (no milk or food).<br>**Day 2.** If the diarrhea has lessened, add applesauce, crushed ripe bananas, precooked rice cereal (mixed with water, *not* milk), and unsalted crackers to the diet.<br>**Day 3.** If the diarrhea has stopped, gradually increase to a normal diet but *omit milk for another 3–4 days.*<br><br>**d.** Emphasize to parents the importance of notifying the clinic *stat:*<br>  –If child appears dehydrated.<br>  –If diarrhea persists and/or vomiting occurs and lasts more than 4 hr.<br>  –If abdominal pain becomes more severe or there are more than the occasional cramps.<br>  –If they are concerned about their child.<br><br>**e.** Ensure that parents have printed instructions and the name and telephone number of the nurse or dr to contact if they have problems.<br><br>**f.** Designated nurse to telephone the parents within the next 24 hr, to check on the child's condition (*see* |

| Usual Problems/Objectives/Timing | Nursing Orders |
|---|---|
| 2. (Continued). | page 304 for Guidelines for Nurse in Follow-up Telephone Calls to Check on Child with Diarrhea or Vomiting). |

# Guidelines for Nurse in Follow-up Telephone Calls to Check on Child with Diarrhea or Vomiting

*Before making the call*, check the child's chart for:

1. Age.
2. Weight (whether average, overweight, or underweight).
3. Level of hydration and activity recorded by dr.
4. Instructions given (e.g., diet, medication, and return appointment).

Do a *nursing assessment* based on the telephone information. By the end of the conversation, you should be sure of your patient's:

1. Level of hydration—intake and output (vomiting, urine, and stools).
2. Level of activity.
3. Parents' or other caretaker's (e.g., baby-sitter's) understanding and ability to cope with the child's needs.

Remember, this is strictly your own judgment. If you are in *any* doubt about the child's condition, or from your assessment you feel he needs medical attention, advise the parents to bring him to the hospital.

If the parents decide to see their family doctor:

1. Record on the chart the name of the family doctor.
2. Tell the parents their child's weight when seen in the hospital, and instruct them to advise their doctor of this.
3. If you feel that the parents need nursing help at home, advise them to call the public health nurse.
4. Record all the information in the child's chart and sign it, stating your title.
5. Notify dr if there are problems.

# Careplan 124 Esophagoscopy and Esophageal Dilation

**Goals for Discharge or Maintenance**

**I.** Patient is receiving adequate nutrition.

**II.** Patient/parents understand the follow-up schedule and can cope with the home care and frequent admissions.

| Usual Problems/Objectives/Timing | Nursing Orders |
|---|---|
| **1.** *Pre-operatively.* | *See* Careplan 17: Pre-operative Care, General. |
| **2.** *Postoperatively.* | *See* Careplan 21: Postoperative Care, General. |
| **3.** Potential perforation of esophagus during surgical procedure.<br><br>**Objectives.** Patient is afebrile, tolerates fluids and pureed foods, and has no pain, discomfort, or dyspnea.<br><br>**Timing.** 6–8 hr. | **a.** Record pulse and respiration q15 min for 1 hr, or until stable; then q4h.<br><br>**b.** Record temperature q4h.<br><br>**c.** Maintain patient on n.p.o. for 4 hr. Then, give water, sugar solution, or ginger ale. *Do not give* apple juice, orange juice, or lemonade. (In case of undetected perforation, any fluids given p.o. must be the least irritating to lung and abdominal cavity.)<br><br>**d.** *Call dr stat* if patient has chest pain, discomfort, pyrexia, or dyspnea. Do not accept telephoned order for analgesic: ask dr to examine patient (analgesics can mask symptoms/signs of esophageal perforation). |
| **4.** Patient and parents anxious about the need for periodic repetition of the procedure.<br><br>**Objectives.** Anxiety lessening; child is socializing.<br><br>**Timing.** As soon as possible. | **a.** For each admission, try to arrange that child is admitted to same ward/room, the same nurses care for him, and his favorite diversions are available.<br><br>**b.** Ensure that his waiting time before entering the OR is as brief as possible.<br><br>**c.** Encourage him to socialize, until shortly before going to the OR and as soon as possible afterward. |
| **5.** Potential mismanagement at home due to lack of understanding or difficulty with care.<br><br>**Objectives.** Patient/parents understand the schedule of treatment and can deal with it.<br><br>**Timing.** Continuing. | **a.** Ensure that all necessary members of the health care team, including outside agencies if appropriate, are involved in care of the child and his family.<br><br>**b.** Allow ample opportunities for parents to discuss their concerns.<br><br>**c.** Reinforce dr's explanations to child/parents. |

**Goals for Discharge or Maintenance**
Parents understand prescribed home care and can cope with it.

| Usual Problems/Objectives/Timing | Nursing Orders |
|---|---|
| **1.** *Isolation.* | **a.** Follow hospital procedure for asepsis.<br>**b.** *See* Careplan 12: Isolation: Psychological Aspects.<br>**c.** Obtain stool specimen for culture, sensitivities, and virology within 24 hr of admission. |
| **2.** Potential dehydration and electrolyte imbalance due to excessive fluid loss.<br><br>**Objective.** Adequate hydration is maintained; early detection of electrolyte imbalance.<br><br>**Timing.** 12 hr. | **a.** Assess hydration level at least q½h during acute stage, then q4h.<br>**b.** Record intake and output accurately.<br>**c.** Ensure at least minimal required intake q4h (p.o. and/or i.v.).<br>**d.** Report if patient is refusing to drink and/or there is a faulty i.v. line.<br>**e.** Observe stools and record frequency, amount, color, consistency, odor, and volume.<br>**f.** Estimate and record volume and description of vomitus.<br>**g.** Report frequent stooling (e.g., more than 3 times per shift) and/or large volumes.<br>**h.** Check electrolyte results as soon as received on ward. If abnormal, notify dr *stat*.<br>**Increased Na⁺.** Convulsions can occur if patient is rehydrated too rapidly.<br>**Decreased Na⁺.** $H_2O$ intoxication can cause convulsions.<br>**Increased or decreased K⁺.** Causes cardiac problems (e.g., arrhythmia). Withhold KCl until patient is voiding, unless specifically ordered otherwise. |
| **3.** Irritability and/or lethargy due to infection, nausea, and/or hunger.<br><br>**Objective.** Patient is interested in environment, staff, and parents.<br><br>**Timing.** By discharge. | **a.** Settle child for naps after meals/feedings.<br>**b.** Comfort the patient with TLC.<br>**c.** Provide age-appropriate toys or activities.<br>**d. Infant.** If n.p.o., give pacifier (unless parents object). |
| **4.** Intolerance of certain foods and/or fluids, due to bowel irritation.<br><br>**Objectives.** Patient tolerates bland diet. Decreased number of stools.<br><br>**Timing.** Day 4. | **a.** Note frequency and characteristics of stools in relation to diet.<br>**b.** Introduce ordered foods gradually.<br>**c. Infant.** Do not introduce any *new* foods in diet.<br>**d.** If stooling increases after a food is given, restrict patient to clear fluids and call dr. |
| **5.** Potential pyrexia due to viral or bacterial infection, and/or dehydration.<br><br>**Objective.** Patient is afebrile. | **a.** *See* Careplan 10: Pyrexia.<br>**b.** Do not administer ASA.<br>**c.** Do not give suppositories. |

| Usual Problems/Objectives/Timing | Nursing Orders |
|---|---|
| **5. (Continued).**<br>**Timing.** Day 4–5. | **d.** Notify dr if patient's temperature is 38.5°C or over. |
| **6.** Potential excoriation of buttocks and perineum, by frequent stooling. | *See* Careplan 41: Diaper Rash. |
| **7.** Parents are concerned about child's illness, hospitalization, and/or treatment.<br>**Objective.** Parents understand and accept treatment methods.<br>**Timing.** By discharge. | **a.** Have dr speak to parents about child's illness, condition, and treatment.<br>**b.** Explain all treatments (e.g., i.v. therapy, need for restraint, diet, need to show stools to nurse for assessment, and blood tests).<br>**c.** Encourage parents to express their feelings about child's admission.<br>**d.** Encourage parents to participate in care (particularly feeding, if patient is an infant).<br>**e.** Teach parents how to modify diet and assess level of hydration if diarrhea recurs at home.<br>**f.** If concerned about home care, request follow-up by public health nurse.<br>**g. Infant.** If discharged on a special formula, arrange instruction of parents by dietitian.<br>**h.** Ensure that parents have a follow-up appointment for their child and know whom to call if his condition causes concern after his return home. |
| **8.** Potential spread of infection to other family members.<br>**Objective.** Parents understand measures to be taken to prevent spread of infection.<br>**Timing.** As soon as possible. | **a.** Instruct parents about precautionary measures to be carried out at home:<br>–Hand-washing, before meals, after using bathroom, before preparing/serving foods.<br>–Careful washing of eating utensils.<br>–Careful washing of linen.<br>–Handling of diapers.<br>**b.** If infection is due to salmonella or shigella organisms ensure that the Public Health Department is notified (they will do follow-up). |

# Careplan 126    Pyloric Stenosis: Surgery

## Goals for Discharge or Maintenance
I. Infant is tolerating formula well.
II. Mother is relaxed when feeding infant.

| Usual Problems/Objectives/Timing | Nursing Orders |
|---|---|
| **1.** *Pre-operatively.* | *See* Careplan 17: Pre-operative Care, General. |
| **2.** Potential dehydration, electrolyte imbalance, and aspiration of vomitus.<br>**Objectives.** Adequate hydration; no aspiration of vomitus.<br>**Timing.** Until surgery. | **a.** Position patient on side or abdomen.<br>**b.** Maintain i.v. fluids as ordered<br>**c.** Record:<br>  –Amount, frequency, and type of vomiting.<br>  –Stools and urine output.<br>**d.** Weigh patient daily.<br>**e.** Notify dr if dehydration develops.<br>**f.** When patient is n.p.o.:<br>  –Give mouth care q2h while he is awake.<br>  –Pick him up and hold him *at least* q4h and when crying.<br>  –Provide opportunities for him to suck on a pacifier. |
| **3.** Parents anxious about the congenital condition.<br>**Objective.** Parents have had the condition explained to them.<br>**Timing.** By time of surgery. | **a.** Reinforce dr's explanations of their baby's condition and need for its correction.<br>**b.** Provide opportunities for parents to express concerns. |
| **4.** *Postoperatively.* | *See* Careplan 21: Postoperative Care, General. |
| **5.** Potential vomiting while feeding, due to gastric irritation and thick gastric secretions.<br>**Objective.** Patient is retaining normal amounts of formula or breast milk.<br>**Timing.** By discharge. | **a.** Do routine care a.c. (bath, diaper change, vital signs, etc.). Avoid disturbing patient p.c.<br>**b.** When introducing oral feedings, give slowly at ordered intervals. First feeding postoperatively is given by nurse, *not parents*.<br>Example of usual feeding routine:<br>  –Start 4–6 hr postop: give 15 ml of full-strength formula or breast milk q4h.<br>  –If previous feed is retained, add 5 ml each feeding.<br>  –If previous feed is not retained, give same amount.<br>**c.** Make sure you are relaxed and comfortable and can take your time with the feeding.<br>**d.** Burp the baby well: before feeding, in the middle of the feeding, after every 15 ml, and p.c.<br>**e.** After feedings, position infant on R side, with head elevated 20 degrees to promote passage of formula through pylorus. Wrap him securely and position him comfortably.<br>**f.** Keep bedside record of feedings and vomiting. (Regurgitation may continue for a short period after surgery.) |

| Usual Problems/Objectives/Timing | Nursing Orders |
|---|---|
| **6.** Parents anxious and concerned about feeding baby at home.<br><br>**Objective.** Parents relaxed when visiting and are feeding baby confidently.<br><br>**Timing.** By discharge. | **a.** Explain feeding routine, burping, and positioning.<br>**b.** Allow parent(s) to feed infant after first tolerated feeding.<br>**c.** Encourage parents to relax and to take time with feeding. Instruct them about adequate burping and positioning p.c.<br>**d.** If mother has breast milk:<br>–Feed breast milk by bottle until baby tolerates feedings. (When dr approves, the mother can resume breast-feeding.)<br>–Breast-feeding: Weigh baby before and after each feeding. Record, and advise the mother.<br>**e.** Reassure parents that baby will be on a normal feeding routine in a few days.<br>**f.** Assist mother with routine infant care p.r.n.<br>**g.** Ensure that parents have written instructions for home care and follow-up, and know whom to contact if they are having problems. |

**Goals for Discharge or Maintenance**
An accurate collection is obtained with a minimum of discomfort to the patient.

| Usual Problems/Objectives/Timing | Nursing Orders |
|---|---|
| | **Note:** This study may be done (a) to assist in the diagnosis of biliary atresia by determining the degree of obstruction and (b) to assess the bile flow after a Kasai procedure (portoenterostomy) in a patient diagnosed with biliary atresia. |
| *Pre-operative collection*<br><br>**1.** Potential delay in confirming diagnosis due to inaccurate urine and stool collections.<br><br>**Objectives.** Specimens are collected as ordered, labeled properly, and delivered promptly to the nuclear medicine laboratory.<br><br>**Timing.** Until test completed. | **a.** Transport patient to the nuclear medicine department on a frame with collection devices in place. Send a quart-size container with patient.<br><br>**b.** Injection of rose bengal sodium $^{131}$I is given in nuclear medicine. Collections start at the time of the injection.<br><br>**c.** Collect urine and stool separately for three 24 hour periods. Place stools in container; discard urine.<br><br>**d.** Ensure that stool is not contaminated with urine. If any stools are contaminated, place them in a separate container for the 3-day period and label as such.<br><br>**e.** Check urine collector q2h and p.r.n. for any signs of leakage. Change collector p.r.n.<br><br>**f.** If metal container/bedpan is used to collect stool, line with plastic wrap (e.g., saran) to prevent uptake of the $^{131}$I by metal and loss of stool. |
| **2.** Potential excoriation of perineum and buttocks due to irritation by collection device.<br><br>**Objective.** Skin clear and intact.<br><br>**Timing.** Until test completed. | **a.** Check buttocks for reddened areas caused by pressure on the Bradford frame.<br><br>**b.** If urine bag is being used, spray skin with silicone skin prep three times before applying the collector. Allow skin prep to dry well between applications.<br><br>**c.** If female adaptor is being used to collect urine, check q4h for skin breakdown at base of adaptor.<br><br>**d.** Notify dr if patient's skin becomes red or excoriated. |
| *Postoperative collection (after Kasai procedure)*<br><br>**3.** Potential errors in results due to inaccurate stool collections.<br><br>**Objectives.** Specimens are collected as ordered, labeled properly, and delivered promptly to the nuclear medicine laboratory.<br><br>**Timing.** Until end of test (3 days). | **a.** Empty stoma appliance before patient receives injection of rose bengal sodium $^{131}$I in nuclear medicine. Collection begins at time of injection.<br><br>**b.** Check stoma appliance q4h and p.r.n. for signs of leakage. Change appliance p.r.n.<br><br>**c.** Collect all portoenterostomy drainage for three 24-hr periods.<br><br>**d.** Record volumes on collection record. Note any losses. |

# Careplan 128    Stomatitis

**Goals for Discharge or Maintenance**

**I.** Parents demonstrate correct home care of child's mouth.

**II.** Patient is able to maintain hydration.

| Usual Problems/Objectives/Timing | Nursing Orders |
|---|---|
| 1. Pain due to ulceration of tongue, lips, and buccal mucosa.<br><br>**Objective.** Mouth lesions are dry and clean.<br><br>**Timing.** 7 days. | **a.** Follow hospital procedure for mouth care.<br><br>**b.** Give patient mouthwashes or irrigations with sodium bicarbonate solutions or N saline, q2h while he is awake.<br><br>**c.** Order soft diet. |
| 2. Potential dehydration due to inadequate oral intake.<br><br>**Objective.** Adequate hydration.<br><br>**Timing.** Throughout hospital stay. | **a.** Offer small amounts of cold fluids, preferably high-protein high-calorie fluids, at least q3h (e.g., fruit-flavored gelatin, popsicles, ice cream, chocolate milk, and "flat" carbonated beverages).<br><br>**b.** Avoid acidic drinks (e.g., orange juice, colas.)<br><br>**c.** Order soft diet as soon as patient can tolerate solid foods.<br><br>**d.** Record intake and output and nutritional intake.<br><br>**e.** Observe for signs of dehydration. |
| 3. Potential mismanagement at home due to lack of understanding of the disease process.<br><br>**Objectives.** Parents demonstrate mouth care correctly, state understanding of need for adequate hydration, and can provide enough suitable fluids.<br><br>**Timing.** By discharge. | **a.** Teach mother the importance of child's mouth care and how to do this.<br><br>**b.** Assist mother in feeding child.<br><br>**c.** Arrange referral to dietitian p.r.n. |
| 4. If herpetic stomatitis is present. | **a.** *See* Careplan 12: Isolation: Psychological Aspects.<br><br>**b.** Follow hospital procedure for asepsis. |

**Goals for Discharge or Maintenance**
See Objectives.

| Usual Problems/Objectives/Timing | Nursing Orders |
|---|---|
| **1.** Potential sepsis, due to contaminated i.v. catheter/cannula and TPN solutions, and/or complications of disease process.<br><br>**Objective.** Prevention or early detection of infection.<br><br>**Timing.** Until TPN is discontinued. | **a.** Ensure that TPN solutions are handled correctly:<br>–Do not make additions to TPN solutions. (All additions are done in pharmacy under a laminar air-flow hood.)<br>–Keep solutions in refrigerator.<br>–Check solutions for discoloration, cloudiness, and turbidity.<br>–Check expiration date before using solution.<br>–Return out-of-date or cloudy solutions to pharmacy.<br>**b.** Use strict surgical asepsis when changing solution, tubing, filter, and dressing (follow hospital procedure).<br>**c.** Ensure that tubing with a glucose filter is used with amino acid–glucose infusion.<br>**d.** Change the TPN administration tubing and filter every 24 hr.<br>**e.** Maintain a dry occlusive dressing over the CV catheter site.<br>**f.** Change peripheral i.v. sites every 72 hr, or as ordered.<br>**g.** Ensure that CV catheter dressings, blood cultures, and heparinization are done by the dr, TPN nurse, or other designated nurse trained in the procedure.<br>**h.** Do not administer i.v. medications through CV catheter unless specifically ordered by the dr.<br>**i.** Do not infuse or withdraw blood through the CV catheter. Do not add stopcocks to the TPN infusion tubing.<br>**j.** Monitor patient's vital signs and urinary glucose levels according to dr's orders. Report any abnormalities to dr.<br>**k.** Observe peripheral sites for infection and thrombophlebitis. Report observations to dr.<br>**l.** If sepsis is suspected, follow dr's orders for septic workup. |
| **2.** Potential fluid imbalance due to:<br>–Incorrect infusion rate.<br>–Malfunctioning infusion device.<br>–Abrupt cessation of infusion because of clots in catheter or disconnection of tubing.<br>–Increased fluid losses or decreased urinary output.<br>**Objectives.** Solutions are infused as ordered. Early detection of problems. | **a.** Check infusion rates at beginning of each shift and with every solution bag change.<br>**b.** Maintain a constant infusion rate with the use of an infusion device on each line.<br>**c.** Notify dr if solutions infuse too rapidly or too slowly. *(Do not alter infusion rates without a dr's order.)*<br>**d.** Maintain accurate intake and output record. Record i.v. intake q1h. Report any fluid imbalance to dr. |

| Usual Problems/Objectives/Timing | Nursing Orders |
|---|---|
| **2. (Continued).**<br>**Timing.** Until TPN discontinued. | **e.** Weigh patient daily and record.<br>**f.** Inspect infusion lines frequently for kinking, occlusion, or disconnection.<br>**g.** Keep i.v. tubing and roller clamps out of patient's reach, tangle free, and away from moving bed rails.<br>**h.** Observe for signs and symptoms of dehydration; report any signs to dr.<br>**i.** Observe for fluid overload (e.g., increased respiration and BP, decreased pulse rate, shortness of breath, edema of feet, hands, face); report any signs to dr. |
| **3.** Potential glucose imbalance due to:<br>−Altered infusion rate (ordered or accidental).<br>−Inability of pancreas to adjust to glucose load.<br>−Possible sepsis.<br>**Objectives.** Solutions are infused as ordered, and normal blood glucose and negative urinary glucose levels are maintained.<br>**Timing.** Early detection of glucose imbalance. | **a.** Maintain glucose concentration and rate as ordered.<br>**b.** Check urinary glucose at each voiding until stable, then q8h. Report elevated levels to dr.<br>**c.** Observe for and report to dr *stat* any signs/symptoms of:<br>−Hypoglycemia (e.g., weakness, pallor, diaphoresis).<br>−Hyperglycemia (e.g., flushed appearance, nausea, weakness, urinary glucose > 2%).<br>**d.** If amino acid-glucose infusion is terminated abruptly, consult dr about hanging another i.v. solution of equal dextrose concentration to prevent hypoglycemia. |
| **4.** Potential electrolyte/metabolite imbalance due to:<br>−Inaccurate infusion rates.<br>−Severe losses related to diarrhea, enuresis, fistulae, trauma, burns, etc.<br>**Objective.** Early detection of electrolyte/metabolite imbalance.<br>**Timing.** Until TPN discontinued. | **a.** Maintain detailed intake and output record.<br>**b.** Record i.v. intake q1h.<br>**c.** Record all urine, stool, enuresis, wound drainage, NG tube losses, etc. Report excessive losses to dr.<br>**d.** Observe, and report to dr, indications of electrolyte/metabolite imbalance:<br>−Changes in vital signs.<br>−Diaphoresis.<br>−Mucosal bleeding or delayed clotting.<br>−Tetany or numbness in extremities.<br>−Headache, weakness, apathy, mental confusion.<br>−Muscle or abdominal cramps.<br>−Edema.<br>−Changes in urinary output. |
| **5.** Potential thrombophlebitis and/or infiltration with *peripheral* TPN, due to irritation from concentrated i.v. solution, and frequent handling or inadequate anchoring of cannula.<br>**Objective.** Early detection of infiltration or thrombophlebitis.<br>**Timing.** Until TPN discontinued. | **a.** Do not leave peripheral cannulae in for longer than 72 hr. Record date and time of insertion on a piece of adhesive tape near the insertion site.<br>**b.** Do not infuse a dextrose solution of >10% through a peripheral vein.<br>**c.** Secure i.v. cannula to prevent undue motion and/or tension. Use restraints to immobilize the limb. |

continued

| Usual Problems/Objectives/Timing | Nursing Orders |
|---|---|
| **5. (Continued).** | **d.** Do not place nonsterile tape directly over the entry site.<br><br>**e.** Observe i.v. site q½–1h. Notify dr if inflammation, swelling, or redness occurs, or if patient complains of pain. If any of these signs/symptoms is present, remove i.v. cannula and restart infusion in another site.<br><br>**f.** If i.v. has infiltrated, remove cannula and apply warm moist soaks to the affected area. If possible, elevate the affected limb. Observe for swelling, redness, darkened skin areas, blisters, and/or weeping areas. If any of these is present, record your observations and inform dr.<br><br>**g.** If phlebitis is suspected, record temperature q2–4h. (Phlebitis could be due to bacterial infection.) |
| **6.** Potential CV catheter problems due to tension on catheter, or nonocclusive CV line dressing.<br><br>**Objective.** CV line remains intact.<br><br>**Timing.** Until TPN discontinued. | **a.** Maintain an occlusive CV catheter dressing. If dressing becomes nonocclusive, call designated person to change dressing.<br><br>**b.** Tape catheter hub-infusion tubing connection securely to patient's chest or abdomen; check it frequently.<br><br>**c.** Prevent tension on infusion tubing.<br><br>**d.** Keep infusion tubing and roller clamps out of patient's reach, tangle free, and away from moving bed-rails.<br><br>**e.** Keep patient dressed with snug-fitting clothing.<br><br>**f.** Observe patient for swelling of chest, limb, neck, and/or facial area; report any swelling to dr.<br><br>**g.** Observe for and report to dr:<br>–Drainage from CV line exit site.<br>–Swelling, tenderness, redness, or gaping. |
| **7.** Potential air embolus due to disconnected i.v. tubing or broken CV catheter.<br><br>**Objectives.** System remains intact and patent. No air embolus.<br><br>**Timing.** Until TPN discontinued. | **a.** Use infusion tubing with Luer lock connections. Secure all slip-fit connections with 2.5 cm white adhesive tape.<br><br>**b.** Keep a padded clamp at the patient's bedside at all times, to clamp catheter and/or infusion tubing if there is a break in the system.<br><br>**c.** Keep silastic CV line repair kit at bedside at all times.<br><br>**d.** When CV line is open, clamp it proximal to the patient.<br><br>**e.** If line breaks, clamp between damaged area and patient and cover damaged area with a gauze 4x4 soaked in povidone-iodine. Notify dr/TPN nurse.<br><br>**f.** Keep sharp objects (e.g., scissors) away from catheter and i.v. infusion tubing. If necessary, keep the tubing out of the reach of the child's teeth.<br><br>**g.** Observe for and report to dr *stat* signs and symptoms of air embolus (e.g., dyspnea, chest pain, diaphoresis, increased pulse or respiration rate). |

| Usual Problems/Objectives/Timing | Nursing Orders |
|---|---|
| **8.** Potential halitosis and/or parotitis due to prolonged n.p.o. and lack of salival stimulation.<br><br>**Objectives.** No halitosis; early detection of oral infection or mucosal breakdown.<br><br>**Timing.** Ongoing. | **a.** Provide mouth care q3–4h and p.r.n.<br><br>**b.** If appropriate, encourage patient to brush teeth at least t.i.d.<br><br>**c.** Observe for and record any mucosal breakdown.<br><br>**d.** Note any halitosis.<br><br>**e.** Provide pacifiers for infants to stimulate production of saliva.<br><br>**f.** Apply lubricant (e.g., petrolatum) to lips to prevent cracking. |
| **9.** Patient/parents anxious and/or depressed due to:<br>–Inability to eat.<br>–Uncertain prognosis.<br>–Lack of understanding of treatment.<br>–Separation anxiety.<br><br>**Objectives.** Anxiety is reduced. Concerns are verbalized.<br><br>**Timing.** As soon as possible. | **a.** Initial teaching about treatment to be done by nursing staff with the aid of medical staff and TPN nurse, emphasizing the positive aspects (weight gain, increased energy).<br><br>**b.** Inform TPN nurse of any difficulties with patient's and/or family's acceptance and/or understanding of therapy.<br><br>**c.** Provide nontreatment time to sit with and encourage patient to verbalize about his diagnosis and treatment.<br><br>**d.** Encourage patient to become involved with diversional activities, especially at mealtimes.<br><br>**e.** Explain all procedures (e.g., lab work, roentgenograms) to patient/family using terminology they understand.<br><br>**f.** Involve patient/family in care as much as possible.<br><br>**g.** Provide appropriate oral experiences for infants to stimulate rooting, sucking, and swallowing.<br><br>**h.** Have dr speak to patient/family regularly, to answer questions about progress, etc.<br><br>**i.** Report and record any behavioral changes of the patient and/or family. |
| **10.** Delayed growth and development due to:<br>–Prolonged hospitalization.<br>–Separation from home and family.<br>–Immobilization due to i.v.<br>–Illness.<br>–Inability to eat.<br><br>**Objective.** Patient maintains growth and development milestones appropriate for age.<br><br>**Timing.** Ongoing. | **a.** Obtain a thorough nursing history at time of patient's admission.<br><br>**b.** Follow patient's home routine and daily activities whenever possible and arrange treatments around this routine.<br><br>**c.** Provide activities suitable to the patient's age and physical activity tolerance level.<br><br>**d.** Encourage parents to bring patient's clothes, toys, etc., from home.<br><br>**e.** Place pictures of family members, pets, etc. on patient's bed.<br><br>**f.** Encourage use of ward playroom, if not contraindicated.<br><br>**g.** If patient is unable to go to ward playroom, contact the recreation department to have a volunteer see patient on a regular basis.<br><br>**h.** To preserve the i.v., restrain infants as necessary |

continued

| Usual Problems/Objectives/Timing | Nursing Orders |
|---|---|
| **10. (Continued).** | while allowing for maximum mobility. (Use mobiles, pictures, music etc. to distract patient from tubing.) |
| | **i.** Remove restraints while patient is supervised. |
| | **j.** Provide range of motion exercises p.r.n. to prevent muscle contractures and wasting due to prolonged immobilization. (*See* Careplan 13: Prolonged Immobilization) |
| | **k.** Consult rehabilitation medicine about appropriate activities for patient (e.g., infant stimulation). |
| | **l.** To ensure maximum consistency, record successful approaches for others to follow. |
| | **m.** Determine whether patient wishes to be away from other patients at mealtimes; if appropriate, arrange diversional activities. |

**Goals for Discharge or Maintenance**
**I.** Infant is adequately nourished and maintaining weight.
**II.** Mother can cope with home care and follow-up.

| Usual Problems/Objectives/Timing | Nursing Orders |
|---|---|
| **1.** Potential aspiration of secretions, fluid intake, and/or barium, due to: | **a.** *The infant must be positioned with his head elevated 45 degrees until the defect(s) have been corrected* [and possibly longer: *see* problem **6c**]. |
| **a. Atresia only:** Overflow of contents of the esophageal pouch into the larynx. | —**Small infant.** Raise the head of the incubator. |
| **b. Atresia and fistula:** Reflux of gastric secretions into the distal esophageal segment, through the fistula, down into the trachea. | —**Large infant.** Support him on a mattress in a sling (e.g., a hiatus hernia sling) within the incubator. |
| **c. Fistula only:** Passage of fluids through the fistula into the trachea. | **b. Esophageal atresia (with or without fistula).** Pass an NG tube into the blind pouch. Maintain straight drainage or intermittent gentle suction of the tube as ordered. |
| **Objective.** No aspiration. | **c. Tracheoesophageal fistula only.** Pass an NG tube into the stomach, to decompress it and to remove accumulating secretions. Maintain straight drainage or intermittent suction as ordered. |
| **Timing.** Until surgical correction of the defect(s). | **d.** Observe continuously for problems of drainage or suction. If the following occur, notify dr *stat*. |
| | —Excessive oral/nasal secretions, or bubbling. |
| | —Moist, rattling respirations. |
| | —Tachypnea. |
| | —Tachycardia. |
| | —Pallor. |
| | —Restlessness. |
| | **e.** Irrigate the tube with air as ordered by dr (usually q2h). |
| | **f.** If the NG tube becomes blocked, change it at once. |
| **2.** Potential dehydration or inadequate nutrition due to the infant's inability to feed p.o. | **a.** Give fluids i.v. as ordered. |
| **Objective.** Adequate hydration and nutrition. | **b.** Report to dr if infant appears overhydrated or underhydrated. |
| **Timing.** Until surgery. | **c.** Be aware of the latest blood test results (electrolytes). Notify dr if imbalance is developing. |
| | **d.** Note the blood sugar (indication of adequacy of carbohydrate intake for metabolic needs). Notify dr if hypoglycemia is developing. |
| **3.** *Pre-operatively.* | *See* relevant problems in Careplan 17: Pre-operative Care, General. |
| **4.** *Postoperatively.* | **a.** *See* relevant problems in Careplan 21: Postoperative Care, General. |
| | **b.** *Be especially alert for signs of infection.* If you suspect infection, notify dr *stat*. (The neonate's immunologic defense mechanisms are immature; even the slightest infection may be overwhelming.) |

**317**

continued

| Usual Problems/Objectives/Timing | Nursing Orders |
|---|---|
| **5.** *Gastrostomy (for esophageal atresia without a fistula).* | |
| **a.** Potential aspiration of fluids from the esophageal pouch.<br><br>**Objective.** No aspiration.<br><br>**Timing.** Until the defect is repaired. | **a.** *See* nursing orders for problem 1. Observe respiratory rate closely.<br><br>**b.** Suction the nasopharynx p.r.n. |
| **b.** Potential tissue damage due to prolonged use of NG tube.<br><br>**Objective.** Tissues are intact.<br><br>**Timing.** Until the NG tube is removed. | **a.** Change the NG tube every 3–5 days.<br><br>**b.** When changing the tube, pass it through the other nostril.<br><br>**c.** Notify dr if the NG secretions contain fresh blood.<br><br>**d.** Observe frequently for trauma to nostril/nasal septum: if present, notify dr. |
| **c.** Potential abdominal distention due to obstruction of the gastrostomy tube or rapid/excessive feedings.<br><br>**Objective.** No abdominal distention.<br><br>**Timing.** Until oral feedings are tolerated after the gastrostomy tube has been clamped. | **a.** Maintain decompression of the stomach:<br>–Attach the gastrostomy tube to the drainage bag.<br>–Hang the bag below the level of the infant (to facilitate drainage).<br><br>**b.** Record the amount of drainage.<br><br>**c.** Prevent obstruction: irrigate the gastrostomy tube as ordered.<br><br>**d.** Before feeding is initiated (usually 24 hr postoperatively):<br>–Remove the drainage bag.<br>–Attach the barrel of a 20-ml syringe to the free end of the gastrostomy tube.<br>–Suspend the barrel 15 cm above the infant's head (Figure 5A). (This allows reflux of fluid/gas if the stomach is overdistended, but it does not empty the stomach of its contents. *Do not clamp the tube.*)<br><br>**e.** Initiate feedings as ordered:<br>–Ensure that the feeds are warm.<br>–Suspend the feeding apparatus above the infant, and regulate flow into the syringe barrel (Figure 5B).<br><br>**f. Continuous feeding**<br>–Infuse regularly and slowly.<br>–Use an infusion pump whenever possible.<br>–Monitor the infusion q1h.<br><br>**g. Intermittent feeding.** Allow the fluid to drip in slowly (usually 15–20 min). (*There must be no sudden influx of fluid*, and the rate of infusion must be determined individually for each infant.)<br><br>**h.** Observe closely for signs that the feed is going in too quickly:<br>–Abdominal distention.<br>–Respiratory distress.<br>–Bradycardia.<br><br>If any of these signs develop, slow the feeding (or stop it temporarily if necessary). |

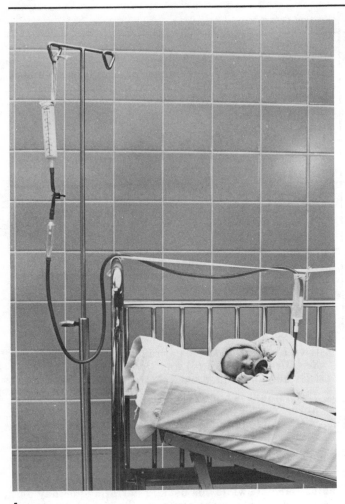

A

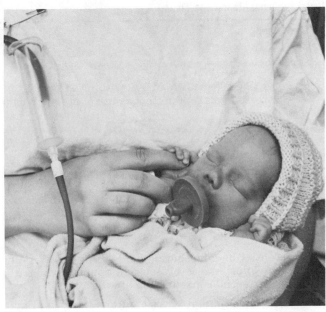

B

**Figure 5.** *Feeding an infant who has tracheoesophageal fistula.*

continued

| Usual Problems/Objectives/Timing | Nursing Orders |
|---|---|
| **5. (Continued).** | **i.** *Leave the gastrostomy tube open* (into the syringe barrel above) *and elevated at all times* until the infant tolerates full feedings. [*See* nursing order 8(a).] |
| **d.** Potential breakdown of skin at insertion site of gastrostomy tube, due to leakage of stomach contents.<br><br>**Objective.** Skin intact.<br><br>**Timing.** Until the gastrostomy tube is removed. | **a.** Observe continuously for leakage around gastrostomy tube.<br><br>**b.** If leakage occurs, stop feeding at once and notify dr *stat*. |
| **6.** *Thoracotomy for ligation of fistula and primary anastomosis of esophageal atresia.*<br><br>**a.** Potential respiratory distress due to obstruction of chest tube. | **a.** Follow hospital procedure for chest drain. |
| **b.** Potential pneumothorax due to rupture of esophageal anastomosis by tension, vomiting, or trauma. Potential consolidation of lung.<br><br>**Objectives.** Minimal tension on anastomosis. Early detection of pneumothorax.<br><br>**Timing.** Until chest drain is removed. | **a.** If an NG tube is in place, irrigate *gently*, to prevent sudden increase in abdominal pressure or rupture of anastomosis.<br><br>**b.** Prevent irritation of the anastomosis. When suctioning the nasopharynx, use catheters marked to the depth determined by dr.<br><br>**c.** Give feedings *slowly* via a transanastomosis NG tube. *See* nursing orders (e) and (f) for problem 5**c.** Keep NG tube unclamped between feedings.<br><br>**d.** If the infant is apneic, keep equipment for intubation at the bedside. *If possible,* avoid manual resuscitation with a bag and mask. (Air forced into the esophagus could rupture the anastomosis.)<br><br>**e.** When oral feedings are instituted, feed infant *slowly* and burp him thoroughly.<br><br>**Note:** Barium swallow is usually performed on day 5 to determine whether the anastomosis/ligated fistula has healed.<br><br>–If healing is incompete, barium swallow will be repeated a few days later.<br><br>–When healing is complete, the NG tube can be removed. |
| **c.** *At a later stage:* Potential aspiration because of interruption of esophageal peristalsis.<br><br>**Objective.** No aspiration.<br><br>**Timing.** Continuing. | **a.** Continue to care for infant in an incubator elevated 45 degrees at the head. *This elevation is particularly important after feedings.* |
| **7.** *Repair or ligation of tracheoesophageal fistula:* Potential breakdown of surgical repair by trauma or vomiting.<br><br>**Objective.** Repair is intact.<br><br>**Timing.** Until the fistula repair has healed. | **a.** *See* nursing orders for problem 6**b.**<br><br>**b.** *If a thoracotomy was performed,* follow hospital procedure for chest drain. |
| **8.** Potential delay in psychosocial and physical development, due to prolonged separation from parents and feeding restrictions imposed by condition (e.g., inability to breast-feed or bottle-feed until defect is repaired and has healed). | *While the infant is being fed via a gastrostomy:*<br><br>**a.** Whenever possible, feed the baby while holding him in the *normal* feeding position (*but with his head elevated*). (It is very important that the baby feels the closeness of his "mother" while feeding.) |

| Usual Problems/Objectives/Timing | Nursing Orders |
|---|---|
| **8. (Continued).**<br><br>**Objective.** Normal development.<br><br>**Timing.** Continuing. | –Keep the syringe barrel 15 cm above the baby's abdomen (e.g., pin it to the shoulder of your gown); attach the feeding equipment to an i.v. pole.<br><br>–If infant is able to handle secretions safely, give him a pacifier to suck, to stimulate oral feeding and develop his sucking and swallowing reflexes. (He will learn to associate these with the sensation of food going into his stomach.)<br><br>**b.** *Between feedings,* walk around with baby in your arms, still keeping the syringe barrel elevated. |
| **9.** Mother concerned about her ability to take over the care of her new baby, who has been separated from her since shortly after birth and has undergone major surgery.<br><br>**Objectives.** Mother handling infant comfortably; understands instructions for home care and follow-up.<br><br>**Timing.** Before discharge. | **a.** Encourage the mother to participate in her baby's care as much as possible as soon as she is able to.<br><br>**b.** Explain all feedings, treatments, etc., to her.<br><br>–Impress on the mother the need to keep her baby in an elevated position (on lap or in bed) *at all times* until she is advised otherwise.<br><br>–Particularly if her baby has had atresia repaired, warn the mother that he may have difficulty swallowing for some time and may vomit some feeds.<br><br>**c.** Ensure that the mother knows how to bathe and feed her baby and is comfortable doing this.<br><br>**d.** See especially the nursing orders for problem 1 in Careplan 1, Stresses of Hospitalization: Infant Stage.<br><br>**e.** Especially if this is the mother's first baby (in which case she may not be certain of what is normal), outline *expected* progress during the next days/weeks.<br><br>**f.** Check that appointments have been made for follow-up in clinic, with public health nurse, etc., and that the mother knows whom to call if problems arise after her baby is discharged from hospital. |

**Goals for Discharge or Maintenance**

**I.** Family members state an understanding of the disease, treatment, and medication.

**II.** They are willing to comply with home care and follow-up regimen.

| Usual Problems/Objectives/Timing | Nursing Orders |
|---|---|
| **1.** Abdominal cramps and tenesmus due to inflammation of the colon.<br><br>**Objectives.** Abdomen relaxed; no tenesmus.<br><br>**Timing.** Before discharge. | **a.** Position patient comfortably. (Some patients prefer to lie on their side, supported by pillows, others on their stomach.)<br><br>**b.** Apply dry heat to patient's abdomen p.r.n. (e.g., warmed towels or, if ordered by dr, a hot-water bottle filled with *warm* water).<br><br>**c.** Notify dr when patient has pain. Record precipitating factors, location, duration, type, and severity of pain.<br><br>**d.** Provide a quiet environment.<br><br>**e.** Give analgesics as ordered (rarely used). |
| **2.** Potential:<br><br>  –Dehydration due to diarrhea, nausea, and vomiting.<br><br>  –Toxic megacolon due to inflammation and/or electrolyte imbalance (this will cause a bowel obstruction that may result in perforation and peritonitis).<br><br>**Objectives.** Hydration maintained/improved. Early detection of toxic megacolon.<br><br>**Timing.** Until discharge. | **a.** Place patient on bed rest if diarrhea is severe.<br><br>**b.** Record number, amount, color, and consistency of stools. Patient must use bedpan throughout entire admission.<br><br>**c.** Record intake and output.<br><br>**d.** Report vomiting to dr.<br><br>**e.** Weigh patient daily, before breakfast.<br><br>**f.** Keep fluids available at bedside unless contraindicated.<br><br>**g.** Assess and record level of hydration q4h.<br><br>**h.** While patient in the acute phase:<br><br>  –Record TPR and BP q4h.<br><br>  –Observe for abdominal distention.<br><br>  –Measure abdominal girth at umbilicus, q12h.<br><br>  –Observe for change in quality of pain, from cramping to severe generalized abdominal pain.<br><br>  Notify dr *stat* if there are significant changes in the patient's condition. |
| **3.** Potential pyrexia due to inflammatory process. | *See* Careplan 10: Pyrexia. |
| **4.** Fatigue and malaise due to:<br><br>  –Rectal bleeding.<br><br>  –Iron deficiency anemia.<br><br>  –Sleep deprivation.<br><br>**Objective.** Patient appears rested and comfortable.<br><br>**Timing.** 2–3 weeks. | **a.** Limit patient's activity during acute phase of illness (bed rest or sitting up in room).<br><br>**b.** Provide a quiet environment and appropriate recreation (e.g., quiet music, books).<br><br>**c.** Limit nonfamily visitors if necessary.<br><br>**d.** Observe and record amount of blood seen in stools and size of blood clots. |
| **5.** Weight loss due to diarrhea and loss of appetite.<br><br>**Objective.** Nutritional status improved. | **a.** Weigh patient daily, before breakfast.<br><br>**b.** Give mouth care q4h if patient n.p.o. or nauseated. |

| Usual Problems/Objectives/Timing | Nursing Orders |
|---|---|
| **5. (Continued).**<br>    **Timing.** 2–3 weeks. | **c.** Establish diet in collaboration with patient, dietitian, and dr. Encourage high-protein, high-calorie choices (patient will avoid foods that cause him distress).<br>**d.** Offer appropriate snacks between meals.<br>**e.** Administer total parenteral nutrition (TPN) if ordered. *See* Careplan 129: Total Parenteral Nutrition. |
| **6.** Embarrassment over frequent, foul-smelling stools and urgency.<br>**Objective.** Embarrassment limited by privacy and consideration of patient's feelings.<br>**Timing.** Throughout hospital stay. | **a.** Keep room well ventilated and free of odor.<br>**b.** Place patient in a single room if possible.<br>**c.** During acute phase, keep a covered bedpan or commode within patient's reach.<br>**d.** Empty and return bedpan promptly.<br>**e.** Check patient frequently at night (often there is an increase in stooling at this time). |
| **7.** Potential perianal excoriation due to diarrhea.<br>**Objective.** Healthy skin.<br>**Timing.** Until discharge. | **a.** Keep perianal area clean and dry. Use soft tissue for wiping.<br>**b.** Check perianal area daily.<br>**c.** Provide sitz baths and apply lubricants locally p.r.n. |
| **8.** Frustration and anxiety due to:<br>  –Difficulty adjusting to acute and chronic implications of the disease.<br>  –Delayed physical and sexual development.<br>  –Possibility of surgery (subtotal colectomy with ileostomy).<br>**Objectives.** Patient/parents express fears and frustration, and state realistic understanding of short- and long-term implications.<br>**Timing.** Before discharge. | **a.** Ensure a consistent assignment of nurses. Designate one nurse to establish rapport with patient and parents.<br>**b.** Provide opportunities for questions and the expression of expectations and concerns. Keep dr informed.<br>**c.** Encourage family involvement in planning and providing care.<br>**d.** Provide information about appropriate support groups (e.g., Canadian Foundation for Ileitis and Colitis). |
| **9.** Potential regression due to illness and hospitalization.<br>**Objective.** Patient regains independence as condition improves.<br>**Timing.** Before discharge. | **a.** Encourage patient's independence in daily routines. Set short-term goals (e.g., choosing diet, getting dressed).<br>**b.** Record, daily, patient's level of activity and family's involvement. Encourage appropriate diversional activity.<br>**c.** Emphasize to family members that they should treat patient as normal, especially as condition improves.<br>**d.** Coordinate activities of health-team members (e.g., social worker, dietitian, and psychiatrist) and confer with them p.r.n.<br>**e.** Refer patient to the school teacher as soon as he is able to return to school work. |

continued

| Usual Problems/Objectives/Timing | Nursing Orders |
|---|---|
| **10.** Possible:<br>–Joint pains associated with acute colitis.<br>–Skin lesions.<br>–Pericholangitis.<br>**Objective.** Early detection of symptoms.<br>**Timing.** Until discharge. | **a.** Notify dr if patient complains of joint pain or joints appear swollen.<br>**b.** To reduce stiffness: Bathe patient in warm water; allow time to soak. Add water periodically to maintain temperature.<br>**c.** Reassure patient and parents that the joint pain will subside as the bowel condition improves.<br>**d.** Check patient's skin daily for lesions. Report any unusual findings to the dr.<br>**e.** Notify dr if patient becomes jaundiced.<br>**f.** If skin is dry, initiate use of bath lubricant and/or skin cream. |
| **11.** Potential difficulties in management at home due to lack of understanding of treatment and long-term implications of the disease.<br>**Objectives.** Patient and parents state realistic understanding of the disease process, treatment, and home care.<br>**Timing.** Before discharge. | **a.** Establish a teaching program for the patient and family based on his treatment regimen.<br>**b.** Encourage patient and parents to participate in giving hydrocortisone retention enemas (Cortenemas) in hospital. Emphasize importance of retaining Cortenemas for the stated time. Reinforce teaching by questioning and by supervising repeated demonstrations.<br>**c.** Reinforce dr's encouragement to resume normal activities (e.g., school, social events).<br>**d.** Reinforce teaching about steroid medication:<br>–The common side effects (e.g., moon face, increased appetite, weight gain, and acne) and that this will resolve once the medication is discontinued.<br>–Taking the medication with milk, food, or an antacid to prevent gastric irritation.<br>–Taking the medication *ONLY* as ordered. Altering dosage or discontinuing drug must not be done without dr's advice.<br>–Notifying dr if patient develops polyuria, polydipsia, or an infection; is exposed to chickenpox; or has recurrence of early symptoms of the disease.<br>–Referral to Medic Alert organization.<br>**e.** Encourage patient to avoid situations that may contribute to relapse (e.g., emotional upsets, fatigue, irregular pattern of daily living, and failure to comply with the medication regimen).<br>**f.** Ensure parent/patient has follow-up appointment.<br>**g.** Refer to public health nurse p.r.n. |

**Goals for Discharge or Maintenance**
Parents can cope with home care and will comply with follow-up instructions.

| Usual Problems/Objectives/Timing | Nursing Orders |
|---|---|
| **1.** Potential dehydration due to fluid and electrolyte loss.<br><br>**Objective.** Adequate hydration.<br><br>**Timing.** By end of first clinic visit. | **a.** Assess patient q15–30 min (depending on patient's condition) for signs/symptoms of dehydration. If these develop, notify dr *stat*.<br><br>**b.** Obtain urine specimen for routine analysis, culture, and sensitivities.<br><br>**c.** Offer patients sips of clear fluid. Observe and report nausea or vomiting.<br><br>**d.** Observe and report to dr if child has difficulty voiding or diarrhea.<br><br>**Note:** Dr will decide whether (and when) the child can go home or should be admitted to hospital. |
| **2.** Potential mismanagement at home, due to parents' lack of understanding of the necessary care.<br><br>**Objectives.** Parents understand the need for the prescribed fluid intake and the reason for diet restrictions.<br><br>**Timing.** By end of first clinic visit. | **a.** Teach parents:<br><br>–How to recognize signs/symptoms of dehydration.<br><br>–Significance of dehydration in children, especially infants.<br><br>–To give only medications ordered by clinic dr.<br><br>**b.** Explain importance of giving fluids to replace those being lost by vomiting.<br><br>**c.** Instruct parents about feeding routine:<br><br>**First 24 hr.** Stop all food, milk, or formula and give clear fluids.<br>For example:<br>**Infants:** Give sugar solution (e.g., corn syrup) or diluted apple juice.<br>**Children over one year.** Give clear tea, flat ginger ale, apple juice, fruit-flavored gelatin, popsicles.<br>Offer frequent small amounts of fluid (e.g., give 30 ml q½h for 1 hr; if this is tolerated, give 30 ml q½h for 2 hr, then increase amount gradually until child is able to take the same amount of clear fluids as he would normally).<br>If child vomits, do not give anything to drink for about ½ hr then try again.<br><br>**Day 2.** When clear fluids have been given for 24 hr and vomiting has stopped, give small amounts of precooked rice cereal (mixed with water, no sugar added), soda crackers, toasted white bread, fruit-flavored gelatin and/or arrowroot biscuits.<br>If child tolerates these, gradually increase to normal diet, excluding milk or formula.<br><br>**Day 4–5.** Introduce milk or formula gradually, as ordered by dr.<br><br>**d.** Instruct parents to notify dr:<br><br>–If child vomits for more than 4 hr.<br><br>–If child is drowsy or irritable. |

continued

| Usual Problems/Objectives/Timing | Nursing Orders |
|---|---|
| **2. (Continued).** | −If child has not passed urine (length of time depends on amount of intake and age of child). |
| | −If the child's mouth looks and feels dry. |
| | −If child looks ill. |
| | **e.** Ensure that parents have printed instructions for home care and the name and telephone of dr or nurse to be contacted if there are problems. |
| | **f.** Designated nurse to telephone the parents within the next 24 hr to check on child's condition (*see* page 304, Guidelines for Nurse in Telephone Calls to Check on Child with Diarrhea or Vomiting). |

# Careplan 133    Arteriovenous (AV) Fistula

**Goal for Discharge or Maintenance**
Parents/patient can cope with home care and follow-up.

| Usual Problems/Objectives/Timing | Nursing Orders |
|---|---|
| **1.** *Pre-operatively.* | **a.** *See* Careplan 17: Pre-operative Care, General.<br><br>**b.** Pay special attention to the child's physical therapy program. |
| **2.** *Postoperatively.* | **a.** *See* Careplan 21: Postoperative Care, General.<br><br>**b.** Pay special attention to the child's physical therapy program. |
| **3.** Potential clotting at fistula, due to poor blood flow.<br><br>**Objectives.** No clotting; bruit heard and felt over fistula incision.<br><br>**Timing.** Continuing. | **a.** Check bruit by stethoscope and palpation, q1h for 48 hr and then q4h, unless contraindicated. If bruit is inaudible, notify dr *stat*. (Follow this routine for subsequent operations; e.g., nephrectomy, transplantation.)<br><br>**b.** Check BP q4h. *Do not use arm with fistula to record BP or to take blood.* If BP is decreased, notify dr *stat*.<br><br>**c.** Do not allow restrictive clothing on limb with fistula.<br><br>**d.** Before any surgical procedure, label arm "AV fistula. Do not use for i.v. or BP" (use adhesive tape).<br><br>**e.** Put patient's arm in sling or support it on pillows for 72 hr.<br><br>**f.** 24 hr after creation of fistula, start limb exercises outlined by the physical therapist. |
| **4.** Potential mismanagement at home due to lack of understanding.<br><br>**Objective.** Parents and/or patient state that they can hear and feel bruit and state their understanding of discharge instructions.<br><br>**Timing.** By discharge. | **a.** Teach parents/patient:<br><br>  –When and how to listen and feel for bruit.<br><br>  –The importance of not exposing the affected limb to trauma (e.g., instruct patient to avoid contact sports; not to take BP on that limb or allow blood to be taken from it; and not to constrict it with tight clothing).<br><br>  –Apply skin-cream (e.g., Nivea) to limb once a day (between dialyses) if skin is very dry.<br><br>**b.** Ensure that parents/patient have written instructions about home care and follow-up and know whom to contact if there are problems. |

# Careplan 134   Arteriovenous (AV) Shunt

**Goal for Discharge or Maintenance**
Parents/patient can cope with home care and follow-up.

| Usual Problems/Objectives/Timing | Nursing Orders |
|---|---|
| 1. *Pre-operatively.* | **a.** *See* Careplan 17: Pre-operative Care, General.<br><br>**b.** Pay special attention to the child's physical therapy program. |
| 2. *Postoperatively.* | **a.** *See* Careplan 21: Postoperative Care, General.<br><br>**b.** Pay special attention to the child's physical therapy program. |
| 3. Potential clotting of shunt, due to poor blood flow.<br><br>**Objective.** No clotting.<br><br>**Timing.** Continuing. | **a.** Check for clotting q1h for 48 hr, then q4h unless contraindicated. Signs of clotting:<br><br>–Cannula cold to touch.<br><br>–No bruit above venous side.<br><br>–Blood in cannula dark or separated.<br><br>–Pain, swelling, or poor circulation in affected limb. (Follow this routine for subsequent operations; e.g., nephrectomy, transplantation.) *If any signs of clotting, notify dr stat.*<br><br>**b.** Check BP q4h. *Do not use limb with shunt to record BP or to take blood.* If BP is decreased, notify dr *stat.*<br><br>**c.** Do not remove bandage from limb.<br><br>**d.** Do not allow restrictive clothing on affected limb.<br><br>**e.** Ensure that bulldog clamps are attached to the shunt dressing at all times.<br><br>**f.** Before any surgical procedure, label affected limb "AV shunt. Do not use for i.v. or BP" (use adhesive tape).<br><br>**g.** 24 hr after creation of shunt, start limb exercises as outlined by physical therapist.<br><br>**h. Arm shunt.** Put patient's arm in sling, or support it on pillows, for 72 hr; then allow activity as ordered by dr.<br><br>**Leg shunt.** Restrict patient to bed (stretcher for visits to physical therapy) as ordered by dr; then allow him to get up, but no weight-bearing, for 2 weeks; then gradually increase exercise as tolerated (e.g., with a walker, hand crutches).<br><br>–While patient is on bed rest, position him on back; turn him on to unaffected side periodically, but ensure that he cannot flex the affected hip (this could restrict circulation to the limb).<br><br>–Forbid use of wheelchair.<br><br>–Prevent constipation. |
| 4. Potential infection of shunt.<br><br>**Objective.** No infection.<br><br>**Timing.** Until discharge. | **a.** Report any signs of infection (redness, swelling, pain, and/or discharge).<br><br>**b.** Do not immerse patient's limb in water.<br><br>**c.** Do not remove bandage from limb. |

continued

| Usual Problems/Objectives/Timing | Nursing Orders |
|---|---|
| **4. (Continued).** | **Dialysis Unit Nurses Only**<br>**d.** Change dressing daily for 1 week.<br>**e.** If any discharge around shunt, send swab for culture and sensitivities.<br>**f.** Follow hospital procedure for care of AV shunt. |
| **5.** Potential mismanagement of shunt, due to lack of understanding.<br>**Objectives.** Parents/patient know the signs and symptoms of clotting, are skilled in care of the shunt, and can use bulldog clamps.<br>**Timing.** Before discharge. | **a.** Teach parents/patient:<br>–How to recognize clotting in a shunt.<br>–How to prevent infection (e.g., never immerse limb in water or remove the bandage at home).<br>–The importance of not exposing the affected limb to trauma (e.g., instruct patient to avoid contact sports; do not take BP on affected limb or allow blood to be taken from it; and do not constrict it in tight clothing).<br>–How to identify the venous and arterial sides of the shunt, and how to apply bulldog clamps if the shunt separates.<br>–How to apply pressure if the shunt falls out.<br>–If shunt separates or falls out, to notify the dr on call for the nephrology service (patient will have to return to hospital immediately).<br>**b.** Record teaching and parents'/patient's progress in managing care.<br>**c.** Ensure that parents/patient have written instructions about home care and follow-up. |

**Goals for Discharge or Maintenance**
See Objectives.

| Usual Problems/Objectives/Timing | Nursing Orders |
|---|---|
| **1.** *Pre-operatively.* | *See* Careplan 17: Pre-operative Care, General. |
| **2.** *Postoperatively.* | **a.** *See* Careplan 21: Postoperative Care, General. <br> **b.** Allow patient to start drinking clear fluids on return from PAR. Increase intake to normal diet 1–4 hr postoperatively. |
| **3.** Difficulty voiding, because of pain, burning, and apprehension. <br> **Objective.** Patient is able to void with minimal discomfort. <br> **Timing.** 24 hr. | **a.** **First voiding postoperatively.** Stay with patient and reassure him. <br> **b.** If patient cannot void, pour warm water over perineum, or sit him in warm tub bath and encourage him to void in water. <br> **c.** If patient still cannot void and is distended or uncomfortable, notify dr *stat*. <br> **d.** Give patient medication or catheterize him, as ordered. <br> **e.** Record fluid intake and output. |
| **4.** Potential hematuria due to surgical trauma. <br> **Objective.** Early detection of hematuria. <br> **Timing.** 24 hr. | **a.** Check urine for blood. <br> **b.** Compare specimens of urine for increased or decreased bleeding. <br> **c.** If hematuria increases markedly, notify dr. |
| **5.** Patient's (and possibly parents') potential embarrassment in relation to urogenital area. <br> **Objective.** Minimal embarrassment during procedures and discussions. <br> **Timing.** Until discharge. | **a.** Do not show embarrassment yourself. Be matter of fact but tactful. <br> **b.** Ensure privacy when needed and show respect for patient. <br> **c.** Illustrate your explanations with diagrams (preferably printed) or models to show that others also undergo cystoscopy. <br> **d.** Use terms the patient/parents understand. |

# Careplan **136** Glomerulonephritis, Acute Poststreptococcal

**Goals for Discharge or Maintenance**
Patient and family understand the nature of the illness and the need for regular follow-up.

| Usual Problems/Objectives/Timing | Nursing Orders |
|---|---|
| **1.** Potential oliguria, with fluid and electrolyte imbalance, due to impairment of renal function.<br><br>**Objective.** Satisfactory fluid balance.<br><br>**Timing.** 4–10 days. | **a.** Encourage patient to void q4h while awake.<br><br>**b.** Ensure that patient receives total fluid allowance and replacement of urinary output, as ordered. Report discrepancies to dr.<br><br>**c.** Record intake and output. Report to dr any increase or decrease in voiding.<br><br>**d.** Record color of urine (e.g., smoky, tea-colored). Notify dr if gross hematuria is present.<br><br>**e.** Save urine specimen daily for examination by dr.<br><br>**f.** Weigh patient daily before breakfast. |
| **2.** Potential hypertension due to fluid retention and/or impairment of renal function.<br><br>**Objective.** BP gradually returns to normal limits.<br><br>**Timing.** Before discharge. | **a.** Measure BP q4h, and more frequently if diastolic pressure is higher than 110 mm Hg.<br><br>**b.** Administer antihypertensive drugs as ordered.<br><br>**c.** Notify dr if diastolic pressure remains high despite antihypertensive medication (dr should indicate level to report).<br><br>**d.** While patient is hypertensive or has gross hematuria, restrict activity (bed or wheelchair) and provide quiet diversions.<br><br>**e.** Observe for signs/symptoms of hypertensive encephalopathy:<br>  –Drowsiness.<br>  –Irritability.<br>  –Vomiting.<br>  –Severe headache.<br>  –Visual disturbances.<br>Notify dr *stat* if any of these are present. |
| **3.** Potential nonacceptance of diet and fluid restrictions.<br><br>**Objective.** Patient accepts restrictions.<br><br>**Timing.** Before discharge. | **a.** Ask dietitian to instruct patient and parents and discuss food preferences.<br><br>**b.** Encourage patient to eat the special diet.<br><br>**c.** Explain to patient and parents the need for restrictions; remind parents not to bring food.<br><br>**d.** Check amount of fluid allowed with amount on tray; remove extras.<br><br>**e.** Give only the fluids allowed (e.g., milk may be restricted). |
| **4.** Potential secondary infection due to debilitated state.<br><br>**Objective.** No secondary infection.<br><br>**Timing.** Until discharge. | **a.** Ensure that roommates are free of infection.<br><br>**b.** Screen visitors for infection.<br><br>**c.** Pay careful attention to hand-washing, etc.<br><br>**d.** Provide good mouth and skin care. |

| Usual Problems/Objectives/Timing | Nursing Orders |
|---|---|
| **4. (Continued).** | **e.** Notify dr if patient has any signs/symptoms of infection (e.g., fever, cough, rash). |
| **5.** Parents'/patient's anxiety and frustration over restrictions (diet and activity) and probable length of illness.<br><br>**Objectives.** Parents'/patient's anxiety reduced; they channel feelings positively.<br><br>**Timing.** As soon as possible. | **a.** Reinforce dr's explanation of probable course of illness and reasons for restrictions.<br><br>**b.** Be aware that parents may have guilt feelings about delay in seeking medical advice for streptococcal infection (e.g., sore throat). Be supportive; spend time with parents allowing them to express concerns.<br><br>**c.** Provide diversions for patient, and quiet games.<br><br>**d.** Arrange for recreationist or volunteer to spend time with patient.<br><br>**e.** Encourage child to socialize with other patients.<br><br>**f.** Prepare patient for discharge. Explain to parents/patient:<br>  –That it is essential to complete course of prescribed therapy.<br>  –Reasons for continued limitation of activity.<br>  –Need for patient to catch up in schooling at home.<br>  –Importance of follow-up.<br><br>**g.** As soon as date of discharge is known, advise dietitian.<br><br>**h.** Advise schoolteacher or public health nurse about need for home schooling. |

## Goal for Discharge or Maintenance
Parents/patient can cope with home care and follow-up.

| Usual Problems/Objectives/Timing | Nursing Orders |
|---|---|
| **1.** *Pre-operatively.* | **a.** *See* Careplan 17: Pre-operative Care, General. <br> **b.** Pay special attention to the child's physical therapy program. |
| **2.** *Postoperatively.* | **a.** *See* Careplan 21: Postoperative Care, General. <br> **b.** Pay special attention to the child's physical therapy program. |
| **3.** Potential clotting of graft, due to poor blood flow. <br><br> **Objectives.** No clotting; bruit heard and felt over fistula incision. <br><br> **Timing.** Continuing. | **a.** Check bruit by stethoscope and palpation, q1h for 48 hr and then q4h, unless contraindicated. If bruit is inaudible, notify dr *stat*. (Follow this routine for subsequent operations: e.g., nephrectomy, transplantation.) <br> **b.** Check BP q4h. *Do not use leg with graft to record BP or to take blood.* If BP is decreased, notify dr *stat*. <br> **c.** Do not allow restrictive clothing on limb with graft. <br> **d.** Before any surgical procedure, label leg "AV fistula. Do not use for i.v. or BP" (use adhesive tape). <br> **e.** 24 hr after creation of access, start limb exercises outlined by the physical therapist. <br> **f.** Restrict patient to bed (or stretcher for transportation) as ordered by dr. <br> **g.** Position patient on back to prevent flexion of hip. Older children may lie on unaffected side for short periods if they will keep affected leg extended. <br> **h.** Allow gradual weight-bearing as ordered by dr. Follow physical therapist's instructions (e.g., about using a walker, hand crutches). |
| **4.** Potential swelling of affected leg. <br><br> **Objective.** No swelling. <br><br> **Timing.** Continuing. | **a.** If dr orders leg bandage, wrap leg, including hip, in tensor bandage, from toes upward. Check with dr whether the child is to have a tensor support stocking (made to measure, to cover the leg and hip, similar to panty hose), to be worn when up. |
| **5.** Potential mismanagement at home due to lack of understanding. <br><br> **Objective.** Parents/patient state that they can hear and feel bruit over incision and state their understanding of discharge instructions. <br><br> **Timing.** By discharge. | **a.** Teach parents/patient: <br> –When and how to listen and feel for bruit. <br> –The importance of not exposing affected limb to trauma (e.g., instruct patient to avoid contact sports, not to take BP on that limb or allow blood to be taken from it, and not to constrict it in tight clothing). <br> –Apply skin-cream (e.g., Nivea) to limb once a day (between dialyses) if skin is very dry. <br> **b.** Ensure that parents/patient have written instructions for home care and follow-up. |

**Goals for Discharge or Maintenance**
See Objectives.

| Usual Problems/Objectives/Timing | Nursing Orders |
|---|---|
| **1.** Potential mismanagement of hypertension at home due to inaccurate recording of BP.<br><br>**Objective.** Parent(s) demonstrate ability to take and record BP accurately.<br><br>**Timing**<br>Nursing orders (a) to (e): By end of first clinic visit.<br>Nursing orders (f), (g): By end of second clinic visit and p.r.n. | **a.** Teach parents how to take and record their child's BP.<br>**b.** Have parents demonstrate procedure and recording at least once.<br>**c.** Give parents Instructions for Parents: Monitoring Blood Pressure (*see* page 336).<br>**d.** Ensure that parents have BP equipment, instructions, record book, and telephone numbers for information.<br>**e.** Advise the public health nurse; home visit(s) will be arranged.<br>**f.** Check BP procedure and records on second visit, then p.r.n.<br>**g.** Ensure that patient brings in his own equipment for checking every 2–3 months. |
| **2.** Potential uncontrolled BP due to incorrect administration of medication.<br><br>**Objective.** Parents understand need to give medication as instructed and side effects of medication.<br><br>**Timing.** By end of first clinic visit. | **a.** Provide *written* instructions about times medication is to be given.<br>**b.** Teach parent(s) to enter medication in record book.<br>**c.** Explain side effects of medication. Stress importance of continuing it even when BP is normal.<br>**d.** Ensure that parents know when to contact dr. (Give names and phone numbers of members of nephrology team or tell parent to call the hospital and ask for the dr on call for nephrology.)<br>**e.** Ensure that parents have prescription/medication.<br>**f.** Arrange the next clinic appointment. |
| **3.** Potential noncompliance with diet (especially salt restriction), due to lack of understanding of disease and treatment and to frustration over chronic nature of disorder.<br><br>**Objective.** Parents understand and are willing to follow prescribed diet.<br><br>**Timing.** By end of first clinic visit. | **a.** Explain why diet restrictions are necessary.<br>**b.** Ensure that *dietitian:*<br>–Interviews parents/patient.<br>–Discusses diet in detail.<br>–Prepares and discusses written instructions.<br>–Does follow-up in clinic. |
| **4.** Potential mismanagement because regimen is not followed at school.<br><br>**Objective.** School personnel are aware of illness and of need for strict adherence to treatment.<br><br>**Timing.** Before return to school. | **a.** Ensure that school nurse knows about child's activity, diet, medication, BP recordings, and whom to contact at the hospital if problems arise. |

# Instructions for Parents: Monitoring Blood Pressure

_____
(Patient's name)

## Blood Pressure Recording

Blood pressure (BP) measures how hard the heart is working to pump blood to the various parts of the body. The blood pressure must be controlled, to prevent damage to the heart and blood vessels. To achieve this, your child must take his medication as instructed, *even when his blood pressure seems normal.* With the medication your child is taking, we expect his normal blood pressure to be about _____.

Dr _____ wishes you to take your child's blood pressure at home _____ times a day. You should check the blood pressure when your child is relaxed and rested. (Excessive activity, excitement, and nervous tension can increase blood pressure.) We have given you two pieces of equipment for measuring your child's blood pressure—a stethoscope and a blood pressure cuff with a dial (see Figure 6A).

## Procedure

Have your child sit on a chair next to a table, so his arm can rest on the table while his blood pressure is being taken. His arm should be level with his heart (see Figure 6B).

Turn the screw next to the rubber bulb to the left (counterclockwise), and press all the air from the cuff. Place the padded part of the cuff on the child's arm above the elbow, with the Velcro (roughened) edges away from the skin. Make sure the dial is face up, then wrap the cuff tightly around the arm. Press the Velcro edges and padded parts together.

Place your fingers on the inside of the elbow and feel the pulse, then place the flat part of the stethoscope on that spot. Put the earpiece of the stethoscope in your ears and listen for the pulse sound.

Turn the screw to the right (clockwise) until it is firmly closed. Pump the bulb of the cuff with one hand until the pulse sound stops; then undo the screw slowly, watching the dial, until you hear the first pulse sound. When you hear this sound, read the number on the dial. This is the systolic blood pressure, the number that goes on top (e.g., 120/—). It indicates the pressure of blood flowing through the blood vessels when the heart is in the contracting phase.

Continue to release the screw slowly until you hear the pulse change from a loud thumping sound to a soft muffled one *or* until the sound disappears. When either occurs, read the number on the dial. This is the diastolic blood pressure, the number that goes on the bottom (e.g., —/80). It indicates the pressure of blood flowing through the vessels while the heart is at rest. If you hear the soft, muffled sound and then the sound disappears, read the dial number at the time of each event.

As soon as you have taken both (or all three) pressures, write them on the chart you have been given. These numbers together record the complete blood pressure. The reading looks like this: e.g., 120/80 or 120/80/60. Remove the cuff and store it and the stethoscope in a safe place.

If you have any problem in hearing the blood pressure or if it is higher than usual, have your child rest for 15 to 30 minutes, then take it again. If the blood pressure measurement is unusually high (around _____)

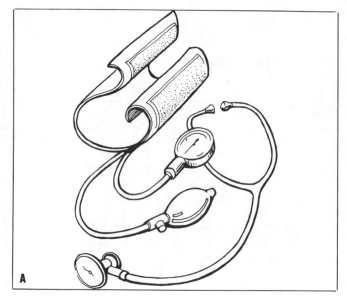

A

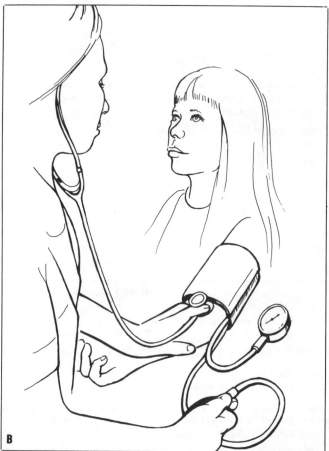

B

**Figure 6.** *Equipment and procedure for recording blood pressure.*

when you recheck it, or if there are other signs of elevated blood pressure (persistent headache, nausea, vomiting, dizziness, and blurred vision), notify

_____ ;

they will give you appropriate instructions.

**Goals for Discharge or Maintenance**
Parents/patient understand the condition and can cope with home care and follow-up.

| Usual Problems/Objectives/Timing | Nursing Orders |
|---|---|
| **1.** *Pre-operatively.* | **a.** *See* Careplan 17: Pre-operative Care, General.<br><br>**b.** Explain:<br>  –Type of catheters that may be used (urethral, suprapubic).<br>  –Bladder spasms.<br>  –Sutures (dissolving type).<br>  –Type of dressing.<br>  –Swelling and discoloration of penile area.<br>  –Use of bed-cradle.<br>  –Need for increased fluid intake.<br>  –Measurement of fluid intake and output. |
| **2.** *Postoperatively.* | **a.** *See* Careplan 21: Postoperative Care, General.<br><br>**b.** Provide a bed-cradle.<br><br>**c.** Ensure that patient's clothing is not touching the operative site.<br><br>**Younger boy:** Pin patient's gown over the cradle edge. |
| **3.** Potential obstruction of urine flow due to blocked catheter.<br><br>**Objective.** Catheter patent.<br><br>**Timing.** Until catheter is removed. | **a.** *See* Careplan 148: Urinary Catheter, Indwelling.<br><br>**b.** Give fluids i.v. until oral intake is tolerated.<br><br>**c.** Start patient on sips of clear fluid then increase to full fluids. If abdomen is not distended, increase to normal diet and push fluids.<br><br>**d.** Offer fluids at mealtimes, between meals, and at least twice during the night. Enlist family's assistance with this.<br><br>**e.** Record fluid intake and output.<br><br>**f.** Check catheter frequently for kinking and to ensure that the suture and tape holding it in place are secure.<br><br>**g.** If urine is mucousy, decrease intake of dairy products.<br><br>**h.** Notify dr if there is little or no urinary drainage. |
| **4.** *If there is no urethral catheter, or when catheter is removed/clamped,* potential development of fistulae due to obstruction of meatus.<br><br>**Objective.** Early detection of meatal obstruction.<br><br>**Timing.** Until discharge. | **a.** Establish voiding routine q2h during the day, q4h at night.<br><br>**b.** **Infant:** *Do not use diapers.* Check at least q1h for evidence of voiding.<br><br>**c.** Observe each voiding for:<br>  –Possible fistulae.<br>  –Crusting at meatus.<br>  –Direction and strength of urinary stream. |

337

continued

| Usual Problems/Objectives/Timing | Nursing Orders |
|---|---|
| **4. (Continued).** | **d.** If crusting occurs, consult dr about using sitz baths or applying mineral oil. |
| | **e.** Notify dr *stat* if patient is unable to void or if a fistula is suspected. If there is a suprapubic catheter, unclamp it. |
| | **f.** If a fistula has developed, be aware that further surgery will be required (usually a few months later); be supportive to parents/patient. |
| **5.** Patient/parents anxious about possible disfigurement, impaired sexual function, and/or sterility.<br>**Objectives.** Patient/parents are able to express their concerns and can cope with explanations given.<br>**Timing.** Before discharge. | **a.** Reassure patient/parents that swelling and discoloration will gradually subside (usually in 7–10 days but may be longer).<br>**b.** Reinforce dr's explanation of anatomical problem and treatment. Use diagrams or body-line drawings if appropriate.<br>**c.** Reassure younger boys that their penis is still there.<br>**d.** Provide opportunities for parents and patient to express concerns (individually or together). Older boys may want to talk to a dr or to a nurse of his choice about possible sexual problems.<br>**e.** Ensure privacy for all discussions and examinations. |
| **6.** Potential boredom and restlessness due to being on bed rest and having to lie flat in bed.<br>**Objective.** Patient is able to participate in activities appropriate for patients on bed rest.<br>**Timing.** 7–10 days. | **a.** Place patient in room with other children who are confined to bed (if possible).<br>**b.** Plan a structured day for the patient, including school, recreation, and visitors.<br>**c.** If family/friends cannot visit, arrange for volunteer assistance.<br>**d.** Provide quiet games, TV, record player, or radio, as appropriate.<br>**e.** Be aware that patients can express their concerns nonverbally (especially fear of castration). Provide board and paper for drawing or painting.<br>**Younger child:** provide water play. Correct misconceptions demonstrated in play. Consult play therapist if appropriate. |
| **7.** Potential mismanagement of home care due to lack of understanding.<br>**Objective.** Parents/patient understand precautions that must be taken to avoid injury in the perineal area.<br>**Timing.** Before discharge. | **a.** Reinforce dr's instructions:<br>–Child must not wear tight-fitting pants; no diapers for infants until ordered by dr.<br>–All straddle-type activities must be avoided (e.g., cycling, seesaws), toddlers must be kept from climbing over bed-sides or playpen, and child must not swim until approved by dr.<br>**b.** Ask parent to bring loose-fitting clothing for child to wear when he goes home.<br>**c.** Check with dr about when patient can return to school (usually 1–2 weeks after discharge).<br>**d.** Ensure that parents have follow-up appointments for clinic or readmission. |

# Careplan 140 Ileal Conduit

## Goals for Discharge or Maintenance
I. Parents/patient demonstrate ability to care for the stoma.
II. They understand the importance of regular follow-up at clinic.
III. They know where to get supplies and whom to call if they have problems.

| Usual Problems/Objectives/Timing | Nursing Orders |
|---|---|
| **1.** *Pre-operatively.* | *See* Careplan 17: Pre-operative Care, General. |
| **2.** Parents/patient anxious about the appearance of the ileal conduit and their ability to cope with it.<br><br>**Objectives.** Parents/patient express concerns, ask questions, and understand the information given.<br><br>**Timing.** Before surgery. | **Designated nurse:**<br><br>**a.** Ascertain parents'/patient's understanding of the operation.<br><br>**b.** Reinforce dr's explanations, including reasons for the operation.<br><br>**c.** Explain briefly to parents/patient the management of a stoma after surgery (e.g., a pouch will be applied directly to the skin until the stoma has shrunk, and then a permanent appliance will be fitted).<br><br>**d.** Notify the enterostomal therapist and explain to child/parents that this person will do the following.<br><br>–Teach them how to cope with the ileal conduit, and provide any necessary assistance.<br><br>–Determine the most suitable site for the stoma, by having the child wear an appliance for a day or two. (This also helps to accustom the child to the appliance. Testing the site is particularly important for those who have other problems, such as postural deformity.)<br><br>–Mark the site most suitable for the stoma. |
| **3.** *Postoperatively.* | **a.** *See* Careplan 21: Postoperative Care, General.<br><br>**b.** Follow the enterostomal therapist's instructions for skin barrier, pouch, etc. |
| **4.** Potential breakdown of ureteral anastomosis.<br><br>**Objective.** Early detection of indications that anastomosis has broken down.<br><br>**Timing.** Day 8–10. | **a.** Check the patency of the ureteral splints q1–2h: check the splints in the stoma, and be sure they are not kinked and there are no occlusive blood clots.<br><br>**b.** Check that the urine bag is firmly in place: if it slips, it could obstruct the stoma.<br><br>**c.** Record fluid intake and output carefully.<br><br>**d.** *Report to dr stat if urine output is diminished.* (This is an early sign of anastomosis breakdown.) |
| **5.** Potential excoriation due to seepage of urine.<br><br>**Objective.** No excoriation.<br><br>**Timing.** Continuing. | **a.** Change the pouch and skin barrier when it leaks and at least every 3 days.<br><br>**b.** At each pouch change:<br><br>–Measure the stoma.<br><br>–Reduce the size of the hole in the pouch and skin barrier gradually (as the stoma shrinks).<br><br>–If the skin is excoriated, consult the enterostomal therapist. |

continued

| Usual Problems/Objectives/Timing | Nursing Orders |
|---|---|
| **5. (Continued).** | **c.** If edema or cyanosis develops at the stoma, notify dr *stat*. If the stoma appears infected, send swabs for culture and sensitivities and notify dr. |
| **6.** Potential urinary tract infection.<br><br>**Objective.** No infection.<br><br>**Timing.** Continuing. | **a.** Encourage patient to drink a lot.<br><br>**b.** Position him to promote free drainage of urine into the pouch (on R side or on his back, with head and trunk elevated).<br><br>**c.** Record characteristics of urine (color, odor, and cloudiness).<br><br>**d.** Notify dr if signs of urinary tract infection develop:<br>–Temperature rising.<br>–Chills.<br>–Diaphoresis.<br>–Flank pain.<br>–Sediment or blood in urine.<br>–Decreased urinary output.<br><br>**e.** Teach parents/patient the signs and symptoms of urinary tract infection. |
| **7.** Potential reluctance to accept the ileal conduit and/or change in body image.<br><br>**Objective.** Patient/parents show some acceptance of the stoma by participating in its care.<br><br>**Timing.** Before discharge. | **a.** Listen to parents'/patient's concerns and answer all questions.<br><br>**b.** Encourage patient/parents to help in managing the stoma. Introduce various aspects *gradually* (e.g., first, skin care; then, changing the pouch; later, emptying the pouch).<br><br>**c.** Explain methods to control the odor of urine (e.g., drinking cranberry juice, soaking appliances in vinegar). |
| **8.** Patient anxious about social acceptance.<br><br>**Objectives.** Patient is planning to return to usual lifestyle and is beginning to take part in age-appropriate social activities.<br><br>**Timing.** Before discharge. | **a.** Reassure child that the ileal conduit cannot be seen when he is dressed and that he will not have to wear diapers.<br><br>**b.** If appropriate, introduce him to another child who has a stoma and has been at home.<br><br>**c.** Encourage child to socialize with his peers in the hospital.<br><br>**d.** Discuss with the patient his plans for returning to school, etc., and resuming activities in the community.<br><br>**e.** Notify the public health nurse in the patient's school district.<br><br>**f.** Give patient/parents the name and address of their local ostomy group and explain its purpose (to meet in a friendly, informal way, to share experiences and learn how to cope). |
| **9.** Potential concern about management of the ileal conduit at home.<br><br>**Objectives.** Patient/parents know how to look after the stoma and equipment and have made the necessary arrangements for home care. | **a.** Teach the parents/patient, and have them demonstrate:<br>–Preparation of the skin around the stoma.<br>–Application of the mounting ring and pouch.<br>–Care of the equipment. |

| Usual Problems/Objectives/Timing | Nursing Orders |
|---|---|
| **9. (Continued).**<br><br>**Timing.** Before discharge. | **b.** Assess the family's ability to cope at home: at least one family member should be able to do stoma care.<br><br>**c.** Check that:<br><br>–Equipment and supplies have been given to family.<br><br>–Parents know where to buy further supplies.<br><br>–They have the equipment manufacturer's printed instructions.<br><br>–They have instructions (written) from the enterostomal therapist.<br><br>–They have follow-up appointment(s).<br><br>–They know whom to call in case of problems.<br><br>**d.** Arrange for appropriate help as necessary (e.g., home care program or public health department, for care with stoma; Easter Seal Society, for financial assistance). |
| **10.** Potential mismanagement of care at home due to failure to comply with instructions about care or to attend follow-up clinic(s).<br><br>**Objectives.** Patient and family are living a reasonably normal life; they can cope with home care and the child attends clinic regularly.<br><br>**Timing.** After discharge from hospital. | **Enterostomal therapist or designated nurse:**<br><br>**a.** Ensure that patient is attending follow-up clinic. Check whether there are problems with transportation, time of clinic, etc. (Many patients with ileal conduits are paraplegic and must attend several clinics.)<br><br>**b.** Stress the importance of attending follow-up clinic to have appliances checked and adjusted.<br><br>**c.** Reinforce instructions from all health care team members.<br><br>**d.** Tell parents to call the enterostomal therapist or other designated person (give name and telephone number in writing) as soon as any problem arises. |

**Goals for Discharge or Maintenance**
Patient/parents understand the outpatient regimen and can cope with home care.

| Usual Problems/Objectives/Timing | Nursing Orders |
|---|---|
| **1.** *Pre-operatively.* | *See* Careplan 17: Pre-operative Care, General. |
| **2.** Parents/patient anxious about the remaining kidney.<br>**Objective.** Parents/patient express their fears and concerns.<br>**Timing.** Continuing until discharge. | **a.** Provide opportunities for patient and family to express their concerns.<br>**b.** Reinforce information given to them by dr (e.g., that one kidney can be adequate).<br>**c.** Use diagrams/pictures to show them how the kidney is connected to the bladder, and give simple explanations of renal system. |
| **3.** *Postoperatively.* | *See* Careplan 21: Postoperative Care, General.<br>–Check BP q4h for 48 hr, then q8h. |
| **4.** Potential oliguria or retention of urine.<br>**Objective.** Adequate output of urine.<br>**Timing.** 12 hr. | **a.** Administer i.v. fluids as ordered.<br>**b.** Record fluid intake and output.<br>**c.** Offer patient a bedpan/urinal q4h while he is awake.<br>**d.** Report if abdomen is becoming distended.<br>**e.** Give analgesic as ordered.<br>**f.** Notify dr if patient has not voided by 8–10 hr postoperatively. |
| **5.** Potential respiratory problems due to patient's reluctance to move.<br>**Objective.** No respiratory problems; patient moves well with decreasing discomfort.<br>**Timing.** Until patient is fully ambulant. | **a.** Observe for and report any signs/symptoms of respiratory problems.<br>**b.** Maintain patient on bed rest for 3 days, or as ordered.<br>**c.** Assist patient with deep-breathing and coughing.<br>**d.** Change patient's position (back, operative side, back) at least q2h.<br>**e.** Gradually introduce ambulation, starting day 4 postoperatively.<br>**First day.** Have patient sit on chair and dangle legs.<br>**Second day.** Have patient walk in room and sit on chair.<br>**Third day.** Have patient walk in corridor and sit on chair.<br>Assist patient with all these activities. |
| **6.** *Heminephrectomy:* Potential spontaneous hemorrhage from remaining part of kidney, due to exertion.<br>**Objective.** Early detection of hemorrhage.<br>**Timing.** Until discharge. | **a.** Record vital signs at least q4h, and observe child frequently.<br>**b.** Enforce bed rest until dr orders ambulation (usually 4 days postoperatively).<br>**c.** Check each specimen of urine for blood.<br>**d.** Help patient do passive and active limb exercises q2h (while he is awake). |

| Usual Problems/Objectives/Timing | Nursing Orders |
|---|---|
| **6. (Continued).** | **e.** Encourage patient to deep-breathe and cough q2h for 24 hr, then p.r.n.<br><br>**f.** Allow patient to lie in any position (preferably on the affected side, to promote drainage).<br><br>**g.** If blood appears in urine, or other signs of hemorrhage develop (e.g., increased pulse rate, fall in BP, pain, or spasms), notify dr *stat* and:<br><br>–Elevate foot of bed.<br><br>–Record vital signs frequently.<br><br>–Observe child closely, reassure him, and keep him as still as possible until dr arrives. |
| **7.** Potential mismanagement at home due to lack of knowledge.<br><br>**Objective.** Parents/patient state their understanding of discharge instructions.<br><br>**Timing.** Before discharge. | **a.** Reinforce dr's instructions for home care.<br><br>**b.** Explain to parents/patient:<br><br>–Need to resume normal activities but to avoid contact sports and any activity (such as heavy lifting) that would affect the remaining kidney (or part of kidney) for 1–2 months.<br><br>–Need to avoid persons with infection (especially upper respiratory tract infections).<br><br>–Symptoms to report to dr (e.g., redness, swelling, fever).<br><br>**c.** Ensure that parents have follow-up appointment(s) in writing.<br><br>**Note:** Further nursing orders depend on the condition that necessitated the renal surgery. |

**Goals for Discharge or Maintenance**
**I.** Patient and parents describe disease accurately.
**II.** Parents can cope with home care and follow-up.

| Usual Problems/Objectives/Timing | Nursing Orders |
|---|---|
| **1.** Potential fluid and electrolyte imbalance due to increased albumin loss, sodium retention, and (later) diuresis.<br><br>**Objectives**<br><br>**a.** No fluid overload during oliguric phase.<br><br>**b.** Adequate hydration during diuretic phase.<br><br>**Timing.** Until discharge. | **a.** Weigh patient daily before breakfast.<br>**b.** Record abdominal girth daily (a.m.).<br>**c.** Record BP q4h when patient is awake.<br>**d.** Record intake and output. Give fluids only as ordered.<br>**e.** Observe for increased edema during oliguric phase and dehydration during diuretic phase.<br>**f.** Consult dr if fluid-replacement orders should be changed (e.g., when diuresis starts).<br>**g.** Save 0700-hr urine specimen daily for examination by dr.<br>**h.** Administer steroids, diuretics, and immunosuppressive drugs as ordered. |
| **2.** Potential infection because resistance is decreased by steroid therapy.<br>**Objective.** No infection.<br>**Timing.** Until discharge. | **a.** Ensure that roommates are free of infection.<br>**b.** Instruct patient to remain on ward, to limit contacts with potential carriers of infection.<br>**c.** Observe patient daily for signs of infection (e.g., elevated temperature). |
| **3.** Potential skin breakdown due to edema.<br>**Objective.** Skin clear and intact.<br>**Timing.** Until discharge. | **a.** Provide meticulous skin care.<br>**b.** If patient is on bed rest, give care to pressure areas (change his position frequently; pay special attention to skin folds).<br>**c.** Provide loose clothing.<br>**d.** Provide special support p.r.n. (e.g., for scrotal edema).<br>**e.** Avoid femoral venipunctures and i.m. injections in buttocks. |
| **4.** Potential unwillingness to accept diet and fluid restrictions.<br>**Objectives.** Patient and parents understand and accept need for **(a)** diet and **(b)** fluid restrictions and comply with them.<br>**Timing**<br>**a.** Before discharge.<br>**b.** Whenever patient is oliguric. | **a.** Explain to patient and parents the reasons for restrictions and need to measure fluid intake and urine. If appropriate, teach child to measure and record these himself.<br>**b.** Work with dietitian to establish diet and fluid requirements.<br>**c.** Refer patient and parents to dietitian for teaching, and reinforce dr's and dietitian's instructions.<br>**d.** Explain reasons for changes in diet as condition improves (e.g., increased fluids and potassium during diureses).<br>**e.** As soon as discharge date is known, advise dietitian. Work with dietitian to establish home care plans. |
| **5.** Potential embarrassment about physical changes due to edema and/or steroids. | **a.** Reassure patient that edema will subside, but that this may take several weeks. |

| Usual Problems/Objectives/Timing | Nursing Orders |
|---|---|
| **5. (Continued).**<br><br>**Objective.** Patient understands reasons for temporary alteration in his appearance.<br><br>**Timing.** By discharge. | **b.** Explain effects of steroids; reassure patient that when medication is reduced the cushingoid appearance will gradually lessen.<br><br>**c.** Encourage socialization with peers. |
| **6.** Parental concern about course of disease and effects of medication.<br><br>**Objective.** Parents express understanding and acceptance of child's condition and are willing to follow dr's plan for home care and follow-up.<br><br>**Timing.** By discharge. | **a.** Reinforce dr's explanation to parents. (Refer to dr for further clarification of prognosis.) Avoid expressing optimism/pessimism about final outcome.<br><br>**b.** Allow plenty of opportunity for discussion, particularly if illness is lengthy.<br><br>**c.** In preparation for discharge, teach parents (and patient if appropriate) about:<br><br>–Medications: side effects and dosage adjustment.<br><br>–Urine: testing for protein, and recording on special sheet.<br><br>–Importance of follow-up, particularly if fever, sore throat, influenza, etc., develops.<br><br>–Precautions for avoiding infections.<br><br>**d.** Ensure that parents have written instructions for home care and follow-up and know whom to contact if they are having problems. |

# 143

**Goals for Discharge or Maintenance**
Parents understand and are willing to follow outpatient regimen.

| Usual Problems/Objectives/Timing | Nursing Orders |
|---|---|
| **1.** *Pre-operatively.* | **a.** *See* Careplan 17: Pre-operative Care, General. |
| | **b.** Reinforce information about type of tension suture that will be used (i.e., button suture or suture with elastic). |
| | **c.** If patient is going to have suture with elastic, explain positioning, eating, drinking, toileting, etc., while suture is attached to thigh (about 7 days). |
| | **d.** Give parents the Information for Parents of Children Undergoing Orchidopexy (*see* page 348). |
| **2.** *Postoperatively.* | **a.** *See* Careplan 21: Postoperative Care, General. |
| | **b.** Remove inguinal dressing 24 hr postoperatively. |
| **3.** Potential retraction of testicle, due to reduced tension on suture. **Objectives.** Constant suture tension; testicle remains in scrotum. **Timing.** Suture removal (2–7 days). | **If tension suture is attached to inner aspect of thigh** |
| | **a.** Check suture tension q2h. |
| | **b.** Use ankle restraints, to keep leg extended. |
| | **c.** Do not raise head of bed. |
| | **d.** Do not allow patient to sit up in bed. |
| | **e.** If patient is unable to void: |
| | **Small boy.** Lift him out of bed with his leg extended. |
| | **Older boy.** Help him slide out of bed with leg extended. |
| | **f.** If patient has difficulty passing stools, allow him to sit on toilet, but ensure that the leg with the tension suture attached remains extended. |
| | **If tension suture is attached to outer aspect of scrotum (button suture)** |
| | **g.** Confine patient to bed for 24 hr (leg does not have to be extended). |
| | **Note:** The patient may sit up and move around after 24 hr. He probably will go home sooner than patient with a thigh suture. |
| | **All patients** |
| | **h.** Provide a bed-cradle. (Pinning the patient's gown over the cradle edge keeps clothing off the operation site and discourages patient from touching the suture.) |
| | **i.** When patient is ambulatory, do not allow underwear or pajama trousers; patient should wear two gowns (one on usual way, and one back-to-front) or a gown and a bathrobe. |
| **4.** If patient is confined to bed, potential anxiety and frustration due to restricted activity. | **a.** Place patient in room with other children who are on bed rest. |

| Usual Problems/Objectives/Timing | Nursing Orders |
|---|---|
| **4. (Continued).**<br><br>**Objective.** Patient is able to cope with usual activities while lying flat or standing.<br><br>**Timing.** Until tension suture is disconnected from thigh. | **b.** Place patient's personal belongings within his reach.<br><br>**c.** Arrange food and snacks so that patient can feed himself (e.g., cut his meat, give him flexible straws for fluids).<br><br>**d.** Provide age-appropriate diversions.<br><br>**e.** If first voiding postoperatively is difficult, patient may stand at side of bed to void. *See* nursing order 3(e).<br><br>**f.** Reassure patient that he will be allowed to get up once the suture is disconnected from the thigh. |
| **5.** Patient's (and possibly parents') potential embarrassment in relation to genitals.<br><br>**Objective.** Minimal embarrassment during procedures and discussions.<br><br>**Timing.** Until discharge. | **a.** Do not show embarrassment yourself. Be matter of fact but tactful.<br><br>**b.** Ensure privacy when needed and show respect for patient.<br><br>**c.** Use terms the patient/parents understand. |
| **6.** Parents anxious about outcome of operation, future development of the testis, and potential sterility.<br><br>**Objectives.** Parents **(a)** express their concerns and **(b)** are kept informed by surgeon.<br><br>**Timing.**<br>**(a)** As soon as possible.<br>**(b)** Until discharge. | **a.** Ensure that surgeon tells parents the results of surgery and expected outcome.<br><br>**b.** Reinforce explanations given by surgeon.<br><br>**c.** Ensure that parents have instructions for home care and an appointment for follow-up.<br><br>**d.** Explain importance of protecting affected area (e.g., child not to wear tight-fitting underpants, avoidance of straddle-type activities).<br><br>**e.** Have parents bring loose-fitting clothes (e.g., track suit) for child to wear home. |

# Information for Parents of Children Undergoing Orchidopexy

### Admission Day

After your child has been admitted to the ward, he will be examined by a doctor who will ask you to sign a consent for surgery. During the evening (around 7:00 p.m.), you will be notified about the time of surgery.

Your child will have a bath before going to bed. Depending on the time of his surgery, he will be given a drink sometime during the night or early morning (usually 6 hours before the operation). After that, he will not be allowed to eat or drink anything.

### The Day of Surgery

Your child will wear a white gown and be taken to the operating room on a stretcher (young children go in their beds). If he is very young or if the surgery is late in the day, your child may have an i.v. (intravenous infusion).

You may go with your son to the elevator; and then you may wait for him in the parents' postoperative waiting room. Your son's surgeon will go to see you there after the operation. After his surgery, your child will spend a few hours in the Recovery Room and then will be brought back to the ward by one of the nurses.

### Return to the Ward

When you see your child back on the ward, he will be awake and able to answer questions. He may have an i.v.,which will probably be discontinued after 24 hours if he is drinking well.

You will notice that your child has a special suture to keep the testicle in place in the scrotum. There are two types of suture.

1. *Suture with elastic attachment.*
    The suture (thread) holding the testicle in place is passed through to the outside of the scrotum and is attached to an elastic. The other end of the elastic is then taped to the inner part of the thigh. This creates a pull or tension on the suture to keep the testicle in its correct place in the scrotum.

It is very important for your child to keep his leg extended (straight) to help maintain this tension on the suture. In about 5 days, the elastic will be cut and your child will then be able to move around more freely. The suture (which is made of catgut) will eventually dissolve as the area heals.

2. *Button suture.*
    The suture (thread) holding the testicle in place is passed through to the outside of the scrotum and is stitched to a button. The button helps hold it in place. Your child will be able to go home in a few days with the suture in place. About 7 days after surgery, he will return to clinic to have the suture removed.

### First Days after Surgery

At first there will probably be some redness, swelling, and discomfort.

If your child has the suture with the elastic attachment, he will have to lie flat in bed until the elastic is detached from the thigh (about 7 days). He will have to eat, be bathed, and use the urinal and/or bedpan while lying flat. He may find this difficult and frustrating to manage; however, the nurses and you can help him and comfort him.

If your child has a button suture, he will be kept in bed for about 24 hours. While he is in bed, he will have to pass urine (void) into a urinal.

### Discharge

When it is time to take your child home, please bring loose-fitting clothing for him to wear (e.g., track suit). Until his next appointment with the doctor, your son will not be allowed to wear tight-fitting underpants and must avoid straddle-type activities and sports that might injure the affected area.

On the day your son is discharged, his nurse will give you specific instructions for follow-up care and information about appointments.

## Goals for Discharge or Maintenance
I. Patient/parents understand reason for peritoneal dialysis, demonstrate competence and confidence in doing procedure, and know how to protect catheter site.
II. Patient/parents can cope with home care and follow-up.

| Usual Problems/Objectives/Timing | Nursing Orders |
|---|---|
| **1.** Insertion of indwelling catheter. | *See* Careplan 17: Pre-operative Care, General *and* Careplan 21: Postoperative Care, General. |
| **2.** Potential infection of peritoneal fluid and/or skin by contaminants.<br><br>**Objective.** No infection.<br><br>**Timing.** Until discharge. | **a.** Maintain strict surgical asepsis when changing dialysis tubing, dressings, and bags, and when adding medication to the tubing.<br>**b.** Ensure that drainage bag is not raised above level of patient's abdomen unless it is clamped.<br>**c.** Record TPR at least q4h.<br>**d.** Observe q4h and p.r.n. for signs/symptoms of infection:<br>–Redness, tenderness, or discharge.<br>–Abdominal pain, nausea, or fever.<br>–Cloudy dialysate returns.<br>Notify dr if any of these occur. |
| **3.** Potential dehydration or overhydration due to fluid/electrolyte imbalance.<br><br>**Objective.** Fluid and electrolyte balance maintained.<br><br>**Timing.** Until treatment is complete. | **a.** Follow hospital procedure for peritoneal dialysis.<br>**b.** Record fluid intake and output accurately.<br>**c.** Observe q4h for confusion, lassitude, edema, fever and/or nausea. Report if any of these are present.<br>**d.** Check BP q4h; notify dr if any sudden decrease or increase. |
| **4.** Potential discomfort related to catheter irritation and abdominal distention.<br><br>**Objective.** Patient states he is comfortable and appears relaxed.<br><br>**Timing.** Until dialysis treatment is complete. | **a.** Place patient in the most comfortable position.<br>**b.** Provide age-appropriate toys or other diversions.<br>**c.** Ensure that dialysate solution is kept warm (37°C).<br>**d.** Run dialysate solution in slowly.<br>**e.** Administer analgesics as ordered. |
| **5.** Potential insomnia because of discomfort.<br><br>**Objectives.** Patient appears to be rested and is sleeping at night.<br><br>**Timing.** Throughout dialysis. | **a.** Provide quiet environment for the patient.<br>**b.** Encourage patient to have fewer naps during day so he will sleep better at night.<br>**c.** Consult dr about giving sedation p.r.n.<br>**d.** *See also* nursing orders for problem 4. |
| **6.** Potential anxiety and/or depression related to altered life-style and body image.<br><br>**Objectives.** Patient voices concerns, understands the disease process and need for treatment, and is able to make the necessary adjustments in life-style.<br><br>**Timing.** Before discharge. | **a.** Explain all procedures carefully.<br>**b.** Allow patient to handle equipment similar to that which will be used during dialysis (e.g., use teaching doll).<br>**c.** Provide ample opportunity for patient to express fears and concerns; be available to answer questions. Do not always focus on dialysis. Emphasize patient's good qualities. |

continued

| Usual Problems/Objectives/Timing | Nursing Orders |
|---|---|
| **6. (Continued).** | **d.** Help patient select clothing that minimizes appearance of dialysis bags and tubing.<br><br>**e.** Encourage patient to socialize with his peers.<br><br>**f.** Ensure that all staff treat patient in an age-appropriate manner (most children with renal disease are small in stature and look younger than they are.)<br><br>**g.** Refer patient/parent to social worker and other members of the health team as appropriate. |
| **7.** Potential mismanagement of diet and/or catheter at home due to lack of understanding and/or failure to comply with instructions because of burnout.<br><br>**Objectives.** Patient/parents skilled in care of the catheter; they select menus consistent with diet.<br><br>**Timing.** Before discharge. | **a.** Arrange for dietitian to reinforce teaching about diet restrictions.<br><br>**b.** Allow patient to select food; supervise, evaluate, and reinforce teaching.<br><br>*Patients on Continuous Ambulatory Peritoneal Dialysis [CAPD]*<br><br>**c.** Instruct patient/parents in care of the indwelling catheter.<br><br>**d.** Emphasize the importance of preventing infection.<br><br>**e.** Teach parent/patient how to recognize symptoms of peritonitis (fever, abdominal pain, tenderness), and other signs of infection (e.g., redness or swelling of catheter site).<br><br>**f.** Patients on home dialysis. Ensure that parents/patient demonstrate competence and confidence in all aspects of treatment and have supplies and equipment.<br><br>**g.** Record teaching and patient's/parents' progress in managing catheter care and diet.<br><br>**h.** Ensure that parents/patient have home care and follow-up appointments in writing and know whom to contact if they have concerns. (Be aware that family may become very fatigued and less careful in technique, etc. It may be advisable to readmit patient so that family can have a break from the time-consuming daily treatment routines.) |

**Goals for Discharge or Maintenance**
See Objectives.

| Usual Problems/Objectives/Timing | Nursing Orders |
|---|---|
| **1.** Patient/family anxious that the renal graft might not function.<br><br>**Objective.** Patient and family discuss their fears with the health care team.<br><br>**Timing.** Throughout hospital stay. | All relevant health care workers cooperate in care; dr talks to patient and family at least once a day.<br><br>**a.** Allow ample opportunity for child and family to discuss their concerns.<br><br>**b.** Ensure that they have access to other staff, particularly social worker, psychiatrist, and nephrologist.<br><br>**c.** Record what information has been given, and by whom, to the child and family. |
| **2.** *Postoperatively.* | *See* Careplan 21: Postoperative Care, General. |
| **3.** *If urinary catheter is in place.* | *See* Careplan 148: Urinary Catheter, Indwelling. |
| **4.** Potential clotting of AV fistula or AV shunt. | *See* Careplan 133: Arteriovenous (AV) Fistula *or* Careplan 134: Arteriovenous (AV) Shunt. |
| **5.** Potential early fluid, electrolyte, and metabolic imbalance, due to malfunctioning of transplanted kidney. (This can occur later, also, if the kidney does not function well.)<br><br>**Objective.** Fluid, electrolyte, and metabolic balance.<br><br>**Timing.** Day 4. | **a.** Record fluid intake and output accurately, q1h until catheter is removed, then q4–8h. If child is not toilet-trained, weigh diapers.<br><br>**b.** Record BP q1h until stable, then q2–4h as ordered.<br><br>**c.** Weigh patient daily (in a.m.), or b.i.d. (a.m. and h.s.) if ordered.<br><br>**d.** Calculate and give fluid replacement as ordered.<br><br>**e.** Notify dr if there is significant increase/decrease in hourly urine output.<br><br>**f.** Take blood daily for laboratory determinations.<br><br>**g.** Collect 24-hr urine specimens daily for 1 week, then twice weekly, or as ordered.<br><br>**h.** Save specimen of first urine voided each day for testing as ordered. |
| **6.** Potential lack of urine because of acute tubular necrosis due to pretransplantation ischemia in transplant.<br><br>**Objective.** Early detection of fluid overload.<br><br>**Timing.** 1 month. | **a.** Record urine output q1h. Notify dr *stat* if oliguria, anuria, or sudden increase in output.<br><br>**b.** Report to dr if signs of fluid overload (e.g., increase in BP, weight, respiratory rate, or apical heart rate; pitting edema of ankles; or facial edema, particularly around eyes). |
| **7.** Potential rejection of kidney. (In early phase, rejection is more likely to be acute and is, therefore, severe.)<br><br>**Objectives.** Patient has some understanding of the rejection process. Early recognition of signs of rejection.<br><br>**Timing.** Continuing. | **a.** Notify dr *stat* if any signs or symptoms of rejection:<br>–Fever.<br>–Decreased urinary output or frank anuria (can occur immediately postop or after several days).<br>–Swelling or tenderness over operation site.<br>–Hypertension.<br><br>**b.** Reassure parents/patient that rejection may respond to treatment. (It is important to be optimistic about the transplanted kidney.) |

351

continued

| Usual Problems/Objectives/Timing | Nursing Orders |
|---|---|
| **8.** Potential infection because resistance is decreased by immunosuppressive therapy.<br><br>**Objectives.**<br><br>**a.** Patient's mouth is free of infection; chest is clear; urine is clear—no organisms; and temperature is normal.<br><br>**b.** Incision is clean and healing.<br><br>**Timing.**<br><br>**a.** Until discharge.<br><br>**b.** By discharge. | **a.** Restrict patient to his own room for 1 week or as ordered after receiving transplant:<br><br>–Limit visitors.<br>–Exclude visitors and staff who might have infections.<br><br>**b.** Give mouth care q4h while patient is on n.p.o., then clean teeth b.i.d.<br><br>–Inspect mouth daily for thrush.<br><br>**c.** Encourage deep-breathing and coughing q2h while patient is awake. Change his position q2h while he is confined to bed.<br><br>**d.** Provide catheter care q8h (*see* Careplan 148: Urinary Catheter, Indwelling). Record urine odor and color and report any change or cloudiness. Send urine specimen for culture and sensitivities twice a week or as ordered.<br><br>**e.** Record temperature q4h: report if elevated.<br><br>**f.** Give patient a bed bath daily.<br><br>**g.** Dress wound daily:<br><br>–Use sterile technique, with gloves and mask.<br>–Report drainage, swelling, and/or redness.<br><br>**h.** If leukocyte count below 2000 per $mm^3$, apply modified reverse isolation (mask and gown). |
| **9.** Potential increased anxiety and emotional lability: the psychological effects of transplantation and, possibly, side effects of steroids.<br><br>**Objective.** Patient/family discuss and can cope with feelings, reactions, and fears.<br><br>**Timing.** Before discharge. | **a.** **Designated nurse.** Spend time with patient/family, giving them opportunities to express their concerns about the transplanted kidney.<br><br>**b.** Observe closely for signs of increased anxiety, depression, or abnormal behavior. Consult social worker and/or psychiatrist as necessary. A psychiatrist who has seen the child and family beforehand will be responsible for psychological aspects of care.<br><br>**c.** Schedule patient's day to include *planned* activities with nurse, recreationist, schoolteacher, and physical therapist.<br><br>**d.** Encourage socializing with other patients who have a renal transplant.<br><br>**e.** Reinforce dr's explanations of any setbacks.<br><br>**f.** If steroids can be reduced, reassure child and family that cushingoid effects will gradually lessen. |
| **10.** Potential depression because of steroid-induced changes in appearance or if complications occur. | *See* Careplan 35: Depression in Adolescence. |
| **11.** Potential urinary frequency and incontinence when catheter is removed, due to lack of use of bladder before surgery.<br><br>**Objective.** Gradual reduction in urinary frequency.<br><br>**Timing.** Before discharge. | **a.** Have bedpan or urinal readily available for patient:<br><br>–Empty promptly.<br>–Provide privacy.<br><br>**b.** Reassure patient that frequency will gradually lessen and continence will improve.<br><br>**c.** **Small child.** Establish regular toilet routine. |

| Usual Problems/Objectives/Timing | Nursing Orders |
|---|---|
| **12.** Weakness due to chronic illness and periodic immobilization.<br><br>**Objective.** Gradual rehabilitation to normal activity.<br><br>**Timing.** Until discharge. | **a.** Encourage ambulation after 48 hr.<br>**b.** Help and encourage patient to perform the program of exercises devised for him by the physical therapist. |
| **13.** Potential mismanagement of home care, due to lack of understanding.<br><br>**Objective.** Patient/parents understand and can cope with all aspects of the program to be followed at home.<br><br>**Timing.** Before discharge. | *See* Careplan 146: Renal Transplantation: Preparation for Discharge. |

## Goals for Discharge or Maintenance
**I.** Patient/parents can cope with home care, including BP recordings, medication, and diet.
**II.** They recognize signs of rejection, will call dr if problems arise, and will attend clinic for follow-up.

| Usual Problems/Objectives/Timing | Nursing Orders |
|---|---|
| **1.** Patient/parents concerned about potential rejection of kidney. (Major or minor rejection may occur at any time but most often during the first 6 months.) <br><br> **Objectives.** Patient/parents understand the importance of antirejection drugs, state knowledge of the signs/symptoms of rejection, and know when and whom to notify if adverse signs/symptoms occur. <br><br> **Timing.** Before discharge. | **a.** Emphasize importance of antirejection drugs. <br><br> **b.** Instruct patient/parents in side effects of these drugs. <br><br> **c.** Instruct patient/parents in signs and symptoms of rejection: <br> –Increased BP. <br> –Rapid weight gain. <br> –Fever. <br> –Decreased urinary output. <br> –Pain over kidney. <br><br> Notify dr if any of these occur. |
| **2.** *Preparation for follow-up in clinic.* | **a.** Give patient/parents a record book; in this book, list drugs, amounts, and times to be given, and specify other information to be recorded (e.g., weight, BP) and names of persons to contact if they have concerns. The patient must bring this book to each clinic visit. <br><br> **b.** If patient and parents are unfamiliar with clinic procedures: <br> –Introduce them to nephrology clinic nurse. <br> –Give them clinic instruction sheet. <br> –Emphasize importance of clinic visits (they will be weekly at first). |
| **3.** Potential hypertension induced by steroids. <br><br> **Objectives.** Parents can take their child's BP and give antihypertensive drugs; they know when they should report BP to dr. <br><br> **Timing.** Before discharge. | **a.** Ensure that parents know how to take BP and record it in the book. Give them the instruction sheet, Information for Parents: Monitoring Blood Pressure (page 336); ensure that dr has completed the specific instructions for your patient. <br><br> **b.** If necessary, arrange for purchase of sphygmomanometer. <br><br> **c.** Instruct patient about antihypertensive medication. List in the book the drugs, amounts, and times to be given. <br><br> **d.** Instruct parents to call dr if BP persists. <br><br> **e.** If patient is on a free diet, discourage very salty foods. |
| **4.** Potential excessive weight gain due to unrestricted diet (after many restrictions) and to increased appetite (sudden well-being). <br><br> **Objectives.** Patient is eating a well-balanced diet; reasonable weight gain. <br><br> **Timing.** By discharge. | **a.** Encourage good eating habits and balanced diet. <br><br> **b.** Discourage overeating and the ingestion of large quantities of aerated drinks. <br><br> **c.** If weight gain is excessive, refer patient for diet counseling. <br><br> **d.** Enlist parents' support and help if a low-calorie diet is necessary. |

| Usual Problems/Objectives/Timing | Nursing Orders |
|---|---|
| **5.** Increased susceptibility to infection, due to immuno-suppressive therapy.<br><br>**Objectives.** Patient is free of infection whenever possible; good personal hygiene.<br><br>**Timing.** By discharge. | **a.** Teach personal hygiene, with special attention to mouth and teeth.<br><br>**b.** Instruct patient/parents to report fevers and minor infections to dr (*Candida*, colds and cold sores, etc.).<br><br>**c.** Instruct patient/parents to avoid large crowds and people with colds and known infections. |
| **6.** Potential injury to the transplanted kidney, due to its more vulnerable position.<br><br>**Objective.** Patient/parents aware of the risk and take steps to avoid injury.<br><br>**Timing.** By discharge. | **a.** Instruct patient to avoid contact sports and activities in which a direct blow to the transplant area is possible.<br><br>**b.** Encourage all other social activities, particularly sports, in which injury to transplant is unlikely.<br><br>**c.** Notify teacher, and others who are involved in child's care at home, of the need for these measures. |
| **7.** Parental overprotection because of the condition's chronicity and their anxiety about the new kidney.<br><br>**Objective.** Parents allow their child to live as normally as possible.<br><br>**Timing.** By discharge. | **a.** **Designated nurse.** Spend time listening to parents' concerns.<br><br>**b.** Encourage patient to increase independence as he feels stronger.<br><br>**c.** Assist parents/patient in making plans for home care.<br><br>**d.** Do not minimize parents' concerns, which have been warranted for a long time. (Readjustment is as difficult for them as for their child.) Help them to increase their child's independence. |

# 147

## Ureteral Reimplants

**Goals for Discharge or Maintenance**
Parents understand and are willing to comply with follow-up care.

| Usual Problems/Objectives/Timing | Nursing Orders |
|---|---|
| **1.** *Pre-operatively.* | **a.** *See* Careplan 17: Pre-operative Care, General.<br><br>**b.** Explain to patient and parents:<br>–i.v. therapy.<br>–Catheters and tubing.<br>–Presence of blood in tubing.<br>–Bladder spasms. |
| **2.** *Postoperatively.* | *See* Careplan 21: Postoperative Care, General. |
| **3.** Potential blocking of urinary drainage by clots and/or mucus in tubing, or by kinks or twists in tubing. | **a.** *See* Careplan 148: Urinary Catheter, Indwelling.<br><br>**b.** **Suprapubic catheter.** Catheter is irrigated by dr. |
| **4.** Potential chest problems due to prolonged anesthesia.<br><br>**Objectives.** Lungs clear; patient can deep breathe and cough.<br><br>**Timing.** By day 4. | **a.** Instruct patient to cough and do deep-breathing exercises q1h for 24 hr, and then q2h for 24 hr. Continue exercises q4h until patient is fully ambulatory. (Support area of incision with pillow or towel, to aid coughing and deep breathing.)<br><br>**Infant.** Stimulate child to cry.<br><br>**Older child.** Encourage patient to blow into paper tissue and blow water bubbles through a straw.<br><br>**b.** Change patient's position q2h for 24 hr (side, back, other side, semi-Fowler's position).<br><br>**c.** Maintain patient on bed rest for 4 days, as ordered, then initiate gradual ambulation (sitting at bedside or in wheelchair, walking in room, etc.).<br><br>**d.** *If patient has tapered (fashioned) reimplants,* maintain bed rest for 2 weeks. |
| **5.** Potential shock due to bleeding.<br><br>**Objectives.** Early detection of bleeding; vital signs stable.<br><br>**Timing.** Until catheter is removed. | **a.** Take TPR and BP q4h for 48 hr, t.i.d. for 24 hr, b.i.d. for 24 hr, then daily.<br><br>**b.** Check dressings q3–4h for blood.<br><br>**c.** Check urine q2h for color and clots. (Blood is always present initially; it decreases gradually and urine is usually clear by day 3 or 4.)<br><br>**d.** If bleeding recurs after clearing of urine, notify dr *stat*, reinstitute complete bed rest, and push fluid intake. |
| **6.** Potential retrograde urinary infection by organisms from suprapubic catheter and/or drain.<br><br>**Objectives.** No crusting around suprapubic catheter; no drainage from stab wound; incision clean and dry. | **a.** Note smell of urine (infected urine has a foul odor).<br><br>**b.** Change dressing daily in a.m.; use antiseptic solution to clean around suprapubic catheter and drain; use aseptic technique when changing drainage bags. |

| Usual Problems/Objectives/Timing | Nursing Orders |
|---|---|
| **6. (Continued).**<br><br>**Timing.** Until after catheter is removed (usually 10–12 days). | **c.** Place corner of gauze pad between suprapubic catheter and skin before applying rest of dressing (prevents catheter from rubbing on skin).<br><br>**d.** Reinforce the tape holding the catheter in position p.r.n. Bring catheter up onto abdomen and then loop it downward.<br><br>**e.** Inspect and record type and amount of drainage.<br>**Usual course**<br>**Day 1.** Much sanguinous drainage from stab wound and incision.<br>**Days 2 and 3.** No drainage from incision; less serous drainage from suprapubic site.<br>**Day 4 or 5.** Drain removed, as ordered by dr.<br><br>**f. When catheter is clamped.** Check TPR q4h. Report elevated TPR or other signs of infection (e.g., chills, irritability, vomiting) to dr. |
| **7.** Potential flank pain due to ureteral swelling or obstruction of catheter splint.<br><br>**Objective.** Patient appears relaxed and does not complain of pain.<br><br>**Timing.** Until catheters and splints removed. | **a.** Observe for flank pain, elevated temperature, and/or decreased urine output. If any of these are present, *notify dr stat.*<br><br>**b.** Notify dr if ureteral splints are not draining.<br><br>–When splint(s) and suprapubic catheter are in place, decreased output through one should be compensated for by the other(s). |
| **8.** Potential postanesthetic nausea and vomiting.<br><br>**Objective.** Patient is tolerating normal diet.<br><br>**Timing.** By day 3–4. | **a.** Give fluids i.v. until oral intake is tolerated.<br><br>**b.** Maintain patient on n.p.o. for 24 hr.<br><br>**c.** Start patient on sips of clear fluids. *Observe for abdominal distention.*<br><br>**d.** Increase to full fluids. If abdomen is not distended, increase to normal diet as tolerated. |
| **9.** Bladder spasms due to irritation by, or obstruction of, catheter.<br><br>**Objective.** Patient can cope with spasms.<br><br>**Timing.** Until catheter removed. | **a.** *See* nursing orders for problem 1 in Careplan 148: Urinary Catheter, Indwelling.<br><br>**b.** When handling suprapubic catheter, hold it firmly; its movement will precipitate spasms.<br><br>**c.** Stay with and comfort patient; divert attention from pain (usually lasts only a few seconds, rarely 1 min). |
| **10.** Potential difficulty passing urine after suprapubic catheter is clamped and/or removed.<br><br>**Objective.** Patient is voiding urine without pain.<br><br>**Timing.** 2 days after catheter is removed. | **a.** Stay with and reassure patient during first attempts at voiding.<br><br>**b.** If patient cannot void, pour warm water over perineum, or sit patient in a tub of warm water and encourage voiding in the water.<br><br>**c.** If patient still cannot void and is distended or uncomfortable, notify dr. |
| **11.** Patient's (and possibly parents') embarrassment in relation to urogenital area.<br><br>**Objective.** Minimal embarrassment during procedures and discussions. | **a.** Do not show embarrassment yourself. Be matter of fact but tactful.<br><br>**b.** Ensure privacy when needed and show respect for patient. |

continued

| Usual Problems/Objectives/Timing | Nursing Orders |
|---|---|
| **11. (Continued).**<br>**Timing.** Until discharge. | **c.** Illustrate your explanations with diagrams (preferably printed) or models to show that others also undergo this operation. |
| **12.** Potential mismanagement at home due to lack of understanding.<br><br>**Objective.** Parents/patient state their understanding of discharge instructions.<br><br>**Timing.** Before discharge. | **a.** Reinforce dr's instructions for home care and follow-up.<br><br>**b.** Instruct parents/patient:<br>–Child to stay at home for one week, and then can return to school.<br>–Child to avoid contact sports and activities (e.g., gym at school) in which a direct blow to the abdomen is possible until approved by dr (usually 4–6 weeks).<br>–To notify dr if child has any difficulty voiding or appears to have a urinary tract infection (e.g., chills, fever, dysuria, flank pain).<br>–To give antibiotic as ordered by dr.<br><br>**c.** Ensure that parents have printed instructions for home care and a follow-up appointment. |

# Careplan 148    Urinary Catheter, Indwelling

**Goals for Discharge or Maintenance**
See Objectives.

| Usual Problems/Objectives/Timing | Nursing Orders |
|---|---|
| **1.** Potential obstruction of urine flow by mucus, clots, twisting, or kink in tubing, because tubing is incorrectly taped, or because catheter is removed accidentally.<br><br>**Objectives.** Catheter and tubing are patent; urine flow is unobstructed.<br><br>**Timing.** Until catheter is removed. | **a.** Check entire drainage system for adequate urine flow q1h and p.r.n. Ensure that the drainage bag is always below the level of the bladder. *If catheter comes out, notify dr stat.*<br><br>**b.** If tubing is kinked or twisted, reposition it. Notify charge nurse if catheter needs retaping.<br><br>**c.** Check taping at least twice a day, at time of bath and dressing change in the morning and when settling for night. Retape p.r.n., allowing for some "give." (Some catheters are taped to patient's abdomen, others to thigh.)<br><br>**d.** Attach tubing to sheet at either side or foot of bed: loop rubber band around tube and pin band to sheet.<br><br>**e.** The tubing must hang straight from the edge of the bed to the drainage bag. Excess tubing between the catheter and the bag must be coiled *on the bed*. When patient is out of bed, position tubing so that coils are between the catheter and the bag *(not on the floor)*. Loop rubber band around the tube and pin the band through a double thickness or seam of dress or shirt —*not to pants/trousers.*<br><br>**f.** Empty bag often enough to prevent pull on rubber band and tubing.<br><br>**g.** Ensure adequate fluid intake; record intake and output.<br><br>**h.** If drainage in tubing is thick with blood or mucus:<br>–"Milk" the tubing q1h.<br>–Increase fluid intake.<br>–Irrigate catheter with 3–5 ml N saline p.r.n. |
| **2.** Potential urinary tract infection by retrograde bacterial flow.<br><br>**Objectives.** No infection; urine is clear, with normal odor.<br><br>**Timing.** Until catheter is removed. | **a.** *Patient with a catheter and no incision*<br>–Give daily tub bath; cleanse urethral meatus with soap and water.<br><br>**b.** *Patient with catheter and incision*<br>–Change dressing daily; remove all crusting, using solution ordered by dr.<br><br>**c.** Use aseptic technique when emptying bag:<br>–Wash hands and wear sterile gloves.<br>–Swab protective sleeve (outlet) with antiseptic solution and remove drain tube (being careful not to touch end of tube).<br>–Drain urine into a clean, graduated receptacle.<br>–After the urine finishes draining, swab the end of the tube and the protective sleeve (on the bag).<br>–Clamp the tube and return it to its sleeve. |

359

continued

| Usual Problems/Objectives/Timing | Nursing Orders |
|---|---|
| **2. (Continued).** | —Record amount of urine drained.<br>—Empty the measuring device and *wash it well* with soap and water.<br>**d.** Ensure adequate fluid intake.<br>**e.** Collect urine specimen for culture just before catheter is removed and weekly if catheter is in place longer than 10 days.<br>**f.** If urine is cloudy, concentrated, or smelly, notify dr. |
| **3.** Potential bladder spasms when catheter is irrigated, or due to obstruction of urine flow and/or constipation.<br><br>**Objectives.** Urine flow is unobstructed; patient understands and can cope with spasms.<br><br>**Timing.** Until catheter is removed. | **a.** *See* nursing orders for problem 1.<br>**b.** Explain bladder spasms to patient and parents. Assure them that the pain, although severe, lasts only a few seconds.<br>**c.** Stay with patient when spasms start. Encourage him to relax, deep-breathe, or pant. Provide quiet diversions (e.g., stories, games, or music).<br>**d.** Support parents and encourage them to help their child through spasms.<br>**e.** Give patient medication as ordered (usually propantheline bromide or oxybutynin chloride).<br>**f.** If no stools by day 3, give enema as ordered.<br>**g.** When a suprapubic catheter is removed, stay with patient and comfort him during the severe bladder spasms that result.<br>**h.** *Never give antispasmodics or anticholinergics after removal of catheter.* (They reduce bladder tone and may cause retention of urine.) |
| **4.** Patient's (and possibly parents') potential embarrassment in relation to urogenital area.<br><br>**Objective.** Minimal embarrassment during procedures and discussions.<br><br>**Timing.** Until discharge. | **a.** Be matter of fact but tactful when doing procedures. Do not show embarrassment yourself.<br>**b.** Ensure privacy when needed and show respect for patient.<br>**c.** Illustrate your explanations with diagrams (preferably printed) or models to show that others also have indwelling urinary catheters.<br>**d.** Use terms the patient/parents understand. |

# Careplan 149     Urinary Incontinence

**Goal for Discharge or Maintenance**
Toilet routine established.

| Usual Problems/Objectives/Timing | Nursing Orders |
|---|---|
| **1.** Nighttime incontinence.<br><br>**Objective.** Reduction in enuresis.<br><br>**Timing.** 2 weeks. | **a.** Observe for:<br>  –Burning on voiding.<br>  –Dribbling urine.<br>  –Foul odor of urine.<br>  –Scratching around anus (may indicate pinworms).<br><br>**b.** Document pattern of enuresis:<br>  –Duration.<br>  –Frequency.<br>  –Nightmares or other precipitating causes (e.g., changes at home).<br><br>**c.** Document parents' handling of child's wetting. (What does it mean to them? Do they punish?)<br><br>**d.** Assess child's feelings about wetting.<br><br>**e.** Do not criticize or punish child for bed-wetting (recognize that child does not deliberately wet the bed).<br><br>**f.** Limit fluid intake after supper. Restrict fluids 2 hr before bedtime (especially colas, because of their diuretic effect.)<br><br>**g.** Establish a time to take child to bathroom during the night (e.g., take child to toilet about 11 p.m.).<br><br>**h.** Give patient a bath in a.m. if wet.<br><br>**i.** Reward child with praise and encouragement if he is dry. |
| **2.** Daytime incontinence.<br><br>**Objective.** Toilet routine is established.<br><br>**Timing.** 2 weeks. | **a.** *See* nursing orders 1(a-d).<br><br>**b.** Record pattern of toileting at home (who does the toileting, where it is done, how often).<br><br>**c.** Assess what incontinence means to child.<br><br>**d.** Note if incontinence is related to preoccupation with activities. (Does he forget to go?) Remind him at regular intervals.<br><br>**e.** Establish a routine for regular toileting.<br><br>**f.** Teach parents routine established in hospital, have them participate, and encourage them to continue routine pattern at home. |

## Goals for Discharge or Maintenance
Parents understand and can cope with home care, including follow-up appointments.

| Usual Problems/Objectives/Timing | Nursing Orders |
|---|---|
| **1.** Potential mismanagement of infection at home due to lack of knowledge.<br><br>**Objectives.** Parents express understanding of need to:<br><br>–Give medication as instructed.<br><br>–Increase fluid intake.<br><br>–Prevent constipation.<br><br>–Cleanse the perianal area as instructed.<br><br>–Keep follow-up appointment(s).<br><br>**Timing.** By end of first clinic visit. | **a. Medication:** Give parents written instructions; emphasize importance of spacing doses. If appropriate, inform public health nurse.<br><br>**b.** Explain that child must increase fluid intake to flush the urinary system; suggest ways of doing this.<br><br>**c.** Emphasize importance of encouraging child to void at frequent, regular intervals (to prevent urinary stasis).<br><br>**d.** Explain that constipation will restrict flow of urine and therefore should be prevented (e.g., by diet).<br><br>**e.** Explain to parents the importance of keeping perianal area clean:<br><br>–Wipe the perianal area, from front to back, after stool or urination.<br><br>–Give patient a tub bath daily; *do not use* bubble-bath solution, oil, or talc.<br><br>–Have patient wear cotton underpants.<br><br>–Change patient's underpants at least once a day.<br><br>–**Infant.** Check diapers frequently; change promptly.<br><br>**f.** Before parents leave clinic, ensure they understand that:<br><br>–They must keep return appointment(s), *even if child is symptom-free.*<br><br>–They should notify the clinic if signs and symptoms are not relieved in 24–48 hr, if child refuses or vomits medication or has a fever, or if they are concerned about any problem.<br><br>**g.** Give parents printed instructions and the names and telephone numbers of dr and clinic nurse *(in writing).* |
| **2.** Potential continuing or recurrent infection due to misunderstanding or noncompliance with treatment plan.<br><br>**Objectives.** Parents appear able to cope with the information given and state willingness to comply with the home care plan.<br><br>**Timing.** As soon as possible. | **a.** Designated nurse (preferably the one who instructed family before) to spend time with family exploring their understanding of the treatment plan.<br><br>**b.** Reinforce previous information given.<br><br>**c.** Ensure parents have follow-up appointment. |

## Goals for Discharge or Maintenance

**I.** Patient and family members are planning how to cope in future.

**II.** They understand and are willing to adhere to plans, which may involve attending another hospital and/or clinics.

| Usual Problems/Objectives/Timing | Nursing Orders |
|---|---|
| **Elective Amputation** | **Designated nurse:** |
| **1.** Grief and anxiety when informed about forthcoming amputation.<br><br>**Objectives.** Patient/parents express grief and anxiety, ask questions about the operation, and begin to discuss after-care.<br><br>**Timing.** Until operation is over. | **a.** Be present when dr tells patient/parents about the operation.<br>**b.** Stay with them after dr has left.<br>**c.** Allow time for reactions to the information.<br>**d.** Encourage questions as soon as appropriate.<br>**e.** The child will probably react by being angry with parents/staff. Prepare parents for this reaction: let them know that this is to be expected and that the nurses will understand.<br>**f.** The parents may react in various ways. Be supportive, remain calm, and do not overreact. |
| **2.** *Pre-operatively.* | **a.** *See* Careplan 17: Pre-operative Care, General.<br>**b.** If appropriate, initiate discussion about the operation.<br><br>**Younger child.** Ask him to show you (using dolls, pictures, etc.) what he thinks will be removed.<br><br>**Older Child.** Ask him to draw his image on a blank piece of paper and indicate what he thinks will be removed. (Children usually think much more is going to be amputated than is the case. Correct this with them.)<br><br>**Note:** Almost all boys (especially schoolage ones) undergoing leg amputation fear castration.<br><br>**c.** Explain that there will be a cast or bandage over the leg/arm and that it will feel as if the limb were still there (phantom pain). Use discretion when using the word phantom; schoolage patients may be upset by it.<br>**d.** Reinforce dr's explanations of the operation and afterward (e.g., whether there will be a prosthesis). |
| **Elective or Traumatic Amputation**<br><br>**3.** *Postoperatively.* | **a.** *See* Careplan 21: Postoperative Care, General.<br>**b.** *See* Careplan 153: Casts, if appropriate.<br>**c.** Observe closely for bleeding q15 min for 12 hr, then q½–1h for 24 hr. |
| **4.** Parents are fearful, grieved, and concerned about their child's future.<br><br>**Objectives.** Parents express their feelings and gradually make realistic plans for the future.<br><br>**Timing.** By discharge. | **a.** Ensure a consistent assignment of nurses.<br>**b.** Designated nurse to spend at least 15–20 min/day with parents, *away from the child's room*, listening to their concerns.<br>**c.** For the first few days, restrict staff entering room to those essential for care. |

| Usual Problems/Objectives/Timing | Nursing Orders |
|---|---|
| **4. (Continued).** | **d.** Recognize that family members may channel anger toward staff. Avoid retaliation; be extra patient.<br><br>**e.** If parents are staying with child:<br>  –Make them as comfortable as possible; provide a bed or bed-chair.<br>  –Assess their level of fatigue.<br>  –Request order for sedation for them p.r.n.<br>  –Encourage them to go for meals, by making sure someone is with their child, accompanying them to cafeteria, etc. |
| **5.** Child is depressed, angry, and anxious about loss of part of self, change in body image, and/or fears of mutilation, castration, and death.<br><br>**Objective.** Child expresses feelings (*negative and positive*).<br><br>**Timing.** Before discharge. | **a.** See especially problem 4 in the patient's Stresses of Hospitalization careplan.<br><br>**b.** Avoid medical discussion in vicinity of patient.<br><br>**c.** Clarify with dr and parents what child has been told. Be consistent with explanations.<br><br>**d.** Answer child's questions truthfully.<br><br>**e.** Encourage and support family participation in care.<br><br>**f.** Provide age-appropriate toys/activities that allow an outlet for child's feelings.<br><br>**g.** Each shift, spend at least 10–15 min just listening to child; allow expression of negative as well as positive feelings.<br><br>**h.** Record on patient's careplan the best methods for preparing him for procedures/tests. Be firm about doing *necessary* procedures, even if child is irritable and demanding. Remain calm; anticipate his needs.<br><br>**i.** Allow patient/parents to decide if and when other patients in the same room are told of the amputation. |
| **6.** Potential flexion deformity of affected leg, due to poor positioning.<br><br>**Objective.** No flexion deformity.<br><br>**Timing.** At time of discharge. | **a.** Give analgesics as ordered (patient will be reluctant to keep his leg in correct position if it is painful).<br><br>**b.** Emphasize importance of positioning immediately postoperatively.<br>  –Reinforce p.r.n.<br><br>**c.** **Above-knee amputation.** Keep patient prone at least 1 hr t.i.d. to prevent hip flexion.<br><br>**d.** **Below-knee amputation.** Elevate *entire* limb and keep knee extended when patient is supine. Ensure that patient performs flexion and extension exercises q1–2h while awake.<br><br>**e.** Provide diversions while patient is in unfamiliar/ uncomfortable position. |
| **7.** Potential distress about phantom pain.<br><br>**Objectives.** Patient and parents express concerns; they understand that *phantom pain is real.*<br><br>**Timing.** By discharge. | **a.** Reinforce explanations that phantom pain is real, even though the limb is not there.<br><br>**b.** Give child analgesic or sedative p.r.n.<br><br>**c.** Stay with and comfort child; divert attention from pain or encourage child to talk about it. |

continued

| Usual Problems/Objectives/Timing | Nursing Orders |
|---|---|
| **8.** Potential increase in swelling and/or malformation of stump, due to incorrect bandaging.<br><br>**Objectives**<br><br>**a.** No undue swelling.<br><br>**b.** Patient/parents know the importance of correct bandaging of stump and are able to do this.<br><br>**Timing**<br><br>**a.** Until discharge.<br><br>**b.** Before discharge. | **a.** Elevate affected stump, supporting hip or shoulder (as appropriate).<br><br>**b.** If cast and/or prosthesis is applied immediately, any pain in stump should be reported *stat*.<br><br>**c.** Dr initiates bandaging of stump. Physical therapist teaches patient/parents how this is done.<br><br>**d.** Prepare patient/parent for appearance of stump.<br><br>**e.** Reinforce importance of correct stump bandaging.<br><br>**f.** Observe patient/parents applying bandages. |
| **9.** Potential lack of acceptance of: (a) prosthesis, due to insufficient knowledge of appearance and use; (b) loss of limb and change in body image.<br><br>**Objectives.** Patient/parents express feelings and are making plans for rehabilitation.<br><br>**Timing.** By discharge. | **a.** If appropriate, arrange a meeting with a child who has had an amputation (of the same limb, if possible).<br><br>**b.** Show patient a film of a child with a prosthesis, or explain using pictures, drawings, or dolls.<br><br>**c.** If patient is to be transferred to a rehabilitation center, try to arrange for patient/parents to visit there beforehand.<br><br>**d.** If a prosthesis will be fitted in present hospital, contact prosthesis department. Accompany patient on first visit (and preferably all visits).<br><br>**Note.** If amputation has been done for malignancy, chemotherapy is usually started before patient is fitted for a prosthesis. Notify the oncology clinic nurse. |

# Careplan 152 Braces

**Goals for Discharge or Maintenance**
Patient and family able and willing to comply with home care and follow-up regimen.

| Usual Problems/Objectives/Timing | Nursing Orders |
|---|---|
| **1.** Potential skin breakdown due to prolonged pressure on parts of body in contact with brace.<br>**Objective.** Clean, healthy skin.<br>**Timing.** Until discharge. | **a.** Gently massage bony prominences q4h.<br>**b.** Observe skin under brace for pressure areas. |
| **2.** Potential rejection of brace: cosmetic reasons and/or lack of understanding of purpose.<br>**Objectives.** Patient and parents express feelings about brace. Patient willing to wear brace.<br>**Timing.** Before discharge. | **a.** Encourage patient when helping him to apply brace.<br>**b.** Initiate conversation about brace with patient and parents. Provide opportunities for them to voice concerns.<br>**c.** Note when and how often patient wears brace.<br>**d.** Check that the brace fits properly and ensure that any necessary adjustments are made (by orthotist, surgeon, etc.).<br>**e.** Advise parents if larger, looser clothing is needed. |
| **3.** Potential incorrect application and care of brace at home, due to inconsistent nursing care instruction.<br>**Objective.** Patient and family apply brace correctly and describe its care accurately.<br>**Timing.** Before discharge. | **a.** Establish and record a consistent method of application and care of brace. Use this as basis for teaching parents and patient.<br>**b.** Provide and explain written instructions for home care. |

**Goals for Discharge or Maintenance**

I. Parents/patient understand and can cope with schedule of follow-up care.

II. Parents/patient understand care and would recognize conditions that need immediate attention.

| Usual Problems/Objectives/Timing | Nursing Orders |
|---|---|
| **1.** *Pre-operatively.* | **a.** *See* Careplan 17: Pre-operative Care, General. <br><br> **b.** Explain to patient: <br>   –Movement, eating and drinking, toileting, etc., while in cast. |
| **2.** *Postoperatively.* | *See* Careplan 21: Postoperative Care, General. |
| **3.** Potential impairment of circulation and/or nerve damage due to constriction of cast. <br><br> **Objectives.** Circulation is not impaired and nerve(s) are undamaged. <br><br> **Timing.** Until discharge. | **a.** Check circulation q1h for 24 hr, then q4h until discharge. Observe: <br>   –Color (of limb *and* extremities), with and without pressure of fingers. <br>   –Sensation. <br>   –Warmth. <br>   –Movement. <br>   –Pulses. <br><br> **b.** Report changes to dr, particularly decreased sensation. |
| **4.** Potential fear and anxiety that the cast may break or that the part obscured by the cast has been altered, removed, or lost. <br><br> **Objectives.** Patient expresses any fears and asks questions; he remains relaxed when cast is touched or moved. <br><br> **Timing.** By discharge. | **a.** Help patient when he needs to be turned and positioned. Do not push or pull on enclosed limb. <br><br> **b.** Reinforce explanations about cast, using pictures, dolls in casts, or other patients in casts. Reassure child that the body part is still there and will look the same (mention scar if appropriate) when the cast is removed, but that the skin will be dry and flaky for a while. <br><br> **c.** Encourage child to socialize with other patients, particularly those now or formerly in casts. |
| **5.** Potential bleeding or infection under the cast. <br><br> **Objective.** Early detection of bleeding or infection. <br><br> **Timing.** Throughout stay. | **a.** Outline blood stains on cast (use pen), add time and date, and sign. <br><br> **b.** Check for spread of stain and report any significant increase. <br><br> **c.** Check cast at least once a day for musty odors (indicating seepage into cast). <br><br> **d.** Report any temperature elevation to dr, and start recording TPR q4h. |
| **6.** Potential pressure sores due to immobility and constant contact with cast. <br><br> **Objective.** No pressure sores. <br><br> **Timing.** Throughout stay. | **a.** Expose cast to air until it is dry. <br><br> **b.** Support cast with sandbags or hard pillows. Make sure that toes, heels, and/or elbows do not dig into bed. <br><br> **c.** Turn patient at least q4h, day and night. <br><br> **d.** Check all bony prominences and other potential pressure areas q4h for signs of skin breakdown. |

| Usual Problems/Objectives/Timing | Nursing Orders |
|---|---|
| **6. (Continued).** | **e.** Report to dr any reddened areas or complaints of burning and pressure. |
| | **f. Toilet-trained patient:** |
| | –Offer bedpan or urinal at least q3–4h when patient is awake. (Use a slipper bedpan.) |
| | –Help child roll on to the bedpan. Tuck a small piece of plastic sheeting or plastic bag under the edge of the cast and fold it toward the back (to help protect the cast). |
| | –Explain importance of keeping cast dry. |
| | **g. Incontinent patient:** |
| | –Cover cast with protective sheeting until dry; tuck sheeting in under cast edges. |
| | –If necessary, place patient on frame with an aperture. Otherwise, cover perineum with disposable diaper or part of an incontinence pad, tucking it in under edges of cast. Change diapers frequently. |
| **7.** Potential soiling of cast by excreta.<br><br>**Objective.** Clean, dry cast.<br><br>**Timing.** Throughout stay. | **a.** As soon as cast is dry, petal its edge with waterproof adhesive tape.<br><br>**b.** After each elimination, check cast for soiling. |
| **8.** Potential concern and embarrassment about appearance of cast.<br><br>**Objective.** Patient expresses concerns and does not appear embarrassed.<br><br>**Timing.** By discharge. | **a.** Provide patient with loose-fitting clothing at all times.<br><br>**b.** Protect patient's privacy.<br><br>**c. Patient in leg cast.** Use diaper, T-binder, or pants with open side-seams. |
| **9.** Potential refracture or dislocation when cast is removed, due to fragility of bones or improper support.<br><br>**Objective.** No complications after removal of cast.<br><br>**Timing.** After removal of cast. | **a.** Help patient during first use of limbs after removal of cast.<br><br>**b.** Provide support for all joints that have been in a cast, and maintain position until dr orders ambulation. |
| **10.** Prolonged immobilization. | *See* Careplan 13: Prolonged Immobilization. |
| **11.** Parents concerned about care of cast at home.<br><br>**Objectives.** Patient and parents understand and accept need for continuing care and can cope with it at home.<br><br>**Timing.** Before discharge. | **a.** Explain home care to child and parents, using Instructions to Parents on Care of Casts (page 370) as guide.<br><br>**b.** Ensure that parents have dr's follow-up instructions.<br><br>**c.** If home schooling will be required, ask public health nurse to arrange this.<br><br>**d.** If parents require home care supplies (e.g., bedpan, special bed) or home nursing instruction, make arrangements and ask public health nurse to visit. |

# Instructions to Parents on Care of Body or Leg Casts

Casts are made of a special type of plaster (white powder), which has been spread on long strips of gauze and then rolled into bandages. When this plaster bandage is soaked in water it becomes mushy, the excess water is squeezed out, then the wet bandage is wrapped around the body where it soon begins to harden.

## Purpose of a Cast

To hold a part of the body in place when treating some types of fractures, dislocations, joint disorders, or skeletal deformities and after some types of surgery.

## Cast Application

A light stockinette is placed over the body area to be covered with the cast and any bony or prominent areas are padded with soft cotton wool to protect them from pressure. Then the plaster bandages are applied by the doctor and a technician.

While the cast is being applied, it feels warm because of the chemical reaction between the plaster and the water. After 10–15 minutes the cast becomes firm to touch; however, it may take 12 to 48 hours to dry, depending on its size. While it is drying, the cast may feel cold and clammy because the water is evaporating.

When the cast is dry, any rough edges will be taped or "petalled" to protect your child's skin from plaster crumbs and rough edges. A nurse will do this, if the cast is dry before your child goes home. If not, you will be shown how to do it at home.

## Cast Care

1. Keep the cast clean and dry.

2. Avoid getting crumbs, coins, food, or small toys under the cast.

3. Your child may have a sponge bath but must not get the cast wet.

4. Check the skin along the cast edges daily for signs of irritation or breakdown.

5. Sharp objects, such as knitting needles or sticks, must never be used as scratchers. If itchiness is severe, get in touch with your child's doctor.

6. Check the cast once a day for any foul, offensive odor.

## Leg Casts

1. When your child is sleeping, resting, or watching television, raise the casted leg on a pillow. This helps reduce any swelling.

2. If your child is allowed to walk with the cast on, the bottom will be protected with a sponge or boot provided by the Hospital.

3. If your child will be using crutches, they will be fitted by a physical therapist. There is a modest charge for the crutches with no refund.

4. A wheelchair will be provided if your child is unable to walk while in the cast. Your child's nurse will discuss your child's needs with you so that arrangements can be made before going home. The wheelchair is provided free on loan from the Easter Seal Society.

5. Forms to arrange transportation to school or for home instruction are available. Your child's nurse will help you with the necessary arrangements.

## Hip Spica Casts

1. The nurse will show you how to help your child turn in his cast. Turn your child (from side to side or from back to stomach) every 4 hours to prevent skin breakdown. Be careful that you do not push or pull on the enclosed leg(s) since this will break or crack the cast.

2. Do not let your child kneel or stand unless the doctor gives permission.

3. A toilet-trained child will need a "slipper" bedpan. This will be supplied by the hospital. You will need to help your child roll onto the bedpan. The cast can be protected by tucking a plastic bag under the back of the cast and folding it back over the cast. Remove the bag when your child has finished using the bedpan.

4. A child who is not toilet-trained will present a few problems. Tuck a disposable diaper into the cast. Change the diaper frequently so the cast won't be soiled.

5. If the cast does become soiled, it can be cleaned with a slightly dampened cloth and cleaning agent (e.g., Comet). Stubborn stains can be covered with white liquid shoe polish. Leave the area exposed to the air until it is dry or use a hair dryer on the "no heat setting." Do not put clothing over the cast until it dries.

## What to Watch For

If any of these problems occur, call your child's doctor or the hospital immediately.

1. *Bluish, cold, or very swollen toes on the affected leg.*

   The toes shoud be pink and warm. Compare the color, temperature, and size with those on the other leg.

2. *Inability to pull toes up and away from the cast.*

   Your child should be able to move his toes as he could before the accident/surgery:

   –Curl toes downwards (plantar flexion).

   –Pull toes (including the big toe) up, away from the cast (dorsiflexion).

3. *Increasing pain or constant pain unrelieved by medication.*

4. *Complaints of numbness, tingling, pins and needles, or "falling asleep" sensations.*

5. *Foul, offensive odor.*

   This may indicate an infection under the cast (rare).

**6.** *Soft or cracked cast.*

The cast should remain hard without cracks.

**Remember** The leg or hip may swell inside the rigid cast and impair circulation.

### Cast Removal and Skin Care

Your child's cast will be removed when healing has occurred, usually after 6 weeks. An electric cast saw will be used. It is large and noisy and might frighten your child. However, the saw is safe and will not cut the skin because it only vibrates and does not cut.

The skin underneath will be dry and flaky. After the cast is removed, wash the skin several times with warm, soapy water. Then apply olive oil or a lanolin-based cream to soften the skin. Avoid vigorous rubbing or scratching as the skin is very tender. After about three or four treatments, the skin will begin to look normal again.

In older children, an unusual amount of hair is often seen when the cast is removed. However, the extra hair falls out within several weeks.

### Follow-up Appointment

Date _____

Time _____

Doctor _____

Clinic _____

Nurse _____

Telephone _____

# Careplan **154** Fractured Femur

## Goals for Discharge or Maintenance
**I.** Parents are taught and are able to turn and lift their child in the cast.
**II.** Parents will follow discharge instructions.
**III.** Necessary equipment is ready at home.

| Usual Problems/Objectives/Timing | Nursing Orders |
|---|---|
| **1.** Patient and parents are fearful and anxious about sudden hospitalization, unfamiliar equipment, and procedures. <br><br> **Objective.** Patient and parents express their fears and concerns. <br><br> **Timing.** By day 3. | **a.** Explain procedures before you start them. <br><br> **b.** Place patient in room with other children on frames or immobilized in other ways to provide companionship when parents or staff not present. <br><br> **c.** Give parents information that explains the usual course of treatment (For example, Information for Parents of a Child with a Fractured Femur, page 374). |
| **2.** Child's potential sleep disturbance and nightmares, reliving accident in which he sustained the injury. <br><br> **Objective.** Restful sleep. <br><br> **Timing.** As soon as possible. | **a.** Wake patient when he is having a nightmare; stay with him until he is asleep again. The next day, encourage him to talk about the nightmare; comfort and reassure him. |
| **3.** Traction. | *See* Careplan 158: Traction. |
| **4.** Prolonged immobilization. | *See* Careplan 13: Prolonged Immobilization. |
| **5.** Fear and anxiety about muscle spasms in affected leg. <br><br> **Objectives.** Patient/parents know why the spasms are occurring and/or can talk about them; spasms are decreasing. <br><br> **Timing.** By day 3. | **a.** Explain why the spasms are occurring and how long they usually last. <br><br> **b.** Avoid jarring bed or patient. <br><br> **c.** Give analgesic or sedative as ordered by dr. <br><br> **d.** While spasms are frequent (particularly the first night), stay with patient and comfort him. <br><br> **e.** Provide age-appropriate activities (talking, toys, games, music, TV) to divert attention from spasms. <br><br> **f.** Take patient (in bed) to playroom whenever possible. |
| **6.** Potential loss of appetite and nausea due to head-down position and immobilization. | *See* Careplan 158: Traction, problem 7. |
| **7.** Potential footdrop due to prolonged pressure on peroneal nerve by traction tapes. <br><br> **Objective.** Patient is moving foot actively. <br><br> **Timing.** Until removal of traction. | **a.** Encourage flexion and circular motion of affected foot q4h while patient is awake. <br><br> **b.** Check pedal pulse q4h or more often if indicated. <br><br> **c.** Report to dr any decrease in usual range of movement or lack of pedal pulse (the tapes may need adjusting). <br><br> **d.** Report to dr *stat* if patient has calf pain. |
| **8.** Potential equinus deformity due to prolonged equinus position of foot. <br><br> **Objective.** Patient's foot is in anatomic position. <br><br> **Timing.** Until discharge. | **a.** Encourage dorsiflexion and plantar flexion of affected foot q4h while patient is awake. <br><br> **b.** Apply foot-board if equinus deformity is developing. Notify dr. |

| Usual Problems/Objectives/Timing | Nursing Orders |
|---|---|
| **9.** Potential difficulty with cast at home.<br><br>**Objective.** Parents and patient demonstrate their understanding of follow-up care.<br><br>**Timing.** By discharge. | **a.** Give parents a copy of Instructions to Parents on Care of Body or Leg Casts (*see* page 370).<br><br>**b.** Explain the information to them and answer their questions.<br><br>**c.** Emphasize to patient and parents the importance of continuing foot exercises as instructed.<br><br>**d.** Ensure that equipment and supplies are available at home (e.g., bedpan, special bed or frame).<br><br>**e.** Assess parents' ability to cope with home care.<br><br>**f.** Arrange for public health nurse to visit if necessary.<br><br>**g.** Ensure that parents have clinic appointment and/or readmission date. |

# Information for Parents of a Child with a Fractured Femur

It takes time for a fracture of the femur (thigh bone) to heal fully. These notes will give you an idea of what to expect. However, they are only a guide to the general plan, which is modified for children of different ages and various types of fractures.

### 1. How will the fractured leg be treated?
First, we put a splint on the leg to support it and lay your child on a special frame on the bed. His head will be lower than his feet: this pulls the leg gently, so the bone will heal in the correct position.

### 2. How long will my child be in hospital?
Most children with this injury spend about 4 weeks in hospital. For about the first 3 weeks, your child will stay on the frame. He will be able to play with others in the ward and playroom, and x-ray films will be taken to ensure that the bone is healing properly. He can make plastic models, play card games and other table games, read, draw, and sew (*this may give you some idea of things to bring*), and will continue schooling.

Next, we shall probably apply a plaster cast—around the waist and down the broken leg to the toes; no anesthetic is needed for this procedure. (Tell the nurse if you wish to see a child who is already in a cast.) Then the fracture frame is removed. For about 2 days, while the cast is drying thoroughly, your child will stay in bed. Then, depending upon the type of fracture (and many other factors), he may be able to start walking with crutches; even if he is not allowed to walk yet, he will be able to sit on the edge of a high stool or lie on a sofa. *Therefore, when the cast is applied, bring a shoe for the other foot; if it is needed, we will apply a shoe-lift to raise it to the height of the cast.* A physical therapist will help your child with exercises and/or instruction in walking with crutches, and the nurses will show you how to cope and what to do. Your child will return home soon.

### 3. What happens next?
The cast remains in place for about another 6 weeks, so the fracture can heal solidly.

**Schooling.** Before your child leaves hospital, we will ask the education authorities to get in touch with you, to arrange teaching at home or transportation to the school. If you have any problems with the arrangements, call the public health nurse at the hospital.

**Orthopedic clinic.** You will be given an appointment to come to the clinic 6 weeks after your child leaves hospital. The cast will be removed and the leg will be x-rayed. If the fracture has healed completely, the cast will be left off. If a little more time is necessary, another cast will be applied; the doctor will tell you how long it will be needed. As soon as the plaster is off, a physical therapist will start your child on a program of exercises and will tell you how you can help.

### 4. The cast is off!
*A leg that has been in a cast is thin and scaly, and its joints are stiff.* Most of the scales will flake off in the bath, and skin cream (any kind; e.g., hand lotion or petrolatum) will soften the skin. The leg will swell a little. The swelling will go down faster if the leg is propped up on pillows when your child is resting.

For the first few days, the best exercise is knee-bending while lying on the abdomen. Encourage your child to exercise all the joints—ankle, knee, and hip. Swimming is excellent exercise.

### 5. How soon will my child walk normally?
At first, children are unwilling to put much weight on the leg. They hop about on crutches for about 1–4 weeks, during which time their strength and confidence return. *At a time that seems right to them,* they will use their crutches less.

Do not hurry your child. By about 6 weeks after the plaster comes off, he will probably be walking without crutches. The leg will be somewhat thinner, and he may have a limp for another 3 months (a total of about 6 months since the bone was broken).

Do not worry if, at first, one leg appears slightly longer than the other. This is normal; if the two legs are likely to grow at different rates after the fracture, the surgeon will take this into account when he sets the leg. Within 6 to 12 months the legs will be of equal length.

# Careplan 155 — Knee Surgery

## Goals for Discharge or Maintenance
I. Patient and family members are able and willing to follow discharge instructions.
II. Patient can do quadriceps exercises and straight-leg raising.
III. Patient walks safely on crutches.

| Usual Problems/Objectives/Timing | Nursing Orders |
|---|---|
| 1. *Pre-operatively.* | **a.** *See* Careplan 17: Pre-operative Care, General.<br>**b.** Teach patient, and have him demonstrate, quadriceps exercises and straight-leg raising.<br>**c.** Instruct patient to keep leg straight postoperatively. (Exercises are established by physical therapist.) |
| 2. *Postoperatively.* | *See* Careplan 21: Postoperative Care, General. |
| 3. Potential impaired circulation, or nerve damage, due to surgical trauma, tight cast, dressing, swelling, or immobility.<br><br>**Objectives.** Toes pink and warm. No edema. No complaint of numbness or tingling in toes. Patient can move ankle and toes as freely as before.<br><br>**Timing.** 48 hr postop. | **a.** Observe toes immediately on return from OR, then q1h for 24 hr, for:<br>–Edema.<br>–Movement.<br>–Warmth.<br>–Circulation (including blanching of nail beds).<br>–Sensation and pain.<br>–Pulses.<br>**b.** Record observations.<br>**c.** Notify dr *stat* if any change in above. |
| 4. Potential knee contracture due to improper positioning; potential weakness of leg muscles (particularly of thigh), due to reluctance to move and failure to adhere to physical therapy program.<br><br>**Objectives.** Patient keeps leg straight (not hyperextended) and maintains muscle tone.<br><br>**Timing.** Until discharge. | **a.** Do not place pillows under patient's knee.<br>**b.** Remind patient to keep leg in good alignment.<br>**c.** Explain to patient that, although difficult and painful, the ordered exercises are necessary, to enhance the surgical result and permit full activity in the future. Give analgesic before therapy.<br>**d.** Emphasize the need to follow dr's orders for physical therapy, etc., to minimize the possibility of complications. |
| 5. Potential injury due to improper crutch-walking, falls, or nerve injury from axillary pressure.<br><br>**Objectives**<br>a. No falls or nerve injury.<br>b. Patient demonstrates safe crutch-walking.<br>**Timing**<br>a. Throughout hospital stay.<br>b. Before discharge. | **a.** Obtain order for physical therapy department to measure patient for crutches and instruct him in their use.<br>**b.** Observe patient for proper crutch-walking technique.<br>**c.** Ensure that crutches are adjusted correctly and are safe to use (rubber tips, padded axilla bar, and no defects in material).<br>**d.** The patient's weight should be on the hands, not armpits, when crutch-walking. |
| 6. *If a cast is applied.* | *See* Careplan 153: Casts. |

# Careplan 156 Osteomyelitis, Acute

## Goals for Discharge or Maintenance
I. Infection has cleared and there is no recurrence.
II. Patient/parents understand and can cope with home care and follow-up.

| Usual Problems/Objectives/Timing | Nursing Orders |
|---|---|
| 1. Immobilization. | *See* Careplan 13: Prolonged Immobilization. |
| 2. Pain in affected bone.<br>**Objective.** Minimal discomfort.<br>**Timing.** 3 weeks. | **a.** Keep patient in bed.<br>**b.** Elevate affected extremity unless contraindicated.<br>**c.** If covers cause discomfort, use a bed-cradle.<br>**d.** Do not jar the bed.<br>**e.** Support affected limb when moving patient.<br>**f.** Give analgesics as ordered. |
| 3. Pyrexia. | *See* Careplan 10: Pyrexia. |
| 4. Pain, potential phlebitis, and emotional upset due to prolonged antibiotic therapy and frequent stabs for i.v. lines.<br>**Objectives.** Pain and emotional upset minimal; no phlebitis. Minimal number of i.v. infusions started.<br>**Timing.** Until i.v. therapy is discontinued (usually 3 weeks). | **a.** Immobilize the limb that has the i.v. line attached.<br>**b.** Check i.v. site often—at least q1h. If the site is red, have the site of the i.v. needle changed.<br>**c.** Whenever possible, have the same person restart the i.v. infusion. |
| 5. *If the wound is draining:* Potential cross-infection.<br>**Objective.** No cross-infection.<br>**Timing.** Until wound is healed. | **a.** Follow hospital procedure for asepsis.<br>**b.** *See* Careplan 12: Isolation: Psychological Aspects. |
| 6. *If surgery is performed.* | *See* Careplan 17: Pre-operative Care, General *and* Careplan 21: Postoperative Care, General. |
| 7. *If irrigation system is used:* Potential edema due to malfunction of drainage system.<br>**Objective.** No edema.<br>**Timing.** Until drainage system is disconnected. | **a.** Before treatment, record circumference of limb (for baseline).<br>**b.** Check drainage system at least q1h. Record inflow and outflow of solution accurately.<br>**c.** Observe for edema q4h (fluid may be leaking into tissues).<br>**d.** If the solution is running well but there is little or no drainage:<br>–*Notify dr stat.*<br>–Slow down the infusion until dr arrives. (Outflow tube must not be irrigated without dr's orders.)<br>**e.** If the outflow is less than the inflow for 2 hr:<br>–Measure circumference of affected limb, and note difference from baseline measurement.<br>–Notify dr. |
|  | **Note.** Before discharge, ensure that follow-up appointment has been made.<br>If appropriate:<br>–Arrange for instruction in crutch-walking.<br>–Teach parent about dressings.<br>–Arrange for help with home care. |

# 157

## Rheumatoid Arthritis in Children
### (Still's Disease)

**Goals for Discharge or Maintenance**
 I. Family members state an understanding of the disease, treatment, and medication.
 II. Family members express realistic plans for home care.

| Usual Problems/Objectives/Timing | Nursing Orders |
|---|---|
| 1. Potential immobility or deformity of affected joints, due to pain and stiffness.<br><br>**Objective.** Immobility/joint deformity not increased.<br><br>**Timing.** Until discharge. | **a.** Maintain patient on bed rest during active phase of disease only.<br><br>**b.** Assess degree of discomfort; request sedation if indicated.<br><br>**c.** While ASA dosage is being stabilized, report any signs of salicylate toxicity; e.g., rapid or heavy breathing (air-hunger), drowsiness, tinnitus, or nausea/vomiting.<br><br>**d.** To reduce gastrointestinal irritation, give salicylates after milk or food.<br><br>**e.** Provide patient's bed with a firm mattress and a low pillow (5 cm or less). Do not raise head of bed or prop pillows under neck.<br><br>**f.** Encourage mobilization, and ensure good body alignment at all times. Emphasize the physical therapy program. Encourage patient to do as much as he can for himself.<br><br>**g.** To reduce stiffness, bathe patient in warm water in the a.m. and p.r.n. Allow time for him to soak, adding water periodically to maintain temperature.<br><br>**h.** Patient should wear splints as ordered (usually during rest periods) and at night. Check for comfort and for pressure areas.<br><br>**i.** Gradually, introduce routine daily activities that may present difficulties (e.g., tying shoe laces, fastening buttons). |
| 2. General malaise and fatigue.<br><br>**Objectives.** Patient appears rested; performs routine daily activities without undue fatigue.<br><br>**Timing.** Before discharge. | **a.** During acute phase, offer fluids and small meals several times a day.<br><br>**b.** Provide a quiet environment.<br><br>**c.** Avoid overtiring the patient. Plan activities and physical therapy so that he has uninterrupted rest periods afterward. |
| 3. Potential pyrexia. | *See* Careplan 10: Pyrexia. (Do not give patient additional ASA.) |
| 4. Patient/parents anxious and concerned about home management.<br><br>**Objective.** Patient/parents state understanding of disease and treatment.<br><br>**Timing.** Before discharge. | **a.** Refer family to physical therapy department for instruction in how to maintain/increase range of movement of affected joints and to strengthen muscles.<br><br>**b.** If occupational and continuing physical therapy is indicated, refer family for home care program.<br><br>**c.** If patient is overweight, refer parents to dietetics department (obesity strains joints further).<br><br>**d.** If activity is severely limited, encourage parents to make adaptations, to promote child's independence in |

**377**

continued

| Usual Problems/Objectives/Timing | Nursing Orders |
|---|---|
| **4. (Continued).** | toileting and dressing (e.g., Velcro fasteners, buttons sewn on with elastic thread, walk-in shower). |
| | **e.** Ensure that parents and child understand the need to avoid strenuous or competitive sports. However, he must move his joint(s), even though this hurts: protection will reduce mobility further and the loss may be permanent. Suggest alternating periods of rest and activity. |
| | **f.** Reinforce dr's teaching program. Help parents and child understand the reasons for treatment, medication, and movement. |
| | **g.** Ensure that parents/patient have written instructions for home care and follow-up and know whom to contact if they have concerns. |
| **5.** Potential decrease in visual acuity, due to inflammatory eye involvement. <br> **Objective.** Visual acuity unaltered. <br> **Timing.** Until discharge. | **a.** Report vision problems to dr. <br> **b.** Encourage patient to wear glasses if prescribed. |
| **6.** Potential discouragement, leading to depression, dependency, regression, and hostility, because of condition's chronicity and change in patient's body image. <br> **Objectives.** Patient is interested in doing things for himself; he accepts realistic limits; and he has normal relationships with other children. <br> **Timing.** Before discharge. | **a.** Designated nurse to establish supportive rapport. <br> **b.** Encourage independence in daily routines and commend accomplishments. <br> **c.** Encourage age-appropriate activities and provide diversions. <br> **d.** Introduce child to other patients and involve him in ward activities. <br> **e.** Do not show anger if the child acts out. Be patient; let him know that you understand his problems, and help him cope with them. <br> **f.** If child wants to talk to you, try to be available. Spend time with him other than for therapy and routine daily activities. <br> **g.** Emphasize to patient and parents that rheumatoid arthritis in children is different from that in adults. <br> **h.** Encourage normality as far as possible, to underemphasize disease; e.g., patient should continue school studies as much as possible. |

**Goals for Discharge or Maintenance**
See Objectives.

| Usual Problems/Objectives/Timing | Nursing Orders |
|---|---|
| 1. Potential anxiety of patient and parents about the equipment, mainly due to ignorance of its purpose.<br><br>**Objectives.** Patient/parents express fears and anxieties, ask questions about the equipment, and understand the purpose of traction.<br><br>**Timing.** 24 hr. | **a.** Explain purpose and importance of traction; e.g., to:<br>–Decrease muscle spasm.<br>–Reduce and stabilize a fracture or dislocation.<br>–Maintain alignment.<br>–Immobilize limb.<br><br>**b.** Demonstrate traction with a doll or visual aids or (preferably) take child/parent to visit a patient in a similar setup. |
| 2. Potential interference with circulation to affected extremities, by swelling and/or pressure of equipment.<br><br>**Objectives.** Affected limb(s) warm and pink and respond to stimuli; no swelling.<br><br>**Timing.** 48 hr after start of traction. | **a.** Check pulse in affected limb(s) q2h, day and night.<br><br>**b.** Check extremities for color, warmth, sensation, and swelling, at least q2h, day and night.<br><br>**c.** If traction is painful, check site, attempt repositioning, and give analgesic as ordered.<br><br>**d.** Report any severe pain to dr *stat*. |
| 3. Prolonged immobilization. | *See* Careplan 13: Prolonged Immobilization. |
| 4. Potential nerve damage due to limb stretching or pressure.<br><br>**Objectives.** Patient describes satisfactory sensation and can move fingers/toes.<br><br>**Timing.** Until traction is removed. | **a.** Check appropriate vital signs and do spinal-cord testing q2h for 24 hr, q4h for 24 hr, then q8h.<br><br>**b. Patient in skull tongs.** Check ability to follow fingers with eyes, to swallow, and to initiate voiding; ensure that taste is unaffected.<br><br>**c.** If any difficulties, remove weights *slowly and carefully*, and notify dr *stat*. |
| 5. Potential delay in healing or loss of alignment, due to malfunction of equipment.<br><br>**Objectives.** Equipment functioning properly; alignment maintained.<br><br>**Timing.** Until traction is removed. | **a.** Check traction each time you visit room (at least q2h). Ensure that:<br><br>–Weights are hanging free.<br>–Pulleys are functioning.<br>–Ropes are not frayed.<br>–Knots are secure. |
| 6. Potential skin breakdown due to continuous contact with equipment and bed linen.<br><br>**Objective.** No skin breakdown.<br><br>**Timing.** Until traction is removed. | **a.** Check areas prone to breakdown, q2h when awake and q4h at night:<br><br>**All traction.** Coccyx, elbows, heels, and ankles.<br><br>**Thomas splint.** Groin and other areas in contact with splint and/or silence cloth (orthopedic felt).<br><br>**Cervical.** Back of head, chin, jaws, and ears.<br><br>**b.** Keep the bed dry, clean, and wrinkle-free.<br><br>**c.** Protect obvious pressure points with sheepskin or gauze; provide alternating-pressure mattress if feasible.<br><br>**d.** If appropriate, encourage patient to change position frequently.<br><br>**Older child.** Provide aids such as a monkey-bar. |

continued

| Usual Problems/Objectives/Timing | Nursing Orders |
|---|---|
| **7.** *Particularly if in head-down position:* Potential nausea and loss of appetite.<br><br>**Objectives.** Adequate nutrition; patient is eating most of each meal; no nausea.<br><br>**Timing.** As long as necessary. | **a.** Allow patient to select foods from menu; help him with choice. (Finger-foods, such as sandwiches, celery sticks, and fresh fruit, are easiest to manage.)<br><br>**b.** Ensure that food tray looks attractive and food is placed within patient's reach.<br><br>**c.** Increase roughage in diet, to prevent constipation.<br><br>**d.** Consult dietitian if poor appetite persists. (Special foods may be ordered, or parents may be allowed to bring selected favorite foods.) |
| **8.** Potential discomfort because of maintenance in unusual position.<br><br>**Objective.** Patient appears reasonably comfortable.<br><br>**Timing.** Until traction is removed. | **a.** Gently massage back q2h while awake.<br><br>**b.** Place narrow, firm pad under lumbar area when patient is supine.<br><br>**c.** Provide enough covers for warmth (equipment may be in the way, permitting drafts). |

## Goals for Discharge or Maintenance
I. Parents/patient understand plan for home care and follow-up.
II. They demonstrate competence in doing physical therapy.
III. Patient is crutch-walking correctly.

| Usual Problems/Objectives/Timing | Nursing Orders |
|---|---|
| 1. *Pre-operatively.* | **a.** *See* Careplan 17: Pre-operative Care, General.<br><br>**b.** Notify physical therapist as soon as patient is admitted.<br><br>**c.** Follow program of exercises established by physical therapist (keep at bedside). Ensure that patient demonstrates correct crutch-walking and appropriate exercises *before* surgery.<br><br>**d.** Explain to patient/parents the usual postoperative course and show them pictures of the Wagner apparatus.<br><br>**e.** If appropriate, introduce patient and parents to another child who has undergone the same operation and is coping well. |
| 2. *Postoperatively.* | *See* Careplan 21: Postoperative Care, General. |
| 3. Potential delay in achieving the desired amount of bone distraction because turning procedure has not been done correctly, or apparatus has been interfered with.<br><br>**Objective.** Distraction procedure is carried out correctly.<br><br>**Timing.** Until apparatus removed. | **a.** Follow dr's orders for rotating the knob (screw turns) on the distraction device. (Usually 1.55 mm per turn per day, 1.00 mm for smaller device.)<br><br>**b.** Maintain a wall-chart in patient's room, and record daily:<br>–Measurement on Wagner apparatus.<br>–Signature of person recording measurement.<br>–Date.<br>Report to dr if measurement level is not being reached.<br>(Patient's BP is also recorded on this chart. *See* nursing orders for problem 7.)<br><br>**c.** If patient has been taught to do screw turns, supervise *each* turn and record it on wall-chart.<br><br>**d.** Check wall-chart frequently for discrepancies in actual and recorded difference in measurements (patient or family member may have interfered with apparatus). |
| 4. Potential skeletal pain (moderate to severe) due to surgery on the bone and/or distraction procedure.<br><br>**Objectives.** Patient is able to cope with pain or discomfort and appears reasonably relaxed.<br><br>**Timing.** Until completion of lengthening procedure. | **a.** Before first screw turn, administer analgesic as ordered by dr.<br><br>**b.** Assess patient's level of pain (and tolerance of the procedure) and give analgesic 1/2 hr before each subsequent screw turn p.r.n.<br><br>**c.** Encourage patient to assist with procedure by doing screw turns (with supervision, and as taught by dr).<br><br>**d.** If procedure is not well tolerated, try dividing the turn into several smaller increments spread out over the day. |

**381**

continued

| Usual Problems/Objectives/Timing | Nursing Orders |
|---|---|
| 5. Potential soft tissue infection around pin sites.<br>**Objectives.** No infection, or early detection of infection.<br>**Timing.** Until pins are removed. | **a.** Observe for signs of infection (e.g., redness, swelling, discharge, odor, elevated temperature).<br>**b.** Change pin site dressings as ordered by dr. |
| 6. Potential skin breakdown due to stretching of limb.<br>**Objective.** Early detection of possible skin breakdown.<br>**Timing.** Until completion of lengthening procedure. | **a.** Check skin around pin sites after each screw turn and p.r.n.<br>**b.** Notify dr if patient's skin is getting very taut (it may be necessary to prepare patient for a skin release procedure). |
| 7. Potential hypertension due to stretching of major vessels.<br>**Objective.** Early detection of hypertension.<br>**Timing.** Until procedure is completed. | **a.** Take patient's BP daily, at the same time each day.<br>**b.** Notify dr if BP is elevated (screw turning may have to be discontinued for a few days). |
| 8. *Femoral traction*<br>  **a.** Potential progressive loss of knee motion due to hamstring tightening (with the gradual lengthening of the bone).<br>    **Objective.** At least 60 degree flexion and less than 10 degree flexion contraction maintained (or as specified by dr).<br>    **Timing.** Until lengthening procedure completed. | **a.** Ensure that the patient's exercise program is carried out (days, evenings, and weekends).<br>**b.** Discourage patient from using a wheelchair once he is ambulant on crutches.<br>**c.** Encourage patient to lie in prone position for 1 hr t.i.d. (with knee extended). |
|   **b.** Potential hip flexion due to prolonged positioning and sitting in wheelchair.<br>    **Objective.** No hip flexion deformity.<br>    **Timing.** Until apparatus removed. | **a.** Encourage patient to lie in prone position for 1 hr t.i.d. (with knee extended) and restrict wheelchair use.<br>**b.** Place pillow under the patient's knee so the leg is extended. Do not leave it there for long periods. |
| 9. *Tibial traction*<br>  **a.** Potential equinus deformity of foot due to heelcord tightening.<br>    **Objective.** No equinus deformity.<br>    **Timing.** Until lengthening completed. | **a.** Encourage patient to do active ankle exercises as instructed by the physical therapist. (Keep close liaison with physical therapist about patient's progress.)<br>**b.** Check dorsiflexion of affected foot after each screw turning. Report to dr any decrease in usual range of movement. |
|   **b.** Potential peroneal nerve palsy due to overstretching of the peroneal nerve.<br>    **Objective.** No peroneal nerve damage.<br>    **Timing.** Until lengthening completed. | **a.** Check strength of dorsiflexion of patient's foot and toes frequently during the day (e.g., each time you are in the room).<br>**b.** Check sensation of foot (in first cleft of toes) daily and p.r.n.<br>**c.** Notify dr if there are any changes in sensation or decreased strength of movement of foot, toes, or knee. |
| 10. *Arm traction*<br>  **a.** Potential progressive loss of elbow motion due to decrease in active motion.<br>    **Objective.** No loss of elbow motion. | **a.** Ensure that patient carries out full program of exercises every day.<br>**b.** Explain importance of maintaining elbow movement |

| Usual Problems/Objectives/Timing | Nursing Orders |
|---|---|
| **10. (Continued).**<br>    **Timing.** Until lengthening completed.<br>  **b.** Potential nerve damage due to overstretching of radial, medial, or ulnar nerves.<br>    **Objective.** No neurological deficit.<br>    **Timing.** Until lengthening completed. | **a.** Note circulation and sensation of hand frequently (especially after apparatus is turned).<br>**b.** Encourage active movement of fingers, wrist, and elbow on affected side. |
| **11.** Potential mood swings due to lengthy hospitalization and lack of mobility.<br>  **Objectives.** Patient expresses feelings, and is able to participate in usual ward activities.<br>  **Timing.** Ongoing. | **a.** Maintain a consistent assignment of nurses.<br>**b.** Place patient in room with other children of same age/interests.<br>**c.** With the patient, establish a daily routine of therapy, school, recreation, etc.<br>**d.** If family members or friends cannot visit, arrange for volunteer visitor(s). |
| **12.** Potential difficulties in management at home due to lack of understanding of treatment and follow-up.<br>  **Objectives.** Patient/parents are able to cope with physical therapy program. Patient demonstrates safe crutch-walking.<br>  **Timing.** Before discharge. | **a.** Ensure that patient/parents have been taught and demonstrate crutch-walking and specific exercises.<br>**b.** Help parents make arrangements for transportation home, for return visits to hospital, and for schooling.<br>**c.** Give parents written instructions and information (e.g., for cast, exercises, returning equipment). |

# Careplan 160 Wired Jaw

## Goals for Discharge or Maintenance
**I.** Parents and patient are able to select appropriate diet and demonstrate correct mouth care.
**II.** They have equipment and supplies and can cope with home care and follow-up.

| Usual Problems/Objectives/Timing | Nursing Orders |
|---|---|
| **1.** *Pre-operatively.* | **a.** *See* Careplan 17: Pre-operative Care, General.<br><br>**b.** Notify physical therapist and dietitian of patient's admission and expected time of operation.<br><br>**c.** Explain to parents/patient:<br>–Swelling and not being able to move jaw.<br>–Wire sutures.<br>–Fluid diet and how this will be given (e.g., syringe and tubing).<br>–Mouth care.<br>–i.v. therapy, blood tests, antibiotics.<br>–Stay in ICU (if appropriate), visiting, etc.<br>–How to communicate. |
| **2.** *Postoperatively.* | **a.** *See* Careplan 21: Postoperative Care, General.<br><br>**b.** Follow surgeon's specific orders for diet and mouth care. |
| **3.** Potential aspiration and asphyxiation because patient is unable to move jaws or open mouth.<br><br>**Objective.** Clear airway maintained.<br><br>**Timing.** By discharge or until wires removed. | **a.** Observe patient closely for any sign of respiratory distress (e.g., restlessness, coughing or choking sounds, gagging, cyanosis).<br><br>**b.** *Ensure that wire-cutters are with patient and clearly visible at all times* (e.g., taped to head of bed, taped to gown).<br><br>**c.** Determine where suction catheter can be inserted (in case needed).<br><br>**d.** Ensure that a nurse or other staff member who knows how and when to cut the wires is in patient's vicinity.<br><br>**e.** Reassure patient and parents that measures can be taken to alleviate choking.<br><br>**f.** If patient is nauseated, sit him up and encourage him to breathe slowly and deeply.<br><br>**g.** Give antiemetic, as ordered (to prevent nausea and vomiting).<br><br>**h.** If patient vomits: Sit him up and tilt his head forward; suction around the wire and suction nasally, if not contraindicated. (Some patients can cope with vomiting and do not aspirate fluids.)<br><br>**i.** If patient cannot cope with emesis and is choking:<br>–Cut the "up" and "down" wires, using the wire-cutters (this will free the jaw).<br>–Suction orally and nasally.<br>–Have someone call the dr *stat*. |

| Usual Problems/Objectives/Timing | Nursing Orders |
|---|---|
| **3. (Continued).** | –Stay with the patient, reassure him, and support his jaw to minimize movement. |
| **4.** Potential mouth infection due to difficulty in performing effective oral hygiene.<br><br>**Objectives.** Mouth clean. No infection.<br><br>**Timing.** Until discharge, or until wires are removed. | **a.** Ensure diligent mouth care, after meals or snacks, at bedtime, and during the night.<br><br>**b.** For mouth care use a water jet (Water Pik®) with water, followed by hydrogen peroxide half-strength. *Do not rinse mouth with water after using peroxide.*<br><br>**c.** While facial swelling is subsiding (about 8 days) brush teeth using a soft toothbrush before using the Water Pik®.<br><br>**d.** Swab the area between teeth and check by using a tongue-depressor to retract the cheek, if not contra-indicated. Use a flashlight to visualize the area.<br><br>**e.** Observe and report any purulent discharge or persistent foul odor from patient's mouth.<br><br>**f.** Teach parents and patient how to do mouth care. Whenever possible the patient should do his own care. (Patient and/or parents must demonstrate ability to do this before discharge from the hospital.) Check patient's mouth each time and reinstruct as necessary. |
| **5.** Potential dehydration and significant weight loss due to inadequate fluid/caloric intake.<br><br>**Objectives.** Adequate hydration. No significant weight loss. (Average acceptable 4–5 kg.)<br><br>**Timing.** Until discharge. | **a.** Maintain i.v. or NG tube fluids as ordered until patient is drinking adequately. Start oral feedings when ordered by dr.<br><br>**b.** Ensure that increased calories and protein are given when patient starts on oral feedings (even when on clear fluids).<br><br>**c.** Order special "wired jaw" diet.<br><br>**d.** List patient's likes and dislikes, give one copy to dietitian and retain one at patient's bedside or on chart.<br><br>**e.** When feeding patient, use a piece of tubing attached to a syringe. Insert tube through a suitable space between the patient's teeth and inject fluids slowly.<br><br>**f.** Teach patient (if appropriate) and parents how to do these feedings. Patient can use a mirror to help him guide the tubing.<br><br>**g.** As facial swelling subsides, patient may drink from a cup or use a straw or a teaspoon. If using a teaspoon place it alongside the patient's mouth. (The food can then be "siphoned" in by the patient.)<br><br>**h.** Ensure that patient's clothes and the bedclothes are protected by a bib or towel.<br><br>**i.** Encourage parents and patient to select foods. Supervise their choices; the patient must eat a well-balanced diet. |
| **6.** Discomfort and potential ulceration, due to wires rubbing on the mucous membranes. | **a.** Check patient's mouth frequently for any rough or protruding wires; coat these with bone wax. |

continued

| Usual Problems/Objectives/Timing | Nursing Orders |
|---|---|
| **6. (Continued).**<br><br>**Objectives.** Patient appears comfortable; no apparent ulceration.<br><br>**Timing.** Until discharge or wires are removed. | **b.** If patient's discomfort persists, notify the dr (the wires may be rubbing on the inner gums). |
| **7.** Potential instability of jaw, due to loose wires.<br><br>**Objective.** Early detection of instability.<br><br>**Timing.** Until discharge or wires are removed. | **a.** Notify dr if wires appear to be loose or if patient is grinding teeth and moving his jaws. Tell patient not to move his jaws. If necessary, support the jaw yourself until dr has checked the wires. |
| **8.** Patient anxious and frustrated because he is unable to communicate clearly.<br><br>**Objective.** Patient looks relaxed and is able to communicate needs.<br><br>**Timing.** Until discharge or wires are removed. | **a.** Place call-bell within patient's reach. Assure him that someone will always be near at hand to help him.<br><br>**b.** Place patient's personal belongings within reach and provide materials to aid communication (e.g., paper and pencil, picture board).<br><br>**c.** If appropriate, have patient in a room with other children. Explain to them patient's inability to communicate clearly and how they can help.<br><br>**d.** Encourage patient to talk, but frame comments/questions so they can be answered in one or two words.<br><br>**e.** Reassure patient and parents that speech will return to normal as swelling goes down and the wires are removed.<br><br>**f.** Answer patient's call promptly. (Patient needs assurance that help is near at hand if he gets into difficulty.) |
| **9.** Potential mismanagement at home, due to lack of knowledge.<br><br>**Objectives.** Patient/parents demonstrate ability in mouth care and selection of diet. They know what has to be done and who is to be called in an emergency.<br><br>**Timing.** Before discharge. | **a.** Ensure that parents/patient demonstrate good mouth care and can cope without supervision.<br><br>**b.** Arrange for parents to meet dietitian. Dietitian will give parents printed information about the high-protein, high-calorie fluid diet. Patient and parents must be able to select foods appropriately and know how to prepare them.<br><br>**c.** Explain to parents and patient what they must do if their child vomits or chokes. Show them how to use the wire-cutters to cut the wires. Emphasize the importance of always having the wire-cutters and a person who can use them with the child (e.g., going to school, in school, when visiting friends).<br><br>**d.** Explain any specific restrictions about activity as ordered by dr.<br><br>**e.** Ensure that parents have:<br>–Printed diet sheets.<br>–Printed instructions for home care.<br>–Water jet (e.g., Water Pik®) and appropriate solutions.<br>–Food blender.<br>–Wire-cutters. |

| Usual Problems/Objectives/Timing | Nursing Orders |
|---|---|
| 9. (Continued). | −Phone numbers and names of person(s) to call in an emergency (in writing).<br>−Follow-up appointment(s).<br>f. Notify public health nurse, if necessary. |

# Appendix

# Vital Signs: Normal Values

## A. Temperature, Pulse, Respiratory Rate

| Age | Temperature | Pulse Rate (per min) | Respiratory Rate (per min) |
|---|---|---|---|
| Newborn | 36.5–37.0°C (rectal) | 85–190 | 30–50 |
| 1–12 mo | 36.5–37.6°C (rectal) | 115–190 | decreasing to 35 |
| 1–3 yr | 37.6°C (rectal) | 100–190 | decreasing to 30 |
| 3–5 yr | 37.6°C (rectal) | 55–145 | 25–30 |
| 5–8 yr | 37°C (oral) | 70–145 | 25–30 |
| >8 yr | 37°C (oral) | 55–115 | 15–20 |

## B. Resting Blood Pressure (Arm) for Boys and Girls at 90th Percentile

| Age | Mean Values (mm Hg) | | |
|---|---|---|---|
| | Systolic | Diastolic | |
| 0–5 mo | 96 | 62 | supine |
| 6–11 mo | 118 | 70 | " |
| 2–5 yr | 110 | 75 | seated* |
| 6–7 yr | 112 | 76 | " |
| 8–9 yr | 118 | 78 | " |
| 10–11 yr | 126 | 82 | " |
| 12–13 yr | 130 | 84 | " |
| 14–15 yr | 136 | 85 | " |
| 16–17 yr | 140 | 87 | " |

*Based on data from report by National Heart, Lung, and Blood Institute's 1977 Task Force on blood pressure control in children.

# Fluid Requirements

Dehydration is often an actual or potential problem in many pediatric conditions. Minimal fluid requirements for maintenance of hydration in normal circumstances are shown in the tables following. Requirements increase with raised temperature, infection, and excessive fluid losses.

## A. Signs of Dehydration
1. Dry mucous membranes
2. Dryness in axillae and groins
3. Increased heart rate
4. Loss of skin turgor
5. Soft, sunken eyeballs
6. Decreased tears
7. Sunken anterior fontanelle
8. Acute weight loss
9. Irritability/lethargy/coma
10. Rapid, shallow respirations
11. Poor peripheral circulation
12. Oliguria and concentrated urine
13. Low blood pressure
14. Fever
15. Shock/coma

## B. Daily Fluid Requirement for Neonates

| Body Weight (g) | Initial Volume (ml) | Frequency | Increase (ml/kg) | Days 1–4 (ml/kg/day) | Days 5–20 (ml/kg/day) |
|---|---|---|---|---|---|
| | | | Fluid Requirement | | |
| Under 1500 | 1–2 | q1–2h | 1 (alternate feedings) | 100–150 | 150–200 |
| 1500–2000 | 2–3 | q2h | 1–2 | 100–150 | 150–200 |
| 2000–2500 | 5 | q2h–3h | 3–5 | 65–100 | 130–175 |
| Over 2500 | 10 | q3h–4h | 5–10 | 65–100 | 130–150 |

## C. Normal Basal Water Requirement, Birth to 16 Years

| Age | Body Weight (kg) | Water Requirement (ml/24 hr) Per kg | Water Requirement (ml/24 hr) Total |
|---|---|---|---|
| Birth | 3.2 | 45 | 145 |
| 10 days | 3.4 | 60 | 205 |
| 2 mo | 5 | 55 | 275 |
| 6 mo | 8 | 50 | 400 |
| 1 yr | 10 | 50 | 500 |
| 3 yr | 15 | 47 | 700 |
| 5 yr | 20 | 45 | 900 |
| 8 yr | 30 | 37 | 1100 |
| 12 yr | 45 | 30 | 1350 |
| 16 yr | 55 | 27 | 1500 |

# Additional Reading

Ack, M. Psychosocial effects of illness, hospitalization, and surgery. *Children's Health Care* 11(4): 132–136, 1983.

Avery, G. B. (Ed.). *Neonatology: Pathophysiology and Management of the Newborn* (2nd ed.). Philadelphia: Lippincott, 1981.

Birch, J. R., et al. Musculoskeletal management of the severely burned child. *Can. Med. Assoc. J.* 115:533, 1976.

Bowlby, J. *Attachment and Loss.* Vol. III. *Sadness and Depression.* New York: Basic Books, 1980.

Bruch, H. *The Golden Cage. The Enigma of Anorexia Nervosa.* Cambridge: Harvard University Press, 1978.

Brunner, L. S., and Suddarth, D. S. *The Lippincott Manual of Nursing Practice* (3rd ed.). Philadelphia: Lippincott, 1982.

Erickson, F. When 6- to 12-year-olds are ill. *Nursing Outlook.* 13(7):48, 1965.

Fontana, V. J. *Somewhere a Child is Crying: Maltreatment—Causes and Prevention.* New York: Macmillan, 1973.

Garfinkel, P. E., and Garner, D. M. *Anorexia Nervosa: A Multidimensional Perspective.* New York: Brunner/Mazel, 1982.

Garfinkel, P. E., Garner, D. M., and Modolfsky, H., The role of behavior modification in the treatment of anorexia. *Journal of Pediatric Psychology* 2(3):113–121, 1977.

Hardgrove C. Emotional inoculation: The 3 R's of preparation. *Journal of the Association for the Care of Children in Hospitals* 5(4):17, 1977.

Hardgrove, C. B., and Dawson, R. B. *Parents and Children in the Hospital: The Family's Role in Pediatrics.* Boston: Little, Brown, 1972.

Hazinski, M. F. Critical care of the pediatric cardiovascular patient. *Nursing Clinics of North America* 16(4):671–697, 1981.

Kempe, C. H., and Helfer, R. E. *Helping the Battered Child and His Family.* Philadelphia: Lippincott, 1972.

Klaus, M., and Fanaroff, A. *Care of the High-Risk Neonate* (2nd ed.). Philadelphia: Saunders, 1979.

Lehmann, A. Anorexia nervosa. Emancipation by emaciation. *Canadian Nurse* 78(11):31–33, 1982.

Mayers, M. G. *A Systematic Approach to the Nursing Care Plan* (3rd ed.). Norwalk, Connecticut: Appleton-Century-Crofts, 1983.

Mayers, M., and El Camino Hospital. *Standard Nursing Care Plans.* Palo Alto, Calif.: K/P Co. Medical Systems, 1974.

McCormick, R., and Gilson-Parkevich, T. (Eds.). *Patient and Family Education: Tools, Techniques, and Theory.* New York: Wiley, 1979.

Menke, E. Schoolaged children's perception of stress in the hospital. *Children's Health Care* 9:80–85, 1981.

Petrillo, M., and Sanger, S. *Emotional Care of Hospitalized Children. An Environmental Approach* (2nd ed.). Philadelphia: Lippincott, 1980.

Plank, E. N. *Working with Children in Hospitals. A Guide for the Professional Team.* Cleveland: Western Reserve University Press, 1962.

Shore, M. F. (Ed.). (National Institute of Mental Health, Bethesda, Md.). *"Red is the Color of Hurting." Planning for Children in the Hospital."* P.H.S. Publication No. 1583. Washington, D.C.: U.S. Government Printing Office, 1967.

Steele, S. (Ed.). *Health Promotion of the Child with Long-Term Illness* (3rd ed.). Norwalk, Connecticut: Appleton-Century-Crofts, 1983.

Thomas, H. *Child Abuse, Neglect and Deprivation. A Handbook for Ontario Nurses.* [Toronto:] Registered Nurses Association of Ontario, 1983.

Tucker, S. M., Breeding, M. A., Canobbio, M. M., et al. *Patient Care Standards* (2nd ed.). St. Louis: Mosby, 1980.

Vaughan, V. C., III, McKay, R. J. Jr., and Behrman, R. E. (Eds.). *Nelson Textbook of Pediatrics* (12th ed.). Philadelphia: Saunders, 1983.

Whaley, L. F., and Wong, D. L. *Nursing Care of Infants and Children* (2nd ed.). St. Louis: Mosby, 1983.

# Index